Religious Identities in Antiquity and the Early Middle Ages

Studies on the Children of Abraham

Series Editor

Antti Laato (*Åbo Akademi University, Finland*)

VOLUME 9

The titles published in this series are listed at *brill.com/stca*

Religious Identities in Antiquity and the Early Middle Ages

Walking Together & Parting Ways

Edited by

Ilkka Lindstedt
Nina Nikki
Riikka Tuori

BRILL

LEIDEN | BOSTON

Library of Congress Cataloging-in-Publication Data

Names: Lindstedt, Ilkka, editor. | Nikki, Nina, editor. | Tuori, Riikka, editor.
Title: Religious identities in antiquity and the early Middle Ages : walking together & parting ways / edited by Ilkka Lindstedt, Nina Nikki, Riikka Tuori.
Description: Leiden ; Boston : Brill, [2022] | Series: Studies on the children of Abraham, 2210-4720 ; volume 9 | Includes bibliographical references and index. |
Identifiers: LCCN 2021038270 (print) | LCCN 2021038271 (ebook) | ISBN 9789004471153 (hardback) | ISBN 9789004471160 (ebook)
Subjects: LCSH: Identification (Religion)–History–To 1500.
Classification: LCC BL85 .R3749 2022 (print) | LCC BL85 (ebook) | DDC 201.70938–dc23
LC record available at https://lccn.loc.gov/2021038270
LC ebook record available at https://lccn.loc.gov/2021038271

Typeface for the Latin, Greek, and Cyrillic scripts: "Brill". See and download: brill.com/brill-typeface.

ISSN 2210-4720
ISBN 978-90-04-47115-3 (hardback)
ISBN 978-90-04-47116-0 (e-book)

This book is printed on acid-free paper and produced in a sustainable manner.

Contents

Notes on Contributors VII

1 Introduction 1
Ilkka Lindstedt, Nina Nikki, and Riikka Tuori

2 A Merchant-Geographer's Identity? Networks, Knowledge and Religious Affinity in the *Expositio Totius Mundi et Gentium* 16
Antti Lampinen

3 Reconstructing the Identity of the Bacchic Group in Athens: οἱ Ἰόβακχοι and IG II^2 1368 41
Elina Lapinoja-Pitkänen

4 Signs of Identity in the Quran: Rituals, Practices, and Core Values 66
Ilkka Lindstedt

5 Sabians, the School of al-Kindī, and the Brethren of Purity 92
Janne Mattila

6 Righteous Sufferer, Scheming Apostate: Traditions of Paul from a Cultural Evolutionary Perspective 115
Nina Nikki and Antti Vanhoja

7 Death in the "Contact Zone": An Analysis of Ibn Ḥanbal's Hadith about a Hairdresser-Mother and Her Sons (*Ḥadīṯ al-Māšiṭa*) 145
Anna-Liisa Rafael and Joonas Maristo

8 Little Big Gods: Morality of the Supernatural in Lydian and Phrygian Confession Inscriptions 186
Jarkko Vikman

9 "One Letter *yud* Shall not Pass Away from the Law": Matthew 5:17 to Bavli *Shabbat* 116a–b 204
Holger Zellentin

General Index 259

Notes on Contributors

Antti Lampinen
(Ph.D.) gained his doctorate in Classics from the University of Turku in 2013, and has since held research fellowships at St Andrews and Helsinki. Since 2018 he has worked as the Assistant Director of the Finnish Institute at Athens. His research deals mostly with ancient historiography, ethnography, religion, and knowledge ordering.

Elina Lapinoja-Pitkänen
(M.Th. 2012) is a doctoral student at the University of Helsinki, writing her dissertation on Pauline Christ-groups as part of the social world of Greco-Roman associations. Her special focus is on the influence of mythical narratives and religious rituals on the social identity formation of religious groups.

Ilkka Lindstedt
(Ph.D. 2013, University of Helsinki), is a University Lecturer in Islamic Theology. He has published on early Islamic history and classical Arabic literature, including a chapter on the medieval Islamic world in *The Cambridge History of Atheism*.

Joonas Maristo
(Ph.D. 2020, University of Helsinki) is postdoctoral researcher specialising in early Islamic historiography both in Arabic and Persian. In the doctoral dissertation he studied transmission of Middle Persian texts into Islamic historiography.

Janne Mattila
(Ph.D.) received his doctoral degree from the University of Helsinki and currently works at the University of Louvain. He specializes in the history of Arabic philosophy during its classical period. He has worked on such authors as al-Rāzī, the Brethren of Purity, al-Fārābī, and Avicenna with a primary focus on ethics, the relation of philosophy and religion, and the technical questions related to the corpus attributed to the Brethren of Purity.

Nina Nikki
(Th.D. 2015, University of Helsinki), is a postdoctoral researcher in Biblical Studies. She is the author of *Opponents and Identity in Philippians* (Brill, 2019) and co-editor of *Magic in the Ancient Eastern Mediterranean* (Vandenhoeck & Ruprecht, 2021).

Anna-Liisa Rafael
(M.Th., University of Helsinki) is a biblical scholar drawn to the study of biblical reception history and the shared scriptural heritage of Jews, Christians, and Muslims. In her dissertation, she examines the story of the mother and her seven sons as a shared narrative tradition.

Riikka Tuori
(Ph.D. 2013, University of Helsinki), is a University Lecturer in Jewish studies. Tuori has published articles on Hebrew literature and Karaite Judaism, including 'Renewal and tradition in devout Hebrew poetry' (*Zutot*, 2019).

Antti Vanhoja
(M.Th. 2017, University of Helsinki) is a doctoral student specializing in Pseudo-Clementine literature and socio-cognitive theories in the field of Biblical Studies.

Jarkko Vikman
(M.Th. 2012, University of Eastern Finland) is a doctoral student at the University of Helsinki. He is writing his doctoral thesis about evolution of cultic expertise in Ephesus during the first three centuries CE.

Holger Zellentin
(Ph.D. 2007, Princeton) is Professor of Religion (Judaism) at the University of Tübingen. He previously taught in Berkeley, Nottingham and Cambridge. His research interests include Talmudic culture and Qur'anic law; his publications include *The Qur'an's Reformation of Judaism and Christianity: Return to the Origins* (2019); *The Qur'ān's Legal Culture: The Didascalia Apostolorum as a Point of Departure* (2013) and *Rabbinic Parodies of Jewish and Christian Literature* (2011).

CHAPTER 1

Introduction

Ilkka Lindstedt, Nina Nikki, and Riikka Tuori

The volume at hand brings together eight articles by scholars of rabbinic Judaism, early Christianity, Islam, and Greco-Roman society and culture with the aim of describing the formation of antique, late antique, and early medieval religious identities and ideas in the Mediterranean geographical context. Since the late twentieth century, scholarly discussions of early Judaism, Christianity, and Islam have successfully shifted away from triumphalist and supersessionist understandings of history. Growing awareness has been placed on the complicated overlappings and blurred boundaries between the three traditions. This volume particularly seeks to participate in this recent trend toward questioning artificial disciplinary and conceptual boundaries and to stress the gray area between and shared nature of many religious traditions.

Much of the nineteenth- and early twentieth-century scholarship produced in Europe and the US still viewed Christianity as superior to the supposedly ossified "Late Judaism" of the first century CE.[1] This tendentious view was eventually replaced by an image of Judaism and Christianity as a parent and a descendant, respectively, a model countered by Daniel Boyarin's portrayal of the two religions as siblings branching from the same origin.[2] The traditional "parting of the ways" paradigm places the final break between the two religions at the end of the first century with the destruction of the Temple and the alleged council of Yavneh, or later at the beginning of the second century with the Bar Kokhba rebellion.[3] Of late, the paradigm of parting ways has fallen under severe criticism. In their seminal essay, Annette Yoshiko Reed and Adam H. Becker criticize even the later, fourth century, proposals for the assumed parting and, instead, suggest that the ample evidence of interaction between, and indeed conflation of, the groups well into the early Middle Ages makes it futile to search at all for "a single turning point that ushered in a global change for all varieties of Judaism and Christianity, in all communities and locales."[4]

1 See the discussion of this change in Reed and Becker 2013, 7–16, and Jokiranta et al. 2018.

2 See Boyarin's (2004, 5) famous portrayal of the relationship between Christianity and Judaism: "Judaism is not the 'mother' of Christianity; they are twins, joined at the hip."

3 A classic proponent of the "partings paradigm" is James D.G. Dunn. See Dunn 1991 and 1992.

4 Reed and Becker 2003, 23.

 | DOI:10.1163/9789004471160_002

Reed and Becker note that the process of "parting" continued to be an ongoing one for so long exactly because the traditions remained close and significant to each other.[5]

New studies are also creating a shift, for example, in the research of rabbinic Judaism. A recent study on Jews and Zoroastrians in Sasanian Iran shows intercultural dynamics between the groups: the formulation of the Babylonian Talmud occurred in this overlapping of several traditions instead of a hermetic or homogeneous Jewish environment.[6] Iran before (and after) Islam is a prime example of a multireligious society where Zoroastrians, Jews, Christians, and various other religious groups rubbed shoulders. The social categorizations and lived realities of the lay people were not always what the religious authorities wished. Believers of different denominations made the pilgrimage to and prayed next to each other in shared sacred spaces.[7]

Rethinking borderlines and early identities has been ongoing in Islamic studies as well. Since the 1990s, Fred Donner has been instrumental in problematizing the idea that Muslims developed and possessed their distinct[8] identity early on, disputing the conventional image that this took place already during the time of the Prophet Muhammad (d. 632 CE). Rather, Donner suggests, Islam did not emerge as a reified religion (and religious identity) separate from Christianity, Judaism, and other faiths until the end of the seventh century.[9] Naming the ingroup is part of this identity building process. For decades, the followers of Muhammad called themselves "Believers"; the appellation "Muslim" starts to be used and gain prevalence as an endonym in the early eighth century CE according to the dated evidence.[10] Though Donner's hypothesis has had a significant impact on the field, it is far from being universally accepted and adopted by scholars. However, recent studies on Syriac literature written

5 Reed and Becker 2003, 23.

6 Secunda 2013.

7 For a myriad of examples of the overlapping and shared practices and spaces in the Islamic era Near East, see Penn 2015, who analyzes the writings of the Syriac Christians. According to him, there are "numerous Syriac references to Muslims requesting Christian exorcists, attending church, seeking healing from Christian holy men, visiting Christian shrines, and endowing Christian monasteries. There are also references to Christians attending Muslim festivals, becoming circumcised, referring to Muḥammad as God's messenger, and draping their altars with a Muslim confession of faith" (Penn 2015, 4).

8 In the sense of being distinct from and articulated in opposition to Jews, Christians, and other religious communities. Donner suggests that the categorizations and borderlines were different (perhaps drastically so) from what they later became.

9 See, in particular, Donner 1998, 2002–2003, 2010, and 2018.

10 Lindstedt 2019, 192.

during the early Islamic era suggest that there were indeed Christians who viewed early Muslims favorably, calling the latter God-fearing and pious and even identifying with them.[11] The borderlines appear to have been anything but clear despite the frequent insistence of later Arabic literary texts to the contrary. Arabic literature such as historiography (produced from the eighth century onward) endeavored to forge an Islamic *social memory*[12] that helped delineate distinct Islamic origins and identity through historical and other literary narratives.

The revision of boundaries should not, however, be restricted to the so-called Abrahamic faiths. Guy Stroumsa, for example, has criticized the narrative of a major change from polytheism to monotheism with the Christianization of the Roman Empire and the way monotheism "is perceived as being at the very core of the great clash between pagans and Christians."[13] Stroumsa directs attention to the constructed nature of the term as well as to the various forms of "pagan monotheism" in late antiquity.[14] On the one hand, neither Christians nor Jews of the time represented a "pure" form of monotheism: Rabbinic Jews discussed "two powers in Heaven"[15] (cf. Bavli, Hagigah 15a) and Christians quickly broke with stringent monotheism by giving Jesus a divine status alongside God the Father and later forming the doctrine of the Trinity. On the other hand, for Platonic philosophers "the pyramid of beings culminated in the One, the supreme god."[16] The lines thus become blurred when looked at more closely, and Stroumsa considers a "conflation of Greek and Israelite forms of monotheism in the Roman Empire" as certain.[17]

Another reason to widen the perspective to include phenomena outside the three religions is the mere variety of religious, cultic, and other practices in the respective environments. The lack of appreciation for this variety is due to the fact that one's own ingroup is generally viewed with more specificity whereas the outgroups tend to be viewed stereotypically.[18] One example of this is the way the early Christ-believing apostle Paul—while able to discuss

11 Penn 2015; Bcheiry 2020.

12 The concept of social memory, much employed in other fields of sociological and historical inquiry, has recently started to be used in Islamic studies. See Borrut 2011; Savant 2013; Savran 2017.

13 Stroumsa 2015, 12–13.

14 See also Crone 2106 and Sinai 2019 for Arabian pagan monotheism.

15 Segal 2002.

16 Stroumsa 2015, 12.

17 Stroumsa 2015, 12.

18 The so-called outgroup homogeneity effect; see Judd, Ryan, and Park 1991.

various aspects of Judaism with nuance—regards all those outside this framework as "Gentile sinners" (Gal 2:15). This underestimation of the enormous variety of religious life in Greco-Roman society has also had a lingering effect on early Christian scholarship.[19] Fortunately, recent interest in Greco-Roman associations, for example, has helped create a more realistic understanding of the variety of interactions and influences in late antique society.[20] As for the study of early Islam, it has recently been understood that the Arabian historical context where the Prophet Muhammad lived and acted was one where different religious identities and persuasions coexisted. There were Jews, Christians, and Jewish Christians as well as polytheist *and* monotheist "pagans."[21] Since the sources at our disposal are far from immune to the homogenizing tendencies common in identity articulation, this diversity of the late antique Arabian religious map would be lost to modern scholars if only one source was used. Rather, an integrated approach is needed: scholars working on pre- and early Islam should take into account epigraphy, archaeology, the Quran, as well as Arabic and non-Arabic literary texts (both poetry and prose).[22]

In recent years, scholars of religion and antiquity have begun to discuss their sources from the point of view of *identity*. In doing so, they have followed a megatrend in the humanities. Studies have emerged on identity articulation and maintenance in Second Temple Judaism, early Christianity, and to a lesser extent in early Islam. The concept of identity has sometimes been judged to be vague.[23] Many studies, however, apply rigorous definitions and established theories of identity, such as the social psychological *social identity approach* (SIA)[24] (consisting of the social identity theory and self-categorization theory), which is utilized in the current volume by Nina Nikki and Antti Vanhoja in their

19 See Kahlos 2016, 68. Robinson (2017, 8) states: "Should we not speak at least of paganisms or polytheisms, particularly when the trend now is to shy away from general terms, so much so that even the use of well-established terms such as Judaism and Christianity are now more likely to be rejected and replaced by the plural forms *Judaisms* and *Christianities*, on the assumption that each was, within itself, diverse," and (2017, 11): "Nuance is probably the first thing to go out the window when a movement draws boundaries to differentiate itself within and from the larger world."

20 See Elina Lapinoja-Pitkänen's article in this volume.

21 See Crone 2015–2016 for Jewish Christians in late antique Arabia and Crone 2016 and Sinai 2019 for Arabian pagan monotheism.

22 As argued and demonstrated by Sinai 2019.

23 Gleason 1983; Handler 1994; Brubaker and Cooper 2000; Hekman 2000; Bendle 2002.

24 See, e.g., Esler 1998 and 2003; Hakola 2007; Tucker 2010 and 2011; Jokiranta 2012; Hakola, Nikki, and Tervahauta 2013; Tucker and Coleman 2014; Hakola 2015; Nikki 2018; Lindstedt 2019.

article on the cultural evolution of pro- and anti-Pauline traditions and Elina Lapinoja-Pitkänen in her investigation into the identity construction of a voluntary association of Dionysos worshippers.

The social identity approach understands the need for *positive distinctiveness*, that is, the feeling of being both different from others and superior to them, to be a central motivation behind social categorization as well as behavior in groups.[25] This basic need is understood to govern strategies of competition between groups in society, which, for its part, is considered as consisting of rival groups with different statuses.[26] Focusing on group identifications rather than personal identities makes the approach particularly suitable for analyzing intergroup relations in collective, and often agonistic, cultures such as those in the ancient Near East and Mediterranean.[27]

An undeniable advantage of the SIA is that it offers a set of empirically tested propositions about human behavior.[28] Since the human cognitive make-up has not changed significantly in the last few millennia, it is legitimate to apply the same notions to ancient phenomena.[29] The SIA was originally developed to explain intergroup hostility. This means that discussions about social identity, and identity in general, often focus on detecting and explaining difference, boundary drawing, competition, and conflict between groups.[30] While this is, of course, a very meaningful task, the law of the hammer should not be forgotten: an approach focused on detecting conflict can easily lead to viewing the sources as ridden with it. However, SIA theorists have also pondered how to reduce intergroup conflict.[31]

One of the most interesting predictions of the SIA concerns groups that are difficult to tell apart when observed from a higher level of abstraction. These similar groups feel a strong pressure to distinguish themselves from each other,

25 "The quest for *positive distinctiveness* means that when people's sense of who they are is defined in terms of 'we' rather than 'I', they want to see 'us' as different to, and better than, 'them' in order to feel good about who and what they are" (Haslam 2004, 20–21).

26 Hogg and Abrams 1998, 13.

27 Nikki 2018, 60–61.

28 Tests in laboratory settings were the basis of early SIA theory and continue to be so in recent developments. For the classic *minimal group paradigm* test which sought to discover the minimal conditions for intergroup discrimination, see Tajfel 1970.

29 See, e.g., Luomanen, Pyysiäinen, and Uro 2007, 20 (and pages 22–25 on the cognitive background of SIA in general). For important correctives to applying results gained from testing members of WEIRD (western, educated, industrial, rich, democratic) societies, see Henrich, Heine, and Norenzayan (2010).

30 Hogg and Abrams (1998, 14) admit that SIA owes more to conflict theorists such as Marx and Weber than consensus theorists such as Comte, Durkheim, Spencer, and Merton.

31 See in particular Gaertner and Dovidio 2000.

which, in turn, generates competition and hostility between them.[32] This is in a very real way the story of early Christ-followers and (other) Jews, whom outsiders, such as the Roman officials, quite naturally lumped together (e.g., Acts 18:12–17). The groups would, in fact, engage in a process of forging distinct identities for centuries. Similarly, in medieval and early modern Judaism, Karaite Jews who had rejected the Oral Torah (Mishnah and Talmud) engaged in fierce literary polemics with Rabbinic Jews and created a separate exegetical tradition, while Rabbinic Jews accused Karaites of heresy. However, non-Jewish (Muslim and later Christian) authorities often observed both groups as Jewish.[33]

It is remarkable that similarity and shared traditions sometimes form the necessary backdrop for emphasis on distinctiveness and competition, which also tend to focus on those overlapping areas. A case in point is the figure of Abraham, which has, in the modern era, inspired the category of Abrahamic religions and also the name of the series at hand. The character of Abraham is indeed highly respected in the various forms of Judaism, Christianity, and Islam—as well as traditions originating with these such as Samaritans, Mormons, and Bahá'ís.[34] The concept of Abrahamic religions has, however, been criticized as a modern construct which conceals the historical disagreements around the figure of Abraham. Aaron W. Hughes, for example, considers the term inappropriate for academic use.[35] According to him, the Abraham of interreligious dialogue is "not the Abraham in whose name or understanding three rival monotheisms have been excluding (and killing) one another for millennia, but a newly repackaged interfaith Abraham who fulfils the modern role of peacemaker."[36] The emic view of the various groups has indeed often (but not always) been one where Abraham has served as a point of contention.[37] Modern people, of course, may choose to put less emphasis on the differing interpretations and see in Abraham first and foremost a widely shared

32 See Haslam 2004, 31–34 for the role of the higher level of abstraction for differentiating groups on lower levels as well as Jetten and Spears 2003, 203–241, on the differences between high and low identifiers in seeking distinctiveness.

33 On Karaite Jewish history in general, see Polliack 2003; on Karaite and Rabbanite coexistence in Fatimid Egypt, see Rustow 2008.

34 Stroumsa, Blidstein, and Silverstein 2015, xiii.

35 Hughes 2012, 16–18.

36 Hughes 2012, 15.

37 "Jews claimed to be the direct descendants of Abraham, Christians to be his spiritual heirs, and Muslims to be the true practitioners of Abraham's original religion. All these claims, however, are predicated on establishing legitimacy in an environment of rival and competing claims of religious superiority" (Hughes 2012, 11).

tradition. In light of the competitive history of these religions and their primary sources, this requires creative criticism and brave renewal of previous traditions.[38] Happily, modern-day inter-religious dialogue—while often motivated by common denominators such as the character of Abraham—does not require the participants to give up their emic perspectives. Accordingly, the goal of Scriptural Reasoning, for example, is not to become unanimous but "to learn to disagree better."[39]

The recent discussion has called for explanations that do not arise from abstract categorizations but take as their starting point the material, lived reality of late antiquity.[40] The category of "religion" itself is questioned as a latecomer and product of Christian thinking, which perhaps Judaism never even agreed to.[41] In a recent book, Carlin Barton and Daniel Boyarin suggest that the word "religion" is fundamentally anachronistic when applied to the ancient Mediterranean world. Ancient Latin or Greek did not have a word that would correspond to the English word "religion." Nor did the ancients have the phenomenon of "religion" in the sense of a system, institution, or complex of attitudes, beliefs, and practices that are distinct from other parts of social life. What we would call "religion" can be said to have permeated the whole life, thoughts, and practices of the people inhabiting the ancient world rather than having been compartmentalized outside of them.[42]

In Western research, the concept of religion has often been based on "the prototype effect of the Judeo-Christian tradition" meaning that scholars have identified phenomena that resemble religion in their own environment as

38 When Hughes exclaims that "to say now, in the present, that there exists a common 'Abrahamic' framework is grossly inaccurate" (2012, 18) he is correct from the viewpoint of historical research. Outside this framework, however, history is constantly rewritten in the present. That an Abrahamic categorization can actually work in reducing tension and conflict between groups has been demonstrated by Kunst et al. 2019.

39 See, for example, the description of the goals of Scriptural Reasoning on the related homepage by the Rose Castle Foundation and the Cambridge Interfaith Program http://www.scripturalreasoning.org/. For academic contributions on Scriptural Reasoning see the University of Virginia-based Journal of Scriptural Reasoning http://jsr.shanti.virginia.edu/.

40 Reed and Becker 2003, 2. Lieu (1994, 108–109), an early critic of the partings paradigm, criticizes the theological, abstract, and Christian apologetic nature of the model and calls for "a more nuanced analysis of the local and specific before we seek to develop models which will set them within a more comprehensive overview." Lieu (1994, 110–114) notes that the ancient Jewish and Christian sources testify to social interaction between the groups precisely by way of forbidding it, and outsiders continually failed to differentiate between the groups.

41 Boyarin 2004, 7–8. On this question, see also the classic work Asad 1993.

42 Barton and Boyarin 2016.

religious.[43] Ilkka Pyysiäinen, for example, argues that while religion is not a *sui generis* category and should be studied as part of human culture, there are "cross-culturally recurrent patterns that are explained under the notion of the 'religious'" and that these similarities can be studied "without committing oneself to any a priori assumptions about the cohesiveness of the category of religion."[44] Pyysiäinen also moves beyond these common patterns to argue for an understanding of religion based on cognitive *explanations* of religion, arriving at a characterization of religion as defined by counterintuitive representations—of *agents* in particular—processed by ordinary cognitive mechanisms and shared by groups of people.[45]

Reed and Becker note that often "the dominant historical assumptions mirror the configuration of disciplinary boundaries, and both have served to reinforce one another."[46] One way to counteract arbitrary boundaries on both disciplinary and conceptual levels is simply to bring scholars from different research backgrounds together. The current volume collects articles from traditionally distinct disciplines and brings them to the same readership. The contributions come from the fields of Islam (Ilkka Lindstedt, Janne Mattila), early Christianity (Nina Nikki and Antti Vanhoja), and various aspects of ancient Greco-Roman society and culture (Antti Lampinen, Elina Lapinoja-Pitkänen, Jarkko Vikman). Several articles also discuss traditions that are shared across religious boundaries (Anna-Liisa Rafael and Joonas Maristo, Nina Nikki and Antti Vanhoja, Holger Zellentin).

∴

Antti Lampinen examines the multifaceted networks of identities and religious affinities in a "merchant-geography" text known in Latin as the *Expositio* and *Descriptio totius mundi et gentium*. This text was originally composed in Greek in the fourth-century but preserved in paraphrased Latin translations that were written centuries later. In addition to the trade and economy of the Roman Empire, the text describes the geography of Roman provinces and lands in the east of the Empire; most likely, the text itself originated from the eastern Mediterranean. Both Latin translators may have been Christian, and one of them omitted many references to non-Christian cults, for example, in the description of the city of Rome. Lampinen shows how the original

43 Pyysiäinen 2003, 1–3.
44 Pyysiäinen 2003, 2, 5. On this topic, see also Pyysiäinen 2009.
45 Pyysiäinen 2003, 235–236.
46 Reed and Becker 2003, 20.

text contains valuable evidence on contemporary perceptions of geography but remains ambiguous in its views on religious identities: the fourth-century author appears to respect all cults and wisdom traditions and thus remains between religious affiliations.

Elina Lapinoja-Pitkänen's article discusses a classical inscription, *The Rule of the Iobakchoi* (IG II^2 1368), which describes the rules and lifestyle of a Greco-Roman voluntary association of Dionysos worshippers. The inscription was engraved on a column in a sanctuary near the Acropolis around 164/165 CE and it describes the rituals, customs, and various regulations of the group. Through the lens of the social identity approach, Lapinoja-Pitkänen seeks to explain how the practices described in the inscription and the inscription itself potentially created a sense of positive distinctiveness for the members through, for example, the ritual re-enactment of the mythic past, the use of the unique vocabulary of the association, and the role of elite benefactors of the group.

In his article, *Ilkka Lindstedt* scrutinizes the Quranic milieu, that is, the Western Arabia of the early seventh century CE. He deals with the Quran's articulation of identity signs—practices, deeds, and visible aspects—that are used to delineate the ingroup ("the Believers") from other groups. He argues that the Quran, perhaps surprisingly, explicitly states that the Jews and Christians ("the People of the Book") also partake in and display many of the signs of identity—praying, doing good deeds, and so on—alongside the Believers. What is more, according to the Quran, many People of the Book subscribe to the same beliefs as the (other) Believers. Lindstedt proposes that the Quran categorizes at least some People of the Book as part of the ingroup, the community of Believers.

Janne Mattila's study discusses the ways in which the religion of the late ancient Ḥarrānian Sabians was interpreted and employed by medieval Muslim philosophers writing in Arabic. Though the Sabians were mostly known for their astral cult, and hence considered "pagan" by Muslim jurists and theologians, the Muslim philosophers argued that they were actually pious monotheists, *ḥanīf*s, and their religion was something that the philosophers, who held astrology in high prominence, could identify with. Writers such as al-Sarakhsī and the Brethren of Purity claimed that the Sabian religion was a philosophical and monotheist one which was, moreover, based on the views of the ancient Greek philosophers. The Sabians and their religion served the Muslim philosophers as a means of legitimizing the practice of philosophy in the Islamic world. The term Sabian itself is found in the Quran, and they are promised a reward in the hereafter (2:62, 5:69). Hence, philosophy is not, the Muslim philosophers argued, pagan and polytheistic at its core. Rather, it was based on the teaching of the ancients who practiced the Sabian religion endorsed by the Quran.

The article by *Nina Nikki* and *Antti Vanhoja* takes as its starting point the general observation that both negative and positive representations of the early Christian apostle Paul have somehow persisted over time. Nikki and Vanhoja explore how the survival and dissemination of these various conflicting perceptions could be explained through cultural evolutionary theory, which understands the variation, selection, and transmission of cultural information as part of a wider process of human biocultural evolution. The positive representations of Paul are illustrated in the essay through the theme of the apostle as a suffering and dying martyr, whereas the negative representations are treated more fully through Pseudo-Clementine, early Islamic, and Jewish literature. The material is discussed on three levels. The first level denotes the selection and transmission of ideas (or "memes") due to their conspicuous nature and memorability; the second level, their selection due to their capacity to enhance the wellbeing and survival of individuals; and the third level, their role in between-group competition. Both the pro- and the anti-Pauline traditions are shown to contain several types of elements that may have offered the themes a selective advantage and ensured their survival through the centuries.

Anna-Liisa Rafael and *Joonas Maristo* look into an interesting Arabic tradition about a hairdresser and her children in the Pharaoh's court. The narrative survives in, for example, Ibn Ḥanbal's (d. 855 CE) collection of Prophetic and other traditions. According to their study, this narrative belongs to the martyrological narrative tradition about "the mother and her seven sons," popular in Christian and rabbinic literature in late antiquity. Specific to this Arabic and Muslim literary context, the mother is a hairdresser, and the story reaches the Prophet Muhammad through a beautiful fragrance on his nocturnal journey. Stories like this that have travelled, been transmitted, told, and retold in the oral and literary corpora of the three Abrahamic faiths give us significant examples of what Rafael and Maristo term "the Jewish-Christian-Muslim contact zone" of shared traditions and common conversations in late antiquity and the medieval era. Rafael and Maristo's novel interpretation extends the narrative tradition of the mother and her seven sons to the sphere of Arabic-Islamic literature.

Jarkko Vikman offers new perspectives on the recent discussion on the birth of the so-called big gods, represented by the omnipotent agents of Abrahamic religions. The development of morally interested gods in human societies has been connected to the rise of upper social classes in complex societies that had a need for religiously based ethics during the Axial Age (600 BCE to 100 CE). However, while masses continued to believe in potent yet amoral supernatural agents, it is possible that the morally interested gods preceded the large-scale societies and, rather, helped build them. Vikman focuses on the morality of divine beings in non-Abrahamic religions, and in his reading of second- and third-century confession inscriptions from traditional cults of Asia Minor, he argues that the morally interested big gods may evolve not only in large societies but also during crises in rural contexts.

Holger Zellentin shows how traditions are shared in the writings of Christian and Jewish authorities. His article studies how early Christian authors received and reformulated a famous passage in the Sermon on the Mount (Matthew 5:17–20) where Jesus proclaims that he has not come to abolish the law but to fulfil it. The Gospel of Matthew was in all probability written for a Jewish audience, and its author presumed that Jews continue to obey the legal obligations of the Torah. The passage in the Sermon on the Mount seems to claim that legal observance is necessary for salvation, and this idea disturbed many of its later Christian readers. Zellentin analyzes how the passage influenced both Western and Eastern Christian legal thought in late antiquity. Studying, then, the satirical Talmudic story (Bavli, Shabbat 116ab) that refers to the Gospels and specifically to Matthew, Zellentin shows how rabbinic legal understanding reformulates and modifies the Greek, Latin, and Syriac Christian traditions of the Matthean passage.

Acknowledgements

The articles in the present collection are the fruit of a symposium organized at the Helsinki Collegium for Advanced Studies on March 12–13, 2018. The symposium was entitled "Ideas and identities in late antiquity: Jews, Christians, and Muslims," though, it must be noted, the presentations also dealt with other religious traditions. What is more, we did not want to keep periodization too restrictive but, rather, welcomed contributions that extended to the medieval era. We wish to thank all those who took part in the symposium, whether as speakers or audience.

The organizers of the symposium comprised the editors of this volume as well as Maijastina Kahlos, to whom we are very grateful for collaboration before, during, and after the symposium. We also thank the Helsinki Collegium for Advanced Studies for providing the financial means and the premises for organizing this fruitful two-day symposium. After the symposium, we were fortunate enough to be able to solicit articles from a few scholars who did not take part in the symposium but who worked on, for example, aspects of identity formation and maintenance.

We wish to thank Heli Alamaunu for formatting and editorial help. Moreover, we are grateful to Jutta Jokiranta and her project "Mediating identities in Judaism, Christianity and Islam" (funded by the Finnish Cultural Foundation) for providing the financial aid required for the editing of this book. We also thank Antti Laato for considering this book for the series "Studies on the Children of Abraham."

Bibliography

Asad, Talal. *Genealogies of Religion: Discipline and Reasons of Power in Christianity and Islam*. Baltimore: Johns Hopkins University Press, 1993.

Barton, Carlin A. and Daniel Boyarin. *Imagine No Religion: How Modern Abstractions Hide Ancient Realities*. New York: Fordham University Press, 2016.

Bcheiry, Iskandar. *An Early Christian Reaction to Islam: Išūʿyahb III and the Muslim Arabs*. Piscataway, New Jersey: Gorgias Press, 2020.

Bendle, Mervyn F. "The Crisis of 'Identity' in High Modernity." *British Journal of Sociology*, 53/1 (2002): 1–18.

Borrut, Antoine. *Entre mémoire et pouvoir: l'espace syrien sous les derniers Omeyyades et les premiers Abbassides (v. 72–193/692–809)*. Leiden: Brill, 2011.

Boyarin, Daniel. *Border Lines: The Partition of Judaeo-Christianity*. Philadelphia: University of Pennsylvania Press, 2004.

Brubaker, Rogers and Frederick Cooper. "Beyond 'Identity.'" *Theory and Society* 29 (2000): 1–47.

Crone, Patricia. "Jewish Christianity and the Quran (I–II)." *Journal of Near Eastern Studies* 74/2 (2015): 225–253 and 75/1 (2016): 1–21.

Crone, Patricia. *The Qurʾānic Pagans and Related Matters*. Leiden: Brill, 2016.

Donner, Fred M. *Narratives of Islamic Origins: The Beginnings of Islamic Historical Writing*. Princeton: Darwin Press, 1998.

Donner, Fred M. "From Believers to Muslims: Confessional Self-Identity in the Early Islamic Community." *Al-Abhath* 50–51 (2002–2003): 9–53.

Donner, Fred M. *Muhammad and the Believers: At the Origins of Islam*. Cambridge, MA: Belknap Press at Harvard University Press, 2010.

Donner, Fred M. "Talking about Islam's origins." *Bulletin of the School of Oriental and African Studies* 81 (2018): 1–23.

Dunn, James D.G. *The Partings of the Ways Between Christianity and Judaism and their Significance for the Character of Christianity*. London: SCM, 1991.

Dunn, James D.G. (ed.). *Jews and Christians: The Parting of the Ways, AD 70 to 135*. Cambridge: Eerdmans, 1992.

Esler, Philip F. *Galatians*. London: Routledge, 1998.

Esler, Philip F. *Conflict and Identity in Romans: The Social Setting of Paul's Letter*. Minneapolis: Fortress Press, 2003.

Gaertner, Samuel L. and John F. Dovidio. *Reducing Intergroup Bias: The Common Ingroup Identity Model*. New York: Psychology Press, 2000.

Gleason, Philip. "Identifying Identity: A Semantic History." *The Journal of American History* 69/4 (1983): 910–931.

Hakola, Raimo, Nina Nikki, and Ulla Tervahauta (eds.). *Others and the Construction of Early Christian Identities*. Helsinki: The Finnish Exegetical Society, 2013.

Hakola, Raimo. "Social Identities and Group Phenomena in Second Temple Judaism." In: Petri Luomanen, Ilkka Pyysiäinen, and Risto Uro (eds.), *Explaining Christian Origins and Early Judaism: Contributions from Cognitive and Social Science*. Leiden: Brill, 2007, 259–276.

Hakola, Raimo. *Reconsidering Johannine Christianity: A Social Identity Approach*. New York: Routledge, 2015.

Handler, Richard. "Is 'Identity' a Useful Cross-Cultural Concept?" In: John R. Gillis, *Commemorations: The Politics of National Identity*. Princeton: Princeton University Press, 1994, 27–40.

Haslam, S. Alexander. *Psychology in Organizations: The Social Identity Approach*. Second edition. London: SAGE Publications, 2004.

Hekman, Susan. "Beyond Identity: Feminism, Identity and Identity Politics." *Feminist Theory* 1/3 (2000): 289–308.

Henrich, Joseph, Steven J. Heine, and Ara Norenzayan. "The Weirdest People in the World?" *Behavioral and Brain Sciences*, 2010: 1–75.

Hogg, Michael A. and Dominic Abrams. *Social Identifications: A Social Psychology of Intergroup Relations and Group Processes*. London and New York: Routledge, 1998.

Hughes, Aaron W. *Abrahamic Religions: On the Uses and Abuses of History*. Oxford: Oxford University Press, 2012.

Jetten, Jolanda and Russell Spears. "The Divisive Potential of Differences and Similarities. The Role of Ingroup Distinctiveness in Intergroup Differentiation." *European Review of Social Psychology* 14 (2003): 203–241.

Jokiranta, Jutta. *Social Identity and Sectarianism in the Qumran Movement*. Leiden: Brill, 2012.

Jokiranta, Jutta, Katri Antin, Rick Bonnie, Raimo Hakola, Hanna Tervanotko, Elisa Uusimäki, and Sami Yli-Karjanmaa. "Changes in Research on Judaism in the Hellenistic and Early Roman Periods." *Studia Theologica—Nordic Journal of Theology*, 72/1 (2018): 3–29.

Judd, Charles M., Carey S. Ryan, and Bernadette Park. "Accuracy in the Judgment of In-Group and Out-Group Variability." *Journal of Personality and Social Psychology*. 61 (1991): 366–379.

Kahlos, Maijastina. *Debate and Dialogue: Christian and Pagan Cultures c. 360–430*. New York: Routledge, 2016.

Kunst, Jonas R. et al. "Can Abraham Bring Peace? The Relationship Between Acknowledging Shared Religious Roots and Intergroup Conflict." *Psychology of Religion and Spirituality* 11 (2019): 417–432.

Lieu, Judith. "'The Parting of the Ways': Theological Construct or Historical Reality?" *Journal for the Study of the New Testament* 56 (1994): 101–119.

Lindstedt, Ilkka. "Who Is in, Who Is out? Early Muslim Identity through Epigraphy and Theory." *Jerusalem Studies in Arabic and Islam* 46 (2019): 147–246.

Luomanen, Petri, Ilkka Pyysiäinen, and Risto Uro. "Introduction: Social and Cognitive Perspectives in the Study of Christian Origins and Early Judaism." In: Petri Luomanen, Ilkka Pyysiäinen, and Risto Uro (eds.), *Explaining Christian Origins and Early Judaism: Contributions from Cognitive and Social Science*. Leiden: Brill, 2007, 1–33.

Nikki, Nina. *Opponents and Identity in the Letter to the Philippians*. Leiden: Brill, 2018.

Penn, Michael P. *Envisioning Islam: Syriac Christians and the Early Muslim World*. Philadelphia: University of Pennsylvania Press, 2015.

Polliack, Meira. *Karaite Judaism. A Guide to its History and Literary Sources*. Leiden: Brill, 2003.

Pyysiäinen, Ilkka. *How Religion Works: Towards a New Cognitive Science of Religion*. Leiden: Brill, 2001.

Pyysiäinen, Ilkka. *Supernatural Agents: Why We Believe in Souls, Gods and Buddhas*. Oxford: Oxford University Press, 2009.

Robinson, Thomas A. *Who Were the First Christians? Dismantling the Urban Thesis*. Oxford: Oxford University Press, 2017.

Reed, Annette Yoshiko and Adam H. Becker. "Introduction: Traditional Models and New Directions." In: Annette Yoshiko Reed and Adam H. Becker (eds.), *The Ways That Never Parted*. Tübingen: Mohr Siebeck, 2003, 1–34.

Rustow, Marina. *Heresy and the Politics of Community: the Jews of the Fatimid Caliphate*. Ithaca, New York: Cornell University Press, 2008.

Savant, Sarah Bowen. *The New Muslims of Post-Conquest Iran: Tradition, Memory, and Conversion*. Cambridge: Cambridge University Press, 2013.

Savran, Scott. *Arabs and Iranians in the Islamic Conquest Narrative: Memory and Identity Construction in Islamic Historiography, 750–1050*. New York: Routledge, 2017.

Segal, Alan F. *Two Powers in Heaven: Early Rabbinic Reports about Christianity and Gnosticism*. Leiden: Brill, 2002.

Sinai, Nicolai. *Rain-Giver, Bone-Breaker, Score-Settler: Allāh in Pre-Quranic Poetry*. New Haven, Connecticut: American Oriental Society, 2019.

Stroumsa, Guy, Moshe Blidstein, and Adam Silverstein. "Introduction." In: Adam Silverstein and Guy Stroumsa (eds.), *The Oxford Handbook of Abrahamic Religions*. Oxford: Oxford University Press, 2015, xiii–xvii.

Secunda, Shai. *Iranian Talmud: Reading the Talmud in its Sasanian Context*. Philadelphia: University of Pennsylvania Press, 2013.

Tajfel, Henri. "Experiments in Intergroup Discrimination." *Scientific American* 223/5 (1970): 96–102.

Tucker, J. Brian and Coleman A. Baker (eds.). *T & T Handbook to Social Identity in the New Testament*. London, New York: Bloomsbury, 2014.

Tucker, J. Brian. *You Belong to Christ: Paul and the Formation of Social Identity in 1 Corinthians 1–4*. Eugene: Pickwick Publications, 2010.

Tucker, J. Brian. *Remain in Your Calling: Paul and the Continuation of Social Identities in 1 Corinthians*. Eugene: Pickwick Publications, 2011.

CHAPTER 2

A Merchant-Geographer's Identity? Networks, Knowledge and Religious Affinity in the *Expositio Totius Mundi et Gentium*

Antti Lampinen

1 Introductory Notes on the *Expositio* / *Descriptio Totius Mundi et Gentium*

This article seeks to identify and discuss indications of religious affinity[1] in a text that preserves the material of its Greek original only in a paraphrased Latin translation. Thus, my contribution should be primarily understood as a kind of thought-exercise. The vanished original of the two extant redactions, known respectively as the *Expositio* and *Descriptio totius mundi et gentium* (*ETMG* and *DTMG*), was a Greek text with an unknown title but with broadly geographical framework; in all likelihood it was written in the late fourth century in the Eastern Mediterranean.[2] The introduction to the text is only preserved in the *DTMG*, which likewise contains a concluding passage (68) that the *ETMG* lacks.[3] From *DTMG* 5 onwards we can compare it with the *ETMG*, which usually gives more details about each region. Whether this represents a fuller transmission of the original, or rather the elaboration or involution of the text at a later stage, is far from clear. What is readily apparent is that *DTMG*'s Latin is more norma-

1 With religious 'affinity' I denote expressions of nearness or respect towards a religious tradition or practice, which despite their range of self-ascribing gestures do not support interpretations of an exclusive or non-fluid self-categorisation of religious identity. Due to the cultural and social embeddedness of ancient religion, several affinities could coexist simultaneously, and in the case of some Late-Antique individuals it may be unnecessary to search for exclusive and definite religious identity. Cf. observations in Cameron 2011, 176–177; Papaconstantinou 2015, xxviii–xxx; McLynn 2003, 226; also MacMullen 1997, 83–84 on the question of 'how much religion?' rather than 'which religion?' being more relevant.

2 Expressions such as 'rituals of the gods [...] are performed' (*deorum mysteria* [...] *perficitur*: *ETMG* 34), with neuter plural arranged with a singular verb make it likely that the text was originally written in Greek; cf. Vasiliev 1936, 2. For the language of *ETMG*, see Hahn 1898.

3 The early debate about the original of the work included Sinko 1904 suggesting that the *ETMG* represents an original Latin text, while Klotz 1906 defended the idea that the surviving texts are based on a Greek original.

 | DOI:10.1163/9789004471160_003

tive and somewhat more polished.[4] The redactor of *DTMG* has, in the passages where we can compare his text with that of *ETMG*, clearly omitted any mention of pagan cults, and thus can be held to have been Christian.[5] Despite the intractable relationship between the Greek original and its Latin renditions, the text is notable for combining technical and utilitarian functions with overt demonstrations of identity. It may thus be of interest to examine some of the ways in which it handles religious affinities in a narratological environment that is, if not exactly linear, then certainly sequential.

The *E/DTMG* has been studied primarily as a valuable testimony for Late-Imperial trade and economy, but while commercial and production-related aspects are very much highlighted throughout the text, it also contains valuable evidence for 4th-century perceptions of geography.[6] The emphasis on trade is foregrounded by the fact that most elements not dealing with production, prices, or the flow of goods around the imperial network of exchange—such as ethnographical, topographical or religious details—seem to be introduced primarily for the sake of *variatio*, or perhaps due to considerations for the requirements of a genre. Understandably, the previous scholarship has tended to view the work as a 'merchant-geography'.[7] The tone of the descriptions is frequently enthusiastic and somewhat breathless, with swift transitions between provinces. The language is extremely repetitive, and although this may be partly due to the translation and condensation of the original text, even many ostensibly central expressions relating to produce, supply, and trade are constantly articulated with barely any variation.[8]

The writer of the original Greek text seems to have lived in a time when the imperial presence was most easily discernible in two different areas of the realm: Antioch and Gaul. He notes that Antioch's abundance of 'all manner of delectations, and especially circus games' is due to the seat of the emperor being located there. Similarly, when moving from Pannonia towards Trier, 'where the emperor is said to reside', the writer explains the presence

4 For the two versions and their publication history, see Klotz 1906, 97–98.

5 Vasiliev 1936, 6. In the passages quoted in this article, clearly Christian interpolations have been marked according to the edition of Rougé 1966, and all the Latin text of the two redactions follows the same edition.

6 Trade and economy: Marasco 1996, 184; evidentiary value for geographical perceptions: Fitzgerald Johnson 2016, 45.

7 Early observations about *Handelsgeografie*, see Sinko 1904; Vasiliev 1936, 34 noted that the term is most apt for the paragraphs from 21 onwards (in other words, the section located in the Roman empire). Now cf. Grüll 2014.

8 E.g. terms referring to abundance, 'all good things', wealth and the natural richness of certain provinces, supply issues, the 'liberal' distribution of goods and services, ebullient trade, and the inhabitants' business acumen.

of the emperor in this city through Gaul's size and it 'always being in need of an emperor'. Due to the imperial majesty's presence (*propter maioris praesentiam*) everything is available there, though prices are high.[9] The idea that Gaul 'needed' an emperor of its own may reflect more common fourth-century sentiments, since it is also expressed in the broadly contemporary collection of imperial biographies known as *Historia Augusta*.[10] These conditions, along with other chronological clues, have in the past been read as indications of the text having been composed under Constantius II and Julian; this chronological context has then been used to interpret some of the *E/DTMG*'s details.[11] Overall, the date of the composition of the original has usually been fixed to between 350 and 362.[12]

2 The Purpose of the *E/DTMG*

The *raison d'être* of the text forms the topic of *DTMG* 1 and 2. The addressee is a 'beloved son' (*carissimus filius*) of the author, at least notionally if not in concrete family terms; the formulation was frequently used among Christians, as is well known, but should by no means be read as a firm indicator of the author's religious affiliation or affinities. The emphasis, expressed in a generalised way, is on a wide set of prior sources, written and oral, and the admirability and usefulness of the data set to follow. The reader will be able to use the details gleaned from the text to 'adorn your wisdom'.[13]

Section 2, outlining the structure of the work, seems to contain an additional promise (possibly added by the redactor) about treating the origins of

9 *ETMG* 32: *Quoniam autem oportet et singula earum describere, quid ad singulas civitates delectabile esse potest, et hoc dicere necessarium est. Habes ergo Antiochiam quidem in omnibus delectabilibus abundantem, maxime autem circensibus. Omnia autem quare? Quoniam ibi imperator sedet, necesse est omnia propter eum*; *ETMG* 58: *Post Pannoniam Gallia provincia, quae, cum maxima sit et imperatorem semper egeat, hunc ex se habet. Sed propter maioris praesentiam, omnia in multitudine abundat, sed plurimi pretii. Civitatem autem maximam dicunt habere quae vocatur Triveris, ubi et habitare dominus dicitur, et est mediterranea.*

10 Rougé 1966 ad loc. pp. 311–312. SHA *Albinus* 1: *quod et ipsi suum specialem principem habent.*

11 Vasiliev 1936, 3; Marasco 1996, *passim*, but e.g. 188–190.

12 Grüll 2014, 630.

13 *DTMG* 1: *Post omnes ammonitiones quas tibi commendavi de studio vitae tuae, carissime fili, incipiens nunc volo tibi exponere historias plurimas et ammirabiles quarum quidem aliquas vidi, ceteras vero ab eruditis auditu percepi, quasdam lectione didici. Haec igitur sensibus comprehendens non solum multa utilia cognoscebis, set et tuam ornare sapientiam ex huiuscemodi rerum varietatibus praevalebis.*

the world, but actually it focuses more on the east-to-west procession of the extant text and the province-based treatment of the *terra Romanorum*. The utilitarian benefit of the work—typically to prefatory statements in texts of technical genres—is further highlighted.[14] The writer promises to describe the 'whole country of the Romans', the provinces of the whole world along with their character and nature (*quales in substantia ac potestate*), what cities these provinces contain, and whatever is noteworthy in each province or city. He notes that this kind of work seems to him useful and worthwhile.[15]

The author's own regional identity has often been argued to be tied into the Syro-Palestinian area, or at least the Levantine seaboard of the Eastern Mediterranean.[16] This area is, indeed, the one described in most detail, and the number of cities—and their special produce—included within the area stands out in comparison with the rest of the empire. The author enumerates a range of different kinds of entertainers hailing from the cities of the Palestinian coast: Tyre and Berytus are noted for their mime artists and Caesarea for its pantomimes, while Heliopolis is famous for its flute players (*choraulas*) who are blessed by the inspiration of the Muses of Mount Lebanon.[17]

Details grow thinner and haphazard as the treatise approaches the western parts of the empire, as will be seen later. Even so, the utilitarian premise and formal justification of E/DTMG demanded that the author should try to say at least something about each node in the network of the empire. We can see an example of this rhetorical gesture—so typical to the technical genres—as the author takes his leave of the Syrian coast:

---

14 On the utilitarian emphasis in Late Antique technical genres, see Formisano 2001, 27–31.

15 DTMG 2: *Quaerentes autem scribere, debemus dicere primum [quando mundus a deo fuerit institutus, dehinc] quae gentes ab oriente usque ad occidentem constitutae sint; post hoc quanta sint genera barbarorum, deinde omnem Romanorum terram, quot sint in omni mundo provinciae, vel quales in substantia ac potestate; quae civitates in singulis provinciis habeant et quid in unaquaque provincia aut civitate possit esse praecipuum. Munificum enim hoc opus et studiosum mihi esse videtur.*

16 Rougé 1966, 27–38 even reconstructs the life stages and hometowns of the author, arguing for Tyre as a crucial centre point. Cf. Mittag 2006, 349 pointing out the author's interest in Carthage, a Tyrian foundation.

17 ETMG 32: [...] *Ecce similiter Laodicia circenses et Tyrus et Berytus et Caesarea; sed Laodicia mittit aliis civitatibus agitatores optimos, Tyrus et Berytus mimarios, Cesarea pantomimos, Heliopolis choraulas, maxime quod a Libano Musae illis inspirent diuinitatem dicendi.* Rougé 1966, 255 noted the similarity of the mention of *mimarios* and *pantomimos* with the contents of SHA *Verus* 8 (*histriones eduxit e Syria [...] adduxerat secum et fidicinas et tibicines et histriones, scurrasque mimarios et praestigiatores, et omnia mancipiorum genera, quorum Syria et Alexandria pascitur voluptate*); likewise, he compared the mention of *choraulas* with Claud. *C. Ruf.* 2.33–35.

> For all [its cities] engage in trade, and their citizens are rich in all goods, speechcraft, public works and virtue. And their climate is temperate. But this suffices about Syria. We have omitted much so as not to seem to prolong our explanation beyond what is appropriate and so as to have the possibility to describe other regions and cities, too.[18]

The mercantile virtues are highlighted, and even if we do not necessarily agree with the idea that the writer was precisely a textile merchant himself—as argued by Tibor Grüll—it seems plausible to claim that commerce (in a narrow sense, and perhaps more broadly the mutualistic exchange of regionally typical produce) is a central concern of the author.[19] But far from being a mere list, the text features, negotiates, and eventually even collapses both diachronical and geographical distance. Indeed, the *E/DTMG* could well be more deeply probed for its implicit ideas of 'regional essentialism',[20] whereby each province of the empire is understood as a symbiotic, functionally specialised part of the whole, and the analogies this thinking has with the broader ways of conceptualising the providentially and essentialisingly presented 'corporeal' unity of the Roman realm during the High and Late Empire. In this article, however, the focus will be on what can be said about the likely identities of the author of this fascinating little text.

3 Mixed Messages: the Religious Affinities of the Author and the Translator(s) of the *E/DTMG*

The religious affinities of the author of the Greek original of the *E/DTMG* are a thorny matter. As Jean Rougé, the 1966 editor of the *E/DTMG*, pointed out, the text's references to 'pagan' religion mostly consist of lists of divinities and brief nods towards certain cults.[21] On the other hand, arguments for a Christian (or Jewish) identity for the author would necessarily be based on similarly meagre indications—mere verbal references to 'the prophets', Josephus, and so on. A redactor certainly removed 'pagan' elements from the DTMG. Yet it is also worth

18 ETMG 33: *Omnes autem per negotia stant et viros habent divites in omnibus et oratione et opere et virtute. Et aeres temperatos habent. Et haec quidem Syriae ex parte. Praetermisimus enim multa, ut non extendere extra opportunum orationem videamur, et ceteras regiones quoque et civitates scribere possimus.*

19 Grüll 2014, esp. 634–636.

20 For essentialism as a useful concept to adopt from the postcolonial scholarship, see Haubold 2013, 34.

21 Rougé 1966, 48.

noting that the ostensibly 'monotheist' names of the *DTMG* 3 are joined by several others who are neither Jewish nor Christian. Especially in the description of Egypt—discussed below—the Jewish or Christian communities of Alexandria are not singled out at all: instead, Egypt of the *ETMG* is a land of ancient, mysterious and expert religious worship, a land of wisdom, and all the more exotic and reverential for that.

In all probability, the translators of the *ETMG* and *DTMG* were Christian, but they may have been centuries removed from the writer of the original. The two translations may well have been completed at different chronological contexts. We must, in any case, remain alert to the possibility that their translators could have added material conforming to the Christian worldview. Yet the fact remains that the *ETMG*, in particular, still retains many references to non-Christian cults, such as Serapis, Asclepius, Jupiter and the Vestal virgins.[22] We can see this in the passage on Rome:

> For in this city of Rome there are seven noble maidens of good families, who take care of the rituals of the gods for the benefit of the city in accordance to the customs of the ancestors. They are called the Vestal Virgins. [...] They [i.e. the inhabitants of Rome] also worship the gods, particularly Juppiter and the Sun, and they are also said to practice the rituals of the Mother of Gods; it is also known that divination of the will of gods is practiced there.[23]

The formulation 'they also worship the gods' (*colunt autem et deos*), followed by the vaguely ethnographicising list of divinities, would seem to distance the author (or his perceived audience) somewhat from the practices of the inhabitants of Rome, but this de-familiarisation cannot be said to be very conclusive. The broadly coeval Ammianus Marcellinus had also treated the city of Rome and its inhabitants through a distancing (and in his case, partly ironic) ethno-

22 Serapis and Asclepius at Alexandria (35, 37), Venus and the Muses on Mount Lebanon (30, 32), Venus and Cupid in Cyzicus (48), Juppiter, the Sun and the Mother of Gods at Rome (55), and Apollo, Leto and Artemis on the Cyclades (63); in addition, Mercury is mentioned as the inventor of the alphabet (34).

23 *ETMG* 55: [...] *Sunt autem in ipsa Roma et virgines septem ingenuae et clarissimae, quae sacra deorum pro salute civitatis, secundum antiquorum morem, perficiunt, et vocantur virgines Vestae.* [...] *Colunt autem et deos, ex parte Iovem et Solem; nec non et sacra Matris deum perficere dicunt, et aruspices ad deos esse certum est.* Rougé (1966. 303 ad loc.) interprets this in the light of Symmachus' approving references to the Vestals, but this sort of preconditioned scholarly projections into our sources of a supposed partisan pagan/Christian clash in the fourth century have been justly criticised by Cameron 2011 (on Vestals, see 41–46).

graphic gaze.[24] Moreover, earlier in the same passage the city of Rome is noted to be 'adorned with divine buildings' (*aedificiis divinis ornata*), which can either be an undefined reference to the city's many temples of different gods, but also—in the light of the various uses of *divinus* in the text—may mean the imperial palaces.[25] This would hardly be in accordance with Christian terminology, although after Constantine's conversion the Christian criticism of the Imperial cult and the emperor's exalted position had toned down remarkably.[26] The emphasis throughout the whole section on Rome is on the antiquity and fame of its practices and specialities.

The beginning of *DTMG*—its corresponding sections in *ETMG* are not preserved, as mentioned above—is prominently adorned with references to Jewish and pagan prophets of the past. The author asks a rhetorical question about how fitting it is to begin his work with the Magi, even if in the following passage this traditionally 'Eastern' group of wise men is not discussed as an entity. Instead, he mentions Berossus, 'the philosopher of Chaldaeans', Manetho, 'the prophet of Egyptians', and Apollonius, 'also an Egyptian philosopher'. After them, and clearly belonging to a second group of literary predecessors, Menander, Herodotus and Thucydides are mentioned.[27]

This passage contains two names that Rougé and later commentators have regarded as later additions, possibly by the translator: Moses and Josephus.[28] There is, however, nothing inherently counterintuitive in Josephus' inclusion in

---

24 See Amm. 14.6; 28.4.

25 Rouge 1966 ad loc. pp. 302–303.

26 On the Christian emperor and things connected with him as *divinus* (corresponding to Greek *theios*), cf. Fishwick 1991, 426, 429, 431; Galinsky 2011, 15; Kahlos 2016, 119–120; De Jong 2016, 38, 46; Van Andringa 2016, 17–20.

27 *DTMG* 3: *Unde ergo nos oportet incipere nisi primum a Magis? Nam priores nostri qui de his rebus scribere conati sunt, aliquanta dicere potuerunt* [*solus autem Moyses, divino spiritu plenus Iudaeorum propheta, quod est certum scripsit. Post hunc*] *de provinciis et temporibus sequentia dixit Berosus, Chaldaeorum philosophus, cuius litteras secuti sunt Manethon, Aegyptius propheta, et Apollonius, similiter Aegyptiorum philosophus*, [*Josephus quoque, vir sapiens, Iudaeorum praeceptor, qui captus a Romanis scripsit iudaïcum bellum.*] *Post istos vero Menander Ephesius et Herodotus ac Thucydides similia conscripserunt, sed non valde de antiquis. Et haec quidem illi. Ego autem de quibus memorati scripserunt, experiar tibi breviter exponere*. Rougé 1966 ad loc. p. 216 reconstructs the unamended paragraph as follows: '*Unde ergo nos oportet incipere nisi primum a magis? Nam priores nostri qui de his rebus scribere conati sunt, aliquanta dicere potuerunt. De prouinciis* […] *et Apollonius, similiter Aegyptiorum philosophus. Post istos* […]'. In his view, Apollonius has to be Apollonius of Aphrodisias, whom the *Suda* (α 3424) calls both a high-priest and a historian (ἀρχιερεὺς καὶ ἱστορικός) and describes as having written a *Karika*, *On Tralles*, and *On Orpheus and his Rites*.

28 Rougé 1966, 121–123; but see also Grüll 2014, 638–639.

such a list of 'barbarian sages' (even under the rubric of *Magi*), especially since most of the authors seem to be historians (cf. the formulation of DTMG 1 in the proem) or other literary figures. The list-form, often interacting with the idea of 'pedigree of wisdom' and its ever-branching derivation among the peoples of the world, is among the most fundamental structures of the Late Antique understanding of 'alien wisdom', as many scholars have noted.[29] Notable is also the reverence that the oldest age of any given wisdom tradition was automatically thought to command.[30] Jews, as Naomi Janowitz has noted, did enjoy something of a reputation as purveyors of 'eastern wisdom', and thus they would fit well in a passage that seeks to lend the text the authority of the prophets and philosophers of old.[31]

It is also worthwhile to mention that DTMG preserves a *titulus* for the work that explicitly calls the author a *philosophus*.[32] It seems clear that the initial chapters, with their emphasis on past philosophers as well as the wisdom traditions of the ancient east, have influenced the *titulus*, possibly only at the later stages of redaction and translation. Yet one wonders whether the Egyptian section—with its constant emphasis on the 'all kinds of philosophers' (*omnem gentem philosophorum*) resident in Alexandria and the author's evident enthusiasm for them—might in fact testify to an original posture of the text's author as a philosopher (in the more expansive Late-Antique meaning of that word). This impression is reinforced by his fairly confident wading into the debate about the merits of wisdom traditions of Chaldaeans and Egyptians, respectively, and the original inventor of writing—despite the eventual *aporia* of his enquiry. This would certainly tally with the programmatic set-up and authority-building in the first three paragraphs of the DTMG.

Does the name-dropping by the author imply any passing familiarity with the philosophers thus evoked? It has been suggested by Tibor Grüll that the listing of Berossus, Manetho, Apollonius, Menander, Herodotus and Thucydides could have been lifted wholesale from Josephus' *Contra Apionem*.[33] While clearly not a Jew himself, the author seems to have been aware of at least this work of Josephus, although not necessarily in any deep way. Rougé posited that it might not have been the writer of ETMG's original himself, but his source, who

29 See Buell 2005, esp. 29–33, 76–80; also Clark 1999; Stroumsa 1999; Broze, Busine and Inowlocki 2006.

30 See Pilhofer 1990.

31 Janowitz 2000, 213.

32 DTMG *titulus*. There is no reason to assume that 'Iunior' accurately preserves the name of the author of the original text.

33 Grüll 2014, 638, suggesting that 'Apollonius' is Apollonius Molon of Rhodes, whom Josephus discussed because of his anti-Semitic opinions.

had referred to Josephus.[34] Yet unlike Josephus, who famously attacks the Greek 'storytellers' (*logioi*) in the proem of his *Jewish War*, the author of ETMG in no way excludes Greek sources of authority for his own endeavour.[35] It seems quite clear why the author of ETMG chose to follow Josephus' list of ancient wise men: they anchor his text firmly into the East, and the list as a whole serves two purposes needed at the beginning of his text—authority-building, and a point of departure that is simultaneously ancient (i.e. historiographical) and eastern (i.e. geographical).[36]

Another reference to Moses occurs immediately in the next paragraph, where it has been added to the original text's discussion of the Eastern group of Camarini. Their land is the origin of a large river (*fluvius maximus*), but in the DTMG another addition introduces the claim that this river divides into four other ones, thus forming the four Biblical rivers of the Paradise.[37] The Camarini are very pious and good (*valde pii et boni*), and among them neither moral nor corporeal blemishes are known. They do not 'use our everyday bread' (*neque pane hoc nostro communi utantur*) or any other similar nourishment, or indeed even fire; they receive their daily bread as a rain from the sky, and drink wild honey and pepper.[38] Both the formulation about the daily bread, and the manna-like bread that the Camarini receive as rain seem securely Biblical.

The early sections on the *Camarini* and other broadly 'Indian' groups tie the origins of state order and power relations into the beginnings of agriculture and possessions.[39] The idea is fairly conventional in the classical literary tradition, and is firmly tied into the 'soft-primitive' idea of the easy life the ancient humans enjoyed before the rise of kingdoms and possessions with their associated vices. There is nothing inherently monotheistic or 'Judeo-Christian' in this notion, even though its implementation in the ETMG seems to work well

34 Rougé 1966, 112–115.

35 Jos. *BJ* 1.13–16. For Josephus' attack, see Mason 2008, 107–108.

36 Cf. Haubold 2013, 35 on the Greek idea of barbarian priests 'commanding a privileged knowledge of history'.

37 DTMG 4: *Gentem aiunt esse Camarinorum in partibus orientis,* [*cuius terram Moyses et Eden nominando descripsit*]; *unde et fluvius maximus exire dicitur* [*et dividi in quattuor flumina, quorum nomina sunt haec: Geon, Phison, Tigris et Euphrates.*].

38 DTMG 4: *Isti autem homines,* [*qui praedictam terram inhabitant,*] *sunt valde pii et boni, apud quos nulla malitia invenitur, neque corporis neque animi. Si autem vis aliquid certius discere, dicunt eos quod neque pane hoc nostro communi utantur, nec aliquo simili cibo, nec igne quo nos utimur; sed panem quidem eis plui per singulos dies asserunt, et bibere de agresti melle et pipere;* [...].

39 ETMG 5: *sunt autem et sine imperio se regentes videlicet;* ETMG 6: *neque seminant, neque metunt.*

as a westward procession from a prelapsarian simple and paradisiacal state of being into more complex yet normative ones.

Interestingly, some of the manuscripts of the Greek *Itineraries from the Paradise of Eden to the Land of the Romans* (Ὁδοιπορία ἀπὸ Ἐδὲμ τοῦ παραδείσου ἄχρι τῶν Ῥωμαίων) include a 'Discourse on the Macarini' ("Εκθεσις λόγων περὶ Μακαρινῶν), which seems to share a common source with the more detailed parts of the DTMG that deal with the Camarini. The apparent metathesis between the ethnonyms has not necessarily changed Μακαρινοί into *Camarini*, but instead the possibly more recent *Itineraries* has attempted to correct the ethnonym to better match the apparently 'blessed' (μακάριος) group.[40] Yet is also equally plausible that the writer of the ETMG was knowledgeable enough about the story of the 'fall from Eden' so as to structure his westward procession along a gradient of increasing complexity and removal from a paradisiacal state.[41] As an important difference from the historiographical or chronicle form of its own era, the ETMG's passages on India and the Eastern edge of the world do not refer to Alexander the Great at all—something which other Christian and non-Christian texts of Late Antiquity (some of them originally composed in Alexandria) did with gusto.[42]

There is, in the ETMG, a clear respect for areas that the classical tradition and other Late Antique writers had associated with learning and wisdom. Whether this is an expression of 'religious' affinity is, of course, quite another matter. Yet much has been made from the references of such authors as Ammianus Marcellinus to the Serapeum of Alexandria, for instance; the authors' attitude to such traditional hubs of 'pagan' learning and cult have been regarded as indicative of their religious stance. A similar attempt can be mounted in order to test the case of the author of the ETMG's original. Egypt, and Alexandria perhaps in particular, hold a tremendous fascination to him. It is no wonder that the lengthy description of Egypt has been taken as the starting point in one important study of ETMG.[43] Egypt combines an almost incredible natural fertility with a vigorous pursuit of religious and philosophical studies.[44]

40 On the *Itineraries* (ed. Klotz 1910), see Pfister 1911; Rougé 1966, 346–355; Braginsky 1998, 368; Kolb and Speidel 2016, 152–153. On the Late-Antique views on the Paradise, see Lozovsky 2000, 50–55. On the *Macarini/Camarini*, see Lampinen 2019, 151–152.

41 Even if India, as such, had been a topical focalization for utopian societies since the Hellenistic era.

42 Cf. *Excerpta Latina Barbari*; even later (and well outside any direct Eastern-Mediterranean influence), see *Cosmographia Aethici*. Despite the silence, cf. Fitzgerald Johnson 2016, 45 on ETMG's notional connections to the Alexander-tradition.

43 Marasco 1996, 184.

44 ETMG 34: [...] *viros similiter nobiles, deos colentes eminenter: nusquam enim deorum mys-*

Yet Alexandria—even though it was a hotbed of theological and ecclesiastical activity in the fourth century, and so described for instance by Ammianus, as well as many others—is not to the author of ETMG in any way a Christian or Jewish city. Its marvels are its learning and (in following paragraphs of the text) the natural wonders of Egypt, the glory of which Alexandria seems to attract to itself metonymically.[45] As for the religious affinities of the author, the statement 'for in fact we know the gods to have lived, or to still live, there' (*etenim ibi deos habitasse aut et habitare scimus*) seems to locate him quite strongly among the non-Christians of his era. Neither does it seem likely on the basis of his description of Egypt that the author hailed from Egypt, himself. Gabriele Marasco has suggested that the text's general emphasis of the traditional cults of Egypt and especially the reference to Serapis means that the author was aware of how Alexandria's Serapeum had become a focal point of religious partisanship.[46] But despite the author's evident enthusiasm and glowing overall assessment, his *Aigyptikos logos* does not give a particularly full picture of Egypt; most of its contents would have been available to any reasonably well-connected person in the Eastern Mediterranean. Other details, such as Alexandria's proneness to sudden outbursts of mob violence, seem like stereotypical talking points that were common in High and Later Empire.[47] Among our sources, Ammianus generally echoes the same impression of Egypt as a volatile country still hosting ancient wisdom.[48]

Rougé suggested that the author's mention of the Chaldaeans as a group possibly worshipping the gods better than even the Egyptians precluded him from having been an admirer of Julian, since Julian's own religion would have come

---

teria sic perficitur quomodo ibi ab antiquo et usque modo, et paene ipsa omni orbi terrarum tradidit deos colere. Dicunt autem Chaldeos melius colere, tamen quos vidimus miramur et in omnibus primos esse dicimus. Etenim ibi deos habitasse aut et habitare scimus. [...] *Tamen viros sapientes prae omnem mundum Aegyptus abundat. In metropoli enim eius Alexandria omnem gentem invenies philosophorum et omnem doctrinam.* [...] *Et impossibile est in quacumque re invenire volueris sapientem quomodo Aegyptium; et ideo omnes philosophi et qui sapientiam litterarum scientes ibi semper morati sunt, meliores fuerunt: non enim est ad eos ulla impostura, sed singuli eorum quod pollicentur certe sciunt, propter quod non omnes omnium, sed quisque sua per suam disciplinam ornans perficit negotia.*

45 Cf. on Ammianus' image of Egypt, Berger 2002, 179–180. On the social context of Late Antique wisdom traditions in Egypt, see MacCoull 2007.

46 Marasco 1996, 190.

47 For this idea, see Haas 1997, 11, and especially 278–330.

48 Amm. 22.16.15. A common source between Ammianus and the author of ETMG was suggested by Vasiliev 1936, 30–31; on the other hand, simply the shared cultural and geographical background for the writers might come some way of explaining the shared features of the two texts.

far too close to the theurgic rituals that were presented as part of the Chaldaean tradition.[49] It should be pointed out that in the text there is no actual disparagement of the Chaldaean arts, but a mere relegation of these to a tightly fought second place in comparison with the Egyptian arts of worship—which is hardly surprising when considering the overall tone of the passage. Besides, the theme of rivalry between Egyptian and Chaldaean priests is a very conventional topic when discussing the pedigree of wisdom among the different peoples of the world.[50] Egypt, in religious terms, was in the Late Roman Empire often perceived in terms roughly analogous to the way in which India is in the modern western popular thinking imagined as the cradle of 'world spirituality'.[51] For this, the author of *ETMG* can again be compared with his close contemporary Ammianus, who wrote about Egypt's pedigree of arcane arts in the following way:

> Here, for the first time and long before others, humans discovered the cradles, so to speak, of the various religions, and the first mysteries of cults are still carefully guarded in secret writings.[52]

Though the author of *ETMG* has a great deal to say about Egypt and Alexandria, he also admits the limits of inquiry—and perhaps credibility—in extolling the particularity of Egypt.[53] This reinforces the idea that he cannot have been an Egyptian provincial himself.[54] Yet it is intriguing how in the sections about Egypt the author seeks to foreground a much more erudite persona than, say, in the Syrian parts of his text. Textual tagging ties Alexandria both to the providential richness of Egypt's nature and to the blessed and luxury-producing areas of the East; the author interweaves these references with his discussion of cults and wisdom.

> For Alexandria is a very large and noteworthy city in its structure, abounding in all goods and rich in food: for it consumes three kinds of fish—

49 Rougé 1983, 162. *ETMG* 34: *Dicunt autem Chaldeos melius colere, tamen quos vidimus miramur et in omnibus primos esse dicimus.*

50 Diod. Sic. 1.28.81, for instance, puts the Chaldaeans to the first position (cf. Diog. Laert. 1.1). See also Broze, Busine and Inowlocki 2006; Haubold 2013.

51 For a telling Victorian iteration, Müller 1883, 13. See Masuzawa 2005, e.g. 259–265. On Late Antique ideas about India and in particular its Brahmins, see Derrett 1960.

52 Amm. 22.16.20: *hic primum homines longe ante alios ad varia religionum incunabula, ut dicitur, pervenerunt et initia prima sacrorum caute tuentur condita scriptis arcanis.*

53 *ETMG* 37: *et est in omnibus civitas et regio incomprehensibilis.*

54 As Wölfflin 1904 suggested.

> riverine, lacustrine and marine—which no other province has. Moreover, in it there is a wealth of all kinds of spices and other foreign trade goods, since beyond it in Thebais it has a tribe of Indians, and receiving [from them] everything it bestows goods to everybody. Gods are worshipped there most eminently, and the temple of Serapis is located there—a unique and singular new marvel in the whole world. For nowhere on earth can such handiwork or such an arrangement of a temple and a cult be found. Due to this it can be seen why the Musaeum was also given to it.[55]

Section 36 soon returns to the topic of religion after an enthusiastic advertisement of the unique blessings of papyrus and the celebration of the fact that Egypt is the only province in the world that can support the demand for supplies during the emperor's Persian war.[56] Despite this, and the eulogy of papyrus, the section of Egypt is markedly less interested in trade than cultural and religious pursuits, and even the details about trade goods are largely to do with empire-wide distribution networks.

The 'divine Egypt'—yet another example of the expansive semantics of *divinus* in the text—is according to the author justly named in this way due to the unique reverence that its inhabitants direct at the gods.[57] Our author seems to appreciate the role of correct ritual action—whether divination or dedication—as a way of ascertaining profitable economic activities.[58] Marasco has even suggested a direct causal link in the author's mind between the providential richness of Egypt's produce and its inhabitants' piety and zeal in the

55 ETMG 35: *Alexandria autem civitas est valde maxima et eminens in dispositione et abundans omnibus bonis et escis dives: piscium enim tria genera manducat, quod altera provincia non habet, fluminale et stagnense et marinum. Omnes autem species aut aromatibus aut aliquibus negotiis barbaricis in ea abundant: supra caput enim habens Thebaidis Indorum genus et accipiens omnia praestat omnibus. Et dii coluntur eminenter et templum Serapis ibi est, unum et solum spectaculum novum in omni mundo: nusquam enim terra aut artificium tale aut dispositio templi talis aut religio talis invenitur; undique autem Musium ei reddi videatur.*

56 ETMG 36: *Constantinopolis enim Thraciae ab ea quam plurime pascitur; similiter et orientales partes, maxime propter exercitum imperatoris et bellum Persarum: propterea non posse aliam provinciam sufficere nisi divinam Aegyptum.*

57 Loc. cit.: *Quem et nominans a diis plus esse puto, ubi deos, uti praediximus, colentes bene historias maxime ⟨eis⟩ offerunt.* The sentence is very problematic—the word *historiae*, in particular, has led to radically different translations: cf. Frankfurter 1998, 19; Grüll 2014, 632.

58 The ties between divination and economic risk are fruitfully examined by Ratzan 2018 (e.g. 254–256).

traditional worship of the gods.[59] While this seems to me to be slightly pushing the boundaries of interpretation, it is nonetheless an argument worth keeping in mind, even if this would essentially represent a return to a previous master paradigm in Late Antique studies—one criticised by scholars such as Alan Cameron—which seeks in each and every Late Imperial text signs of religious partisanship and either overt or covert choosing of sides.[60]

Still in ETMG 36, the author offers a vivid sensory description of the display of traditional sacrifice, which seems like a strong argument against any overtly Christian religious affinity on the author's part. There are all kinds of rituals and richly decorated temples in Egypt; there is an abundance (one of the favourite words of the writer/translator) of temple-wardens, priests, sacrificial assistants, soothsayers, worshipers and excellent diviners. One can see altars constantly glowing with fire, full of sacrificial offerings and incense, sacrificial fillets of cloth, and censers heaped with aromatics and bestowing a heavenly (*divinum*) odour.[61] It is quite interesting that the redactors of the text have not been particularly bothered to remove this section that so explicitly approves of a sacrifice in the pagan style.

If the author indeed conceived of produce and providentiality as causally linked, the passage on Egypt might also explain why he used such elevated language and gestured towards such prestigious generic predecessors for his text; his perceived role as a writer showcasing the richness and usefulness of Roman provinces may have approached the general Late-Antique image of a sage-author.

4 'Hodological' Text as a Way of Charting Paths between Different Late Antique Religious Identities

One may—perhaps with very good justification indeed—remain sceptical about whether a route- or network-based commercial manual of the Late Roman Empire could ever offer conclusive indications of its author's religious identity. This suspicion is compounded by the fact that the extant redacted translations, ETMG and DTMG, are likely to contain indications of the transla-

59 Marasco 1996, 186.

60 Cf. Cameron 2011.

61 ETMG 36: *Et sunt sacra omnia et templa omnibus ornata; aeditimi enim et sacerdotes et ministri et aruspices et adoratores et divini optimi abundant; et fit omnia ordine: aras itaque invenies semper igne splendentes et sacrificiorum et ture plenas, vittas simul et turibula plena aromatibus divinum odorem spirantia invenies.*

tors' and redactors' religious affinities instead of—or in addition to—those of the original author. In the early section between India and the Empire this latter objection is partly alleviated by the fact that already the original of the E/DTMG seems to have used as its source a text that is related to the *Itineraries from the Paradise of Eden to the Land of the Romans* type.[62] Here, we are not dealing with any recognisable type of utilitarian mercantile geography, but instead with a more 'hodological' or 'hodoiporic' text—an *itinerarium*, essentially—that makes several forays into moralising rhetoric. The progression from one area to the other is set out in the proem to be the guiding principle to the whole structure of the text, as the author cites Berossus and other ancient sages who 'discussed the provinces and epochs in succession'.[63] The 'progressional' approach ties the ETMG not only with such pictorial depictions as the Peutinger Table, but also the compendious gestures that the geographical tradition was replete with—a connection brought to the forefront by Scott Fitzgerald Johnson.[64]

As for the combination of such a linear guide, measuring the Eurasian expanse in units of *mansiones* (distances between halting places or inns), with the more subjective geography of the very differently narrated product- and service-oriented spatial relations of the Roman Empire, there is nothing quite similar surviving to us from the fourth century. As far as references to Christian or Jewish material go, it should be noted that it is the early, hodoiporic part that contains much of the passages cited as evidence. One example already mentioned is the reference to 'daily bread' (*neque pane hoc nostro communi utantur*), which is couched in the discussion of the Camarini in our Latin version and might derive from a Christian Ὀδοιπορία text. Alternatively, it may simply be an addition of the redactor or translator under the influence of a broader Biblical idiom.[65]

Such additions were a low-threshold way of giving at least a Christian veneer onto a text that otherwise is framed through a more complex set of source authorities—as we saw above. The ETMG does contain unambiguous expressions of identity, but these are not of 'religious' nature in the strictest sense; instead, they are those of a utilitarian instructor, a technical writer, a commentator on wisdom traditions, and a mercantile expositor of provincial character-

62 See above.

63 DTMG 3: *de provinciis et temporibus sequentia dixit.*

64 Fitzgerald Johnson 2016, 45. Also very valuably discussed in Kolb and Speidel 2016.

65 *Exodus* 16.4 (cf. *Proverbs* 30.8). It is worth noting that Rougé (1966, 50 and ad loc. p. 217) considered the phrase original, not a later interpolation.

istics. Some of these are identities which in all likelihood would not have been very salient to the translators and redactors of the Greek text, leading to a lack of emphasis or even a muted transmission.[66]

As a hodoiporic text approaching the Roman world from the East, *ETMG* exhibits a predictable gradient of increasing familiarisation, combined with indications of similarly increasing antagonism as the populations described approach the Roman frontier. These come to a head in the description of the Persians, especially in the *ETMG*'s more elaborately condemnatory account, which says that tales have often mentioned their many evils (*qui historiantur valde in malis omnibus*). *DTMG* includes the condemnation of Persian close-kin marriages.[67] The general disparagement of Persian morals is not surprising, considering both the long Greco-Roman tradition of casting the Persian, Parthian, and Sassanid empires as the morally bizarre opposite of their own societies, and also the heightening of the Romano-Persian conflicts in the late fourth century, the likely time of production of the Greek original.[68]

Despite this scathing assessment of the Persians in general, we should remember that the author had begun his hodoiporic section from the *Magi* (*DTMG* 3). Yet the reference is not unambiguously followed up by another use of the tag.[69] What was intended with this brief prefatory declaration about the Persian sages? Moses, to be sure, was often taken in the classical world to have been a magician—but the mention may well be a later addition to the text, and certainly cannot derive from Josephus, as many of the other 'sages'.[70] Are we to take it to mean that in the author's view, Berossos, the 'philosopher of the Chaldaeans', represents the Magi, and thus his enquiry is

66 Which would, of course, be an *argumentum ex silentio* and should thus be left aside.

67 *ETMG* 19: *Post hos sunt Persae, Romanis propinquantes, qui historiantur valde in malis omnibus* [...] *et in bellis esse fortes. Et impietates ab eis magnas agi dicunt: non cognoscentes naturae dignitatem, sicuti muta animalia, matribus et sororibus condormiunt. Et impie faciunt in illum qui fecit eos deum. Aliam autem abundare dicuntur in omnibus; data enim potestate negotii gentibus adpropinguantibus suae regionis, ad eos omnia abundare videntur.* Cf. *DTMG* 19: *Post hos sunt Persae Romanis propinquantes, quos historiae tradunt pessimos esse et fortes in bellis, qui, non cognoscentes dignitatem naturae, sicuti muta animalia matribus et sororibus nefando concubitu sociantur. Data propinquis gentibus potestate negotii, bonis omnibus abundare videntur.*

68 Ammianus gives in 23.6.1–88 a more mixed assessment of Persian moral state, while Agathias, centuries later, again echoes a more unambiguously hostile view. See Den Boeft 1999; Cameron 1970.

69 On the Syriac (though primarily Christian) perspectives on the Magi, see Yoshiko Reed, 75–82.

70 On Moses as a magician and Josephus' attitude towards this tradition, see Feldman 1992, 307.

tied to a pedigree of wisdom that goes all the way back to the Chaldaeans? This seems like a veritable overkill in terms of building authority, but it does find certain parallels in the way in which Ammianus Marcellinus wrote about the *translatio* of Brahminic knowledge, through Zoroaster, to the Magi of Persia.[71] The likeliest explanation is that the 'Magi' denotes a category for the first group of earlier sources singled out by the author. This seems to be the only thing linking the mentions of Berossus 'the philosopher of Chaldaeans', Manetho 'the prophet of Egyptians', and Apollonius 'also an Egyptian philosopher'. From these, the author proceeds to his second category of sources, the historians, with the addition of Josephus locating him squarely among the sages.

In the later, province-based section of the *ETMG/DTMG*, the author's construction of identities and affinities seems to waver between identifying with the nodes of the network, and the network itself. Each province is assumed to have its own specialities—whether manufactured, providentially nature-given, or human. Occasionally it even seems like the purpose of the text's latter half is to provide a 'conversation manual' for an enterprising merchant, who will be able to appear knowledgeable about any province or region of the empire, at least among his peer group. These locally specific nodes, then, form the Imperial network of trade and mutual supply, which arguably is the aspect for which the author reserves his most awestruck appreciation.[72] In such a scheme, the first, hodoiporic part of the text would form an exotic prelude to a system that covers the whole world and all the necessities of human life.

If we think about the narratology of the *ETMG* in its entirety, one might also suggest that the way in which the Roman Empire's network of exchange and its excellent products connect with the hodoiporic and exoticising prior part of *ETMG*, produces a heightening of value and prestige to goods which in some ways could have seemed humdrum. This may partly have been why it made

---

71 Amm. 23.6.32–33: *In his tractibus Magorum agri sunt fertiles, super quorum secta studiisque, quoniam huc incidimus, pauca conveniet expediri. Magiam opinionum insignium auctor amplissimus Plato machagistiam esse verbo mystico docet, divinorum incorruptissimum cultum, cuius scientiae saeculis priscis multa ex Chaldaeorum arcanis Bactrianus addidit Zoroastres, deinde Hystaspes rex prudentissimus Darei pater. Qui cum superioris Indiae secreta fidentius penetraret, ad nemorosam quandam venerat solitudinem, cuius tranquillis silentiis praecelsa Brachmanorum ingenia potiuntur, eorumque monitu rationes mundani motus et siderum purosque sacrorum ritus quantum colligere potuit eruditus, ex his, quae didicit, aliqua sensibus magorum infudit, quae illi cum disciplinis praesentiendi futura per suam quisque progeniem posteris aetatibus tradunt.*

72 On the Imperial-era rhetoric of the 'local', see Whitmarsh 2010.

sense for the author to speak about 'divine bread' (DTMG 4) of the Camarini in India. Egypt, for its part, has wisdom as its own 'ethnic product'—almost as a sort of 'India within the Empire': as noted above, Upper Egypt was even presented as contiguous with 'Indians' (i.e. with Ethiopia).[73] The exceptionality of the 'riches of the east' trickled through the described caravan routes of *mansiones* right into the heart of the empire, and even all the way to the Atlantic seaboard, where the enquiry of the author fizzles out as it encounters the unmappable expanse of the Ocean:

> Here, it is said, lies the Ocean, along with the part [of the world] which no human can describe. But what could exist there? For it is uninhabited, and as they say, the end of the world is there.[74]

A sense of not merely a geographical but also an epistemological *aporia* takes over the writer at the thought of the western Ocean. Nothing to go towards—nothing to say: the network thinking of the author cannot really take in an area that is uninhabited or deserted (*desertum*)—a word which might well evoke notions of unproductivity, as well. The work that has begun in the East in a way that is not only geographical but also civilizational and chronological (the primacy of the East), ends up having nothing much to say about the western margin of the *oikoumene*.

Yet neither the Jewish nor the Christian notions of certain geographical spaces or landscapes being particularly imbued with holiness (though such ideas were still under development in texts such as *Itinerarium Egeriae* during the very lifetime of the author of the E/DTMG) seem to accurately reflect the spatial conceptions of the text at hand.[75] A certain kind of blessedness seems implied in the case of individual provinces, but this is mediated through their rich products, as well as the providential mosaic of the Roman world as a self-sufficient network. In his own spatial scheme, the author—himself a native of the Eastern Mediterranean where many cities are said to pursue trade fervently (*ferventer*)—creates connections between the fabulous eastern fringes of the world and the whole network of the Roman provinces, but contrasts this with the image of the West as a fringe where provinces such as Spain are 'considered by many to be poor'.[76] Our author is not interested in connecting ideas of spir-

73 For this so-called 'confusion of Indias' (as e.g. in Mayerson 1993), see now Schneider 2016.

74 ETMG 59: *Inde Oceanum esse dicitur et huius partem quam nemo hominum narrare potest. Sed quid ibi esse potest? Est enim desertum et, sicut aiunt, est ibi finis mundi.*

75 For Egeria, see Lozovsky 2000, 46.

76 ETMG 59: *apud multos autem debilis esse videtur.*

ituality with such barren lands, and neither does he indicate any connections between abundance and sin, the way many Christian historiographers did—a device which in itself was a classical topos used to debate the moral effects of luxury (*luxuria*).[77]

5 Concluding Remarks

ETMG and DTMG both render a Greek original text that occupied an ambiguous position to the religious identities of its own era. What makes the author of the original so fascinating is the fact that he seems to have been a figure with no vested religious identity in a time—the age of Constantius II, Julian, and Jovian—that such identities had become more prominently foregrounded than perhaps at any previous point. Religion, in the ETMG, obtains a role that is more focused on sightseeing and curiosities than any systematic coverage of holy places: churches and other sacred locales of Christianity are not mentioned. The pride of place is taken instead by the produce of each region, for which the most enthusiastic praise is reserved. *Divinus* is frequently used as a term of approval—even in contexts where it might have appeared vulgar and disrespectful to any religiously-minded monotheist of Late Antiquity; this has led Grüll to wryly observe that the author (or the translator, at any rate) does not seem to have been aware of the third commandment of the Decalogue about not taking the name of the Lord in vain.[78]

Interesting cases of their own are the instances in which the probably Christian translators and redactors of the ETMG have not cared to remove mentions of pagan divinities or rituals. In the case of the ETMG's story of the 'awarding' of the Musaeum to Alexandria as the result of a competition between Greeks and Egyptians, the surviving narrative has kept the mention of Asclepius; another example are the voluminous compliments paid to the Egyptians for their traditions of divine worship. The redactor or translator of the ETMG—unlike that of DTMG[79]—clearly did not see it worthwhile to expurgate all these, perhaps because the 'archival aesthetic' of the ETMG's initial sections. The pitching of the work as something standing in linear derivation from the ancient prophets and sages of old, and as being a text of great worth, could have made the Musaeum a useful symbol for the work as a

77 See Ahern 2017, especially 613–614 on the fourth and fifth centuries.

78 Grüll 2014, 639.

79 Cf. Vasiliev 1936, 6.

whole.[80] The writer's use of Christian-sounding phrases seems to testify to the author's awareness of at least some Christian ways of expression, but it should also be remembered that these, too, could stem from the later Latin translators.

As for the author himself, it may be useful to keep in mind the option that he was neither Christian nor pagan—inasmuch as such religious affiliations existed in any monolithic way, in any case—but instead belonged to the possibly quite sizable portion of the population for whom it was expedient (or sufficient) to remain respectful of all cults and wisdom traditions.[81] We should not expect there to have only been narratives of conversion even in this intensely religious era: for some people, remaining in-between religious affiliations and being ready to recognise whatever was noteworthy in any religious tradition, could certainly have seemed like the best option. Stability in religious affinities during the fourth century should not be overstated. Neither should we close our eyes to the benefits of non-conversion in contrast to conversion. If conversion, at least when narrated, functions to create differences, the *E/DTMG* is not interested in articulating such religious differences: the range of variety it is preoccupied with is instead of a material kind.[82] The author's enthusiasm and loyalty seems to be devoted to the flow of goods, services and local specialities in the imperial network, into which the presence of the emperor(s) created nodes of particularly heightened intensity and providentiality. Yet rather than seeing this side of the writer's identity as a decisive identifier of a 'merchant-geographer', it might be better to understand the network aspects of *ETMG* as an 'archival' ordering principle which was reinforced by the usages of other contemporary texts—and possibly even by maps. The trade and exchange in the text is almost as much about knowledge than about commodities: the recipient of the text is offered a tool to being prepared and informed in the ways that

80 As an analogy one could point to how Pomponius Mela takes the labyrinth as a metaphor and cipher for his own ordering of the meandering and cryptic, but eventually solvable riddle that is the World (cf. Romer 1998, 9–13).

81 Although Cameron 2011, 177 notes the difficulty of assessing the numbers of 'committed' vs. 'centrist' practitioners (and non-practitioners), the existence of many individuals who did not feel inclined to commit exclusively to Christianity is well recognised. On religious ambiguity and utilitarianism in Late Antiquity: Papaconstantinou 2015, xxix; Sizgorich 2015, 163–165; cf. Kahlos 2007, 26–28; Cameron 2011, 176–177. On how the majority of the population of the empire are unrepresented by our religiously-tinged sources: MacMullen 1997, 64, 75–76; their practices often avoided choosing firmly between one tradition and the next: Sizgorich 2009, 115; White 2011, 200.

82 Conversion narratives geared towards 'making a difference': Sizgorich 2015, 165 (cf. Kahlos 2007, 83–85).

the Late Roman Empire linked together. Wisdom, the text seems to imply, was one commodity among others. The author's praise of papyrus is at least partly explicable through it constituting a major kind of 'information technology'.

Overall, then, it might be worthwhile to envision the religious affinities of the author of *E/DTMG*'s original as a genuinely utilitarian and contingent set of professed opinions. Indeed, there is little reason to expect something else. Things of great antiquity, whether in Rome or Alexandria, were of great interest to the author, and he made particular remarks of pagan cults at several sites. This, as well as the reverential gesturing towards the sages of old in the beginning of his work bring him close to the vaguely 'monotheistic' Late Antique appreciation for any wisdom traditions provided that they are old enough.[83] The linkages between the oldest wisdom of the east were already showcased at the very outset of *DTMG*, and the later shift from the exotic goods and ethnographic curiosities of the similarly eastern hodoiporic sections of the text to the vibrant exchange network of the Empire are all very confidently handled, and we would be hard pressed to detect any indication of religious or identity-related insecurity in the way our anonymous, excitable Eastern-Mediterranean author inhabits the complex networks through which he scampers.

Bibliography

Ahern, Eoghan. "Abundance, *Luxuria*, and Sin in Late Antique Historiography." *JECS* 25 (2017): 605–631.

Berger, Denis. "Les paradis orientaux d'Ammien Marcellin." *RÉL* 80 (2002): 176–188.

Braginsky, Vladimir. "Two Eastern Christian Sources on Medieval Nusantara." *Bijdragen tot de Taal-, Land- en Volkenkunde* 154 (1998): 367–396.

Broze, Michéle, Aude Busine and Sabrina Inowlocki. "Les catalogues de peuples sages. Fonctions et contextes d'utilisation." *Kernos* 19 (2006): 131–144.

Buell, Denise Kimber. *Why This New Race. Ethnic Reasoning in Early Christianity*. New York: Columbia University Press, 2005.

Cameron, Averil. "Agathias on the Sassanians." *DOP* 23/24 (1970): 67–183.

Cameron, Alan. *The Last Pagans of Rome*. New York: Oxford University Press, 2011.

Clark, Gillian. "Translate into Greek: Porphyry of Tyre on the new barbarians". In: Richard Miles, *Constructing Identities in Late Antiquity*. London: Routledge, 1999, 112–132.

83 Cf. Pilhofer 1990.

Den Boeft, J. "Pure Rites—Ammianus Marcellinus on the Magi." In: Jan Willem Drijvers and Edward David Hunt (eds.), *The Late Roman World and Its Historian: Interpreting Ammianus Marcellinus*. London: Routledge, 1999, 207–215.

Derrett, John Duncan Martin. "The history of 'Palladius on the Races of India and the Brahmans'." *Classica et mediaevalia, separatum*. Oslo: Gyldendal, 1960, 64–135.

Feldman, Louis H. "'Josephus' Portrait of Moses." *The Jewish Quarterly Review* 82 (1992): 285–328.

Fishwick, Duncan. *The Imperial Cult in the Latin West*, vol. 2.1. Leiden and New York: Brill, 1991.

Fitzgerald Johnson, Scott. *Literary Territories. Cartographical Thinking in Late Antiquity*. Oxford and New York: Oxford University Press, 2016.

Formisano, Marco. *Tecnica e scrittura: le letterature tecnico-scientifiche nello spazio letterario tardolatino*. Rome: Carocci, 2001.

Frankfurter, David. *Religion in Roman Egypt. Assimilation and Resistance*. Princeton: Princeton University Press, 1998.

Galinsky, Karl. "The Cult of the Roman Emperor: Uniter of Divider?" In: Jeffrey Brodd and Jonathan L. Reed (eds.), *Rome and Religion. A Cross-Disciplinary Dialogue on the Imperial Cult*. Atlanta: Society of Biblical Literature, 2011, 1–21.

Grüll, Tibor. "*Expositio totius mundi et gentium*. A peculiar work on the commerce of Roman Empire from the mid-fourth century—compiled by a Syrian textile dealer?" In: Zoltán Csabai (ed.), *Studies in Economic and Social History of the Ancient Near East in Memory of Péter Vargyas*. Budapest: L'Harmattan, 2014, 629–642.

Haas, Christopher. *Alexandria in Late Antiquity. Topography and Social Conflict*. Baltimore and London: Johns Hopkins University Press, 1997.

Hahn, Ludwig. *Die Sprache der sogenannten Expositio totius mundi et gentium*. Bayreuth: E. Mühl, 1898.

Haubold, Johannes. '"The wisdom of the Chaldaeans': reading Berossos, *Babyloniaca* Book 1." In: Johannes Haubold, Giovanni B. Lanfranchi, Robert Rollinger and John M. Steele (eds.), *The World of Berossos*. Wiesbaden: Harassowitz, 2013, 31–46.

Janowitz, Naomi. "Rethinking Jewish Identity in Late Antiquity." In: Stephen Mitchell and Geoffrey Greatrex (eds.), *Ethnicity and Culture in Late Antiquity*. London and Swansea: Duckworth and The Classical Press of Wales, 2000, 205–219.

De Jong, Janneke. "Emperor Meets Gods: Divine Discourse in Greek Papyri from Roman Egypt." In: Maijastina Kahlos (ed.), *Emperors and the Divine—Rome and its Influence*. Helsinki: COLLeGIUM 20, 2016. [https://helda.helsinki.fi/handle/10138/161314], 22–55.

Kahlos, Maijastina. *Debate and Dialogue: Christian and Pagan Cultures c. 360–430*. Aldershot: Routledge, 2007.

Kahlos, Maijastina. "The Emperor's New Images—How to Honour the Emperor in the Christian Roman Empire?" In: Maijastina Kahlos (ed.), *Emperors and the Divine—*

Rome and its Influence. Helsinki: COLLeGIUM 20, 2016. [https://helda.helsinki.fi/handle/10138/161319], 119–138.

Klotz, Alfred. "Über die *Expositio totius mundi et gentium*." *Philologus* 65 (1906): 97–127.

Klotz, Alfred. "'Οδοιπορία ἀπὸ 'Εδὲμ τοῦ παραδείσου ἄχρι τῶν 'Ρωμαίων." *RhM* 65 (1910): 607–616.

Kolb, Anne and Michael A. Speidel. "Perceptions from Beyond: Some Observations on Non-Roman Assessments of the Roman Empire from the Great Eastern Trade Routes." In: Daniëlle Slootjes and Michael Peachin (eds.), *Rome and the Worlds Beyond Its Frontiers*. Leiden: Brill, 2016, 151–179.

Lampinen, Antti. "Cultural Artefacts in Transit: Notes on the Transmission and Translation of Ethnonyms in the Greco-Roman Eastern Mediterranean." In: Jaakko Hämeen-Anttila and Ilkka Lindstedt (eds.), *Translation and Transmission. Collection of Articles*. The Intellectual Heritage of the Ancient and Mediaeval Near East 3. Münster: Ugarit-Verlag, 2019, 139–179.

Lozovsky, Natalia. *"The Earth is Our Book". Geographical Knowledge in the Latin West ca. 400–1000*. Ann Arbor: University of Michigan Press, 2000.

Mayerson, Philip. "A Confusion of Indias: Asian India and African India in the Byzantine Sources." *Journal of the American Oriental Society* 113/2 (1993): 169–174.

McLynn, Neil. "Seeing and Believing: Aspects of Conversion from Antoninus Pius to Louis the Pious." In: Kenneth Mills and Anthony Grafton (eds.), *Conversion in Late Antiquity and the Early Middle Ages. Seeing and Believing*. Rochester, NY and Woodbridge: University of Rochester Press, 2003, 224–270.

MacCoull, Leslie S.B. "Philosophy in its social context." In: Roger S. Bagnall (ed.), *Egypt in the Byzantine World, 300–700*. Cambridge: Cambridge University Press, 2007, 67–82.

MacMullen, Ramsay. *Christianity and Paganism in the Fourth to Eight Centuries*. New Haven and London: Yale University Press, 1997.

Marasco, Gabriele. "L'*Expositio totius mundi et gentium* e la politica religiosa di Costanzo II." *Ancient Society* 27 (1996): 183–203.

Martelli, Fabio. *Introduzione alla "Expositio totius mundi". Analisi etnografica e tematiche politiche in un'opera anonima del IV secolo*. Bologna: Giorgio Barchigiani Editore, 1982.

Mason, Steve. "The Greeks and the Distant Past in Josephus' *Judaean War*." In: Gregg E. Gardner and Kevin Lee Osterloh (eds.), *Antiquity in antiquity: Jewish and Christian pasts in the Greco-Roman world*. Tübingen: Mohr Siebeck, 2008, 93–130.

Masuzawa, Tomoko. *The Invention of World Religions; or, How European Universalism was Preserved in the Language of Pluralism*. Chicago: University of Chicago Press, 2005.

Mittag, Peter Franz. "Zu den Quellen der *Expositio Totius Mundi et Gentium*. Ein neuer Periplus?" *Hermes* 134 (2006): 338–351.

Müller, Friedrich Max. *India. What can it teach us? A Course of Lectures Delivered before the University of Cambridge*. London: Longmans, Green, and Co., 1883.

Papaconstantinou, Arietta. "Introduction." In: Arietta Papaconstantinou, Neil McLynn and Daniel L. Schwartz (eds.), *Conversion in Late Antiquity: Christianity, Islam, and Beyond*. Farnham: Ashgate, 2015, xv–xxxvii.

Pfister, Friedrich. "Die Ὁδοιπορία ἀπὸ Ἐδὲμ τοῦ παραδείσου und die Legende von Alexanders Zug nach dem Paradies." *RhM* 66 (1911): 458–471.

Pilhofer, Peter. *Presbyteron Kreitton. Der Altersbeweis der jüdischen und christlichen Apologeten und seine Vorgeschichte*. Tübingen: Mohr, 1990.

Ratzan, David M. "Freakonomika: Oracle as Economic Indicator in Roman Egypt." In: AnneMarie Luijendijk and William E. Klingshirn (eds.), *My Lots are in Thy Hands: Sortilege and its Practitioners in Late Antiquity*. Leiden and Boston: Brill, 2018, 248–289.

Romer, Frank E. *Pomponius Mela's Description of the World*. Ann Arbor: University of Michigan Press, 1998.

Rougé, Jean. *Expositio totius mundi et gentium*. Paris: Éditions du Cerf, 1966.

Rougé, Jean. "Compte-rendu de Fabio Martelli, *Introduzione alla 'Expositio totius mundi'*." *Revue des Études Anciennes* 85 (1983): 161–162.

Schneider, Pierre. "The So-called Confusion between India and Ethiopia: The Eastern and Southern Edges of the Inhabited World from the Greco-Roman Perspective." In: Serena Bianchetti, Michele R. Cataudella and Hans-Joachim Gehrke (eds.), *Brill's Companion to Ancient Geography*. Leiden: Brill, 2016, 184–202.

Sinko, Thaddäus. "Die *Descriptio orbis terrae*, eine Handelsgeographie aus dem 4. Jahrhundert." *Archiv für lateinische Lexikographie und Grammatik* 13 (1904): 531–571.

Sizgorich, Thomas. *Violence and Belief in Late Antiquity. Militant Devotion in Christianity and Islam*. Philadelphia: University of Pennsylvania Press, 2009.

Sizgorich, Thomas. "Mind the Gap: Accidental Conversion and the Hagiographic Imaginary in the First Centuries A.H." In: Arietta Papaconstantinou, Neil McLynn and Daniel L. Schwartz (eds.), *Conversion in Late Antiquity: Christianity, Islam, and Beyond*. Farnham: Ashgate, 2015, 163–174.

Stroumsa, Guy G. "Philosophy of the Barbarians: On Early Christian Ethnological Representations." In: Guy G. Stroumsa (ed.), *Barbarian Philosophy: The Religious Revolution of Early Christianity*. Tübingen: Mohr Siebeck, 1999, 57–84.

Van Andringa, William. "Rhetoric and Divine Honours: On the "Imperial Cult" in the Reigns of Augustus and Constantine." In: Maijastina Kahlos (ed.), *Emperors and the Divine—Rome and its Influence*. Helsinki: COLLeGIUM 20, 2016. [https://helda.helsinki.fi/handle/10138/161313], 10–21.

Vasiliev, A.A. "*Expositio Totius Mundi*. An Anonymous Geographic Treatise of the Fourth Century A.D." *Seminarium Kondakovianum* 8 (1936): 1–39.

Yoshiko Reed, Annette. "Beyond the Land of Nod: Syriac Images of Asia and the Historiography of 'The West'." *History of Religions* 49 (2009): 48–87.

White, Michael L. "Capitalizing on the Imperial Cult: Some Jewish Perspectives." In: Jeffrey Brodd and Jonathan L. Reed (eds.), *Rome and Religion. A Cross-Disciplinary Dialogue on the Imperial Cult*. Atlanta: Society of Biblical Literature, 2011, 173–214.

Whitmarsh, Tim. "Thinking local." In: Tim Whitmarsh (ed.), *Local Knowledge and Microidentities in the Imperial Greek World*. Cambridge: Cambridge University Press, 2010, 1–16.

Wölfflin, E. "Bemerkungen zu der *Descriptio orbis*." *Archiv für lateinische Lexikographie und Grammatik* 13 (1904): 574–578.

CHAPTER 3

Reconstructing the Identity of the Bacchic Group in Athens: οἱ Ἰόβακχοι and IG II[2] 1368

Elina Lapinoja-Pitkänen

The classical inscription IG II[2] 1368, *The rule of the Iobakchoi*,[1] offers us a rare insight to the world of Greco-Roman religious voluntary associations.[2] It was engraved on a column around 164/165 of the Common Era,[3] and it includes explanations of rituals, customs, and regulations of a voluntary association devoted to the worship of Dionysos. This article examines how the inscription IG II[2] 1368 may have influenced the identity of the group. Regulations, elite benefactors, rituals, and mythical narratives remembered and re-enacted

1 Now also known as the "Regulations of the Iobakchoi."

2 Some suggested reasons for the origins of religion are: 1) religion explains the world, its origins, good and evil, it gives reason for suffering; 2) religion has a comforting capability; 3) religion offers social order; and finally, 4) religion is an illusion based on superstition. Geertz 2004, 359–360. Indisputably the concept or term "religious" in the context of antiquity is a difficult one, and it has been argued, for instance, by Philp A. Harland, that the terms "religion/religious" should not be used at all, the main argument being that the term "religion" is a modern scholarly concept often observed from one's own religious background. Another issue making the use of the terms or concepts "religious/religion" difficult is the overlapping nature of the religious and secular lives of Hellenistic and imperial times. From the cultural point of view, separating religion from everyday life is impossible, as Harland argues. Harland 2013; Ilkka Pyysiäinen points out that the concept of religion is indeed an academic construct, used to categorize phenomena that one is studying. Pyysiäinen 2003, 1–2. For further discussion, see Smith 1982; Anttonen 2000. However, Pyysiäinen continues, explaining that, even though the categorization of "religion/religious" is an academic construct based on one's own expectations of what religion should be like, this does not mean that the phenomenon itself does not exist. He notes that "Religious beliefs, behaviours, etc. do have a real existence, independent of the academy, and are understood by believers as distinctive domain"; Pyysiäinen 2003, 1–2. Thus, I also use the term "religion" to describe associations whose members' primary connection can be traced back to a sanctuary/temple or to religious activities.

3 For further detail, see *GRA* 2011, 241. For discussion on the dating of the column and its inscription, see GRA page 248 starting from note 1.2 where Kloppenborg and Ascough discuss the dating of this inscription through archons and the priest Herodes Attikos (II). In 1894, Sam Wide published an article discussing the dating of the inscription by using the diacritics on the iota, arguing that iota adscript indicates the latter half of the second century CE. Wide 1894, 248–282; GRA 2011, 241.

 | DOI:10.1163/9789004471160_004

through ritual, were all part of the everyday life of the *Iobakchoi*. However, they also played a part in the construction and re-formation of the social identity of the association.

1 Greco-Roman Associations

The term association has been well established in discussions of ancient organizations (ἔρανον, κοινόν, *collegium*, etc.) and the adjective "voluntary" has been added to distinguish associations from institutions (state, city, or family).[4] To make sense of the vast amount of inscriptional material, researchers have categorized associations based on different distinguishing factors. Traditionally, associations have been categorized into three groups based on their main function: occupational, cultic, and funerary associations.[5] However, categorization based on the main functions has challenges, and in more recent research it has been discarded as insufficient.[6] During the last decades scholars have offered alternative classifications where the focus has shifted from associations' main functions to their members and membership networks. John S. Kloppenborg suggests a categorization based on membership profile, introducing three main sources of membership: common household connections, shared occupation, and common cult.[7] Philip Harland uses Kloppenborg's typology

4 For instance, Wilson 1996, 1. However, it is important to note that the adjective *voluntary* is somewhat misleading, and in recent years the term has often been substituted with either unofficial associations or private associations. See Kloppenborg 2019, 1; Last and Harland 2020, 9–10.

5 Earlier studies were done, for instance, by Paul-François Foucart, in 1873 and Erich Ziebarth in 1910.

6 First, because the boundaries of associations were obscure, all associations were somewhat religious/cultic, and distinguishing that aspect from occupational associations or funerary associations would not be supported by evidence, (see Wilson 1996, 7). For example, an association of Roman merchants was an occupational association, but their texts also show clear indications that they also worshiped certain gods and hence were also a religious association (GRA 2011, 297. SEG 1:282). Second, there is lack of evidence of associations that were solely devoted to funerary practices until the time of Hadrian. For further, Kloppenborg 1996, 20–23. Furthermore, there is evidence that so-called religious associations and occupational associations also buried their dead. One example of an occupational association that buried their dead is found in SEG 32:488 (GRA 2011, 287). See also IG II^2 13232012, 10; AGRW 25 = PHI 27703; AGRW 2012, 34.

7 Kloppenborg 1996, 18–26. The members of these associations did not participate exclusively joint meetings of only one type of association but were more likely to belong to several associations. In his article *Associations, Guilds, Clubs*, published in 2018, Kloppenborg also discusses neighbourhood and diasporic associations as basic types. Kloppenborg 2018, 155.

in developing his own categorization based on members' principal social network connections, ending up with five common types of associations: Household connections, ethnic or geographic connections, neighbourhood connections, occupational connections, cult or temple connections.[8] Even though these categories offer a way to comprehend and study the Greco-Roman associations, they are still scholarly hypotheses, and as such cannot be taken too strictly.[9]

2 The Character of Dionysos

Dionysos was a popular deity throughout the centuries, and even though he was not part of the original Greek or Roman pantheon, his character was introduced already at an early date to Greco-Roman mythology.[10]

Gradually the worship of Dionysos spread, first to the eastern and later to the whole Mediterranean area, being particularly popular in Ionia.[11] It has been argued that one reason behind the success of the cults of Dionysos was the fact that Alexander the Great was intrigued by narratives and the character of Dionysos.[12] Besides being well advertised by Alexander, another, perhaps more

8 Harland 2013, 25–52. See also Ascough 2002, 1–2.

9 One issue complicating categorization, in addition to fragmentary evidence, is the nature of social networks and how people belonged to several social networks, thus being members of several different associations. Wilson 1996, 9–10; Harland 2003, 52–53. Harland points out that his own classification is not exact and that it cannot be taken as the final word.

10 The first mentions of Dionysos and the mythological narratives of his past come from two Linear B tablets found at Khania and Pylos. Cole 2007, 327–341. The second appearance is a small part in Homeric epic by the time myths of Dionysos are already well established. Thus, the author does not offer extended explanations of the character of Dionysos as is done in the case of a few other deities the author introduces. Bremmer 2013, 6.

11 Cole 2007, 328. See, for instance, the following inscriptions: IG VII 686 "Grave of Galatas Prepared by Dionysiasts (250–200 BCE)" Trans. John F. Kloppenborg. *Associations in the Greco-Roman World,* Accessed 30 September 2019, http://www.philipharland.com/greco-roman-associations/?p=4495; IG VII 107 "Honors by a Baccheion for Flavia Lais and Flavia Apollonia" (after 117 CE) || Megara—Attica. Trans. Philip Harland. *Associations in the Greco-Roman World* Accessed 30 September 2019. http://www.philipharland.com/greco-roman-associations/?p=23167; SEG 41 (1991), no. 1064 "Grave of a Leader of a Bacchic Association" (III CE) || Daskyleion—Mysia and the Troad. Trans. Philip Harland. *Associations in the Greco-Roman World* Accessed 30 September 2019. http://www.philipharland.com/greco-roman-associations/?p=20464.

12 Dalby 2003, 78.

plausible reason why Dionysiac associations were able to maintain their popularity over centuries was connected to the fluid and flexible character of the deity. Dionysos is described being a multipurpose deity: He was the god of wine, but also a god of life and death, who was said to have been born two or three times.[13] He descended to Hades to collect his mother and eventually moved to Olympus.[14] In writings and in art, Dionysos is portrayed as a God of opposites: male and female, popular and underrated. He is often pictured wearing clothing more suitable for women, like a saffron yellow garment, but he is also described as being very seductive and conquering women as easily as cities.[15] Dionysos was worshiped in popular public festivals,[16] but archaeological and epigraphical evidence proves that Dionysos was also worshiped in private and semi-private voluntary associations.

---

13 Depending on the version, Dionysos was born one, two or three times: two times as a baby, and the third time as a child. First, he was born from his burning mother as a premature baby and given to her sister. Another, later, storyline says that the baby was put into Zeus' thigh and he was born from there a second time in two months' time. (This version is told at least by Lucian, a satirist of the second century CE.) See Dalby 2003, 29–35. According to some ancient writers (Nonnos, *Dionysiaka* 6.163–205; Diodoros of Sicily, *Historical Library* 3.62.6–8; Pausanias, *Guide to Greece* 8.37.3; Hyginus, *Fables* 167.), Dionysos, around the age of two, was killed by Titans at the time of the death of his foster mother. There are two different storylines connected to this death and rebirth of the child Dionysos; both have a similar beginning: First, Dionysos, as a boy, was killed by Titans; they cut him into seven pieces and tossed the pieces into a cauldron. According to the more common account, he was saved by Gaia or Demeter, who assembled him again. The second storyline comes from the philosopher Proklos. In the version that he recorded in his *Hymns*, Titans boiled and even ate the poor Dionysos. The remains of Dionysos were given to Apollo by Zeus to be buried. Apollo buried the remains near his shrine at Delphos. Dionysos' heart was the only part that the Titans did not eat, and it was still beating, Athene came and rescued the heart, and from this heart a new Dionysos came to life. Dalby 2003, 42–43. Proklos, *Hymns* 7.11–15; see also West 1985, 87–90.

14 The outline of.Dionysos' travels to the underworld and back are told by Hyginus, but parts of it can be observed in various ancient writers. For a longer discussion about this trip, see Dalby 2003, 107–117.

15 Dalby 2003, 72–74.

16 For example, in Athens the famous Dionysos theatre was located in the sanctuary area of Dionysus Eleuthereus or 'The Liberator.' Worship of the deity is thought to have spread during the rule of Peisistratus in the 6th century BC. Worship of the god was originally a rural festival in the ancient city of Eleutherae in Attica. For more details,

Papastamati-von Moock 2014, 15–76. The Sanctuary of Dionysus in Athens played host to one of the largest theatrical festivals in the ancient world. Its influence shaped the spread of theatre to many other areas of the world and pioneered the genres and format of theatrics that we use today.

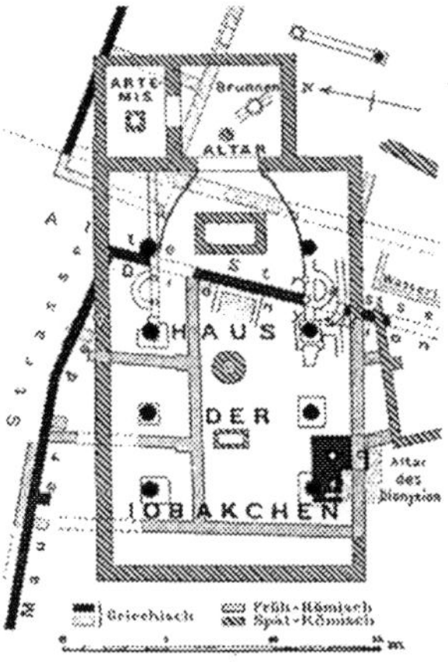

FIGURE 3.1
Building plan of the Bakcheion, apse and colonnade emphasized
JUDEICH 1905, 261

3 The Bakcheion and IG II^2 1368

The inscription IG II^2 1368 was found in an apse inside a sanctuary devoted to the worship of Dionysos.[17] The *Bakcheion* (Βακχεῖον), as the sanctuary is addressed in the inscription, was located near the western slope on the main road leading to the centre of the Acropolis.[18] The Bakcheion measured around 198 m^2 having two rows of columns, as can be seen in the floorplan, and a semi-circular recess or the apse where the column with the inscription was found.[19]

The column itself is 99.5 cm in height, and 31 cm in diameter, which makes this inscription one of the longest readable inscriptions describing activities of voluntary associations. The stele was erected by a group of people addressing themselves as οἱ ἰόβακχοι, i.e. the worshippers of Bacchus, and it contains rules and regulations of the said association.

The inscription begins (lines 1–32) with customary greetings and continues by explaining how the stele come to be. It states that the priest read the statutes made by former priests, and then members voted on the need to combine the

17 The site was first excavated in the late 19th century by Wilhelm Dörpfeld. Dörpfeld 1895, 161–206. The archaeological report can be found on Philip Harland's internet site: http://www.philipharland.com/greco-roman-associations/?p=23404.

18 Dörpfeld 1895, 176–180; Travlos 1980, 274–277, 332; GRA 2011, 241. The Bakcheion was most likely built on an older triangular sanctuary that was no longer in use (GRA 2011, 241). The previous sanctuary has been identified as being either a sanctuary of Herakles Alexikakos or of the Dionysos of the Marshes. Dörpfeld 1895, and many following him believe this to have been the sanctuary also mentioned by Thucydides in his *History of the Peloponnesian war* 2.15.4: "τὸ ⟨τοῦ⟩ ἐν Λίμναις Διονύσου".

19 An altar decorated with images arising from the mythological narratives of Dionysos was also found in the apse. For a complete list of the findings, see Schäfer 2002.

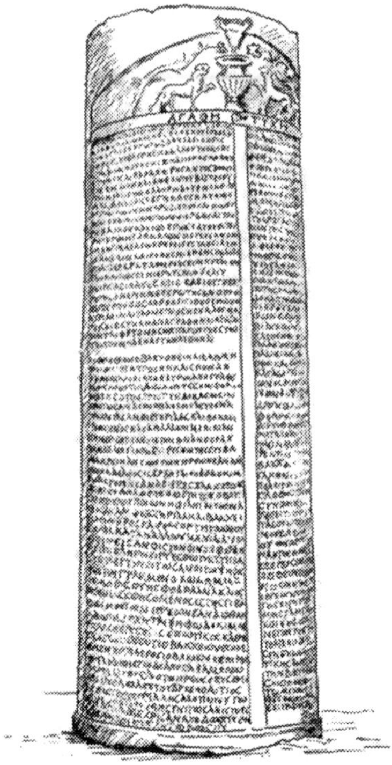

FIGURE 3.2
Column with the rules of the Iobakchoi
HARRISON 1906, 90, FIG. 25

information from these previous statutes together on one large stele, which was then done. After this explanation, the inscription moves on to deal with the manifold rules and regulations of the association.[20] Altogether the inscription consists of 163 lines:

32–62 Explanations covering the meeting days and entrance qualifications.
63–110 Rules and regulations concerning the actual meetings.
111–127 Instructions for leaders of the association and explanations of rituals.
127–136 List of special situations when a member is required to make a libation to the God.
136–159 Explanations of acceptable behaviour during the meetings and instructions on different positions held by the members.
159–163 discussion on how the association honors their deceased members.[21]

20 Dennis Smith discusses the previous statutes, highlighting the inconsistencies present in the stele: Smith 2003, 111–112.

21 For the whole inscription and translations see, for instance, *GRA* 2011 or *AGRW 2012*. Both GRA and AGRW 2012 include translations and comments. For a German translation, see Ebel 2002, 87–101.

4 Activities of the Association[22]

The Iobakchoi (Οἱ ἰόβακχοι) had a manifold hierarchical structure created over decades and now finally engraved on one collective stele. The stele functioned as a catalogue of their rules, but also as a reminder for present and future members of the importance of their association. In contrast to many other Dionysian associations this association was open only to (freeborn) men and boys.[23] In order to become a member and a part of the Iobakchoi, one had to go through a three-stage initiation process. The first step was registration, after which current members of the group would vote on whether the new candidate was suitable to enter their association.[24] If the candidate is approved, he must then pay an entrance fee of 50 denarii and make a libation, or if one's father is a member and the candidate is underage then the fee is 25 denarii and a libation.[25] After the payment was made, the priest would give the new member documentation proving his membership. The association had elite members, but it was not just a hub for the elite to get together but was also open to the middle class if they could afford to pay the entrance fee. The entrance fee of 50 denarii was reasonably small, indicating that it was not meant to create boundaries that only the elite could cross. Rather, the entrance fee and other additional fees were meant to gain lifelong members from a variety of socioeconomic levels.[26] Another clear indicator that the Iobakchoi had members from

22 See also Dennis Smith's most important discussion on the meetings and regulations of this association. Smith 2003, 111–123.

23 Underage boys were also welcome if they were able to meet the entrance requirements. When they come of age, they were expected to make an additional libation (line 130: ἐφηβείας). GRA notes that many later (CE) Dionysiac associations were heterogenous, having both male and female members from a variety of social levels. GRA 2011, 294.

See, for example, AGRW 25 = IG IV 207; GRA I 61 = IG IX,1² 670; GRA I 71 = IPhilippiP II 340/L589; GRA I 80 = IG X,2.1 506.

24 μηδενὶ ἐξέστω ἰόβακχον εἶναι, ἐὰν μὴ | πρῶτον ἀπογράψηται παρὰ τῷ ἱερεῖ | τὴν νενομισμένην ἀπογραφὴν καὶ || δοκιμασθῇ ὑπὸ τῶν ἰοβάκχων ψή|φῳ, εἰ ἄξιος φαίνοιτο καὶ ἐπιτήδειος | τῷ Βακχείῳ (lines 33–37). See also, for instance, IG II² 1369 where the president, head of the club, secretary, treasurer and advocates are meant to examine candidates to find out if they are pure, pious, and good. AGRW 2013, 17.

25 For all the fees and penalties collected by the association, see note 44. Inscriptional evidence seems to suggest that collecting either an entrance fee, annual fees or both was a fairly common practice with voluntary associations. See, for instance, IG IX/1² 670 (GRA 2011, 293); IG II²1339 (GRA 2011, 217) where the fee was 30 denarii; or the association in SEG 31:122 (GRA 2011, 235) whose members when entering the association were expected to offer a large food sacrifice. The association in IG II² 1301 lets us understand that they used annual fees. GRA 2011, 136.

26 At the beginning of the second century CE, the yearly salary for common solders was

different socioeconomic levels comes from the special situations libation list in lines 125–136.[27] The additional libation lists cover all the situations when members need to offer an extra libation, and one of these special situations is the gaining of citizenship (πολειτείας). The citizenship mentioned here is in all probability the Roman citizenship, which would mean that there were members who did not have Roman citizenship. By the second century CE, the Athenian elite already had Roman citizenship, but the middle class were still earning theirs.[28] Thus, having regulations covering the gaining of citizenship would speak for members' varied socioeconomic backgrounds.

At the time of the inscription, the association was led by Herodes Atticus II,[29] one of the wealthiest men in Athens, who, in addition to being the priest of Dionysos, also acted as a benefactor of the association.[30] Including the priest, this inscription introduces six to eight different roles or positions held by the members, depending on how one counts the bouncers (as its own category or as a subcategory to order-keeper (εὔκοσμος)) and secretary. Some were meant for life, while others were short-term appointments. The roles of

---

300 denarii which would be around 339 drachmas. (1 denarius = 1.132 drachma). So, the entrance fee would be the one-sixth of the yearly salary for someone from the lower middle class earning around 300 denarii a year. However, during the second and third century CE inflation was rapid and by the third century the yearly salary of a solder was already 750 denarii per year. For a longer discussion on money and inflation in the second and third century CE See Katsari 2011.

27 ὃς δ' ἂν τῶν ἰοβάκχων λάχῃ κλῆ|ρον ἢ τειμὴν ἢ τάξιν, τιθέτω τοῖς ἰο|βάκχοις σπονδὴν ἀξίαν τῆς τάξεως, || γάμων, γεννήσεως, Χοῶν, ἐφηβείας, | πολειτείας, ῥαβδοφορίας, βουλείας, ἀ|θλοθεσίας, Πανέλληνος, γερουσίας, | θεσμοθεσίας, ἀρχῆς ἧσδηποτεοῦν, | συνθυσίας, εἰρηναρχίας, ἱερονείκου, || καὶ εἴ τίς τι ἐπὶ τὸ κρεῖσσον ἰόβακχος ὢν | τύχοιτο.

28 There were a few traditional ways to gain citizenship: 1) by birth: in the case of citizenship as a birth right, the child's parents must have been married and citizens; in mixed marriages, the child would follow the father's citizenship if the mother was a plebeian, patricians or Latin (Livy 4.1; Adams 2008, 310), 2) by manumission (Adams 2008, 310). By the end of the first century CE, Roman citizenship or granting it had become an integral part of the policy of aggrandizement, and, according to Tacitus, in 47 CE there were 5.9 million citizens (Tacitus, *Ann.* 11.25).

29 In the inscription Herodes is address as κράτιστον "his excellency," highlighting his elite status. Herodes Atticus (Lucius Vibullius Hipparchus Tiberius Claudius Atticus Herodes) (101–177 CE) was a famous benefactor, orator, sophist, and teacher of Marcus Aurelius and Lucius Verus. He was a friend of the emperor Hadrian and acted as a consul in 143 CE. See GRA 2011, 250; https://www.britannica.com/biography/Herodes-Atticus.

30 When compared to other associations, especially to Roman professional guilds, the elite benefactors, like Herodes Atticus II, were more often honorary members, rather than actual participants. Thus, it is interesting to observe that in the case of the *Iobakchoi* the benefactor seems to be active in the meetings since he also acts as the priest directing the meetings. Kloppenborg 2018, 160.

priest (ἱερεύς), vice-priest (ἀνθιερεύς), *archibakchos* (ἀρχίβακχος) and president (προστάτης) were somewhat juxtaposed positions of power. The priest was the head of the association, directing meetings and controlling the initiation ritual. He was most often chosen for life, except in the case of Nikomachos, who stepped down in favour of Herodes, taking up the role of vice-priest.[31] The vice-priest was similarly a high-ranking position, working alongside the priest in maintaining order during the meetings. Kloppenborg and Ascough discuss the possibility that the role of the vice-priest might have been a stepping stone to the position of the priest.[32] The archibakchos (ἀρχίβακχος or as written in line 11 ἀρχίβαχχος) directed the meetings alongside the priest, and he was in charge of the yearly sacrifices made on the 10th day of the month of Elaphebolion (see line 117).[33] The role of the president (προστάτης) is left ambiguous in this inscription, but most likely he held a position of power in this association. At the very least, arranging elections would fall under the job description of the president.[34] However, interestingly, the president is left out when naming those who get a part of the sacrificial meat.[35] Altogether, the position of president is rare in contexts of religious associations but more common in inscriptions listing functionaries connected with education.[36]

Another uncommon position mentioned in the inscription is the role of order-keeper *eukosmos* (εὔκοσμος). His job was to maintain order during the meetings and banquets. In addition to this inscription, there is only one other association inscription mentioning εὔκοσμος as a position held by a member.[37]

---

31 For interesting speculation on why this happened, see: GRA 2011, 254. On nominations of priests for life, see, for instance, AGRW 287 = IDelta I 446; AGRW 129 = TAM V 972 (slightly different contexts); IG VII 107 = CIG 1059 (also priest for life); AGRW 60 = GRA I 60.

32 GRA 2011, 254.

33 προστάσσοντος | τοῦ ἱερέως ἢ τοῦ ἀρχιβάκχου. With inscriptions mentioning sacrificing or sacrifices, it is often the priest or priestess who performs the sacrifice rituals. See, for instance, IG II^2 1283, IG II^2 1315, IG II^2 1334; all can be found on the *Associations in the Greco-Roman World* = AGRW internet site http://philipharland.com/greco-roman-associations/.

34 καὶ ἐπερώτησεν ὁ πρό|εδρος Ῥοῦφος Ἀφροδεισίου· ὅτῳ δοκεῖ | κύρια εἶναι τὰ ἀνεγνωσμένα δόγμα|τα καὶ ἐν στήλῃ ἀναγραφῆναι, ἀράτω | τὴν χεῖρα.

35 Lines 123–125.

36 GRA I 2011, 250. See, for instance, AGRW 279 = IAlexandriaK 96 and IAlexandriaK 92 = AGRW 283.

37 That is, inscription *IPerg* 374.b (GRA II 111 = IPergamon 374): "The keeper of order (*eukosmos*) will also supply wreaths for the hymn singers on the monthly celebration of Augustus' birthday and on the remaining birthdays of the emperors. He will supply wreaths in the hymn singers' meeting place and wreaths for the hymn singers and their sons each day during the mysteries, as well as cakes, incense and (20) lamps for Augustus." See GRA 2011, 252; Robert 1937, 58.

In the case of the Iobakchoi, the order-keeper was chosen either by casting lots or being nominated by the priest. He was given the wand of the God (τὸν θύρσον τοῦ θε|οῦ),[38] and he would, after being approved by the presider (most likely the priest, vice-priest, or archibakchos), lay his wand upon the one causing the disturbance, in which case the troublemaker would have to leave. To help the *eukosmos* with his order-keeping job, the priest named two bouncers (ἵπποι) to escort the troublemaker outside.[39]

The Iobakchoi chose a treasurer for a two-year term (ταμίαν δὲ αἱρείσθωσαν οἱ ἰόβακ|χοι ψήφῳ εἰς διετίαν,) and he was given all the property of the association, which he was then required to write down and keep a record of. Once his term ended, he was expected to pass the records and all the possessions to his successor. If he wanted, he was allowed to appoint a secretary, but at his own risk. And if he chose to have a secretary, his own part of the sacrificial meat would go to the secretary, who would also be liberated from annual fees for his term of office.[40] In addition to keeping a list of all the property of the association, the chosen treasurer was also required to cover the cost of lamp oil for all the meetings during his term of office.[41]

The association met regularly on the 9th day of the month and on the 10th of the month of Elaphebolion and on special occasions (such as the festival of Return—Katagogia or in the case of the death of a member).[42] The special days notwithstanding, the association had different types of meetings: business meetings to discuss the general affairs of the association and maintaining their sanctuary, disciplinary meetings called together when needed, and regular banquets (στίβας).[43] Members were required to pay a contribution

38 See For 'The term Βάκχος and Dionysos Βάκχιος' published in *Redefining Dionysos*, ed. Alberto Bernabé, et al., (De Gruyter, Inc., 2013). The thyrsos, or sacred wand tipped with a pinecone, was used in cultic settings, particularly associated with Dionysos. (GRA 2011, 253.)

See also Burkert and Raffan 1985, 162–163; Casadio and Johnston 2009.

39 Another mention of *hippoi* as bouncers can be found in IG II[2] 236 (GRA 2011, 257–261).

40 αἱρείσθω δὲ γραμμα|τέα, ἐὰν βούληται, τῷ ἰδίῳ κινδύνῳ, | συνκεχωρήσθω δὲ αὐτῷ ἡ ταμιευ|τικὴ σπονδὴ καὶ ἔστω ἀνείσφορος | τὴν διετίαν (lines 155–159).

41 IG II[2] 1325 mentions a treasurer who also acted as a benefactor, using his own funds for the good of the association. The same treasurer-benefactor is mentioned in IIG II[2] 1326. Both can be found from AGRW internet site.

42 GRA 2011, 255. See also Deubner 1932, 138–142.

43 GRA 2011, 255. Interestingly, we have only a little evidence of voluntary associations calling disciplinary meetings. On the meaning of the word στίβας, see Smith 2003, 114–115.

for the meetings (a fixed amount of wine), and if a member did not pay the predetermined fee, he was not allowed to enter until the fee was paid or he obtained special permission from the priest to be excused from the payment. No one could be absent from meetings, except in case of sickness, travel, or mourning. If a member skipped a meeting without an acceptable reason, he would have to pay a fine of 50 light drachmas.[44]

The regular assemblies were directed by the priest or by the archibakchos and no one could "sing, cause a disturbance, or applaud. Rather, with all order and decorum members shall speak and do their parts, as the priest or the head of the Bacchic devotees directs."[45] Moreover, fighting, disorderly behaviour, or sitting in someone else's seat was also forbidden.[46] If a member did break these rules, he was then ordered either to pay a fine of 25 light drachmas (in a case of disorderly behaviour, or sitting in someone else's place) and not to come to the meetings until paid, or to pay a fine of up to 25 silver denarii (in cases of fist fights) and "[t]he offender shall be penalized by not being permitted to enter for a time—as long as it seems appropriate."[47] The member who did not initiate the fight was required to report it as soon as possible to the priest, so that the penalty could be carried out. However, if the offended party did not report the fight, but rather went to public court "[t]he same penalty shall also be applied to [him]."[48]

Besides rules and regulations covering the meetings and banquets of the Iobakchoi, this inscription also explains how the association is to remember its deceased members. Members of the group were expected to participate in funerals, and afterwards those members who attended the funeral shall receive "a single jar of wine," but if someone is absent from the burial, he cannot just attend the memorial meeting and collect his wine. Similarly, a wreath worth five denarii shall be made for a deceased member.[49] However,

---

44 Kroll argues that by the second century the light drachma was equivalent to the old obol (Kroll 1993, 84) and the obol was one sixth of a drachma. See https://coinweek.com/education/worth-purchasing-power-ancient-coins/ and https://www.unitconverters.net/weight-and-mass/denarius-biblical-roman-to-drachma-biblical-greek.htm.

For someone from a lower economic class, the sum of 8.33 drachmas would be a substantial amount of money; however, members from the middle and upper classes could pay it without much inconvenience.

45 This and further translations made by John F. Kloppenborg and Philip A. Harland. GRA 2011, 247.

46 One's seating place was most likely connected to one's status and years of membership, as was often the custom in meetings.

47 Trans. Kloppenborg GRA 2011, 247.

48 Trans. Kloppenborg GRA 2011, 247.

49 γεινέσθω στέφανος αὐ|τῷ μέχ⟨ρ⟩ι (δην.) ε'. Some sort of remembrance for the death of mem-

it seems that the group did not pay for the funerals, as, for instance, an association mentioned in inscription IG II^2 1323 did.[50]

5 How the Inscription Reveals Methods of Identity Construction

The group's social identity is constructed and re-evaluated in relation to outsiders, in other words, the outside context matters. If social contexts encourage competition, groups are more likely to exhibit ingroup favouritism and outgroup discrimination.[51] The association mentioned in IG II^2 1368 had various ways to enhance members' Dionysiac-identity and consolidate their commitment to the association and its rules.[52]

The first topic to be discussed as regards identity construction is the location of the stele. It was placed inside the sanctuary, not outside. Associations often erected steles, statues, and gilded plates to be showcased outside their sanctuary so that passers-by could see them. This was done especially when the inscription mentioned famous benefactors or had praise directed to the benefactor.[53] However, even though this inscription mentions its famous benefactor, clearly indicating the high status of the group, it was still located inside the sanctuary. The column with its inscription reminds current (and future) members of the importance of their association and helps the group to remember

---

bers was fairly common with voluntary associations. See, for instance, the association mentioned in IG II^2 1369 that set up something (line damaged) in memory of its dead members. AGRW 2012, 17.

50 For example, in IG II^2 1323 members honor their treasurer because he has paid for the funerals of deceased members from his own resources: "—and, further, he has paid immediately the burial expenses for those who have died."

IG VII 685: Over the body of Lykaon. The Athena-devotees (*Athenaistai*) buried him (trans. Kloppenborg).

IG VII 686: Galatas. The Dionysos-devotees (*Dionysiastai*) buried him (trans. Kloppenborg).

IG VII 687: Farewell, Hippomachos! The butchers (*mageiroi*) who sacrifice together (*synthytai*) buried him. (trans. Harland).

IG VII 688: Elpis. The synod (*synodos*) of Athena-devotees (*Athenaistai*) buried her (trans. Kloppenborg). In addition to these, see, for instance, IG VII 2725 = Koehler, *MDAI*(*A*) 3 (1878) 299–300; Roesch 1982, 166–167 (no. 22); Roesch 1982, 125 (no. 4) = Marchand 2015, 261 (no. 8); AGRW 42 = IPhilippiP II 029/G215; AGRW 54 = NewDocs IV, p. 215 (no. 17). All inscriptions mentioned can be found from AGRW internet site.

51 Tajfel and Turner 1979, 41; Haslam 2004, 21.

52 For discussion on the Bacchic language, especially the term Βάκχος and the verb Βακχευειν, see San Cristóbal 2013.

53 Kloppenborg 2018, 158–159.

their past benefactors, but also offers an opportunity for those mentioned in the text to be remembered in the future. In other words, it creates and enhances the group's social memory.[54] Van Eck concludes:

> The sociology of remembering also indicates that there is an interrelationship between memory, identity and narrative: identity (e.g. of a group) is constructed by the remembering (retelling) of narratives from the past, and the present is reframed (identity) by telling (narrative) through remembering (memory).[55]

In the case of this association, the stele would enhance the process of remembering and retelling of the narratives of the past, while also reminding members of the mythological narratives of their deity.[56]

As discussed earlier, the Iobakchoi had strict rules and sanctions for rule-breakers, which is not uncommon for voluntary associations.[57] However, besides keeping meetings and members in order, these regulations were used to create and reinforce ingroup salience. The regulations effectively force members to participate in and bring the fixed amount of wine to the meetings on the 9th of each month, thus controlling a certain amount of members' resources (time and money), strengthening the individual's commitment to the activities of the association while also signalling this commitment to other members.

A clear example of rules having an impact on social identity formation comes from lines 90–94, where it is highlighted that members are, at the risk of being fined, encouraged to resolve quarrels inhouse rather than using public courts. Therefore, becoming an Iobakchoi requires limiting the use of one's

54 Memory is a complex process, which can include both individual and social processes. It is the individuals who do the act of remembering (collected memory), but the social contexts are what often activates the act of remembering, while also modifying the memory (social memory). Fentress and Wickham 1992, x; Olick, Vinitzky-Seroussi, and Levy 2011.

55 van Eck 2011, 201. A typical example of a collected memory could be for instance an incident from one's childhood—e.g., I can remember the first time my mom took the training wheels off my bike.

56 Marco Cinnirella argues that groups are motivated to "re-interpret and re-contract the past, present and future" in order to create a sense of temporal continuity. Cinnirella 1998, 235. For a longer discussion, see, for instance, Nikki 2018; Esler 2003, 175.

57 Kloppenborg 2018, 162. Many associations had fines for misbehaviour, such as disorderly conduct, missing meetings, failure to assist a member in distress, striking a fellow member, or sexual interference with the member's family, etc. Kloppenborg notes that interestingly the fine one has to pay after misconduct is always directed to the association, not to the injured party. See also Arnaoutoglou 2003, 135–136.

legal rights for the benefit of the group.[58] One's willingness to relinquish inherent rights for the benefit of the group is directly proportional to the value attached to belonging to the group. The more meaningful the group is to the individual's self-concept, the more he is inclined to exhibit ingroup favouritism and de-personalizing in order to fit in.[59] In other words, the more the member has to gain by being a part of the Iobakchoi (ἰόβακχοι), the more he is willing to limit the use of his legal rights. In the case of fighting, he is willing to resolve matters inhouse, even if the injured party has legal rights to bring charges in public courts. Meanwhile, having public courts resolving matters connected to their association would have been shameful and hence lower their status in comparison to other groups, which again would make it more difficult to obtain donations and elite members.[60]

Having patrons or benefactors from the elite was essential for the survival of an association, but having elite patrons, like the Iobakchoi had, was not just a question of survival, rather it also influenced the social identity of the group. Having such an elite benefactor as Herodes Atticus II was an excellent advertisement for the association; furthermore, it offered a rare opportunity for members from lower classes to socialize with the elite. Being able to rub shoulders with the elite would increase the value of belonging to this association, enhancing the level of member commitment and making members more likely to exhibit ingroup favouritism and outgroup discrimination. Besides benefiting individual members, having elite patronage would also benefit the association as an entity, strengthening its positive distinctiveness. Their benefactor was a "celebrity" willing to use his resources for the benefit of their group. And since social identity develops in connection and in competition with similar reference groups, having an elite benefactor would advance the group's position in objective and social competition, thus impacting the group's social identity.[61]

Besides the above-discussed regulations and elite patronage influencing social identity formation, the inscription reveals a unique level of language

58 Accepting the limitation of one's legal rights can be understood as one type of commitment signalling. Uro 2016 and, especially with regard to applying the theory to religious groups, page 143.

59 Baker 2011, 5; Hogg and Abrams 1988, 7.

60 This same tendency can be observed in Paul's letter to the Corinthians: "When any of you has a grievance against another, do you dare to take it to court before the unrighteous, instead of taking it before the saints?" (1 Cor 6:1).

61 Israel and Tajfel 1972, 299; See also Tucker, 2010; Hogg and Abrams 1988, 50.

meant to separate their association from other Dionysiac associations. The group used their own way of addressing their members as οἱ ἰόβακχοι and in singular ὁ ἰόβακχος, which is rare in the case of Dionysiac associations.[62] In addition to naming their association directly through the name of their deity, the title of archibakchos (ἀρχίβακχος) is also unique to this inscription.[63] The use of ἀρχί- prefix was fairly common way to accentuate the leader of the group role, like chief-sacrificer (ἀρχιιεροθυτήσας) or the head of the synagogue (ἀρχι-συνάγωγον); however, in Dionysian contexts only this association uses the form archibakchos to indicate the leader of a Bacchus group.[64] Similarly, the association uses the name Bakcheion (Βακχείον) in reference to their group and/or their sanctuary (see, for instance, lines 8, 37, 56, 148). Kloppenborg notes that, of the Attic inscriptions known to us, this is the only one using this designation.[65] However, the wording of the sentence would indicate that the members, or at least some of them, were aware of other groups addressing themselves as Bakcheion. Whether these exceptional tittles (*Iobakchoi, archibakchos* and *Bakcheion*) were intentional or not, they effectively fortify the distinctiveness of this association, highlighting its separation when compared to other Dionysiac associations in the area.

Showing ingroup favouritism and outgroup discrimination is often unconscious or semi-unconscious behaviour, highlighting the excellence of one's own group while downplaying other rival groups.[66] However, instead of just subtle hints and subordinate clauses, this inscription showcases a new, direct level of competition and ingroup favouritism: "Now we are the best of all the

62 More commonly, especially in the Greek-Macedonian area, members of associations devoted to Dionysos are addressed as βουκόλοι, βουκόλος, βουκολᾳ. The masculine boukolos is somewhat more common than the feminine version found in texts of Dionysos associations. See AGRW 30: regulations of a Dionysian association where men are addressed as boukoloi; IAegThrace E18 from GRA 2011, 381 presents a leader called ἀρχιβουκολος. For boukola, see AGRW 25.

63 Smith 2003, 116. We have evidence of different name variations to describe the head of the association: ἀρχιβουκολοι, archisynagogos, ἀρχιιεροθυτήσας (ILindos 219); however, only one association in addition to ἰόβακχοι uses the form ἀρχιβάκχος: IPergamon 488.

64 For for ἀρχιιεροθυτήσας, ILindos 219; for ἀρχισυνά|γωγον, SEG 46:800. Both examples can be found on the AGRW internet site.

65 Outside of Attica, we have some inscriptions mentioning the Βακχείον as their name. GRA 2011, 249. See, for example, the inscriptions G VII 107 (Megara, II CE); IGBulg III/2 1865.4–5 (Malko Tarnovo); IGBulg 5579.2 (Augusta Traiana); IGLScythia 80.2 (Kallatis [Scythia Minor], 50–100 CE); IG XII/1 155.49 (Rhodes, I BCE); IKyme 30.4 (Kyme, II BCE). For a longer list, see GRA 2011, 249.

66 Tajfel and Turner 1979, 41; Haslam 2004, 21.

Bakcheion" (–νῦν πάντων πρῶτοι | τῶν Βακχείων.)[67] This verse is part of a larger section where the members vote on the need to make the stele and shout praise after the decision has been made. Since this stele was situated inside the sanctuary, its message was mostly directed to members of the group (and some visitors). Therefore, the reminder that now they are the best of all the Bacchеion would also be directed to the ingroup. It was done to highlight their originality and position in comparison to other religious (Dionysian) associations, but it also created and consolidated the social identity of the association by re-forming and reinforcing members' image of their group. Using distinctive language is one way to amplify a group's identity, thus creating positive distinctiveness for the group.[68]

6 Rituals and Ritualistic Behaviour as Methods of Creating Ingroup Cooperation and Salience

As Risto Uro has noted, rituals are one of the driving forces of religious movements, strengthening cooperation inside religious groups.[69] Commitment signalling theory, which is an established theory developed to analyse and predict how religious practices motivate cooperation, offers a suitable framework for investigating the rituals mentioned in the inscription.[70] Lisa Maurizio argues

67 Lines 26–27.

68 One of the definitions of social memory is the idea that this memory is never an actual representation of history or the past, but rather a modification to fit the needs of the present day. Williams 2011, 189–200. According to van Eck: "social identity is constructed by the remembering and retelling (configuration) of narratives from the past, and the present is reframed (refiguration) by telling the narrative through memory" (van Eck 2011, 201).

69 As Paul Post points out, historical research into ritual and ritualistic behaviour can also be one form of ritual studies. Post 2015, 16. See also Uro 2018. For a critical approach to using ritual theories in studying historical occurrences, see Philippe Buc in his *The Dangers of Ritual*, published in 2001.

John Kloppenborg defines rituals as "practices that are performed, formalized, repetitive, differentiated from the ordinary, collective, and designed to mark association members as distinct from others." Kloppenborg 2018, 155. He notes that these rituals or ritualistic behaviour acted out in voluntary associations often mimic political (city or state) and to some extent domestic rituals or ritualistic behaviour. Kloppenborg 2018.

70 See, for instance, Taussig 2009; Lamoreaux 2013; Turley 2015; Uro 2016. For more on religious rituals operating as honest, hard-to-fake signals enhancing cooperation in religious groups, see Irons 2001; Sosis and Alcorta 2003, 264–274; Bulbulia 2004, 19–42; Bulbulia, and Sosis 2011, 363–388; Heimola 2012.

that Dionysian rituals included theatrical elements and occurred in time and space separated from daily routines.[71] Although Maurizio bases her argument on literary sources rather than epigraphical ones, Maurizio's argument coheres with this inscription.

The first clear form of ritualistic behaviour present in the inscription is the initiation ritual, during which the candidate is evaluated by the members to determine if he is worthy and suitable for the Bakcheion. Whether it meant that one had to have enough money and be from a suitable background or that one had to have some qualities that the group was looking for, the process of vetting the candidate is a clear initiation ritual.[72] Going through the evaluation and paying the entrance fee signals the candidate's commitment to the group and his willingness to be categorized by his connection with the association. Joining the group is a costly commitment signal indicating that one is willing to accept the rules, including the fees, fixed meeting times, and inhouse problem resolution; in other words, one is willing to use some of his limited resources (time and money) for the group. This is especially true in the case of middle-class members, for whom the 50 denarii entrance fee was a much heftier investment than for someone coming from the elite, thus indicating their level of commitment to the association. After one was accepted, the new member would obtain documentation proving his membership. Receiving membership documentation is rare, and within Dionysiac groups this association is the only one handing out membership documentation.[73] Having documentation proving one's membership was an important clarification of one's status as a member of the group.[74] Richard Sosis argues that religious groups with stricter or restricted entrance qualifications are more likely to outlast those with little or

71 Maurizio 2016, 413.

72 "The phrase 'if he appears to be worthy (*axios*) and suitable (*epitēdeios*)' (ll. 36–37) leaves little doubt that some sort of test was applied. Since the Iobakchoi engaged in Dionysiac performances, 'suitability' (*epitēdeios*) might have to do with the ability to perform in the play; but *axios* suggests a moral standard. A few lines later (ll. 53–55), it is stipulated that if the brother of a member applies, he likewise would have to undergo vetting." Kloppenborg 2018, 156–157.

He also argues that vetting the new candidates most likely originates with or is mimicking the ritualized vetting of a candidate for Athenian city office, a practice of the Athenian *boulē* (council). Kloppenborg 2018, 156. See also Aristot., *Const. Ath.* 55.3.

73 ᾧ δὲ ἀπογραψαμένῳ | καὶ ψηφοφορηθέντι διδότω ὁ ἱερεὺς ἐπισ||τολὴν ὅτι ἐστὶν ἰόβακχος, ἐὰν πρῶτον | δοῖ τῷ ἱερεῖ τὸ ἰσηλύσιον, ἐνγραφομένου | τῇ ἐπιστολῇ τὰ χωρήσαντα εἰς τόδε τι.

74 Why did the group hand out documentation proving membership? Was it something members were required to bring with them to meetings? Or was it meant to be showcased in one's home?

no specific entrance qualifications.[75] In other words, one is more likely to commit to the activities of the group if gaining entrance is not self-evident. This might be one reason why this group had survived and been able to attract elite members.[76]

Besides the initiation ritual, this document showcases a number of rituals connected with the meetings of the association. On lines 111–117 the inscription presents rituals including customary services i.e. *liturgia* (λιτουργία) and *theologia* (θεολογία).

> The priest shall perform the customary services (*litourgia*) of the stibas and of the yearly festival in a fitting manner; he shall set before the gathering (stibas) one libation of the Festival of Return (Katagogia), and shall give the discourse about the god (*theologia*), which the former priest Nikomachos inaugurated out of his zeal.[77]

Smith argues that "a major role was played by the religious rituals,"[78] and making the libation and performing customary services were important parts of the regular banqueting meetings. Besides the litourgia and theologia, the inscription introduced surprisingly detailed descriptions of a sacrificial ritual held on the 10th day of the month of Elaphebolion. This meat sacrificial ritual was performed by the priest and archibakchos together with selected voluntary members of the group:

> The archibakchos shall sacrifice the victim to the god and make a libation on the tenth day of Elaphebolion. When the parts (of the sacrificial victims) are distributed, let them go to the priest, the vice-priest, the archibakchos, the treasurer, the one playing the cowherd (boukolikos), "Dionysos," "Kore," "Palaimon," "Aphrodite," "Proteurythmos." Let these roles be apportioned among all by lot. (lines 117–124)[79]

---

75 He also states that religious groups with strict entrance qualifications are clearly more likely to outlast their secular counterparts. Bulbulia and Sosis 2011, 367–368.

76 The initiation ritual acted as a boundary crossing ritual uniting the members through a shared experience. Members from the outgroup can be incorporated into the ingroup as long as they are able to cross the identity boundary and re-categorize themselves in terms of their new identity.

77 Trans. Kloppenborg GRA 2011, 247. For other translations see: Smith 2003, 116 and AGRW 2012, 16.

78 Smith 2003, 116.

79 If the treasurer has chosen to have a secretary, then his meat would go to him. Trans.

What it meant to play a role in the ritual is unclear, but most likely the ritual itself was not a complete play, but rather a ritual including play-like aspects. Judging from the roles to play—boukolikos,[80] Dionysos, Kore, Palaimon,[81] Aphrodite, Proteurythmos[82]—the play derived its basis from the mythical narratives connected to Dionysos, which were then re-enacted and (re-)remembered during the ritual itself.[83] Remembering and reactivating the group's social memory through shared ritual using mythological narratives of Dionysos is an effective way to influence members' social identity and to tie them more firmly to the affairs of the association. The specific ritual arising from this shared mythology works as a unifying agent in intragroup and intergroup relations. From the social identity point of view, reflections of mythology in rituals and in language have two distinct, but cognate purposes: 1) Reflections of mythology create history for the group. They link present members to past ones and to the myths of their god(s). This creates social history, which is important for the self-understanding and self-value of the group. 2) Similarly,

Kloppenborg GRA 2011, 248. There might also be hints of this ritual in lines 64–66, where everyone is reminded that "but with all order and decorum members shall speak and do their parts, as the priest or the archibakchos directs."

80 The term *boukolikos* has two cognate translations or meanings: firstly, it is linked to cowherds, who in mythical narratives have been converted to servants of Dionysos by witnessing a miracle (Rutherford 2000, 106–110, see also Eur., *Bacch.* 660–774), but it also refers to the transformation of Dionysus from human into animal form, especially into the form of a bull (Rutherford 2000, 106–110 [Eur., *Bacch.*, 616–622; Plut., *Quaest. Graec.* 299b]). The word itself is most often linked to the Greek word for bull βοῦς, bulls being important animals in the Dionysiac narratives. Dionysos, much like his father Zeus, was able to metamorphose into an animal and he often chose a bull. Additionally, the bull is linked to the mythology of Dionysos' boyhood years. The story goes that he was to first one to harness a bull to work for man. He did it as revenge on behalf of his best friend Ampelos, who was killed by a bull.

81 Palaimon is the god-name of Dionysos' cousin and adopted brother Melicertes, who become a sea god after his mother was forced to jump off a cliff still holding the toddler Melicertes. Ancient storytellers hint that Hera's idea was to condemn Ino to the lowest level of Tartaros, which is reserved for child killers. However, Poseidon took pity on them and transformed the mother Ino into Leukothea and Melicertes into Palaimon (Dalby 2003, 37–40). Several ancient writers mention the story; see, for instance, Homer, *Odyssey* 5.333; Pseudo-Apollodorus, *Bibliotheca* 3.28; Pausanias, *Description of Greece* 1.44.7.

82 Martin Nilson argues that "it might be guessed that he [Proteurythmos] was Orphic or a god of dance; we know nothing for certain" Nilsson 1957, 60–61. GRA 2011, 253.

83 During the ritual the archibakchos would sacrifice the meat and distribute it to selected dignitaries and the ones playing parts in the ritual. Smith argues that after the sacrificial ritual was completed the leftover meat would be divided amongst the members of the group. Smith 2003, 116.

retelling the myth, even in small parts through the name of the association, and through rituals, amplifies togetherness, and for the duration of the ritual it separates the members from outsiders.[84]

In addition to the two distinct ritual or ritualistic behaviours introduced, the inscription also reveals several smaller rituals. The most explicit is the recurring wine-libation ritual, which was most likely part of the regular meetings on the 9th of each month. It is possible that this ritual was acted out by every member, for their own part.

Similarly, the inscription mentions, unfortunately only in a passing remark in line 54, an uninitiated boy active in sacred services (ἱερὸς παῖς).[85] We do not have any other evidence of what these sacred services were, whether they were a separate ritual or connected to sacrificial rituals, but it seems that the association had a ritual where an underage boy had a role to play. At the end, the inscription mentions rituals connected with the burial of members:

> If an Iobakchos dies, a wreath worth up to five denarii and a single jar of wine shall be provided for those who attend the funeral. But no one who is absent from the funeral itself shall have any wine.[86]

The wreath would be for the deceased member and the wine was most likely used in some sort of memorial ritual; sadly, we do not have any other indication of what this memorial service looked like. However, it does indicate that the group expected to have lifelong committed members, while on its part the association promised to honor and remember its dead members.[87]

According to Rappaport, participation in rituals is fundamentally an act of acceptance: "by performing a liturgical order the participants accept, and indicate to themselves and to others that they accept whatever is encoded in the canon of that order."[88] Altogether, participating in rituals acts as a commitment signal, communicating the level of commitment the member shows towards

---

84 Social memory is used to create cohesion in the ingroup and it can be used to define boundaries. Van Eck 2011, 211.

85 ἀν δὲ ἱερὸς παῖς ἐξωτικὸς καθεσ|θεὶς ἀναλώσῃ τὰ πρὸς τοὺς θεοὺς καὶ τὸ Βακχεῖον, | ἔστω μετὰ τοῦ πατρὸς ἰόβακχος ἐπὶ μιᾷ | σπονδῇ τοῦ πατρός. See GRA 2011, 252; Wide 1894, 273.

86 Translation by Harland and Kloppenborg. ἐὰν δέ τις τελευτή||σῃ ἰόβακχος, γεινέσθω στέφανος αὐ|τῷ μέχ⟨ρ⟩ι (δην.) ε', καὶ τοῖς ἐπιταφήσασι τι|θέσθω οἴνου κεράμιον ἕν, ὁ δὲ μὴ | ἐπιταφήσας εἰργέσθω τοῦ οἴνου (lines 159–163).

87 GRA 2011, 255–256.

88 Rappaport 1999, 119. Rappaport argues that the acceptance shown by liturgical performance is more profound than can expressed by words alone. Uro concludes that Rappa-

the group, thus enhancing the level of cooperation which in turn promotes and reinforces the ingroup salience.[89] Uro argues that according to commitment signalling the religious rituals promote group cohesion by requiring members to engage in behaviour that is too costly to fake.[90]

7 Conclusions

The inscription IG II^2 1368 introduces a group that had an elite benefactor, a hierarchical structure, and its own sanctuary. The group had monthly meetings and additional gatherings when needed. The *Iobakchoi* as a group use unique and rare language choices and have strict rules one is expected to obey after going through the initiation ritual. However, because of the multidimensional, context-dependent nature of social identity and the challenges presented by the epigraphical and archaeological evidence, one must be careful when discussing the social identity development of the Iobakchoi. Nevertheless, what is clear and what I have argued in this article is that the stele and the inscription written on it had potential to influence the social identity formation of the association, strengthening the positive distinctions of the ingroup. Through rituals, and recalling the mythic narratives, the Iobakchoi association offered a communal expression of people's devotion. Rituals and recalling the myth produce religious experiences for the members, but they also influence and reshape the worshippers' identity. Participating in religious rituals and religious rituals altogether are a form of communication where members communicate their commitment to the association, strengthening group cohesion and influencing the levels of cooperation within the Iobakchoi.

Abbreviations

AGRW — Richard S. Ascough, Philip A. Harland, and John S. Kloppenborg (eds.). *Associations in the Greco-Roman World: A Sourcebook*. Waco and Berlin: Baylor University Press and De Gruyter, 2012.

port's emphasis comes close to what signalling theorists call honest signalling. "In expressing acceptance (Rappaport's term) by ritual public performance, the participants are also indicating commitment (the term used in Signalling Theory)." Uro 2018, 132.

89 See Uro 2018; Taussig, 2009; Lamoreaux 2013.

90 Uro 2018, 134.

AGRW internet site	Richard S. Ascough, Philip A. Harland, and John S. Kloppenborg (eds.). *Associations in the Greco-Roman World*, http://www.philipharland.com/greco-roman-associations/.
GRA	John S. Kloppenborg and Richard S. Ascough (eds.). *Greco-Roman Associations: Texts, Translations, and Commentary: Attica, Central Greece, Macedonia, Thrace*. Berlin and New York: De Gruyter, 2011.
GRA II	Philip A. Harland (ed.). *Greco-Roman Associations: Texts, Translations, and Commentary. II, North Coast of the Black Sea, Asia Minor*. Berlin and Boston: De Gruyter, 2014.

Bibliography

Adams, Sean A. "Paul The Roman Citizen: Roman Citizenship in The Ancient World and Its Importance for Understanding Acts 22:22–29." In: Stanley E. Porte (ed.), *Paul: Jew, Greek, and Roman*. Leiden: Brill, 2008, 309–326.

Anttonen, Veikko. "Sacred." In: W. Braun and R.T. McCutcheon (eds.), *Guide to the Study of Religion*. London and New York: Cassell, 2000, 271–282.

Arnaoutoglou, Ilias N. *Thusias Heneka Kai Sunousias: Private Religious Associations in Hellenistic Athens*. Athens: Academy of Athens, 2003.

Ascough, Richard S. "Greco-Roman Philosophic, Religious, and Voluntary Associations." In: Richard N. Longenecker (ed.), *Community Formation in the Early Church and the Church Today*. Peabody: Hendrickson, 2002, 3–19.

Ascough, Richard S., Philip A. Harland, and John S. Kloppenborg. *Associations in the Greco-Roman World: A Sourcebook*. Waco, TX: Baylor University Press, 2012.

Baker, Coleman A. *Identity, Memory, and Narrative in Early Christianity: Peter, Paul, and Recategorization in the Book of Acts*. Eugene, Or.: Pickwick Publications, 2011.

Bremmer, Jan, N. "Walter F. Otto's Dionysos (1933)." In: Alberto Bernabé et al. (eds.), *Redefining Dionysos*. Boston and Berlin: De Gruyter, 2013, 4–22.

Burkert, Walter and John Raffan. *Greek Religion: Archaic and Classical*. Oxford: Blackwell, 1985.

Bulbulia, Joseph. "Religious Costs as Adaptations that Signal Altruistic Intention." *Evolution and Cognition* 10 (2004): 19–42.

Bulbulia, Joseph and Richard Sosis. "Signalling Theory and the Evolution of Religious Cooperation." *Religion* 41 (2011): 363–388.

Casadio, Giovanni and Patricia A. Johnston. *Mystic Cults in Magna Graecia*. Austin, TX: University of Texas Press, 2009.

Cinnirella, Marco. "Exploring the Temporal Dimension of Social Identity: The Concept of Possible Social Identities." *European Journal of Social Psychology* 28 (1998): 227–248.

Cole, Susan Guettel. "Finding Dionysos." In: Daniel Ogden (ed.), *A Companion to Greek Religion*. Malden, MA: Blackwell, 2007, 327–341.

Dalby, Andrew. *Bacchus: A Biography*. London: The British Museum Press, 2003.

Deubner, Ludwig. *Attische Feste*. Berlin: Akademie Verlag, 1932.

Dörpfeld, Wilhem. "Die Ausgrabungen am Westabhange der Akropolis. II. Das Lenaion oder Dionysion in den Limnai." Athenische Mitteilungen 20 (1895): 161–206.

Ebel, Eva. "Der Stein und die Steine: Methodische Erwägungen zur Benutzung von epigraphischen Quellen am Beispeil IG II 2 1368." In: Peter Pilhofer (ed.), *Die frühen Christen und ihre Welt: Greifswalder Aufsätze 1996–2001*. Tübingen: J.C.B. Mohr, 2002, 11–22.

Eck, Ernest van. "Social Memory and Identity: Luke 19:12b—24 and 27." *Biblical Theology Bulletin* 41 (2011), 201–212.

Esler, Philip Francis. *Conflict and Identity in Romans: The Social Setting of Paul's Letter*. Minneapolis, MN: Fortress Press, 2003.

Fentress, James and Chris Wickham. *Social Memory*. Oxford: Blackwell, 1992.

Foucart, Paul-François. *Des Associations Religieuses chez les Grecs: thiases, éranes, orgéons: avec le texte des inscriptions relatives à ces associations*. Paris: Chez Klincksieck, 1873.

Geertz, Armin. "Cognitive Approaches to the Study of Religion." In: Peter Antes, Armin W. Geertz, and Randi R. Warne (eds.), *New Approaches to the Study of Religion: Volume 2, Textual, Comparative, Sociological, and Cognitive Approaches*. Berlin: De Gruyter, 2004, 349–399.

Harland, Philip A. *Associations, Synagogues, and Congregations: Claiming a Place in Ancient Mediterranean Society*. Minneapolis, MN: Fortress Press, 2003.

Harland, Philip A. *Associations, Synagogues, and Congregations: Claiming a Place in Ancient Mediterranean Society*. Second edition. Ontario: Kitchener, 2013.

Harrison, Jane Ellen. *Primitive Athens as Described by Thucydides*. Cambridge: Cambridge University Press, 1906.

Haslam, S. Alexander. *Psychology in Organizations: The Social Identity Approach*. Second edition. London: SAGE Publications, 2004.

Heimola, Mikko. *Religious Rituals and Social Norms in the Making of Adaptive Systems: Empirical and Theoretical Synthesis on Revivals in the 19th Century Finland*. Dissertation at the University of Helsinki, 2012.

Hogg, Michael, and Dominic Abrams. *Social Identifications: A Social Psychology of Intergroup Relations and Group Process*. London and New York: Routledge, 1988.

Israel, Joachim, and Henri Tajfel (eds.). *The Context of Social Psychology: A Critical Assessment*. London: Academic Press, 1972.

Judeich, Walther. *Topographie von Athen*. Munich: C.H. Beck, 1905.

Katsari, Constantina. *The Roman Monetary System: The Eastern Provinces from the First to the Third Century AD*. Cambridge: Cambridge University Press, 2011.

Kloppenborg, John S., and Richard S. Ascough (eds.). *Greco-Roman Associations: Texts, Translations, and Commentary: Attica, Central Greece, Macedonia, Thrace* = GRA. Berlin and New York: De Gruyter, 2011.

Kloppenborg, John F. "Collegia and Thiasoi—Issues in Function, Taxonomy and Membership." In: John S. Kloppenborg and Stephen G. Wilson (eds.), *Voluntary Associations in the Greco-Roman World*. London: Routledge, 1996, 16–30.

Kloppenborg, John F. "Associations, Guilds, Clubs." In: Risto Uro et al. (eds.), *The Oxford Handbook of Early Christian Ritual*. Oxford: Oxford University Press, 2018, 154–170.

Kloppenborg, John F. *Christ's Associations: Connecting and Belonging in the Ancient City*. New Heaven and London: Yale University press, 2019.

Lamoreaux, Jason T. *Ritual, Women, and Philippi: Reimagining the Early Philippian Community*. Eugene, OR: Cascade Books, 2013.

Last, Richard, and Philip A. Harland. *Group Survival in the Ancient Mediterranean: Rethinking Material Conditions in the Landscape of Jews and Christians*. London: T&T Clark, 2020.

Maurizio, Lisa. *Classical Mythology in Context*. Oxford: Oxford University Press, 2016.

Nikki, Nina. *Opponents and Identity in Philippians*. NovTSup 173. Leiden: Brill, 2018.

Nilsson, Martin P. *The Dionysius Mysteries of the Hellenistic and Roman Age*. Lund: C.W.K. Gleerup, 1957.

Olick, Jeffrey K., Vered Vinitzky-Seroussi, and Daniel Levy. *The Collective Memory Reader*. New York: Oxford University Press, 2011. Print.

Papastamati-von Moock, Christina. "The Theatre of Dionysus Eleuthereus in Athens: New Data and Observations on Its 'Lycurgan' Phase." In: Eric Csapo et al. (eds.), *Greek Theatre in the Fourth Century BC*. Berlin: De Gruyter, 2014, 15–76.

Pyysiäinen, Ilkka. *How Religion Works: Towards a New Cognitive Science of Religion*. Leiden: Brill, 2003.

Rutherford, Ian. "Formulas, Voice, and Death in *Ehoie*-Poetry, the Hesiodic *Gunaikon Katalogos*, and the Odysseian *Nekuia*." In: M. Depew and D. Obbink (eds.), *Matrices of Genre, Authors, Canons, and Society*. Cambridge, MA: Harvard University Press, 2000, 81–96.

Schäfer, Alfred. "Raumnutzung und Raumwahrnehmung im Vereinslokal der Iobakchen von Athen." In: Ulrike Egelhaaf-Gaiser and Alfred Schäfer (eds.), *Religiöse Vereine in der römischen Antike: Untersuchungen zu Organisation, Ritual und Raumordnung*. Tübingen: Mohr Siebeck, 2002, 161–180.

Smith, Dennis Edwin. *From Symposium to Eucharist: The Banquet in the Early Christian World*. Minneapolis: Fortress Press, 2003.

Smith, Jonathan Z. *Imaging Religion*. Chicago: Chicago University Press, 1982.

Sosis, Richard and Candace Alcorta. "Signaling, Solidarity, and the Sacred: The Evolution of Religious Behavior." *Evolutionary Anthropology* 12 (2003): 264–274.

Tajfel, Henry and John Turner. "An Integrative Theory of Intergroup Conflict." In: William G. Austin and Stephen Worchel (eds.), *The Social Psychology of Intergroup Relations*. Monterey, CA: Brooks/Cole, 1979, 33–47.

Taussig, Hal. *In the Beginning Was the Meal: Social Experimentation and Early Christian Identity*. Minneapolis, MN: Fortress Press, 2009.

Travlos, John. *Pictorial Dictionary of Ancient Athens*. New York: Hacker Art Books, 1980.

Tucker, J. Brian, *You Belong to Christ: Paul and the Formation of Social Identity in 1 Corinthians 1–4*. Eugene, OR: Pickwick publications, 2010.

Turley, Stephen R. *The Ritualized Revelation of the Messianic Age*. London: Bloomsbury T&T Clark, 2015.

Uro, Risto. *Ritual and Christian Beginnings: A Socio-Cognitive Analysis*. First edition. Oxford: Oxford University Press, 2016.

Uro, Risto. "Introduction: Ritual in the study of early Christianity." In: Risto Uro et al. (eds.), *The Oxford Handbook of Early Christian Ritual*. Oxford: Oxford University Press, 2018, 3–17.

West, Martin L. "The Orphic Poems." *The Classical Review* 35 (1985): 87–90.

Wide, Sam. *Inschrift der Iobakchen*. Mitteilungen des Deutschen Archäologischen Instituts, Athenische Abteilung 19, 1894, 248–282.

Williams, Ritva. "BTB Readers' Guide: Social Memory." *Biblical Theology Bulletin* 41 (2011): 189–200.

Wilson, Stephen G. "Voluntary Associations: An Overview." In: John S. Kloppenborg and Stephen G. Wilson (eds.), *Voluntary Associations in the Greco-Roman World*. London: Routledge, 1996, 1–15.

Ziebarth, Erich. *Aus der antiken Schule: Sammlung griechischer Texte auf Papyrus*. Bonn: A. Marcus und E. Weber's Verlag, 1910.

CHAPTER 4

Signs of Identity in the Quran: Rituals, Practices, and Core Values

Ilkka Lindstedt

1 Introduction*

The study of early Islamic identity is a burgeoning field. A number of articles and monographs that deal with or touch upon the issue explicitly have come out in recent years.[1] The most important contributions have, in my opinion, been those by Fred Donner (2002–2003, 2010, 2018). Fred Donner begins his, by now classic, article entitled "From Believers to Muslims" (2002–2003, 9) with the following sentence: "Studies of early Islam, by Muslim and non-Muslim scholars alike, have almost without exception taken as axiomatic that Islam from its earliest days constituted a separate religious confession distinct from others—in particular, distinct from Judaism, Christianity, Magianism [Zoroastrianism], and of course from the *mushrikūn*, those who 'associate other beings with God.'" This axiom he then goes on to refute, arguing for a piecemeal and somewhat slow identity-articulating process that took decades to accomplish. He dates the delineation of Islam from other faiths—the "parting of the ways," to use a phrase from early Christian studies—to the late seventh century CE.[2]

Although Donner's views on the tardiness of reified Islamic identity have received praise and affected the arguments of my studies immensely, they have not been accepted by all, as can be seen from the critical stances taken by other heavyweights of the field, such as Amikam Elad (2002), Patricia Crone (2010),

* I thank Ismo Dunderberg, Jaakko Hämeen-Anttila, Jutta Jokiranta, Nina Nikki, Kaj Öhrnberg, Riikka Tuori, and Holger Zellentin for comments on an earlier draft of this article.

1 To mention some of the studies that explicitly deal with or touch upon the issue of identity: Hoyland 1997, Nevo and Koren 2003, Lecker 2004, Griffith 2008, Imbert 2011, Shoemaker 2012, Zellentin 2013, G. Fowden 2014, Lamptey 2014, Neuwirth 2014, Sirry 2014, Penn 2015, Stroumsa 2015, Crone 2015–2016, Crone 2016, Shaddel 2016, Webb 2016, Sinai 2017, Munt 2017, Shoemaker 2018, Weitz 2018, Sinai 2019.

2 In this article, I mostly use Common Era dates. In some instances, I give both the Islamic and Common Era dates, in this order, e.g.: 123/741.

 | DOI:10.1163/9789004471160_005

Nicolai Sinai (2017, e.g., 187, n. 90), and Robert Hoyland (2017). I have discussed and taken issue with Elad and Crone's criticism of Donner's argument of a slow identity-making process elsewhere (Lindstedt 2019), so I will only deal with Hoyland and Sinai's contributions to the debate here.

In his 2017 primer on the Quran, Nicolai Sinai follows Donner in using the word "Believers" as a translation of the endonym of the Quranic ingroup, which is most commonly called *mu'minūn* in the Quran (and other seventh-century CE evidence). However, in contrast to Donner, Sinai suggests that the Believers formed a group set apart from other communities. According to Sinai, a reified, bounded Muslim community existed from very early on, though they did not yet call themselves Muslims at this stage. Sinai proposes that the formation of the "Believers' communal distinctness from Jews and Christians" occurred in the Medinan period (Sinai 2017, 200), that is, during the years 622–632 CE. Although he allows for a certain symbiosis between the ritual practices of the early Medinan Believers and Judaism, this overlap diminishes as the Medinan phase advances. According to him,

> what is at stake in Medinan polemics against the Jews and Christians as well as in the Medinan surahs' establishment of distinctly Qur'anic rituals, such as the fast of Ramaḍān and the Meccan *qiblah* [prayer direction], is ultimately the very existence of the Believers as *an independent religious community* that was more than a group of gentile monotheists orbiting around Medinan Judaism with its *fully formed communal identity*.
>
> SINAI 2017, 200, emphasis added

Thus, the full and total demarcation of Islam from other faiths was, according to Sinai, accomplished during the Medinan phase of the Prophet's life through Quranic polemics against other religions as well as the establishment of distinct rituals that only the Prophet's community of Believers performed and that marked them out as different and distinct from Jews and Christians.

I agree with Sinai in that the censure of Jews and Christians has to do with religious identity formation but an identity that is still developing and that accepts some of the earlier monotheists as part of the ingroup.[3] What is more, I do not see the polemics as quite as encompassing as Sinai does, as I will argue in this study. I will deal with the Quranic rituals in this article one by one and

3 Quranic social categorizations are a complex and multifaceted issue which I tackle in Lindstedt, forthcoming b.

suggest that there is, on the basis of the Quran, much evidence that Jews and Christians also partook in those rituals and shared the same group beliefs. It should be noted in passing that Sinai seems to mostly follow the conventional narrative that, interestingly enough, does not remember many Christians living in and around Mecca and Medina, allocating the role of earlier monotheists to the Jews alone, who were ubiquitous in Medina. This narrative seems to go against what the Quran supposes, with its rather many references to the Christians.[4]

Robert Hoyland's 2017 article is a rich reflection on the nomenclature and discourse on early Islam and Muslims, considering endonyms and exonyms as well as emic and etic points of view. He comments on both the ethnic and religious identities as well as considers what the conquests initiated and carried out by the early Arabian Believers should be called. Hoyland, like Sinai, dates the beginning of distinct Islamic identity to the time of the Prophet Muhammad. He states that in his opinion "Muhammad had already initiated this process [of Islamic identity development] when he changed the *qibla* [prayer direction], opted for Ramadan as the month of fasting and instituted the hajj [pilgrimage], as these sort of practices tend to mark out people as different" (Hoyland 2017, 131, n. 78). Like Sinai, he cites the examples of prayer direction and fasting during Ramadan, but also adduces the pilgrimage; I suppose that Hoyland understands this as meaning the pilgrimage to the shrine of the Kaʿba in Mecca. In this article, I will discuss these three rituals in addition to other markers of identity. I will reconsider how distinctive an identity they actually create.

My earlier articles on issues of early Muslim identities have used a social psychological theory called the social identity approach.[5] It was promulgated by Henri Tajfel (e.g. Tajfel 1981) and has turned out to be a fruitful avenue of research with a large amount of literature.[6] According to my research, Fred Donner's proposal of the late formation of distinct identity stands the test.

One of my articles (Lindstedt, forthcoming b) deals with group categorizations in the Quran. There, I put forward that the Quran often classifies Jews and Christians—the "People of the Book"—as part of the ingroup, called Believers. I

4 For a new dated pre-Islamic (sixth century CE) inscription from northwest Arabia showing the presence of Christianity in the region, though still rather far away from Mecca and Medina, see Nehmé 2017, 124–131.

5 See Brubaker and Cooper 2000 for a criticism of vague use of the word "identity" in humanities and social sciences. However, in my opinion a defined and theoreticized employment of the word is justifiable and indeed beneficial.

6 For a lucid introduction to the social identity approach, see Haslam 2004.

also draw attention to the fact that the Quranic censure of Christianity is rather muted. Though some Christian dogma (trinitarianism, Jesus as God) are denigrated, these beliefs are, in the Quran, not in fact ascribed to the Christians except in a few instances. The door is left open for Christians as well as Jews to become part of the Believer affiliation.

In another article, I discuss the so-called Constitution of Medina, which has to do with contacts and relations with the Medinan Jews (Lindstedt, forthcoming a). This text has been accepted by the majority of the scholars of early Islam as authentic and early, that is, stemming from the Medinan phase of the Prophet. I agree with this dating, though the surviving recensions of the text have been, in all likelihood, reworded to a degree. The text is a treaty document between the Gentile and the Jewish Believers of Medina.

I suggest that the "Constitution of Medina" creates a recategorized and superordinate Believer identity ("one people to the exclusion of others") which was open to sub-identities. The participants in the treaty document were Gentile and Jewish Believers. In that article, I also look at the Quranic evidence of re- and decategorization and suggest that whereas the earliest layers of the Quran welcome sub-identities totally and, hence, employ recategorization as an identity-building device, the later strata are not so accepting of them. The Medinan Quran, on the other hand, uses decategorization rather than recategorization of Jews and Christians as an identity discourse. By decategorization I mean that Jews and Christians could still affiliate with the community of Believers without undergoing a formal conversion ritual but their group identities as Jews and Christians were somewhat suspect, though not completely rejected.

In the third article (Lindstedt 2019), I concentrate on the early Islamic-era Arabic inscriptions, which form an extremely significant but still underused set of evidence. My focus is on the circa 100 Arabic inscriptions dated by their writers to the 640s–740s. In the study, I conclude (Lindstedt 2019, 201):

> To summarize the timeline for the development of the Muslim identity as reflected in epigraphy in a simplified manner: we have indeterminate pious formulae up to the 70s/690s, when the first instances of the emphasis on the Prophet surface. Simultaneously, designations referring to different outgroups appear in the 70s–90s/690s–710s. Following this, in the 80s–100s/700s–720s, we have mentions of specifically Muslim rites such as pilgrimage, prayer, and fasting. The processes of boundary-drawing and group designation are brought to a close around 100s–110s/720s–730s, when the words Muslims and Islam appear as clear references to a specific group. The idea that the Muslims formed a distinct community is

> attested by, for example, one writer of a graffito of the year 123/741 who asks God to bless the totality of Muslims (*ʿāmmat al-muslimīn*) and to let them into Paradise.

Thus, I suggest, the epigraphic evidence tallies well with Fred Donner's arguments. While Donner dates the articulation of particularly Islamic identity to the late seventh century CE, I propose that it might be dated somewhat later, to the early decades of the eighth century. By this I mean that, according to the dated historical evidence, beginning from that time most of the Muslims self-categorized themselves as part of the Muslim group which was apart from other religious communities.

If Donner's and my arguments are accepted, it follows that some reconceptualization of how we understand Islamic origins is required. Just to mention one example: According to the chronicles and other literary evidence, the Caliph ʿUmar II (r. 717–720 CE) stipulated that Jews, Christians, and other communities dress differently from Muslims.[7] Usually in scholarship, this is understood as *maintaining* communal boundaries that were already in place: Muslims, Jews, Christians, Zoroastrians, and others all agreed on communal boundaries and categorizations, and these sartorial orders only made those social categorizations more visible. However, I would argue that these identity-politics acts of ʿUmar II (if it was indeed he who tried to enforce the dress stipulations) should be seen as part of the process of *creating* the Muslim affiliation and *delineating* communal boundaries rather than merely sustaining or bolstering them. Since, according to the dated documentary evidence, it is during the decades of the 700s–730s that Muslims start to emphasize their distinctive rituals and call themselves "Muslims" and their religion "Islam," we cannot suppose (if new evidence does not surface) that the social categorizations of Muslims versus non-Muslims were already in place and widely accepted before and when ʿUmar II tried to enforce his sartorial stipulations. Naturally, the seeds of a distinctive identity were already there, but it should not be supposed, I argue, that the religious and other affiliations were understood in the same way as later.

In this article, I will do something different from my earlier studies, offering a new approach to the question of social identities in the early Islamic era. It is not my aim to repeat the social categorizations in the Quran and early Arabic evidence or to concentrate on group nomenclature. Instead, I will look at specific Quranic identity signs (such as prayer, almsgiving, and fasting) and core

7 See Levy-Rubin 2011 for a thorough study on ʿUmar II's stipulations. However, Yarbrough 2014 remarks that these rulings are also attributed to earlier and later rulers in the literature, so the historical date and actual authenticity of these rules remains questionable.

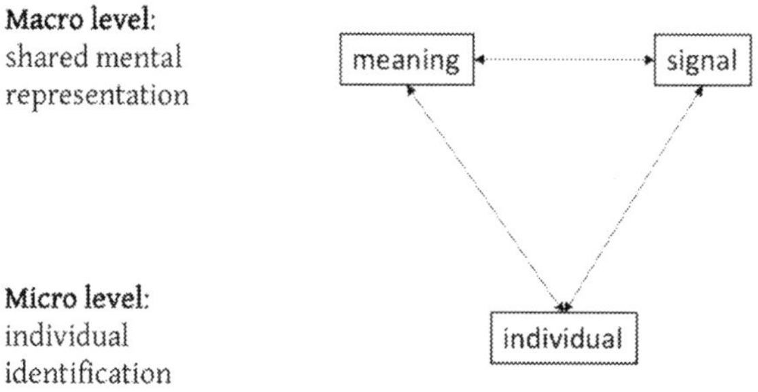

FIGURE 4.1 The tripartite structure of the identity sign
ADAPTED FROM EHALA 2018, 62

values (such as the belief in God, the last day, and the Prophet[s]). My aim is to probe which groups share these core values and signs of identity according to the Quranic evidence.

2 Theoretical Framework: Identity Signs

The recent theory of identity signs has been put forward by Martin Ehala (2018). This framework proffers tools to analyze and specify the identity markers of different groups: what makes a group differ from other groups (real or imagined) and through what processes and acts?

Ehala has formulated a theory on identity performance, utilizing the concept of *sign*, a term borrowed from linguistics. The identity sign is divided into two parts: *signal* and *meaning*. Furthermore, the identity sign is context dependent (Ehala 2018: 54). To give an example, in Finnish society in the year 2019 (context), wearing a cross necklace (signal) is widely understood as signifying that the person with the cross is indicating that she is a believing Christian (meaning). The meaning assigned to the signal can of course differ in the minds of the signaler and the receiver of the signal. While for the person with the cross the identity sign in all likelihood carries positive meanings, an ardent atheist, for example, might scoff at it. Thus, we have to take into account not only the signal and signaler but also the receivers of that signal (see figure 4.1).

Meanings and signals work on both macro (societal) and micro (individual) levels. In the above example, the necklace-wearing Christian and the atheist are both individuals on the micro level that project different meanings to the cross necklace, though they also in all likelihood share some cultural, macro-level, conceptions and understandings of the item in question. Both understand it as marking Christian faith, though the significations that they allocate to this signal differ. The above figure and its two-way arrows are meant to indicate that identity signaling and the assignment of meaning to a signal are always a socially contextualized and negotiated process. The figure also suggests that identity signaling is a feature of both social identity and self identity.[8]

Different meanings (positive, negative, neutral, and so on) can be given to religious and other symbols signaling identity, such as wearing a cross necklace, by different individuals either sending or receiving that signal, though there are some shared conceptualizations of them as well. This is especially true for signs that are stigmatized or stereotyped. One needs only to think of the multifaceted meanings attached to wearing a Muslim headscarf in 21st-century Europe, for instance.

In addition to manifesting identity signaling, groups also hold a number of *core values*[9] that (possibly) set them apart from other groups. Core values, Ehala (2018, 4) explains, refer to

> what people with these identities are supposed to think and believe, in broad terms ... Core values provide a moral scale to assess and evaluate other identities: whether individuals having these identities behave in a respectable manner, whether they are warm or cold in social relations, and whether they are competent or not.

This does not mean that groups are in agreement about the core values; however, they often aim for consensus. Social identity theorists speak of self-stereotyping, meaning that the members of the group often start to act like the perceived prototype of the group.[10] In any case, the core values and identity signs are in a constant state of negotiation.

In what follows, I suggest some *core values* and *identity signs* that I see as pivotal in the Quranic communication. To anticipate the results of my inquiry, the *meaning* that the Quran assigns to these values and signs is, by and large, *piety and ingroup belonging* both in this life and the next. Now, it must be understood that this is how the Quran articulates these signs. We have no way of telling exactly how the audience of the Quran and the individuals

8 By social identity, I refer to an individual's understanding of herself as a member of a group or groups. Self identity, on the other hand, indicates an individual's understanding of herself as different from the other ingroup members.

9 These could also be called "group beliefs." For the definition of core values and their types, see Ehala 2018, 10–11, 91–96.

10 There is a discussion of self-stereotyping in Haslam, Reicher, and Platow 2011, 52–55, 60.

among the community of the Believers received, interpreted, and performed these signals since contemporary evidence for these issues does not exist. Hence, I am only dealing with the *Quranic articulation* of the Believer affiliation and the signs of identity related to belonging to that group. I would suggest, however, that the Quranic message was of utmost importance for the early Believers and they took its communication and social categorizations in earnest.[11]

3 Core Values in the Quran

For the purposes of this study, I treat the following core values, which I deem are central in the Quran: belief in God and the last day; belief in earlier Messengers, Prophets, and revelations as well as belief in the Prophet Muhammad and his message; and submitting to God. These are organized into three subsections below. Other core values could of course be suggested as being more key in the Quranic communication than those I have laid out here,[12] but I think is safe to say that these themes would be considered significant by all interpreters of the Quran and warrant analysis here.

3.1 *Belief in God and the Last Day*

Belief in God and the last day (*al-īmān bi-llāh wa-l-yawm al-ākhar*) is a widely recurring premise for ingroup affiliation. The centrality of this belief is so essential that it gives the group the most commonly used endonym of the Quranic text, "Believers," *al-muʾminūn* or *alladhīna yuʾminūna*.

That the same belief is ascribed to Jews and Christians is rather widely attested in the Quran. For instance, verses 3:113–114 read:

> There are some among the People of the Book who are upright, who recite God's revelations during the night, who bow down in worship, who

11 I strongly agree with Fred Donner (1998, 85): "The strong concern for piety and morals visible in the Qurʾān, which I take to be evidence of the values prevailing in the earliest community of Believers, did not die out in the period following the death of Muḥammad and the codification of the Qurʾān. Rather, the preoccupation with piety survived among the Believers."

12 Other commentators have proposed somewhat different sets of Quranic core values (though not using this specific concept). For Lamptey (2014), for instance, *taqwā* or God-consciousness is central. See also Izutsu (1959) and Fazlur Rahman (1980), who offer rich, by now classic, discussions of ethical and religious concepts, themes, and values in the Quranic communication.

> believe in God and the last day, who order what is right and forbid what is wrong, who are quick to do good deeds. These people are among the pious.[13]

While belief in God and the last day might not be an attribute of all Jews and Christians, according to the Quran some do indeed believe (the same is implied, for example, in verses 2:62, 5:69, and 74:31). The common faith in one God is emphasized in verse 29:46, which enjoins the audience of the Quranic message to say to the People of the Book: "our God and your God are one."

There are some Quranic verses, however, that imply that the People of the Book, or at least some of them, do not believe. Verse 3:70 asks why the People of the Book do not believe in God's signs, even though they clearly see them. Not only that, but they scheme to deceive the Believers (Q. 3:72). Verse 2:105 notes: "Neither those People of the Book who disbelieve nor the associators would like anything good to be sent down to you from your Lord, but God chooses for His grace whoever He will: His bounty has no limits" (see also 98:6). Other passages, such as 5:82–86, appear to make a distinction between the Jews and the Christians: the latter are said to believe, while the former are said to detest the Believers.

Nonetheless, the Quranic verses imputing disbelief to the People of the Book never state that the disbeliever category applies to all of them but only those among them who do not believe. Hence, all in all, in the Quran Jews and Christians (the People of the Book) are not marked out categorically as different or distinct from the Believers because of their faith (or lack of it). The majority of the People of the Book might be transgressors, but among them are also Believers (*minhum al-muʾminūn,* Quran 3:110). It should be noted that the arguably contemporary "Constitution of Medina" also indicates that the participants in that treaty—Jewish and Gentile Believers in Medina—shared the faith in God and the last day (Lindstedt, forthcoming a). Shared belief in God (*Allāh*) is naturally what one would assume.[14]

---

13 Quotations of the Quran are from the translation of Abdel Haleem, with some modifications.

14 In this connection, it should be noted that there is some (epigraphic) evidence that the pre-Islamic Arabic-speaking Christians usually called God *al-Ilāh* though *Allāh* is attested in poetry as well; see most recently Sinai 2019, 7–9. The words *al-Ilāh* and *Allāh* were used by pagans as well to refer to a deity. As for Yemen, Jews and Christians often designated God with the Ancient South Arabian word *raḥmānān,* which corresponds with Arabic *al-Raḥmān,* "Merciful" (Sinai 2019, 59).

3.2 *Belief in Earlier Prophets, Revelations, and the Prophet Muhammad*

It might not be surprising that the Quran credits the Jews and Christians with faith in God and the last day, as noted in the previous subsection. It might also not be striking that the Quran narrates that the Jews and Christians believed in earlier Prophets. What is more remarkable, perhaps, is that the Quran also ascribes to them belief in the Prophet Muhammad and the current revelation. Surprising or not, such is the case.

Indeed, belief in the past revelations and in the most recent one is often conjoined. Above, I referred to verse 29:46, but the whole passage 29:46–47 should be adduced in this connection:

> Say [plural]: 'We believe in that which has been revealed to us and you. Our God and your God is one; we submit to Him.' Thus We have sent you the Book. Those that have received the Book [before] believe in it, and among them are those that believe in it. Only the disbelievers reject Our signs.

In these verses, the People of the Book are described as believing in the current revelation and are set apart from the disbelievers, who reject the "signs" (or, perhaps, "revelations," *āyāt*) of God.

Strikingly, the People of the Book's belief in Muhammad and the truth of his message is reiterated in quite a few verses: for instance, in 6:114: "Those to whom We have given the Book know that this [Muhammad's revelation] is revealed by your Lord with the truth, so do not be one of those who doubt." The same is emphasized in 3:199: "Some of the People of the Book believe in God, in what has been sent down to you and in what was sent down to them: humbling themselves before God, they would never sell God's revelation for a small price. These people will have their rewards with their Lord: God is swift in reckoning." Verse 13:36 says that the People of the Book "rejoice" (*yafraḥūna*) because of Muhammad's revelation, but "some factions deny parts of it"—hardly a categorical statement.

To conclude, Jews and Christians are not, in the Quran, singled out as groups distinct from other Believers in matters of faith (*al-īmān*). Quite interestingly, even belief in the Prophet Muhammad and the veracity of the revelation given to him is not seen as a divisive feature that would set the People of the Book apart—outside the boundaries of the ingroup affiliation—since key verses indicate that some of them accepted Muhammad and his revelation.

3.3 *Submitting to God* (al-islām)

Submitting to God (*al-islām*) is a rather significant group belief in the Quranic communication. As Quran 3:19 states, "the religion,[15] in God's eyes, is *al-islām*." It is an especially interesting matter to take into consideration here since, as is well known, it later gives the appellation "Islam" to the religion of the group. Scholars arguing for early Islamic identity development (that is, the supposition that the group demarcation was already in place during the life of the Prophet) might take the Quranic concept of *al-islām* to claim that it is one of the aspects that delineates the ingroup from Jews and Christians. As I have argued in the introduction of this article, I do not believe that contemporary evidence supports such an early partitioning of Islam from other faiths.

Here, as in the other core values considered above, we encounter the fact that, according the Quranic communication, the People of the Book take part in *al-islām*, submission to God. Verses 28:52–53 refer to the People of the Book, saying that they believe in the Prophet's revelation and, "when it is recited to them, say, 'We believe in it, it is the truth from our Lord. Before it came we had already submitted (*muslimīn*) [to God].'" Furthermore, Quran 29:46 says that the People of the Book and the (other) ingroup members believe in the same God, confirming that "we [all] submit to Him."

Since *al-islām* later became the widely used name of the religion, it might be reasonable to suppose that the Quran excludes this concept from the People of the Book. As I have stated, this is not the case. Rather, *al-islām* marks the People of the Book as well. Quran 28:53, moreover, states that they have been submitters even before the most recent revelation. Hence, verses such as 3:19—"the religion, in God's eyes, is *al-islām*"—that are quite often adduced as evidence for a specifically and distinctly Islamic identity in the Quranic communication turn out to be not exclusive at all since the People of the Book also receive the approbation of submission to God. Even the continuation of 3:19—"those who were given the Book disagreed out of rivalry, only after they had

15 Or, perhaps "law," *al-dīn*. The terms *al-dīn* and *al-islām* have been treated quite extensively in modern scholarship; see, e.g., Baneth 1971; Esack 1997, 126–134; El-Badawi 2013, 49–50. Cole (2019, 419) argues that the word *al-islām* should be understood to mean the "prophetic tradition of monotheism" rather than submission. Though I might take issue with that exact rendering, Cole and I agree on the point that, in the Quran, *al-islām* does not refer to a specific religion followed by the Prophet and his community. Cole (2019, 423) states: "Far from being an attribute only of Muhammad's believers, *islām* characterizes all monotheists throughout history" in the Quranic communication.

been given knowledge"—does not affect my reading, since the disagreement could be understood to be an aspect among them, not disagreement with the Believers. Naturally, after "Islam" became the dominant name for the religion (in the early eighth century, as I argue in Lindstedt 2019), verse 3:19 was one among many that was used to demarcate religious boundaries. But this must be understood as an interpretive process that postdates Muhammad by a century or so.

4 Identity Signs in the Quran

Above, I argued that the Quran ascribes all of its ingroup core values to the People of the Book as well (in addition to other Believers). But what about the identity signs properly speaking, such as rituals and dietary regulations? The evidence is more mixed but there is still substantial overlap.

4.1 *Doing Good Deeds and Being Pious*

Doing good and pious acts, indicated with Arabic verbs and nouns from the roots *ḥ-s-n*, *ṣ-l-ḥ*, and *kh-y-r*, is an important Quranic identity marker that the Believers should possess and indicate. Doing good is often equated with, accompanied by, or connected with other Believer affiliation identity signs, such as pilgrimage (verses 2:158 and 197), fasting (2:184), fighting against the enemy (2:194–195), and spending for charity (2:215).

Doing good is mentioned as a prerequisite for the paradisal reward in many verses of the Quran, for instance in verse 10:26: "Those who do well (*alladhīn aḥsanū*) will have the best reward and more besides. Neither darkness nor shame will cover their faces: these are the companions in Paradise, and there they will remain." Or consider 3:133–134: "Hurry towards your Lord's forgiveness and a Garden as wide as the heavens and earth prepared for the righteous, who give, both in prosperity and adversity, who restrain their anger and pardon people—God loves those who do good (*al-muḥsinīn*)."

Thus, belief, doing good, and other pious deeds are connected in the Quranic communication and are described as leading to Paradise. There are not many verses that explicitly indicate that Jews and Christians (rather than the Believers in general) are also among the good-doers. But there are a few Quranic sections that will be dealt with in the following.

Quran 3:114 was cited above, but let us repeat the passage: it states that some of the People of the Book are "quick to do good deeds (*yusāriʿūna fī al-khayrāt*). These people are among the pious (*al-ṣāliḥīn*)." The same is implied in verses 2:62 and 5:69 that state that those of the Believers, Jews, Christians, and Sabians,[16] who believe in God and the last day and do pious deeds (*ʿamila ṣāliḥan*) will get their reward in the hereafter.

Quranic verses 5:82–85 make a distinction between the pious, good-doing, and amicable Christians on one hand and hateful Jews and associators on the other. As was stated above, the Quranic theology links doing good and being accepted in Paradise. Likewise here:

> You are sure to find that the most hostile to the Believers are the Jews and those who associate other deities with God; you are sure to find that the closest in affection towards the Believers are those who say, "We are Christians," for there are among them people devoted to learning and ascetics. These people are not given to arrogance, and when they listen to what has been sent down to the Messenger, you will see their eyes overflowing with tears because they recognize the Truth. They say, "Our Lord, we believe, so count us amongst the witnesses. Why should we not believe in God and in the Truth that has come down to us, when we long for our Lord to include us in the company of the righteous?" For saying this, God has rewarded them with Gardens graced with flowing streams, and there they will stay: that is the reward of those who do good (*al-muḥsinīn*).

This is a rather categorical ascription of the identity marker "doing good" (*iḥsān*) to the Christians (though it is denied to the Jews in this Quranic passage). Another verse (2:83) addresses the Israelites in connection with *iḥsān*: "Remember when We took a pledge (*mīthāq*) from the Children of Israel: 'Worship none but God; be good to your parents (*bi-l-wālidayn iḥsānan*) and kinsfolk, to orphans and the poor; speak good words to all people; keep up the prayer and pay the prescribed alms.' Then all but a few of you turned away and paid no heed." Granted, here the context is historical (as is often the case when the Quran talks of the Children of Israel), but the verse also seems to speak to the time of the revelation. It should be noticed that while the majority of the Israelites are indeed said to have "turned away" from the virtues described in Quran 2:83, a few (*qalīl*) of them did not. Hence, while 5:82–85 counts the category "Christians" as good-doers, 2:83 implies that there are good-doers among the Israelites/Jews as well. Likewise, verses 2:62, 3:114, and 5:69 extend the attribution of good and pious acts to the Jews and Christians.

---

16 The identity of this group has been debated in both classical Islamic tradition and modern scholarship. See, e.g., de Blois 2002. Janne Mattila's article in this volume deals with how later Muslim scholars understood this group.

4.2 *Giving Alms and Praying*

The identity signs of almsgiving (*zakāh*) and prayer (*ṣalāh*) are very important in the Quran, though they are not subject to detailed rules and regulations concerning how they should be performed. These practices are not often credited to Jews and Christians, but there are a few occurrences.

Verses 2:40 ff. address the Israelites, enjoining them to remember the blessing and covenant of God toward them. The whole passage is rather positive in tone. Verse 2:43 mentions the practices of almsgiving (*zakāh*) and prayer (*ṣalāh*), stating that the Israelites should uphold them and bow down with others who bow down in worship (*wa-rkaʿū maʿa al-rākiʿīn*). There is no suggestion that the Israelites are not currently giving alms and prayer; I would argue that the implication is that they indeed are and that they should continue to do so. The phrase used (*aqīmū al-ṣalāh wa-ātū al-zakāh*) resembles other Quranic verses that enjoin the Believers to maintain their rites.[17]

Verse 3:113, discussing the People of the Book in general, says that some of them recite God's "revelations" (or "signs," *āyāt*) during the night and bow down (*yasjidūna*) in worship. Although the Quranic evidence is slight (consisting of only 2:43 and 3:113), it is suggestive of the possibility that, during the lifetime of the Prophet Muhammad, the almsgiving and prayer practices of Jews and Christians were deemed acceptable. If this is an appropriate interpretation, it signifies that the potential differences among Jews, Christians, and other Believers in the details of how the prayer was performed and alms given were not a hindrance for a shared sense of community as Believers. Jews and Christians were not automatically relegated to the outgroup.

Above, it was mentioned that both Sinai and Hoyland view the diverging directions of prayer of the People of the Book and other Believers mentioned in Quran 2:145[18] as clear signals of distinct communal practices and identities. Nevertheless, the Quran does not offer completely clear evidence concerning the prayer direction and its difference. Nor is it clear how much weight as an identity marker and what meaning the Quran gives to the prayer direction. The Islamic tradition holds (and, if I understand him well, Hoyland concurs)

17 For instance, Q. 2:277: "Those who believe, do good deeds, keep up the prayer, and pay the alms (*aqāmū al-ṣalāh wa-ātaw al-zakāh*) will have their reward with their Lord: no fear for them, nor will they grieve." See also verses 6:72, 7:170, 8:3, 9:18, 9:71, 11:114, 13:22, 14:31, 31:4, 35:29, 42:38, and 98:5.

18 "Yet even if you brought every proof to those who were given the Book, they would not follow your prayer direction, nor will you follow theirs, nor indeed will any of them follow one another's direction. If you [Prophet] were to follow their desires, after the knowledge brought to you, you would be doing wrong."

that Muhammad's followers prayed towards Jerusalem but, later, the prayer direction was changed toward the temple of the Kaʿba in Mecca. Now, it is true that Quran 2:142–144[19] indicates that the prayer direction of Muhammad's community changed at some point, and 2:145 says that the People of the Book differ from it in their prayer direction. However, other verses from the same surah (and hence, probably more or less contemporary with verses 2:142–145)[20] explicitly deny the role of prayer direction as a distinction-making identity sign. The verses in question are 2:115 and 2:177, the latter of which I will quote in full:

> Goodness does not consist in turning your face towards East or West. The truly good are those who believe in God and the last day, in the angels, the Scripture, and the Prophets; who give away some of their wealth, however much they cherish it, to their relatives, to orphans, the needy, travellers and beggars, and to liberate those in bondage; those who keep up the prayer and pay the prescribed alms; who keep pledges whenever they make them; who are steadfast in misfortune, adversity, and times of danger. These are the ones who are true, and it is they who are aware of God.

Crucially then, the Quran itself seems to reject the role of prayer direction ("turning your face towards East or West") in assessing the righteousness of the people and hence limits its exclusiveness as an identity signal. The content of belief and practice trumps the form, these Quranic verses state, according to my interpretation. The meaning of the exact prayer direction is not of utmost importance for group affiliation and piety.

---

19 "The foolish people will say, 'What has turned them away from the prayer direction they used to face?' Say, 'East and West belong to God. He guides whoever He will to the right way.' We have made you into a just community, so that you may bear witness [to the truth] before others and so that the Messenger may bear witness [to it] before you. We only made the direction the one you used to face [Prophet] in order to distinguish those who follow the Messenger from those who turn on their heels: that test was hard, except for those God has guided. God would never let your faith go to waste, for God is most compassionate and most merciful towards people. Many a time We have seen you [Prophet] turn your face towards Heaven, so We are turning you towards a prayer direction that pleases you. Turn your face in the direction of the Sacred Mosque: wherever you may be, turn your faces to it. Those who were given the Scripture know with certainty that this is the Truth from their Lord: God is not unaware of what they do."

20 In fact, there is no way of knowing which came first: verses 2:142–145, which ascribe to the prayer direction the role of an identity marker, or verse 2:177, which denies this role.

4.3 *Fasting and Making the Pilgrimage*

The Quran does not say that Jews and Christians fast or perform the pilgrimage. Nonetheless, it does not say that they do not, either. It is worthwhile to probe fasting and pilgrimage as Quranic signs of identity at some length.

The first question I will ask is: What are the *meanings* and *exclusivity* of Ramadan as the month of fasting and the pilgrimage to Mecca as identity signs? Here, too, we find a certain amount of ambiguity in the Quran. Fasting, in the Quran, is a very common ritual practice, definitely not exclusive to the month of Ramadan (which is mentioned as a fasting month in 2:185). Fasting is prescribed as a means of replacing other religious duties such as shaving the head during the pilgrimage (2:196), doing penance after killing another Believer (4:92), hunting during the pilgrimage (5:95), or breaking an oath (5:89). Nowhere is it said to be *forbidden* to fast at other times too. We can hypothesize (although we of course have no evidence of this) that Jews and Christians joining the Believer's group could have continued their existing traditions of fasting.

The same applies to the pilgrimage (*ḥajj*): although the importance of the local cult is emphasized, the Quran never excludes pilgrimages to other places. Once again, these other places visited by the Arabian Believers are in the realm of hypothesis only since they are not mentioned in the Quran, but they could have included other Arabian sanctuaries or Jerusalem, for example. In fact, there is actually rather little in the Quran that would tie the pilgrimage to the shrine of the Kaʿba in Mecca. Quran 2:158 does mention al-Ṣafā and al-Marwa, two hills next to the Kaʿba, and Quran 5:97, preceded by verses dealing with the *ḥajj*, reads: "God has made the Kaʿba—the sacred shrine—a means of support for people," possibly thereby linking the pilgrimage and the Kaʿba, although the expression is somewhat open to interpretation. Other verses mentioning the *ḥajj* do not mention any toponyms or simply mention "the sacrosanct place of prostration" (*al-masjid al-ḥarām*, Q. 2:196) or "the shrine" (*al-bayt*, 3:97). If Medina (along with other Arabian localities) was also counted as a *ḥaram*, sacred enclave, it is not impossible to interpret these verses (according to the traditional dating, revealed in Medina!) as referring to a local temple instead of that in Mecca. Notably also, verse 2:197 says that the "pilgrimage takes place during the prescribed months," not simply one month (the *dhū al-ḥijja*), as in later tradition. It is plausible that, during the life of the Prophet and for some time afterwards, the Believers held somewhat alternating views as to where a pilgrimage could and should be made and when.

As Arabic poetry evinces, pilgrimage (*ḥajj*) to Mecca was a pre-Islamic tradition (see, e.g., Miller 2016, 104). When the Quran stipulated the *ḥajj* as a ritual, it was confirming and continuing what was already in place in Western Arabia.

Robert Hoyland (2017, 131, n. 78), as mentioned above, says that the Prophet Muhammad "instituted" the *ḥajj*. This is not exactly the case, since his community was, it appears, maintaining prevalent West Arabian traditions. What is more, the connection of the Kaʿba with the figure of Abraham, suggested by the Quran (2:127), might have been a shared narrative and memory already in pre-Islamic times.[21] If this is the case, we can suppose that Arabian Jews and Christians too might have made the pilgrimage to the Kaʿba and linked it with Abraham before Muhammad started to recite his prophetical revelations. Moreover, as I have argued, the Quran does not exclude other pilgrimages either and is somewhat vague as to the exact time and place of the *ḥajj*, which might have been a more encompassing concept than it later became. In the case of the *ḥajj* too, I think it is justifiable to doubt just how much this Quranic ritual actually "mark[s] out people as different" (to borrow Hoyland's phrase, 2017, 131, n. 78).

Recently, Nicolai Sinai (2019, 53–56) has catalogued instances of pre-Islamic (*jāhiliyya*) poetry where God (*Allāh*) is mentioned as the patron deity of Mecca and the Meccan shrine. Now, the authenticity of the corpus of pre-Islamic poetry has been debated in scholarship for around a century. However, it appears that a consensus is emerging that the poetical corpus includes authentic material, though we must accept that the poems were reworked during the two centuries of oral or oral–written transmission (Sinai 2019, 19–26). The poems surveyed by Sinai suggest that Arabian pagans deemed the Kaʿba and its environs holy places vouchsafed and protected by God (*Allāh*) (Sinai 2019, 54–55). Strikingly, also the Christian poet ʿAdī ibn Zayd swears by "the lord of Mecca and of the cross" (*rabbi makkata wa-l-ṣalībī*; Sinai 2019, 52)

Sinai (2019, 54) concludes: "In sum, there is poetic evidence associating Allāh with a pilgrimage sanctuary in general and with the Meccan Kaʿba specifically, and with rites like sacrifice and circumambulation that also figure in the Quran." If these poetic snippets are authentically pre-Islamic, as is probable in at least some of the cases, it follows that Mecca and the Kaʿba constituted a local pilgrimage center that was venerated by Arabians belonging to different religious orientations, including Christians.[22] This practice was accepted

21 I thank Nathaniel Miller for suggesting this to me; see Miller (forthcoming).

22 The idea that both Christians and "pagans" (and perhaps others as well) might have venerated the Kaʿba and made the pilgrimage there in the pre-Islamic era might strike the reader odd at first glance. However, this would be customary in the history of religions: Christians have always borrowed and continued practices from non-Christians and vice versa. Shared holy places are not uncommon. Just to give one example, Heyden 2020 discusses the case of Mamre in late antique Palestine. The sanctuary of Mamre was connected with

and continued by the Quran. When the Quran speaks of pilgrimage rites taking place at the Kaʿba, I do not necessarily see this as drawing a distinction from other communities. I see cultural continuity and sharedness.

4.4 *Following the Law and Dietary Regulations*

Though the Quran is not a law book per se, the notion of law (referred to with Arabic words such as *dīn* and *shirʿa*) is rather central in Quranic conceptualizations of communal life. The Quran appears to allow some plurality in how different communities organize their laws as well as categorize their permissible and forbidden things. However, the idea that these legislations are God-given is at least implied.

This is elaborated at length in Quran 5:44–49. This is a long passage, but I will quote it in its entirety because of its significance:

> We revealed the Torah with guidance and light, and the prophets, who had submitted to God, judged according to it for the Jews. So did the rabbis and the scholars in accordance with that part of God's Book which they were entrusted to preserve, and to which they were witnesses. So do not fear people, fear Me; do not barter away My messages for a small price; those who do not judge according to what God has sent down are rejecting [God's teachings]. In the Torah We prescribed for them a life for a life, an eye for an eye, a nose for a nose, an ear for an ear, a tooth for a tooth, an equal wound for a wound: if anyone forgoes this out of charity, it will serve as atonement for his bad deeds. Those who do not judge according to what God has revealed are doing grave wrong.

Abraham and Sarah and was esteemed and visited during pilgrimage by Jews, Christians, and others. The similarities to the Kaʿba are not difficult to see. See also E. Fowden 2002 on the issue of sharing holy places.

For the (often messy and unsuccessful) articulations of borders between Christians and "pagans" in the late antique world, see, e.g., Kahlos 2007 and 2020. Kahlos argues that Christians interacted with "pagans" at festivals and in places deemed holy: "In the reality of late antique communal life, Christians tended to make their decisions on a situational basis: in situations where they felt belonging to their Christian community was important enough, they 'activated' their Christian 'identity'. The same persons can be seen as taking part in both 'pagan' (or what was seen as pagan) and Christian festivities, probably without any particular scruples—or at least they would have had no scruples if bishops had left them to continue their celebrations in peace. Put bluntly, the often discussed identity crisis of late antique Christians was more of a headache for ecclesiastical leaders than a problem for ordinary people. Practices that in the eyes of bishops appeared incompatible with Christian conduct were not irreconcilable for the participants themselves" (Kahlos 2020, 177).

> We sent Jesus, son of Mary, in their footsteps, to confirm the Torah that had been sent before him: We gave him the Gospel with guidance, light, and confirmation of the Torah already revealed—a guide and lesson for those who take heed of God. So let the followers of the Gospel judge according to what God has sent down in it. Those who do not judge according to what God has revealed are lawbreakers.
>
> We sent to you [Muhammad] the Book with the truth, confirming the Books that came before it, and with final authority over them: so judge between them according to what God has sent down. Do not follow their whims, which deviate from the truth that has come to you. We have assigned a law and a path to each of you. If God had so willed, He would have made you one community, but He wanted to test you through that which He has given you, so race to do good: you will all return to God and He will make clear to you the matters you differed about. So [Prophet] judge between them according to what God has sent down. Do not follow their whims, and take good care that they do not tempt you away from any of what God has sent down to you. If they turn away, remember that God intends to punish them for some of the sins they have committed: a great many people are lawbreakers.

This extensive passage expounds the idea of legislation given to different communities: Jews, Christians, and Muhammad's community. God has "assigned a law and a path to each of you." The Torah of the Jews and the Gospel of the Christians (as the Quran calls these scriptures) are portrayed as valid laws and scriptures with which to organize communal life. Remarkably, Jews and Christians are enjoined to judge according to their scriptures rather than adopting that of the Prophet Muhammad. What is more, Muhammad's Book does not supplant but merely confirms the earlier divine Books. Verse 5:66 states that the failure of some of the People of the Book is to reject the Torah and the Gospel. Their mistake is *not*, it should be underscored, that they have repudiated the Book revealed to Muhammad.[23]

Hence, the People of the Book (or some of them) abide by a God-given law. Interestingly too, the Quran portrays them as sharing the same notions of dietary regulations with other Believers. Intermarriage, too, is permissible. Verse 5:5 proclaims: "Today all good things have been made lawful for you. The food of the People of the Book is lawful for you as your food is lawful for them.

23 It should be remembered that the Quran specifically states that some People of the Book actually accepted Muhammad's revelation, as I have argued above.

So are chaste, believing, women as well as chaste women of the people who were given the Book before you, as long as you have given them their bride-gifts and married them, not taking them as lovers or secret mistresses."[24]

The importance of food regulations and, in particular, partaking in eating together is of much importance in the ancient and late ancient discourse of Near Eastern religions but it has not been conceptualized enough in the study of the Quranic communication and early Islam. Fortunately, Zellentin has recently (2018) authored an extensive and insightful article on the topic of dietary discourse in the Quran and earlier traditions. His treatment develops from the so-called Apostolic Decree (cited in the New Testament, Acts of the Apostles 15:23–29) and the Hebrew Bible tradition. In the New Revised Standard Version translation, verses 28 and 29 in Acts of the Apostles 15 read as follows: "For it has seemed good to the Holy Spirit and to us to impose on you no further burden than these essentials: *that you abstain from what has been sacrificed to idols and from blood and from what is strangled and from fornication.* If you keep yourselves from these, you will do well" (emphasis added). Zellentin notes that many Christian texts written in late antiquity uphold these dietary regulations, proscribing blood and strangled animals (often understood to mean carrion), among other things.

The Quranic dietary regulations are hence intimately connected with the late ancient Judeo-Christian legal discourse. Quran 5:3 prohibits "carrion; blood; pig's meat; any animal over which any name other than God's has been invoked; any animal strangled, or victim of a violent blow or a fall, or gored or savaged by a beast of prey, unless you slaughter it; or anything sacrificed on idolatrous altars" (see also verse 6:145). These accord by and large with the dietary regulations of the Apostolic Decree, adding a few details as well as prohibiting pork.[25] Hence, the Quranic food stipulations in all likelihood were quite familiar to and acceptable to (or already accepted by) many Jews and Christians that were living during the time of the Prophet Muhammad. The Quranic dietary discourse does not, I contend, proffer a distinctive but a shared sign of identity.

In this subsection, I have argued that the Quran seems to allow for parallel legal systems. Moreover, Quran 5:5 allows intermarriage and table fellowship

24 The discourse of verse 5:5 is highly gendered: male believers are the implied addressee. In classical Islamic jurisprudence, the verse (and related Quranic passages) are taken to mean that Muslim men can marry women from among the People of the Book but not vice versa.

25 Pork is not censured in the New Testament as such but prohibited in Leviticus 11:7 and rejected in some late antique Christian texts, see Zellentin 2018, 147. It appears that some (many?) late antique Christians eschewed pork. Such Christians might have been present in Western Arabia as well.

TABLE 4.1 The shared core values and identity signs in the Quran

Core values and identity signs	Believers	(at least some among) Jews and Christians / People of the Book
Believe in God	X	X (e.g. Q. 3:114)
Believe in the last day	X	X (e.g. Q. 3:114)
Believe in the previous prophets and revelations	X	X (Q. 5:44, 6:114)
Believe in God's messenger (i.e., Muhammad) and his revelation	X	X (Q. 3:199, 13:36, 28:52–53, 29:47)
Submit to God	X	X (Q. 28:53, 29:46)
Do good deeds and are pious	X	X (e.g. Q. 3:114)
Pray	X	X (kneel, Q. 3:113, see also 2:43, 98:4–8)
Give alms	X	maybe (Q. 2:43, 98:5)
Fast during Ramadan and other times	X	?
Make the pilgrimage	X	?
Follow the law	X	maybe (5:44–47, 66); dietary regulations shared (5:5)
(Are rewarded in the afterlife)	X	X (e.g. Q. 2:62)

between the People of the Book and other Believers (see also Zellentin 2018, 157–158). When it comes to food and marriage, there are no rigid boundaries but mostly shared practices and traditions.

5 Social Categorizations in the Hereafter

Social categorizations transcend the division of this world from the next, continuing to function in the hereafter as well, according to the Quran. Verse 22:17 reads: "As for the Believers, the Jews, the Sabians, the Christians, the Magians, and the idolaters, God will differentiate them (*yafṣilu baynahym*) on the Day of Resurrection; God witnesses all things." After reading this verse, the expectation might be that the Believers are set aside from the other communities and only the former be the object of the paradisal reward. This is not necessarily the case. In fact, the differentiation mentioned in 22:17 seems to be better interpreted as something that happens between individuals rather than between groups, that is, separating the wheat from the chaff.

There are multiple passages that promise salvation to the pious and faithful among the People of the Book. The soteriology of the Quran, like its legal discourse, is rather pluralistic (to use an anachronistic term).[26] This assurance of the hereafter is communicated in verses 2:62, 3:115, 3:199, 5:69, and 28:54, many of which have been referred to in the preceding. These verses promise the People of the Book their reward (*ajruhum*, Quran 2:62, 3:199) for their good deeds (3:115), adding (2:62, 5:69) that they shall not fear nor grieve (supposedly, in the afterlife). Verse 28:54 promises the People of the Book a double reward (*ajrahum marratayn*), "because they are steadfast, repel evil with good, give to others out of what We have provided for them, and turn away whenever they hear frivolous talk, saying, 'We have our deeds and you have yours. Peace be with you! We do not seek the company of ignorant people'" (28:54–55).

Thus, the Quran not only ascribes positive qualities and attributes of believer-ness and piety to some People of the Book in this world but also suggests that they will receive a reward (or even a double reward) for their good deeds in the world to come. The Quran does not present or articulate the religious communities as being totally separate but rather as overlapping in diverse ways; as Quran 3:110 asserts: the categories "the People of the Book" and "the Believers" are not really mutually exclusive. This applies to both this world and the next.

6 Conclusions

In this study, I have applied the concept of identity signs (Ehala 2018) to the Quran. I have argued that, in fact, identity signs marking a difference[27] between Jews, Christians, and other Believers are, by and large, absent in the Quran.

Perhaps strikingly, (at least some among) the People of the Book share *each and every* one of the aspects that I have termed the core values of the Quranic normative definition of the Believer affiliation. What is more, I have put for-

26 Classical Islamic theological discourse, on the other hand, usually emphasized that only Muslims will receive the heavenly reward. The promise to the People of the Book was interpreted as applying to people before the lifetime of the Prophet Muhammad. However, there were some voices among early Muslim scholars that deemed the People of the Book fit for salvation; see Esack 1997, 163. For a well-argued Islamic theology of pluralism, see Lamptey 2014.

27 Such identity signs can be called "boundary features" or "distinctions"; see Ehala 2018, 80.

ward that the Quran also ascribes to the People of the Book many of the identity signs, such as rituals, that belong to the description of the Believers. I would argue that the conclusion to be drawn based on this is quite simple: the Quran categorizes some People of the Book as part of the ingroup, the community of Believers.

Naturally, this was not how classical Islamic thought understood the Quranic social categorizations. Rather, Jews and Christians were considered by the majority of Muslim scholars as being beyond the pale. Though this question is beyond the scope of my inquiry, I will end with a quotation from Farid Esack (1997, 114–115), who describes this process of social categorization in classical Islamic interpretive tradition as follows: "One of the manifestations (and consequences) of the process of Islamic theology becoming more and more rigid was the reification of terms such as *islam*, *iman* and *kufr* [disbelief]. In other words, these words are no longer seen as qualities that individuals may have; qualities that are dynamic and vary in intensity in different stages of an individual's life. Instead, these terms are now regarded as entrenched qualities of groups."

Bibliography

Abdel Haleem, M.A. (transl.). *The Qur'an*. Oxford: Oxford University Press, 2004.

Baneth, D.Z.H. "What Did Muḥammad Mean When He Called His Religion 'Islam'? The Original Meaning of *aslama* and Its Derivatives." *Israel Oriental Studies* 1 (1971): 183–190.

de Blois, François. "*Naṣrānī* (*Ναζωραῖος*) and *ḥanīf* (*ἐθνικός*): Studies on the Religious Vocabulary of Christianity and of Islam." *Bulletin of the School of Oriental and African Studies* 65/1 (2002): 1–30.

Brubaker, Rogers and Frederick Cooper. "Beyond 'Identity.'" *Theory and Society* 29 (2000): 1–47.

Cole, Juan. "Paradosis and Monotheism: A Late Antique Approach to the Meaning of *islām* in the Quran." *Bulletin of the School of Oriental and African Studies* 82/3 (2019): 405–425.

Crone, Patricia. "Among the Believers." *Tablet* (August 10, 2010), http://www.tabletmag.com/jewish-news-and-politics/42023/among-the-believers.

Crone, Patricia. "Jewish Christianity and the Qurʾān (I–II)." *Journal of Near Eastern Studies* 74/2 (2015): 225–253 and 75/1 (2016): 1–21.

Crone, Patricia. *The Qurʾānic Pagans and Related Matters*. Leiden: Brill, 2016.

Donner, Fred M. *Narratives of Islamic Origins: The Beginnings of Islamic Historical Writing*. Princeton: Darwin Press, 1998.

Donner, Fred M. "From Believers to Muslims: Confessional Self-Identity in the Early Islamic Community." *Al-Abhath* 50–51 (2002–2003): 9–53.

Donner, Fred M. *Muhammad and the Believers: At the Origins of Islam*. Cambridge, MA: Belknap Press at Harvard University Press, 2010.

Donner, Fred M. "Talking about Islam's Origins." *Bulletin of the School of Oriental and African Studies* 81 (2018): 1–23.

Ehala, Martin. *Signs of Identity: The Anatomy of Belonging*. London and New York: Routledge, 2018.

Elad, A. "Community of Believers of 'Holy Men' and 'Saints' or Community of Muslims? The Rise and Development of Early Muslim Historiography." *Journal of Semitic Studies* 47/1 (2002): 241–308.

El-Badawi, Emran. *The Qur'an and the Aramaic Gospel Traditions*. London: Routledge, 2013.

Esack, Farid. *Qur'ān, Liberation and Pluralism: An Islamic Perspective of Interreligious Solidarity against Oppression*. Oxford: OneWorld, 1997.

Fazlur Rahman. *Major Themes of the Qur'an*. Minneapolis: Bibliotheca Islamica, 1980.

Fowden, Elizabeth Key. "Sharing Holy Places." *Common Knowledge* 8 (2002): 124–146.

Fowden, Garth. *Before and After Muhammad: The First Millennium Refocused*. Princeton: Princeton University Press, 2014.

Griffith, Sidney H. *The Church in the Shadow of the Mosque: Christians and Muslims in the World of Islam*. Princeton: Princeton University Press, 2008.

Haslam, S. Alexander. *Psychology in Organizations: The Social Identity Approach* (2nd ed.). London: SAGE Publications, 2004.

Haslam, S. Alexander, Steve D. Reicher, and Michael J. Platow. *The New Psychology of Leadership: Identity, Influence and Power*. New York: Routledge, 2011.

Heyden, Katharina. "Construction, Performance, and Interpretation of a Shared Holy Place: The Case of Late Antique Mamre (Rāmat al-Khalīl)." *Entangled Religions* 11.1 (2020). Available at https://doi.org/10.13154/er.11.2020.8557 (accessed on May 21, 2020).

Hoyland, Robert. *Seeing Islam as Others Saw It: A Survey and Evaluation of Christian, Jewish and Zoroastrian Writings on Early Islam*. Princeton: Darwin Press, 1997.

Hoyland, Robert. "Reflections on the Identity of the Arabian Conquerors of the Seventh-Century Middle East." *Al-ʿUṣūr al-Wusṭā* 25 (2017): 113–140.

Imbert, Frédéric. "L'Islam des pierres: l'expression de la foi dans les graffiti arabes des premiers siècles." *Revue des mondes musulmans et de la Méditerranée* 129 (2011): 57–78.

Izutsu, Toshihiko. *The Structure of the Ethical Terms in the Koran*. Tokyo: Keio Institute of Philological Studies, 1959.

Kahlos, Maijastina. *Debate and Dialogue: Christian and Pagan Cultures c. 360–430*. London: Routledge, 2007.

Kahlos, Maijastina. *Religious Dissent in Late Antiquity, 350–450*. Oxford: Oxford University Press, 2020.

Lamptey, Jerusha Tanner. *Never Wholly Other: A Muslima Theology of Religious Pluralism*. Oxford: Oxford University Press, 2014.

Lecker, Michael. *The "Constitution of Medina"*. Princeton: Darwin Press, 2004.

Levy-Rubin, Milka. *Non-Muslims in the Early Islamic Empire: From Surrender to Coexistence*. Cambridge: Cambridge University Press, 2011.

Lindstedt, Ilkka. "Who Is in, Who Is out? Early Muslim Identity through Epigraphy and Theory." *Jerusalem Studies in Arabic and Islam* 46 (2019): 147–246.

Lindstedt, Ilkka. "'One People to the Exclusion of Others': Recategorized Superordinate Identity in the Medinan Community." In: Isaac W. Oliver et al. (eds.), *Proceedings from the Second and Third Early Islamic Studies Seminar Meetings*. De Gruyter (forthcoming a).

Lindstedt, Ilkka. "Religious Groups in the Quran." In: Raimo Hakola, Outi Lehtipuu and Nina Nikki (eds.), *Common Ground and Diversity in Early Christian Thought and Study: Essays in Memory of Heikki Räisänen*. Tübingen: Mohr Siebeck (forthcoming b).

Miller, Nathaniel. *Tribal Poetics in Early Arabic Culture: The Case of Ashʿār al-Hudhaliyyīn*. Dissertation at the University of Chicago, 2016.

Miller, Nathaniel. "Yemeni Inscriptions, Iraqi Chronicles, Hijazi Poetry: A Reconstruction of the Meaning of *Isrāʾ* in Qurʾan 17:1." *Journal of Royal Asiatic Society* (forthcoming).

Munt, Harry. "What Did Conversion to Islam Mean in Seventh-Century Arabia?" In: A.C.S. Peacock (ed.), *Islamisation: Comparative Perspectives from History*. Edinburgh: Edinburgh University Press, 2017, 83–101.

Nehmé, Laila. "New Dated Inscriptions (Nabataean and Pre-Islamic Arabic) from a Site Near al-Jawf, Ancient Dūmah, Saudi Arabia." *Arabian Epigraphic Notes* 3 (2017): 121–164.

Nevo, Y.D. and J. Koren. *Crossroads to Islam: The Origins of the Arab Religion and the Arab State*. Amherst: Prometheus Books, 2003.

Neuwirth, Angelika. *Scripture, Poetry, and the Making of a Community: Reading the Qurʾan as a Literary Text*. Oxford: Oxford University Press, 2014.

Penn, Michael P. *Envisioning Islam: Syriac Christians and the Early Muslim World*. Philadelphia: University of Pennsylvania Press, 2015.

Shaddel, Mehdy. "Qurʾānic *ummī*: Genealogy, Ethnicity, and the Foundation of a New Community." *Jerusalem Studies in Arabic and Islam* 43 (2016): 1–60.

Shoemaker, Stephen J. *The Death of a Prophet: The End of Muhammad's Life and the Beginnings of Islam*. Philadelphia: University of Pennsylvania Press, 2012.

Shoemaker, Stephen J. *The Apocalypse of Empire: Imperial Eschatology in Late Antiquity and Early Islam*. Philadelphia: University of Pennsylvania Press, 2018.

Sinai, Nicolai. *The Qur'an: A Historical-Critical Introduction*. Edinburgh: Edinburgh University Press, 2017.

Sinai, Nicolai. *Rain-Giver, Bone-Breaker, Score-Settler: Allāh in Pre-Quranic Poetry*. New Haven, Connecticut: American Oriental Society, 2019.

Sirry, Mun'im. *Scriptural Polemics: The Qur'an and Other Religions*. Oxford: Oxford University Press, 2014.

Stroumsa, Guy G. *The Making of the Abrahamic Religions in Late Antiquity*. Oxford: Oxford University Press, 2015.

Tajfel, Henri. *Human Groups and Social Categories: Studies in Social Psychology*. Cambridge: Cambridge University Press, 1981.

Webb, Peter. *Imagining the Arabs: Arab Identity and the Rise of Islam*. Edinburgh: Edinburgh University Press, 2016.

Weitz, Lev. *Between Christ and Caliph: Law, Marriage, and Christian Community in Early Islam*. Philadelphia: University of Pennsylvania Press, 2018.

Yarbrough, Luke. "Origins of the *Ghiyār*." *Journal of the American Oriental Society* 134 (2014): 113–121.

Zellentin, Holger. *The Qur'ān's Legal Culture: The Didascalia Apostolorum as a Point of Departure*. Tübingen: Mohr Siebeck, 2013.

Zellentin, Holger. "Judaeo-Christian Legal Culture and the Qur'ān: The Case of Ritual Slaughter and the Consumption of Animal Blood." In: Francisco del Río Sánchez (ed.), *Jewish Christianity and the Origins of Islam*. Turnhout: Brepols, 2018, 117–159.

CHAPTER 5

Sabians, the School of al-Kindī, and the Brethren of Purity

Janne Mattila

The Sabian religion of Ḥarrān evoked considerable interest in the intellectual circles of the Islamic world during the 9th and 10th centuries. As described by the Arabic authors, the inhabitants of Ḥarrān in northern Mesopotamia practiced a pagan religion of pre-Islamic origins with its peculiar doctrines and rituals.[1] The Ḥarrānians were known in particular for an astral cult with an elaborate festival calendar determined by the positions of the stars and the planets.[2] An offshoot of the Ḥarrānian Sabians was also operating in Baghdad, as represented by the translator and mathematician-astronomer Thābit Ibn Qurra (d. 901) and his descendants.[3] Against this background, it is not surprising that many philosophers operating in Iraq were also fascinated by the Sabian religion. Among them, al-Kindī (d. ca. 870) and his pupil al-Sarakhsī (d. 899) on the one hand, and the anonymous group of philosophers known as the Brethren of Purity (Ikhwān al-Ṣafā'; 9th–10th-cent.) on the other, showed particular interest in the pagan religion of Ḥarrān.

Both al-Sarakhsī and the Brethren of Purity discuss the religious beliefs and practices of the Sabians in some detail. Like other contemporary authors, they tell us that the Sabians venerate the planets, and describe some of their astrologically determined cultic practices. But while the Arabic accounts often manifest a critical or neutral stance with regard to the Sabian religion, it is immediately apparent that these philosophical authors present the Ḥarrānian astral cult in a particularly positive light. Moreover, they attribute to the Sabians largely philosophical views, and appear to think that the major doctrines to which they attest are more or less correct. This raises two questions. First, why are these philosophers interested in the Ḥarrānian religion in the first place?

1 There is a voluminous secondary literature on Ḥarrān and the Sabians since the grand work of Chwolsohn 1856. See in particular Hjärpe 1972; Green 1992; Gündüz 1994, 15–54, 125–191; van Bladel 2009, 64–114.

2 Hjärpe 1974.

3 For Thābit Ibn Qurra and his works, see Ibn al-Qifṭī 1903, 116–122, and for his descendants, Roberts 2017.

 | DOI:10.1163/9789004471160_006

In contrast to the other authors discussing the Sabians, they are neither historians nor heresiographers,[4] and presumably their primary interest does not lie in a doxographical account of the Sabian religion. This leads to the second question: Is there a philosophical reason for their interest in the Sabians, and could the Sabian religion even represent a doctrinal influence on their thought? This study will consist of three parts. I will first present the general background for the relation between the Sabian religion and the school of al-Kindī and the Brethren of Purity. Second, I will present the accounts that these authors offer on the Ḥarrānian religion. Third, I will see in what sense their accounts should be interpreted in the general context of their philosophical thought.

1 Sabians and Philosophy

The fact that these particular philosophers accord the Sabians such high regard is interesting also due to the various doctrinal affinities between the thought of al-Kindī and his disciples on the one hand,[5] and the Brethren of Purity on the other.[6] Some of these affinities might be related to their interest in the Sabian religion. Both accord high prominence to astrology, in contrast to many authors operating within the Aristotelian tradition, such as al-Fārābī (d. 950) and Avicenna (Ibn Sīnā; d. 1037),[7] and consequently endorse the view that particular events are celestially determined and that it is possible to predict them.[8] Both authors attest to the doctrine of cosmic harmony in the form of microcosmism, or the idea that the cosmos constitutes a single living being analogous to the human being as exemplified in very specific correspondances between the

4 While the Brethren's 42nd epistle, *On Beliefs and Doctrines* (*Fī al-ārā' wa-l-madhāhib*), is partly heresiographical or doxographical in nature, the authors do not in it explicitly address the Sabian religion. For the surprisingly positive view on religious diversity manifested by this epistle, see Mattila 2017.

5 For the general features of the school of al-Kindī, see Adamson 2007b.

6 For some parallels, see Alfred Ivry's introduction and commentary in al-Kindī 1974, 20, 21, 170, 174. See also de Vaulx d'Arcy 2019, 13–63, for the argument that the *Epistles* of the Brethren of Purity should be attributed to al-Sarakhsī.

7 For their refutation of astrology, on ontological and epistemological grounds respectively, see Druart 1978 and 1979; Avicenna 2006.

8 For the primacy of astrology in al-Kindī, see Adamson 2002 and 2007a, 191–206. The interest in astrology prevailed also in al-Kindī's students: Abū Maʿshar al-Balkhī (d. 866) is the most influential astrologer in early Islamic history, and a treatise by the title *On the Main Principles of Philosophy and the Establishment of Astrology* (*Kitāb arkān al-falsafa wa-tathbīt aḥkām al-nujūm*) is attributed to al-Sarakhsī (for which treatise see Rosenthal 1943, 120–121).

parts of the cosmos and of the human body and soul.[9] Both also accord high status to mathematics, in the specific sense that they emphasize ontological arithmology, harmonic mathematical relations, and the study of mathematics as philosophical propadeutics.[10] When taken together, these three aspects distinguish al-Kindī and the Brethren of Purity at least from the kind of Aristotelianism that came to prevail in Baghdad during the 10th century. The primacy of astrology and the idea of cosmic relations prevailing between the celestial and earthly spheres might be related to their interest in the Sabian astral cult, given that the central tenet of the Ḥarrānian religion is the worship of planets and stars. The third aspect may similarly have some relation with Ḥarrān due to the city's alleged position as a conduit for the transmission of Neo-Pythagorean and Platonic thought in the Islamic world.[11] The doctrinal parallels between al-Kindī and the Brethren of Purity are undoubtedly to a large extent explained by their reliance on common sources, but they nevertheless indicate that they shared similar philosophical inclinations.[12]

The question about the doctrinal affinities between al-Kindī's school and the Brethren of Purity inevitably leads to the problem concerning the dating of the *Epistles* of the Brethren of Purity (*Rasāʾil Ikhwān al-Ṣafāʾ*). The work is an encyclopedia of the philosophical sciences in 51 or 52 epistles, each of which is devoted to a different science or field of knowledge. A major part of the scholarly debate on the work has revolved around the interrelated problems of its dating and the identity and doctrinal affiliation of the author or authors.[13] While there is still no scholarly consensus on any of these questions, until recently, the most common view was to date the work to the second half of

9 For microcosmism in al-Kindī, see Adamson 2007a, 172–180, and in the Brethren, Nokso-Koivisto 2014.

10 For these doctrinal tendencies in the school of al-Kindī and the Brethren of Purity, see Endress 2003, 127–135, and for Neo-Pythagorean ideas in al-Kindī, see also Adamson 2007a, 27–28, 173–180.

11 See the discussion below.

12 These common sources include the so-called Hermetic corpus, and, in case of the Neo-Pythagorean tendencies, Nicomachus of Gerasa's (2nd cent. CE) *Introduction to Arithmetics* (*Arithmetikē Eisagōgē*). As regards the former, the Arabic sources mention Hermes as a prophet of the Ḥarrānians since the 9th century, and both al-Sarakhsī and the Brethren similarly identify Hermes as one of the chief Sabian prophets. The question whether Ḥarrān in fact played any role in the transmission of the treatises attributed to Hermes, however, still remains open, and is analyzed critically in van Bladel 2009, 79–114.

13 For concise and up-to-date overviews of these questions, see Baffioni 2008 and de Callataÿ 2013a.

the tenth century. However, since it now seems probable that the *Epistles* was introduced in al-Andalus by the mid-tenth century,[14] its Iraqian origins must be temporally close to the milieu of al-Kindī's circle of students, even if the final redaction of the work might still have taken place later. This, in turn, fits in well with the doctrinal parallels between the *Epistles* and the Kindian tradition.

But what is the Sabian religion that al-Sarakhsī and the Brethren of Purity are talking about? The term Sabian itself is founded on Quranic authority (5:69; cf. 2:62, 22:17): "For those who believe, Jews, Sabians, and Christians who believe in God and the judgment day and do righteous works, have no cause for fear and will not grief." The Sabians are, then, a religion of the book, alongside the Jews and Christians, that enjoys protected status under Islamic rule. Since the object of the Quranic reference was no longer clear by the 9th century, Arabic authors came to employ the term in reference to various unrelated pagan religions in Iraq, including the Mandeans and Ḥarrānians.[15] To increase the ambiguity, the Arabic sources also employ the term in an even wider sense to refer to pagan religions in general, such as Buddhism or the religion practiced by the ancient Greeks.[16] Moreover, some Arabic authors, including al-Sarakhsī and the Brethren of Purity, identify the Sabians further with *ḥanīf*s, another Quranic term with a sometimes ambiguous referent. While the original Semitic meaning of the term seems to be 'pagan,' in the Quran it is attributed in particular to Abraham, and has the entirely positive sense of pre-Islamic monotheists, who are neither Jewish nor Christian.[17] When al-Sarakhsī and the Brethren of Purity speak about the Sabians, their primary frame of reference is nevertheless clearly the religion practiced in Ḥarrān. But at the same time, the wider

14 See Fierro 1996, 94–95, 106–108; de Callataÿ 2013b. The Andalusian alchemical and magical treatises of *Rutbat al-ḥakīm* and *Ghāyat al-ḥakīm* cite from and explicitly refer to the *Epistles*, and Fierro has argued convincingly that these treatises should be attributed to Maslama al-Qurṭubī (d. 964). The re-attribution coincides with the statement in *Ghāya* that the author wrote *Rutba* in 343–348 A.H. (954–960 C.E.), although unfortunately in some manuscripts the dates are given as 434–438.

15 For a new assessment of the genesis and early history of the Mandean religion, see van Bladel 2017.

16 Hence, Hämeen-Anttila 2006, 50, refers to it as an "umbrella term" for pagan religions. See also de Callataÿ 2017 for Ṣā'id al-Andalusī's (d. 1070) presentation of all of the seven primeval nations as Sabians distinguished by their worship of idols representing the astral bodies.

17 For the Quranic and later Islamic use of the term, and an interpretation of its pre-Islamic Semitic etymology, see Blois 2002, 16–27. For the employment of the term by Muslim authors in its original sense of 'pagan,' and as synonymous with the term 'Sabian,' see in particular Ibid, 19–20.

extension of the term, entangled with the term *ḥanīf*, allows them to expand its meaning to encompass also the religion practiced by the ancient Greek philosophers.

The relation between Ḥarrān and the classical philosophical tradition involves further confusions. Since Chwolsohn, many scholars have posited in Ḥarrān a Hellenistic system of beliefs and rites that mixes together Aristotelian, Neoplatonic, Neo-Pythagorean, and Hermetic influences, either existing alongside the more plebeian astral cult of Mesopotamian origin,[18] or perhaps fused with it.[19] Tardieu went even further to argue that the Platonic Academy lived on in Ḥarrān well into the Islamic era.[20] According to the well-known narrative, emperor Justinian (r. 527–565) closed the Academy in Athens in 529, after which its last representatives, including Damascius (d. after 538) and Simplicius (d. ca. 560), left for the court of the Sāsānid king Khosrow Anūshirwān (r. 531–579) in Persia.[21] Disappointed with the Persian court, they soon headed back towards the Roman Empire, and, according to Tardieu's influential hypothesis, found a new home in Ḥarrān.

There is little evidence, however, that there was a Platonic philosophical school in Ḥarrān either in Late Antiquity or in early Islamic times.[22] The most important support for the hypothesis is founded on a passage by the historian al-Masʿūdī (d. 956):

> And in this group (*ṭāʾifa*) known as the Ḥarrānians or the Sabians there are philosophers, but they are lowly and common philosophers (*ḥashwiyyat al-falāsifa wa-ʿawāmmuhum*) who differ in their beliefs with the elite of their sages (*khawāṣṣ ḥukamāʾihim*). For we relate them to philosophers (*aḍafnāhum ilā al-falāsifa*) because of their ancestry (*nasab*), not because of their wisdom. They are Greek, but not all Greeks are philosophers,

18 Chwolsohn 1856, II, 717–802; Hjärpe, 1972, 39; Green 1992, 162–190.

19 Pingree 2002.

20 The thesis was first proposed in Tardieu 1986 and 1987. It has been accepted mainly by classicists, such as Shaw 1995, 5 and Hadot 1996, 37–47, but more cautiously also in Pingree 2002.

21 For a critical re-evalution of this story, see Cameron 1969. According to Cameron's reading of the Neoplatonic sources, it is not clear that Justinian closed the philosophical school of Athens, although it was closed at some point, nor did the Persian trip necessarily have anything to do with its closure. For a more recent reconstruction of the events based on the available evidence, and an extensive bibliography, see Wildberg 2006, 329–333.

22 See in particular van Bladel 2009, 70–79.

> although the philosophers are the sages among the Greek (*ḥukamāʾuhum*).[23] I have seen written in Syriac on the knocker over the door of a Sabian temple (*majmaʿ*) in the city of Ḥarrān a saying by Plato (*qawl li-Aflāṭūn*) which Mālik b. ʿUqbūn and others among them explain as follows: 'whoever knows herself becomes like a god' (*man ʿarafa dhātahu taʾallaha*).[24]

Due to the ambiguity of the Arabic, Tardieu interprets the first part of the passage to state that the Ḥarrānians consisted of the "vulgar" (*ḥashwiyya*) philosophers on the one hand and sages (*ḥukamāʾ*) on the other, the latter of which he claims were the later followers of Simplicius. Yet, this clearly is not what al-Masʿūdī says. What he says instead is that there were philosophers in Ḥarrān, although they were not particularly good philosophers, and that their opinions were at variance with those of the Ḥarrānian savants.[25] The last sentence of the passage states that al-Masʿūdī witnessed a Platonic slogan inscribed over the doorway of a Sabian "gathering-place" (*majmaʿ*), probably a temple, advocating self-knowledge as a path to approach divinity.[26] Tardieu reads this as a reference to the Platonic Academy, whose leader he claims was undoubtedly the stated Mālik b. ʿUqbūn that helped al-Masʿūdī to understand the meaning of the alleged inscription.[27] In consequence, Ḥarrān came to form an important philosophical center which played an essential role for the genesis of the Arabic philosophical tradition, in particular as a conduit of oral transmission, thus complementing the literary channel by means of the translation of texts.[28] Clearly, al-Masʿūdī's eyewitness account, albeit interesting, falls far short of establishing the existence of Platonic Academy in Ḥarrān. While Hellenistic culture undoubtedly survived in Ḥarrān well into the Islamic era, as it did in

---

23 For the Arabic employment of the term 'Greek' (*yūnānī*) as referring either to ethnically Greek or to pagans in general, see van Bladel 2009, 73–74.

24 Al-Masʿūdī 1966–1974, II, 393 [my translation].

25 For the refutal of Tardieu's reading, see also Lameer 1997, 187–188; van Bladel 2009, 72.

26 The aphorism probably goes back to the Delphic maxim, as well as, as suggested in Tardieu 1986, 15, *Alcibiades I*, 330C: "Then this part of the soul [= wisdom] resembles god, and whoever looks at this, and comes to know all that is divine, will gain thereby the best knowledge of himself."

27 Tardieu 1986, 18.

28 Hence, Tardieu 1986, 39: "Son rôle historique est immense. Restée païenne jusqu'au bout et attachée à trois grandes langues de civilisation, elle est un maillon de la chaîne de tranmission de la science antique à l'islam médiéval." Marquet 1966 claims a similarly central role for Ḥarrān in the philosophical education of the Brethren of Purity, to which thesis we will return later.

various other places, there is little evidence to show that Ḥarrān played a central role in the transmission of philosophical knowledge.[29]

It is nevertheless incontestable that al-Kindī, al-Sarakhsī, and the Brethren of Purity associate both the Sabians in general and Ḥarrān in particular with the heritage of the ancient philosophers. It is not known that any of them visited Ḥarrān,[30] and thereby possessed first-hand knowledge about the Sabian religion. The presence of Thābit Ibn Qurra and his kin at the caliph's court in Baghdad certainly enabled acquaintance with the Ḥarrānian Sabians, at least for al-Sarakhsī.[31] Alternatively, their knowledge might at least to a large extent be based on the 'Sabian narrative' transmitted by textual sources. Given the major historiographical problems that concern the Arabic descriptions of the Sabians, it is in fact not at all clear that this narrative would correspond in any simple sense to the historical reality. Moreover, insofar as the Sabians for the philosophical authors served a primarily instrumental purpose, as I will argue, it seems quite likely that they were not even pursuing an objective description of the Sabian religion.

2 Al-Sarakhsī and the Brethren on the Sabians

With the possible exception of a treatise on the kingly conduct, none of al-Sarakhsī's works have reached us through the manuscript tradition.[32] But the bibliographical sources attribute to him a work by the title *Description of the Doctrines of the Sabians* (*Risāla fī waṣf madhāhib al-ṣābiʾīn*). The *Catalogue* (*Fihrist*) of Ibn al-Nadīm (d. before 998) transmits a short testimony by al-Sarakhsī on the Sabian religion, as conveyed "on the authority of al-Kindī" (*ḥakāhā ʿan al-Kindī*),[33] which seems to be based on al-Sarakhsī's lost treatise.

29 For a rebuttal of the idea of Ḥarrān as a conduit of non-literary transmission of Platonic and Neo-Pythagorean ideas, see also De Smet 2010 and 2011. Endress 2003, 126–127, nevertheless suggests that the Ḥarrānian mathematicians in Baghdad might have played some role in the transmission of Platonic influences among scientists and philosophers. See also Ibid, 128, for Thābit Ibn Qurra's extensive knowledge on Plato's *Meno*.

30 Rosenthal 1943, 22, 65, suggests that al-Sarakhsī might have when he accompanied the ʿAbbāsid prince al-Muʿtaḍid in the prince's military expedition to Syria.

31 See van Bladen 2009, 89, note 107, for the evidence of a personal relation between al-Sarakhsī and Thābit Ibn Qurra.

32 The available evidence for al-Sarakhsī's life and works has been collected in Rosenthal 1943, complemented in Rosenthal 1951, 1956, 1961, 1995; Moosa 1972. See also Biesterfeldt 2012.

33 Ibn al-Nadīm 1872, 318–320. The text has been translated, along with the variant accounts, in Rosenthal 1943, 41–51.

What is interesting at the outset is that al-Sarakhsī authored such a treatise, and that, according to Ibn al-Nadīm, it was based on the authority of al-Kindī, as this attests to a continuing interest in the Sabian religion within the school of al-Kindī.

Like other Arabic testimonies on the Sabian religion, al-Sarakhsī's account covers both religious beliefs and ritual practices. As regards their religious doctrines, the Sabians believe, first, that the world has a single unitary and eternal cause which is transcendent in the sense that He cannot be described in positive terms and that attributes of the caused beings cannot be related to Him.[34] Second, God has chosen from among the "people of discernment" (*ahl al-tamyīz*) some to act as prophets in order to guide people towards the true faith (*al-ḥanīfiyya*), and to exhort them about His reward and warn them against His punishment. The Sabian prophets are of perfect bodily and mental constitution, and include Arānī, Agathodaimon, and Hermes, and, according to some, Solon who is claimed to be Plato's grandfather.[35] Third, the Sabians believe that the afterlife is restricted to the spirits (*arwāḥ*) only, and that the soul is subject to an immediate, as opposed to postponed, reward and punishment in the afterlife.[36] In sum, despite minor divergences, the Sabians believe in the three major Islamic articles of faith: monotheism, prophecy, and reward and punishment in the afterlife. As regards monotheism, the Sabians do not worship planets in themselves: they believe that the heavenly motions are voluntary and intellectual,[37] and that they act as intermediaries of God's providence (*mutawassiṭ fī al-tadbīr*),[38] which is of course the standard Aristotelian view. Moreover, they attest to the divine transcendence and negative theology reminiscent of the Muʿtazilite theological school, which also characterizes al-Kindī's theological thought,[39] and restrict afterlife only to the soul together with most Muslim philosophers.[40]

As for the Sabian religious legislation, al-Sarakhsī, first, informs us that it is directed towards the essentially philosophical ends of investigation of wisdom (*baḥth al-ḥikma*) and acquisition of the four Platonic cardinal virtues.[41] On the

34 Ibn al-Nadīm 1872, 318, 320.

35 Ibid, 318, 319.

36 Ibid.

37 Ibid, 318.

38 Ibid, 319.

39 Adamson 2003.

40 For al-Kindī's explanation of the Platonic afterlife in *Al-Qawl fī al-nafs al-mukhtaṣar min kitāb Arisṭū wa-Aflāṭūn wa-sā'ir al-falāsifa*, see al-Kindī 1950, 277–278. For al-Kindī nevertheless affirming the possibility of bodily resurrection, see Adamson 2007a, 63–64.

41 Ibn al-Nadīm 1872, 318.

whole, the ritual aspect of the Sabian religion is in part determined by the positions of the planets and stars. The Sabian rites include three daily prayers (*ṣalāt*), at sunrise, noon, and sunset, directed towards the north pole,[42] to be performed in a due state of purity, and all of which are accompanied with a specific amount of bendings (*rakʿa*) and prostrations (*sujūd*).[43] They have three yearly fasts of differing lengths that coincide with the conjunctions of the Sun and the Moon, four yearly days of sacrifice to honor the planets, and a number of yearly festivals.[44] They adhere to strict regulations concerning ritual purity, especially as concerns menstruating women, as well as with regard to which animals are held to be licit for food and sacrifice, cock being the most important sacrificial animal. As regards their social legislation, men and women share equal inheritance, while incest, polygamy, and circumcision are prohibited. When taken as a whole, then, in part the Sabian ritual sounds surprisingly Islamic, such as in what concerns the prayer movements and requirements of ritual purity. Although many aspects clearly diverge from the Islamic practice, these hardly seem particularly abhorrent from the perspective of a Muslim intellectual, such as al-Kindī or al-Sarakhsī. In both its doctrinal and ritual aspects, the Sabian religion differs from the Islamic belief and practice only to an extent that falls well within the normal variation between the licit monotheistic religions. This impression is confirmed by the fact that the Ḥarrānian religion is explicitly identified as the *ḥanīf* religion of Abrahamic monotheism.

The concluding passage of al-Sarakhsī's account is, however, the most surprising:

> Concerning matter, elements, form, non-being, time, space, and movement, the Sabians hold the same opinions as Aristotle in *Physics*. The heaven, in their opinion, is a fifth nature, not composed of the four elements. It neither disintegrates nor perishes. This opinion is in agreement with Aristotle's opinion in *On the Heavens*. The four natures, in their opinion, perish for the propagation of plants and animals … This opinion is in agreement with Aristotle's opinion in *On Generation and Corruption*. Their opinion concerning the supernal influences (*al-āthār al-ʿulwiyya*) and the events in the sublunar sphere, is in agreement with Aristotle's opinion in *Meteorology*. The soul, in their opinion, is perceptive, unperishable, and an incorporeal substance to which no attributes of the body

42 In most of the Arabic accounts, the Sabians direct their prayers towards the south pole (see Gündüz 1994, 164–166).

43 Ibn al-Nadīm 1872, 318–319.

44 Ibid, 319.

> attach. This opinion is in agreement with Aristotle's *On the Soul*. Their opinion concerning true dreams and similar things, and the senses and the sensibles, is in agreement with Aristotle in *On Senses and the Sensibles*. God, in their opinion, is one, no attribute can be applied to Him, and no positive statement can be made about Him, and therefore He does not fit into any syllogism. This opinion is in agreement with Aristotle's *Metaphysics*. Their opinion concerning demonstrations of things is in agreement with what Aristotle stipulated in *Apodeictic*. Al-Kindī said that he had examined a book which these people consider authoritative, namely some treatises of Hermes about divine unity (*tawḥīd*), which Hermes had written for his son. It was utterly proficient on the subject of divine unity, so much so that the philosopher no matter how he tried would have to accept it.[45]

Al-Sarakhsī, then, makes the remarkable claim that, not only is the Sabian religion conformant with a philosophical interpretation of religion in general terms, but its doctrines concerning the cosmos, nature, soul, prophecy, and God agree perfectly with specific Aristotelian works. The doctrines about the immortal soul and transcendent God attributed to Aristotle certainly require a heavily Platonized reading, and the Platonic element in the Sabian religion is also attested to by their adhering to the Platonic cardinal virtues. Since the Sabians also hold Hermes to be both a prophet and doctrinal authority, the Sabian doctrine would, then, be founded on an eclectic mixture of Aristotelian, Platonic, and Hermetic thought. One could argue that this supports the thesis about the Ḥarrānian religion as a syncretistic mix of various Hellenistic philosophical currents, or even the continuity of a Platonic school in Ḥarran,[46] or perhaps al-Kindī and al-Sarakhsī might derive their information from Thābit Ibn Qurra's philosophized interpretation of the Ḥarrānian religion. But at the same time, while the general features of the Sabian doctrine and ritual in al-Sarakhsī's account coincide with the other Arabic accounts, no other sources attribute to the Sabians these specific philosophical beliefs. And most remarkably, in both its classical sources and doctrinal views, al-Sarakhsī's Sabian religion is conspicuously similar with the thought system prevailing in al-Kindī's philosophical school.

---

45 Ibid, 319–320 [translation Rosenthal 1943, 49–51, with modifications].

46 Despite the Platonism of the late ancient schools in Athens and Alexandria, their members wrote more commentaries on Aristotle than Plato, and the physical works in al-Sarakhsī's account, while excluding botany and zoology, are arranged in the late ancient curricular order.

The Brethren of Purity provide their account of the Sabians in their final 52nd epistle on magic.[47] In this context, the Sabians are introduced as the last chain of the authorities that attest to the veracity of magic, following sections based on the story of Gyges in Plato's *Republic*, and on 'Abbāsids, the Quran, and Jews and Christians. Among the Greeks, the believers in the veracity of talismans are said to be called the Sabians, Ḥarrānians, or *ḥanīf*s, who had learned their art from the Babylonians and Egyptians.[48] Their ancient chiefs include Agathodaimon, Hermes, Homer (*Ūmahris*), and Aratus. Later on, however, the Sabians were divided into Pythagoreans, Aristotelians, Platonists, and Epicureans (*afiqūrūsiyya*).[49] Elsewhere in the *Epistles*, the Brethren inform us further that Pythagoras was a monotheist (*muwaḥḥid*) sage who originated from Ḥarrān.[50] Clearly, then, the Brethren employ the term Sabian simultaneously in a specific sense to refer to the inhabitants of Ḥarrān, and in an impressively wide sense that embraces ancient Greeks, both mythical sages and later philosophers, and further identifies all Sabians with pre-Islamic monotheists (*ḥanīf*). Moreover, Sabians form a link through which the art of magic at least passed on from the Babylonians and Egyptians to later nations.[51]

The Brethren's account of the Sabian religion again provides a list of some of their specific doctrinal beliefs and ritual practices. First, with regard to the cosmos, the Sabians believe that the universe is spatially finite and spherical in

47 The manuscript tradition in fact conveys three completely different versions of the epistle on magic. The account of the Sabians is included in epistle 52a, which has been edited in Ikhwān al-Ṣafā' 2012, while the editions of versions 52b and 52c are currently in preparation. De Callataÿ, in the introduction (pp. 5–10), argues that 52a is likely to be authenticly Ikhwānian, but at this stage of our knowledge its authentic attribution is not beyond doubt. Since many scholars now support the hypothesis of a redaction process lasting as long as a century, it is not clear what 'authenticity' even means here—it is possible that the three versions are all written by different authors, but two or even all three of them are still 'authentic' in the sense of pertaining to distinct stages within the redaction process, as opposed to being later additions introduced by the copyists.

48 Ikhwān al-Ṣafā' 2012, 44–45.

49 Ibid, 45. As noted by de Callataÿ (Ikhwān al-Ṣafā' 2012, 44), and Marquet before him, the inclusion of Epicureans is strange since the knowledge of Epicureanism in the Islamic world was slight, nor are there any Epicurean influences to be found in the *Epistles*. Baffioni 1992, 15–16, suggests an alternative reading of the word (with *aq'ūrūsiyya*, as it appears in many manuscripts) rendering Greek *arkhontikoi*, which she connects with the pagan, as opposed to philosophical, Sabians, but this seems excessively speculative.

50 Ikhwān al-Ṣafā' 2015, 17.

51 Cf. the account in al-Fārābī 1983, 88, about philosophy passing from the Chaldeans of Iraq through Egyptians to the Greeks, and from the Greeks through the Syrians to the Arabs. Since for the Brethren the Sabians are apparently identified with the Greeks, the order of passage is roughly similar.

form, that it has only one primary principle, and that it is causally dependant on the Creator.[52] Second, as regards the celestial world, they believe that the heavens are constituted of nine spheres, inhabited by incorporeal souls which are divided into angels and demons, as well as of souls attached to the spheres, and that the celestial souls and bodies influence the terrestrial events.[53] Third, as concerns the sublunary world, its existents and events are explained by 1) four elements, 2) souls, 3) effects of the celestial beings bringing about the generated beings, and 4) divine providence.[54] It is nevertheless ultimately the different combinations of the planets, fixed stars, and the zodiacs that directly determine terrestrial events.[55] Fourth, with regard to the human afterlife, the Sabians attest to the doctrine of reincarnation, and believe that the human soul after the demise of its body will pass to the "sea of Ṭāwus" in the sphere of ether,[56] in order to either reincarnate in another body corresponding to the character traits it acquired during the worldly life, or ascend towards the spheres.[57] Since the context of the account is magic, the Brethren's aim is not to give a comprehensive account of the Sabian religion, but relate what is relevant for the astrological and causal basis of magic.[58] Yet, it is noteworthy that the doctrinal beliefs that the account attributes to the Sabians are essentially philosophical in nature: Ptolemaic-Aristotelian cosmology, Aristotelian physics, and Platonic eschatology in terms of the soul's progressive reincarnations and gradual ascent.[59] Even more strikingly, all of these views are characteristic of the

---

52 Ikhwān al-Ṣafāʾ 2012, 45–46. I read *mabdaʾ thānin*, along with the Beirut edition, for *mabdaʾ wa-thānin*, in the phrase *laysa li-wujūdihi mabdaʾ thānin wa-innamā huwa mutaʿalliq bi-l-bāriʾ taʿalluq al-maʿlūl bi-ʿillatihi*. The reading in the Oxford edition, based on two manuscripts, which de Callataÿ translates (118) as "there is no commencement to its existence and no second one," makes no sense. The former reading can be understood here to affirm that the world has a single cause, God, *contra* the dualists, such as Zoroastrians and Manicheans, against whom the Brethren polemize elsewhere in the *Epistles* (e.g., Ikhwān al-Ṣafāʾ 1957, III, 461–464).

53 Ibid, 47–49.

54 Ibid, 46–47.

55 Ibid, 47–48.

56 It is unclear what the "sea of Ṭāwus," or possibly Ṭāʾus, or even Ṭaws, as it appears in the Beirut edition, is. However, the passage locates it in the sphere of the ether, which the *Epistles* situate between the sublunary world and the lowest sphere of the Moon, meaning that it occupies an intermediate position between the sublunar and celestial worlds.

57 Ibid, 50–54.

58 Ibid, 55. For the Brethren's largely astrologically founded explanation for the efficacy magic, see Lory 1992.

59 For two somewhat similar Arabic eschatological accounts based on Plato's *Phaedo* (107c–108c, 112e–115a) in the Kindian tradition, see al-Kindī 1950, 277–278; al-ʿĀmirī 1988, 154–160.

Brethren of Purity, including the specifics of both spherical and incorporeal souls inhabiting the celestial world,[60] astrological determinism, and the doctrine of reincarnation.[61]

Consequent on the doctrinal views, the ritual aspect of the Sabian religion is founded on an entirely astrological basis. The aim of the Sabian rites is to approach the good celestial souls and appease the bad ones, and for this end they have designated special invocatory prayers (*duʿāʾ*), incences, and rites (*siyāqat ʿamal*), which correspond to the nature of a particular celestial entity, and by means of which they may therefore be reached.[62] They have constructed temples for the planets and the fixed stars, and practice sacrifices and religious feasts the particulars of which are determined by the astral positions and the needs of each astral divinity.[63] In particular, the account devotes a long section for a minute description of the temple of Jirjās, constructed at the point when all seven planets were at their dignities, which is ornamented with the twelve zodiacal signs and images of the seven planets.[64] The account furthermore includes a similarly detailed account of the initiation rite into the Sabian religion performed in that temple, which includes in particular a sacrifice of a cock, which practice is explicitly linked with a passage in *Phaedo* (118A) in which Socrates urges the sacrifice of a cock for Asclepius in his death bed.[65] Although the Sabian ritual is, then, centered around the veneration of the celestial entities, it is still compatible with monotheism, because the Sabians, like the Brethren themselves, consider them to be intercessors of the divine will, rather than independently acting divinities.

For the Arabic knowledge on and employment of the *Phaedo*, see Biesterfeldt 1991 and Rowson's introduction and commentary in al-ʿĀmirī 1988, 29–42, 304–314.

60 For the Brethren's angelological views, see Ikhwān al-Ṣafāʾ 2013, 395–404 and Baffioni 2003. The fact that the Sabians believe the celestial souls to be both good and evil, however, seems harder to reconcile with the *Epistles*. But insofar as the first principle is entirely good, and the celestial souls and bodies are the intermediaries that realize its providential purposes in the world, it would seem that the celestial souls cannot be truly evil for the Sabians either. The Brethren also include among the angels, for example, the wrathful angel of hell, which, however, serves some beneficial purpose in the context of the providential order.

61 The Brethren are probably deliberately ambiguous about this subject, but see Marquet 1999, 383–392, for the passages that support the view that they believe in the transmigration of souls. Marquet himself changed his view from earlier articles where he had claimed that the Brethren deny the doctrine of reincarnation.

62 Ibid, 48–49, 56–57.

63 Ibid, 59–66, 82–84.

64 Ibid, 66–69.

65 Ibid, 66–79.

3 Sabian Influence in the School of al-Kindī and the Brethren

When the two accounts are compared, it it clear, first, that they share with each other many general features of the Sabian religion, such as astral worship, prayers, sacrifices, and feasts, as well as some specific features, such as Agathodaimon and Hermes as Sabian prophets and the prominence of the cock as a sacrificial animal. All of these are present also in other Arabic accounts, and could go back to the textual tradition about the religion of Ḥarrān, although it is also true that the Brethren's minute descriptions of specific temples and rites are unique to the *Epistles*. Second, it is equally clear that the two accounts differ both in their general emphasis and specifics, and that they therefore are not based on any direct common textual source. Thus, for example, the Brethren do not mention God's transcendence as a Sabian doctrine, while al-Sarakhsī makes no reference to reincarnation. Third, the two accounts nevertheless share a general attitude towards the Sabian religion, which is not present in other Arabic accounts at least in its entirety. Both authors agree that the Sabians are *ḥanīf*s, that they adhere to the three fundamental Islamic doctrines of monotheism, prophecy, and reward and punishment in the afterlife, and that their astral cult does not thereby breach monotheism. Moreover, for both the Sabian beliefs are philosophical in origin and rational in nature: al-Sarakhsī relates the Sabian doctrine to Aristotle in particular, while the Brethren identify the Sabians with four ancient philosophical schools and locates Pythagoras in Ḥarrān. Fourth, and as a consequence of the former point, both view the Sabians to be essentially correct in their beliefs. Neither account gives the slightest hint that their authors would find anything to reproach in the Sabian religion from a Muslim perspective. On the contrary, al-Kindī considers the Hermetic opus that the Sabians regard as their authority to be philosophically irrefutable, while the Brethren resort to the Sabians as one of their authorities that attest to the veracity of magic.

Does this mean that the Sabian religion in some sense constitutes a doctrinal influence for the school of al-Kindī and the Brethren of Purity, perhaps as regards the prominence that they accord to astrology in particular? There is some further evidence to support this view. As regards al-Kindī, his astrological writings include a treatise with the title *Determining the Appropriate Time in which the Prayer is Answered from the View Point of Astrology* (*Taḥrīr waqt yurjā fīhi ijābat al-duʿāʾ wa-l-taḍarruʿ ilā Allāh taʿālā min jihat al-tanajjum*).[66] The work is founded on the view that the "non-Muslim monotheist philosophers"

66 Al-Kindī 1976.

(*al-falāsifa al-muwaḥḥidūna alladhīna hum ʿalā ghayr millatinā*) were of the opinion that the planetary positions would indicate the times when prayers are answered because they viewed the planets as intermediaries (*wasāʾiṭ*) between the Creator and the humankind.[67] In the preamble, al-Kindī explains further that the belief of the philosophers in the planets as intercessors between God and the material world led them to sacrifice and construct temples for the seven planets, and Socrates to prescribe sacrificing a cock to Venus in *Phaedo*.[68] This seems to be a clear reference to the astrologically determined ritual of the Sabian religion, which al-Kindī also identifies with the religion practiced by the ancient philosophers. Al-Kindī continues, however, that in the subsequent generations devoid of philosophy (*ʿādimūna li-l-falsafa*) this original practice based on the idea of intercession deteroriated into idol worship in the true sense in that people started to devise idols (*ṣanam*) for the planets, and direct their prayers and sacrifices to the idols themselves.[69] Al-Kindī's, relatively mild, disapproval is directed against idol worship, while the original philosophical idea of astral intercession is entirely correct. In this particular treatise al-Kindī, moreover, employs the idea to assess the propitious times determined by the celestial bodies for Muslim supplicatory prayer (*dūʿāʾ*), listing the astrological views on the auspicious planetary positions for each particular petition, just as al-Kindī's other astrological works offer practical instructions on propitious signs to initiate other kinds of activities.[70] While al-Kindī is not endorsing the worship of planets as such, the Sabian astral worship still seems to provide him with a model for the application of astrology into Islamic religious practice.

There is similar evidence for the Brethren of Purity. In fact, because many of the doctrines that the Brethren attribute to the Sabians are ones that they endorse themselves, Yves Marquet has argued that Ḥarrān constitutes the primary conduit through which the Brethren of Purity adopted their knowledge of Greek philosophy.[71] Since there is no evidence that they ever even visited Ḥarrān, Marquet's claim remains entirely speculative.[72] But there is one particularly revealing example that seems to suggest that the Brethren go even further than al-Kindī in their esteem of the Sabian astral worship. In their 50th

67 Ibid, 66.

68 Ibid.

69 See Genequand 1999, 110, for al-Masʿūdī's depiction of a similar devolution from the idea of intercession to idolatry.

70 Burnett 1993.

71 Marquet 1966 and 2006.

72 See especially De Smet 2007.

epistle, the Brethren of Purity endorse those of their followers that have proceeded sufficiently far in their intellectual and moral development to adopt the practice of philosophical rites of worship (*al-ʿibāda al-falsafiyya al-ilāhiyya*) to complement the Islamic ritual practice.[73] These include philosophical feasts, rites of sacrifice, and prayers directed towards the north pole, which are clearly at least in part modeled on the Sabian ritual devoted to astral entities. This would suggest that the Brethren go much further than merely considering the Sabian religion to be an acceptable form of monotheism: they view the Sabian ritual to constitute an inherently rational form of worship, perhaps even more so than the Islamic ritual, given that they advocate their philosophically gifted followers to adopt some of its rites.

It would, then, seem possible that al-Kindī, al-Sarakhsī, and the Brethren of Purity were influenced in their philosophical views by the Sabian religion, whether their knowledge on it was based on literary sources, Thābit Ibn Qurra, or even some direct acquaintance with Ḥarrān. But it is perhaps more likely that the direction of influence goes to the opposite direction, and that it is in fact the philosophical opinions of these authors that influence the religious doctrines that they attribute to the Sabian religion. For both al-Sarakhsī and the Brethren of Purity, the Sabian religion that they describe sounds almost like a utopian religion of the philosophers: It is founded on the authority of the ancient philosophers, and its beliefs and practices are justified by reason.[74] Moreover, it draws on the philosophical authorities they attest to themselves, and endorses the doctrinal views they themselves more or less subscribe to. Accordingly, many of the differences between the two accounts on the Sabian religion coincide with differences of emphasis between the philosophical inclinations of the school of al-Kindī and the Brethren of Purity. The Brethren accord particularly high status to Pythagoras, therefore Pythagoras is from Ḥarrān, while for al-Sarakhsī the Sabians follow the late ancient Aristotelian curriculum that al-Kindī also subscribes to in his *On the Quantity of Aristotle's Works* (*Risāla fī Kammiyyat Kutub Arisṭūṭālīs*).[75] Al-Kindī emphasizes divine transcendence, therefore the Sabian religion endorses negative theology, the Brethren believe in reincarnation, thereby the Sabians endorse it too. In part, the Sabian narrative, then, seems to serve the instrumental purpose of validating the authors' own philosophical beliefs.

73 Mattila 2016.

74 Thus, in its rationality, it may be compared with al-Fārābī's (d. 950) famous virtuous religion (*milla fāḍila*), in which both religious beliefs and ritual practice are ultimately derived from philosophy (see in particular al-Fārābī 2001, 46–47).

75 Al-Kindī 1950, 363–384.

But the primary motivation for all of these philosophers to raise the Sabians to such a prominent position is in all likelihood to legitimate the practice of philosophy in more general terms. Al-Kindī famously prefaces his theological-metaphysical treatise *On First Philosophy* (*Fī al-falsafa al-ūlā*) with a plea for the legitimacy of philosophy:

> We ought not to be ashamed of appreciating the truth and acquiring it wherever it comes from, even if it comes from races distinct and nations different from us (*al-ajnās al-qāṣiya ʿannā wa-l-umam al-mubāyina lanā*). For the seeker of truth nothing takes precedence over the truth.[76]

Al-Kindī's apologetic tone suggests that the pagan Greek origin of philosophy was problematic for many of his Muslim contemporaries.[77] But what if the ancient philosophers practiced a Sabian monotheistic religion that was no more different from Islam than Christianity and Judaism, and which is likewise legitimated by the authority of the Quran? Clearly the pre-Islamic origins of philosophy would be much less suspicious, in that the religious beliefs and practices of the ancient philosophers would agree with the Islamic ones in their essential aspects, and only disagree on the specifics.

According to the literate-philosopher al-Tawḥīdī's (d. 1023) testimony, the premise underlying the aims of the philosophical-religious group of the Brethren of Purity was the belief that religion (*sharīʿa*) had become stained with ignorance and error, and that it must therefore be purified by means of Greek philosophy and science.[78] To this end, the *Epistles* repeatedly makes the claim that ancient philosophers and prophets have throughout history agreed on all the primary questions, while their disagreements have only concerned the non-essential particulars.[79] Evidently, for its authors the *Epistles* represent this truth that is sanctioned by prophets and philosophers alike. The notion that the ancient philosophers were Sabian monotheists forms an essential component of this thesis, since it shows that, far from being pagan polytheists, they practiced a Quranically sanctioned monotheistic religion of Abrahamic origins.

---

76 Al-Kindī 1950, 103.

77 For the strategies of legitimizing the practice of philosophy in general from al-Kindī to Averroes (Ibn Rushd; d. 1192), see Endress 1990.

78 Al-Tawḥīdī 1939–1944, II, 4–11.

79 Ikhwān al-Ṣafāʾ 1957, IV, 126.

4 Conclusions

The medieval Arabic testimonies on the Sabian religion of Ḥarrān are highly problematic in historiographical terms, and it is far from clear that it is possible to reconstruct a reliable picture of what the Ḥarrānian religion was like during the first Islamic centuries from them. The assumption that Ḥarrān was an important philosophical center with a central role in the transmission of classical philosophy in the Islamic world is particularly suspect, because there is little evidence for it from outside the Sabian narrative. The views of al-Kindī, al-Sarakhsī, and the Brethren of Purity on the Sabians are highly interesting from this perspective, since these authors share many doctrinal views, in particular the prominence of astrology, which could potentially be explained by the influence of the Sabian astral cult, and some of their writings explicitly support the view that they were influenced by the Sabians in their philosophical ideas.

The accounts of al-Sarakhsī and the Brethren of Purity on the Sabian religion share many general and specific aspects with each other and other Arabic testimonies, and the Brethren also transmit detailed descriptions of specific Sabian temples and rites. Obviously their testimonies are therefore not entirely fictitious, but they rather probably draw on some Arabic tradition on the Sabian religion which quite possibly corresponds to some extent to the astral worship still practiced in Ḥarrān during their time. But rather than being influenced by the Sabians in their philosophical views, it seems much more likely that precisely these philosophers took particular interest in the Sabian religion because of the astrological inclinations they already had. Their overall accounts of the Sabian religion as a philosophical religion based on the views of the Greek philosophers is clearly too implausible to be taken at face value, especially because both authors project to the Sabian religion precisely the philosophical views that they themselves endorse. Al-Sarakhsī and the Brethren of Purity are not historians, and their primary aim is not to describe the Sabian religion objectively. The Sabians, then, serve them the instrumental purpose of justifying the practice of philosophy in the Islamic world against its potential critics, by asserting that the pre-Islamic sources of their philosophical thought do not lie in pagans with suspect polytheistic beliefs and practices, but rather in ancient monotheistic philosophers who practiced the Sabian religion sanctioned by the Quran.

Bibliography

Adamson, Peter. "Abū Maʿšar, al-Kindī and the Philosophical Defence of Astrology." *Recherches de théologie et philosophie médievales* 69 (2002): 245–270.

Adamson, Peter. "Al-Kindī and the Muʿtazila: Divine Attributes, Creation and Freedom." *Arabic Sciences and Philosophy* 13 (2003): 45–77.

Adamson, Peter. *Al-Kindī*. Oxford: Oxford University Press, 2007a.

Adamson, Peter. "The Kindian Tradition: The Structure of Philosophy in Arabic Neoplatonism." In: Cristina D'Ancona (ed.), *Libraries of the Neoplatonists*. Leiden and Boston: Brill, 2007b, 351–370.

Al-ʿĀmirī. *A Muslim Philosopher on the Soul and Its Fate: Al-ʿĀmirī's Kitāb al-Amad ʿalā al-Abad*. Edited and translated by Everett Rowson. New Haven, Ct: American Oriental Society, 1988.

Avicenna. *Réfutation de l'astrologie*. Edited and translated by Yves Michot. Beirut: Albouraq, 2006.

Baffioni, Carmela. "Traces of 'Secret Sects' in the *Rasā'il Ikhwān al-Ṣafā'*." In: F. De Jong (ed.), *Shīʿa Islam, Sects and Sufism: Historical Dimensions, Religious Practice and Methodological Considerations*. Utrecht: M.Th. Houtsma, 1992, 10–25.

Baffioni, Carmela. "The Angelology System in the Iḫwān al-Ṣafā'." In: Simeon Evstatiev et al. (eds.), *Arabistika i isljamoznanie, 2: Studii po slučaj 60-godišninata na Penka Samsareva*. Sofia: Universitetsko izdatelstvo S. Kliment Ohridski, 2003, vol. II, 435–442.

Baffioni, Carmela. "Ikhwân al-Safâ'." In: Edward N. Zalta (ed.), *The Stanford Encyclopedia of Philosophy* (https://plato.stanford.edu/entries/ikhwan-al-safa/). 2008.

Biesterfeldt, Hinrich. "Phaedo Arabus: Elemente griechischer Tradition in der Seelenlehre islamischen Philosophen des 10. und 11. Jahrhunderts." In: G. Binder and B. Effer (eds.), *Tod und Jenseits im Altertum*. Trier: Verlag Trier, 1991, 180–202.

Biesterfeldt, Hinrich. "Aḥmad ibn aṭ-Ṭaiyib as-Saraḫsī." In: Ulrich Rudolph (ed.), *Philosophie in der islamischen Welt*. Basel: Schwabe Verlag, 2012, vol. I, 150–156.

van Bladel, Kevin. *The Arabic Hermes: From Pagan Sage to Prophet of Science*. Oxford: Oxford University Press, 2009.

van Bladel, Kevin. *From Sasanian Mandaeans to Ṣābians of the Marshes*. Leiden and Boston: Brill, 2017.

de Blois, François. "Naṣrānī (*Ναζωραῖος*) and *ḥanīf* (*ἐθνικός*): Studies on the Religious Vocabulary of Christianity and of Islam." *Bulletin of the School of Oriental and African Studies* 65 (2002): 1–30.

Burnett, Charles. "Al-Kindī on Judicial Astrology: 'The Forty Chapters.'" *Arabic Sciences and Philosophy* 3 (1993): 77–117.

de Callataÿ, Godefroid. "Brethren of Purity (Ikhwān al-Ṣafā')." In: Kate Fleet et al. (eds.), *Encyclopedia of Islam Three*. Leiden: Brill, 2013a, vol. 4, 84–90.

de Callataÿ, Godefroid. "Magia en al-Andalus: *Rasāʾil Ijwān al-Ṣafāʾ*, *Rutbat al-ḥakīm* y *Gāyat al-ḥakīm (Picatrix)*." *Al-Qanṭara* 34 (2013b): 297–344.

de Callataÿ, Godefroid. "The Ṣābi'ans of Ṣāʿid al-Andalusī." *Studia graeco-arabica* 7 (2017): 291–306.

Cameron, Alan. "The Last Days of the Academy at Athens." *Proceedings of the Cambridge Philological Society* 15 (1969): 7–29.

Chwolsohn, Daniel. *Die Ssabier und Ssabismus*. St. Petersburg: Buchdruckerei der kaiserlichen Akademie der Wissenschaften, 1856.

De Smet, Daniel. "Yves Marquet, les Iḫwān al-Ṣafāʾ et le pythagorisme." *Journal Asiatique* 295 (2007): 491–500.

De Smet, Daniel. "Le Platon arabe et les Sabéens de Ḥarrān: la 'voie diffuse' de la transmission du platonisme en terre d'Islam." *Res Antiquae* 7 (2010): 73–86.

De Smet, Daniel. "L'héritage de Platon et de Pythagore: la 'voie diffuse' de sa transmission en terre d'Islam." In: P. Derron, R. Goulet, and U. Rudolph (eds.), *Entre Orient et Occident: La philosophie et sciences gréco-romaines dans le monde arabe*. Genève: Vandoeuvres, 2011, 87–133.

Druart, Therésè-Anne. "Astronomie et astrologie selon Farabi." *Bulletin de philosophie médiévale* 20 (1978): 43–47.

Druart, Therésè-Anne. "Le second traité de Farabi sur la validité des affirmations basées sur la position des étoiles." *Bulletin de philosophie médiévale* 21 (1979): 47–51.

Endress, Gerhard. "The Defense of Reason: The Plea for Philosophy in the Religious Community." *Zeitschrift für Geschichte der Arabisch-Islamischen Wissenschaften* 6 (1990): 1–49.

Endress, Gerhard. "Mathematics and Philosophy in Medieval Islam." In: Jan P. Hogendijk and Abdelhamid I. Sabra (eds.), *The Enterprise of Science in Islam: New Perspectives*. Cambridge, MA and London: MIT Press, 2003, 121–176.

Al-Fārābī. *Kitāb Taḥṣīl al-saʿāda*. Edited by Jaʿfar Āl Yāsīn. Beirut: Dār al-Andalus, 1983.

Al-Fārābī. *Kitāb al-Milla wa-nuṣūṣ ukhrā*. Edited by Muhsin Mahdi. Beirut: Dar al-Mashreq, 2001.

Fierro, Maribel. "Bāṭinism in al-Andalus: Maslama b. Qāsim al-Qurṭubī (d. 353/964), Author of the 'Rutbat al-Ḥakīm' and the 'Ghāyat al-Ḥakīm' (Picatrix)." *Studia Islamica*, 84 (1996): 87–112.

Genequand, Charles. "Idolâtrie, astrolâtrie et sabéisme." *Studia Islamica* 89 (1999): 109–128.

Green, Tamara. *The City of the Moon God: Religious Traditions of Harran*. Leiden: Brill, 1992.

Gündüz, Inası. *The Origins and Early History of the Mandeans, Their Relation to the Sabians of the Qur'ān and to the Harranians*. Oxford: Oxford University Press, 1994.

Hadot, Ilistraut. *Simplicius: Commentaire sur le manuel d'Épictète*. Leiden: Brill, 1996.

Hjärpe, Jan. "Analyse critique des traditions arabes sur les Sabéens ḥarrāniens." Dissertation at the University of Uppsala, 1972.

Hjärpe, Jan. "The Holy Year of the Harranians: Some Remarks on the Festival Calendar of the Harranian Sabians." *Orientalia Suecana* 23 (1974): 68–83.

Hämeen-Anttila, Jaakko. *The Last Pagans of Iraq: Ibn Waḥshiyya and His Nabatean Agriculture*. Leiden: Brill, 2006.

Ibn al-Nadīm. *Kitāb al-Fihrist*. Edited by Gustav Flügel. Leipzig, Verlag von F.C.W. Vogel, 1872.

Ibn al-Qifṭī. *Tārīkh al-ḥukamāʾ*. Edited by Julius Lippert. Leipzig, Dieterichsche Verlagsbuchhandlung, 1903.

Ikhwān al-Ṣafāʾ. *Rasāʾil Ikhwān al-Ṣafāʾ wa-Khullān al-Wafāʾ*. Edited by Buṭrus al-Bustānī. Beirut: Dār Ṣādir, 1957.

Ikhwān al-Ṣafā. *Epistles of the Brethren of Purity: On Magic 1: An Arabic Critical Edition and English Translation of Epistle 52a*. Edited and translated by Godefroid de Callataÿ and Bruno Halflants. Oxford: Oxford University Press and Institute of Ismaili Studies, 2012.

Ikhwān al-Ṣafāʾ. *Epistles of the Brethren of Purity: On the Natural Sciences: An Arabic Critical Edition and English Translation of Epistles 15–21*. Edited and translated by Carmela Baffioni. Oxford: Oxford University Press and the Institute of Ismaili Studies, 2013.

Ikhwān al-Ṣafāʾ. *Epistles of the Brethren of Purity: Sciences of the Soul and Intellect: Part 1: An Arabic Critical Edition and English Translation of Epistles 32–36*. Edited and translated by Paul E. Walker. Oxford: Oxford University Press and the Institute of Ismaili Studies, 2015.

Al-Kindī. *Rasāʾil al-Kindī al-falsafiyya*. Edited by Muḥammad Abū Rīda. Cairo: Dār al-Fikr al-ʿArabī, 1950.

Al-Kindī. *Al-Kindī's Metaphysics: A Translation of Yaʿqub ibn Ishaq al-Kindi's Treatise "On First Philosophy."* Translated by Alfred I. Ivry. Albany, NY: State University of New York Press, 1974.

Al-Kindī. "Taḥrīr waqt yurjā fīhi ijābat al-duʿāʾ wa-l-taḍarruʿ ilā Allāh taʿālā min jihat al-tanajjum." Edited by Muhsin Mahdi. In: ʿUthmān Amīn (ed.), *Nuṣūṣ falsafiyya*. Cairo, 1976, 65–78.

Lameer, Joep. "From Alexandria to Baghdad: Reflections on the Genesis of a Problematic Tradition." In: Gerhardt Endress and Remke Kruk (eds.), *The Ancient Tradition in Christian and Islamic Hellenism: Studies on the Transmission of Greek Philosophy and Science Dedicated to H.J. Drossaart Lulofs on His Ninetieth Birthday*. Leiden: Research School of Asian, African and Amerindian Studies, 1997, 181–191.

Lory, Pierre. "La magie chez Iḫwān al-Ṣafāʾ." *Bulletin d'études orientales* 44 (1992): 147–159.

Marquet, Yves. "Sabéens et Iḫwān al-Ṣafāʾ." *Studia Islamica* 24 (1966): 35–80.

Marquet, Yves. *La philosophie des Iḫwān al-Ṣafāʾ: Nouvelle edition augmentée*. Paris and Milan: S.É.H.A. and Archè, 1999.

Marquet, Yves. *Les "Frères de la pureté" pythagoriciens de l'Islam: La marque du pythagorisme dans la rédaction des Épîtres des Iḫwān aṣ-Ṣafāʾ*. Paris: S.É.H.A. and Edidit, 2006.

Al-Masʿūdī. *Murūj al-dhahab*. Edited by Charles Pellat. Beirut: Publications de l'Université Libanaise, 1966–1974.

Mattila, Janne. "The Philosophical Worship of the Ikhwān al-Ṣafāʾ." *Journal of Islamic Studies* 27 (2016): 17–38.

Mattila, Janne. "The Ikhwān al-Ṣafāʾ on Religious Diversity." *Journal of Islamic Studies* 28 (2017): 178–192.

Moosa, Matti. "A New Source on Aḥmad Ibn Ṭayyib al-Sarakhsī: Florentine MS Arabic 299." *Journal of the American Oriental Society*, 92 (1972): 19–24.

Nokso-Koivisto, Inka. "Microcosm-Macrocosm Analogy in *Rasāʾil Ikhwān al-Ṣafāʾ* and Certain Related Texts." Dissertation at the University of Helsinki, 2014.

Pingree, David. 2002. "The Ṣābians of Ḥarrān and the Classical Tradition," *International Journal of the Classical Tradition*, 9, no. 1: 8–35.

Roberts, Alexandre M. 2017. "Being a Sabian in Court in Tenth-Century Baghdad," *Journal of the American Oriental Society*, 137: 253–277.

Rosenthal, Franz. *Aḥmad b. aṭ-Ṭayyib as-Saraḫsî*. New Haven, Ct: American Oriental Society, 1943.

Rosenthal, Franz. "From Arabic Books and Manuscripts IV: New Fragments of as-Sarakhsī." *Journal of the American Oriental Society* 71 (1951): 135–142.

Rosenthal, Franz. "From Arabic Books and Manuscrips VI: Istanbul Materials for al-Kindī and as-Sarakhsī." *Journal of the American Oriental Society* 76 (1956): 27–31.

Rosenthal, Franz. "From Arabic Books and Manuscripts VIII: as-Sarakhsī on Love." *Journal of the American Oriental Society* 81 (1961): 222–224.

Rosenthal, Franz. "From Arabic Books and Manuscripts XVI: as-Sarakhsī (?) on the Appropriate Behavior for Kings." *Journal of the American Oriental Society* 115 (1995): 105–109.

Shaw, Gregory. *Theurgy and the Soul: The Neoplatonism of Iamblichus*. University Park, PA: Pennsylvania State University Press, 1995.

Tardieu, Michel. "Ṣābiens coraniques et "ṣābiens" de Ḥarrān." *Journal Asiatique* 274 (1986): 1–44.

Tardieu, Michel. "Les calendriers en usage à Ḥarrān d'après les sources arabes et le commentaire de Simplicius à la Physique d'Aristote." In: Ilistraut Hadot (ed.), *Simplicius: sa vie, son oeuvre, sa survie: Actes du Colloque International de Paris (28 sept.–1er oct. 1985)*. Berlin and New York: De Gruyter, 1987, 40–57.

Al-Tawḥīdī. *Kitāb al-imtāʿ wa-l-muʾānasa*. 3 vols. Edited by Aḥmad Amīn and Aḥmad al-Zayn. Beirut: Dār Maktabat al-Ḥayāt, 1939–1944.

de Vaulx d'Arcy, Guillaume. *Les Épîtres des Frères en Pureté (Rasāʾil Ikhwān al-Ṣafāʾ): Mathematique et philosophie*. Paris: Les Belles Lettres, 2019.

Wildberg, Christian. "Philosophy in the Age of Justinian." In: Michael Maas (ed.), *The Cambridge Companion to the Age of Justinian*. Cambridge: Cambridge University Press, 2006, 316–340.

CHAPTER 6

Righteous Sufferer, Scheming Apostate: Traditions of Paul from a Cultural Evolutionary Perspective

Nina Nikki and Antti Vanhoja

1 Introduction*

On 28 June 2007, Pope Benedict XVI declared the year starting from June 2008 "the Year of Paul." This special celebration would honor the bimillenary of the apostle's traditional date of birth. It was announced that the year would include "a series of liturgical, cultural and ecumenical events ... all inspired by Pauline spirituality."[1] This recent Jubilee year is proof of a fact well known: two thousand years after his life and work, Paul is celebrated by an overwhelming majority of Christians as an exemplary man of faith and a champion of orthodoxy.

On the other hand, Paul is hardly adored universally either within or outside of Christianity.[2] Even though there is no mention of Paul in the Quran,[3] some early Islamic sources, including one of the first to mention Paul, criticize him for distorting the true doctrines of Jesus.[4] Some later writers share the critical

* We want to thank Dr. Martin Whittingham for sharing notes from his book *A History of the Muslim Views of the Bible* before its publication in 2020 and allowing us to cite the audio lecture he gave on the topic (see note 5). His help was indispensable and much appreciated.

1 See Eastman 2011, 1.

2 According to Pervo (2010, 185), he is considered by some "a nefarious villain." We are aware of Pervo's criminal conviction of possession and distribution of child pornography and understand the ethical problems of citing his work. While research by Pervo is essential for this article, we do not want to let the abuser off the hook by avoiding mentioning his crimes. We believe it is important to acknowledge his conviction in order to protect the direct and indirect victims of Pervo and to support the survivors of sexual abuse in academia.

3 Some interpreters of the Quran identify the third missionary mentioned in Surah 36:13–14 as Paul and the city mentioned therein as Antioch. Al-Masʿūdī (d. 345 AH/956 CE) and Ibn Kathīr (d. 774/1373) both make note of this interpretation, though the latter considers the tradition unsound. Whittingham 2020, 87. The dates of Muslim authors are given in this article according to both the Islamic era (AH) and Common era (CE).

4 Whittingham (2015, lecture recording) states that the perception of Paul as a false teacher is common throughout the history of Islam. For the early Islamic account of Paul referred to here, that of Sayf ibn ʿUmar's account, see below.

 | DOI:10.1163/9789004471160_007

stance, as exemplified in the following quote by modern-day Muslim philosopher Sayyid Muḥammad Naqīb al-ʿAṭṭās:

> So in the Holy Qur'ān God did not charge Jesus (on whom be Peace!) with the mission of establishing a new religion called Christianity. It was some other disciples and the apostles including chiefly Paul who departed from the original revelation and true teachings based on it, and who began preaching a new religion ... which later came to be called Christianity.[5]

In this essay, we hypothesize *explanations* for the survival and success of the positive and negative perceptions of Paul with the help of cultural evolutionary theory. The cultural evolutionary approach is a multidisciplinary field that seeks to explain the variation, selection, and inheritance of cultural representations from a Darwinian perspective. Proponents of cultural evolutionary theory often apply statistical analysis and computer modeling to big data to analyze changes in culture over time. They sometimes also produce phylogenetic trees to illustrate the descent of variations from a common ancestor and the relationships between different variants. While the construction of a phylogenetic tree for Pauline and anti-Pauline representations would be a welcome project, our essay takes as a point of departure the general observation that both negative and positive representations of Paul have somehow persisted over time. We instead focus on exploring different types of explanations cultural evolutionary theory can offer to the success of cultural representations and how they might explain the survival and dissemination of various, contrary perceptions of Paul.

We limit our discussion to the spread of the idea of Paul as a positively and negatively understood person. That is, we will not attempt to tie Paulinism or anti-Paulinism to specific religious denominations or cultural phenomena, such as "Jewish Christianity" or "Pauline Christianity." In fact, our sources reveal that both negative and positive images of Paul appeared in the early stages of different religious traditions. Thereafter, ideas about and perceptions of Paul quickly took on a life of their own, subject to the laws of cultural change. Connections to the historical Paul and his authentic letters are also not our main interest. Like its counterpart in the field of biology, the cultural evolutionary perspective advances from population thinking, breaking from essentialist notions concerning species. That is, in the cultural evolutionary approach, a species is not treated as a timeless and unchangeable category. Instead, the members of a population are considered to be tied to one another through

5 al-ʿAṭṭās 1978, 28.

common ancestry, with variation taken as a norm—not as a deviation from a predetermined category or as an imperfect imitation of some "original."[6]

The paper begins with a general introduction to cultural evolutionary theory, with a more detailed presentation of the different levels of analysis (viz., gene/meme, individual, and group), at which the different reasons for the success or failure of a given cultural content can be pursued. The positive and negative depictions of Paul are then dealt with in the subsequent sections. Because the positive depictions of Paul in later tradition are practically innumerable, these treatments are assessed mainly through the single theme of Paul as a suffering martyr. The aspect is chosen not because it is the only one by which Paul is remembered but because it is a prominent theme in positive perceptions of Paul that lends itself well to cultural evolutionary analysis. The aim of a cultural evolutionary approach is then to explore how the cultural success of a particular theme might be explained. The negative portrayals of Paul, on the other hand, are fewer and less known to the general audience and scholars alike. Therefore, these traditions will be examined in greater detail, meaning that the image of Paul as a "villain" will, in this article, be more comprehensive and nuanced than that of Paul as a "hero."

2 What is Cultural Evolution?

What is evolution and what does it have to do with cultural change? Charles Darwin's most succinct formulation of evolution was that it is "descent with modification."[7] This definition reveals the very basic Darwinian observation: that offspring, in some sense, resemble their parents but are also different, modified versions of them. Laurence Moran's recent formulation is more precise, describing evolution as the process by which a population experiences changes over time, with those changes having been inherited from previous generations. Moran offers a minimalistic definition of evolution as "a process that results in heritable changes in a population spread over many generations."[8] It is important to note that the scientific understanding of evolution often differs radically from its everyday understanding and terminological use by non-scientists. From a scientific perspective, evolution does not denote development, improvement, purpose, or direction—only changes at the pop-

6 Richerson and Boyd 2005, 5–8; Ylikoski and Kokkonen 2009, 92–97.

7 The term functions as a name for the general theory in, e.g., Darwin 1859 (1st ed.), vii, ix.

8 Moran 2007.

ulation level.[9] Natural selection does produce adaptation, but this takes place in relation to a local and ever-changing environment.[10] Furthermore, there are evolutionary mechanisms that do not result from adaptation—for example, genetic drift, which results instead from random sampling.[11]

István Czachesz notes that evolution is not restricted to a particular medium, such as living matter. Rather, he views evolution as a "philosophical rather than an empirical matter" that describes and explains a wide range of phenomena. This "universal algorithm" of variation, selection, and inheritance can explain changes in computer programs, culture, and perhaps even multiple universes.[12]

The three basic functions of the algorithm—variation, selection, and inheritance—are also the minimum criteria to describe evolution instead of some other type of change (e.g., the erosion of rocks, which does effect change but is not heritable).[13] Alex Mesoudi argues that the evolution of culture[14] can be viewed as analogous to biological evolution precisely because it meets these three macro-evolutionary principles:

1. Like in nature, there is immense variation in culture—a good example is the variation in languages already noted by Darwin.[15]

---

9 Moran 2007. Similarly, Czachesz 2017, 25: "Evolution is free of value: whatever traits become widespread in evolution must be good enough to be selected for, but do not have to be regarded as superior to other traits or optimal in any sense. This is not to say that evolution does not produce astonishingly complex and well-adapted organisms." Mesoudi discusses the differences between Darwin and Herbert Spencer, his contemporary. Spencer, and some early anthropologists follow him, viewed societies as developing towards increasing complexity through fixed stages of inevitable progress. Unfortunately, misrepresentations of evolution have persisted in the study of cultural evolution longer than in that of biological evolution (Mesoudi 2011, 37–38).

10 In the words of Mesoudi (2011, 38), adaptation "does not necessarily translate into global increases in fitness, and does not result in inevitable and entirely predictible evolutionary change along a prespecified course."

11 Moran (2007), for example, strongly criticizes definitions of evolution which take into account only the mechanism of natural selection.

12 Czachesz 2017, 24. Already Darwin refers to the evolution of languages (1859, 300–301). See also Daniel Dennett's (1995, 48–52) discussion of "natural selection as an algorithmic process", whose power derives from its "*logical* structure, not the causal powers of the materials used in the instantiation" (emphasis Dennett's).

13 An example by Czachesz 2017, 25.

14 Mesoudi (2011, 3–4) defines culture as "information that is acquired from other individuals via social transmission mechanisms such as imitation, teaching, or language." Richerson and Boyd (2005, 5) define culture as "information capable of affecting individuals' behavior that they acquire from other members of their species through teaching, imitation, and other forms of social transmission."

15 For a fascinating example of variation within a specific cultural phenomenon and a phylo-

2. Culture also goes through selection and competition—some languages, for instance, gain speakers every day, while others become extinct. Natural selection is the best-known force behind cultural change but is not the only one.[16]
3. Culture is also "inherited" in the sense that people acquire beliefs, values, behavior, and knowledge from other people—languages are not genetically inherited but learned, which makes the matter one of cultural transmission.[17]

Differences between cultural and biological evolution do emerge, however, when considering some of the more recent advances in scientific understanding of genetic inheritance, the Neo-Darwinian micro-evolutionary level.[18]

1. Whereas learned content cannot be inherited through genes, cultural transmission works in the opposite way: it is Lamarckian, based on the transmission of learned information.[19] This also means that, whereas genetic information is inherited vertically, from parents to offspring, cultural information can be adopted horizontally across peers.[20]
2. In biology, variation is random and is produced blindly. This means that genes do not have a direction or "a plan"—that is, they are non-adaptive. Cultural information, on the other hand, is quite often created purposefully.[21]
3. Genetic inheritance is particulate. A gene is one unit, or something close to it.[22] As for cultural content, however, a person is likely to inherit (= learn) a blended version from several people. It is still an open question whether a particulate unit of cultural information, sometimes called a

genetic analysis of the material, see Christopher Buckley's study on a tradition of weaving patterns in Southeast Asia (2012).

16 Natural selection takes place, when a trait/gene becomes selected because it has a positive effect on the organism's reproductive success (see Czachesz 2017, 25). Other evolutionary forces include e.g. random drift.

17 Mesoudi 2011, 27–34.

18 For the discussion below, Mesoudi 2011, 40–47, who summarizes the conclusion in a heading: "Cultural evolution is Darwinian but not Neo-Darwinian" (2011, 46).

19 The different inheritance systems have been helpfully classified by Jablonka and Lamb (2005), who distinguish the following systems: genetic, epigenetic, behavioural, and symbolic. The last two represent areas in which learned content can be inherited.

20 Mesoudi 2011, 58–61.

21 Robert Boyd and Peter Richerson have coined the term "guided variation" to describe the intentional nature of cultural variation. Boyd and Richerson 1985, 9. See also Mesoudi 2011, 63–64.

22 For up-to-date views on the definition of "gene," see Gerstein et al. 2007.

> "meme," can be detected, for example, in human cognition.[23] Czachesz notes that, even though we do not yet understand the essence of "memes" or the mechanisms of their inheritance, we can still talk about cultural evolution. After all, Darwin himself was able to discuss biological evolution without knowing about genes.[24]

While it is helpful to view the evolution of culture as analogous to biological evolution, this is ultimately an incomplete image. Cultural content is always strongly connected to humans as biological creatures, though culture can, in fact, be understood as an *extended human phenotype*.[25] For this reason, we follow the so-called dual inheritance theory, or biocultural evolution, which stresses the interconnectedness of culture and biology through *human cognition*, an interaction that results in cultural variation and the horizontal adoption thereof. A biocultural theory also considers human cognition to be simultaneously embodied,[26] encultured, extended, and distributed—thus creating a true interface between biology and culture.[27] Dan Sperber, for example, finds it "unrealistic to think of culture as something hovering somehow above individuals—culture goes through them, and through their minds and their bodies and that is, in good part, where culture is being made."[28]

3 Levels of Evolution

Evolution, both biological and cultural, takes place at different levels: that of genes and memes, that of individuals, and that of groups.[29] At the first level, a

23 According to Mesoudi (2011, 42), it is the future task of neuroscientists to understand "how information is represented in the brain and how it is transmitted from one brain to another."

24 Czachesz 2017, 27. The difficulty of defining "meme" has been one of the criticisms launched against memeticist theories by Richard Dawkins, Daniel Dennett, and Susan Blackmore. For an overview of the criticisms of meme theories, see Heylighen and Chielens (2009, 4), who also provide a defence of the approach in their article.

25 The concept of the extended phenotype was introduced by Dawkins in a 1982 book by the same name.

26 Embrainment and embodiment denote "the foundational fact that the mind and brain are one and the same and that both are firmly anchored in the body, with all that it entails" (Kundtová Klocová and Geertz 2018, 75).

27 For an overview of biocultural theories of religion, see Geertz 2010 and Turner et al. 2017.

28 Sperber 2011 (interview).

29 The idea that natural selection takes place on more than one level goes back to Darwin, and the theory is currently known by the name "multilevel selection theory" (Wilson and Wilson 2007, 328). For a helpful overview, see Czachesz 2017, 29–30, who calls the first

gene or a meme does not spread because it increases the success of an individual organism or a group. Rather, something in the variant itself makes it more successful than other variants. Czachesz mentions bad jokes as an example for memes: telling one may not benefit someone who tells the joke as an individual, but the joke may still survive to be retold, perhaps because it provoked disgust or other strong emotions in the listeners and is therefore easy to remember.[30] Unlike genes, memes cannot compete against each other independently.[31] Rather, they are always embedded in human cognition, contending for space in human memory.[32] According to Czachesz, emotional arousal and minimal counterintuitiveness in particular contribute to the memorability of ideas.[33] The concept of minimal counterintuitiveness has been used to demonstrate that memorability is enhanced when ideas contain a mild violation of innate ontological expectations.[34] Biblical material offers a host of examples of this phenomenon, such as Bileam's talking donkey or Jesus walking on water. In the early Christian context, miracle-stories or apocalyptic texts in particular can also be categorized as narratives that evoke strong sentiments like empathy, fear, abhorrence, and relief. Minimally counterintuitive or emotionally provocative stories are ideal for (oral) transmission, especially in the form of short narratives, as is the case with the Gospel of Mark or the Acts of John.[35] Petri Luomanen, who has sought to explain the relative success of Mark and Matthew compared to the so-called Q source of Jesus's sayings (which did not survive independently), sees the two traits taken up by Czachesz as preliminary requirements for a successful text. He points out, however, that there was a high number of emotionally laden and minimally counterintuitive narratives in Antiquity and, therefore, considers it necessary to augment Czachesz's the-

level "the replicator level." The term does, however, unfortunately create the impression that memes copy themselves independently of their passive human "vehicles." Here, the interest is on the level of selection.

30 Czachesz 2017, 30.

31 Czachesz (2017, 29) takes up the meiotic drive as an example of genetic competition at the replicator level.

32 Richerson and Boyd 2005, 73.

33 Czachesz 2011; 2017, 31, 44.

34 The role of minimal counterintuitiveness in religious ideas was first discussed by Boyer in 1994 and 2001. For later research into violations of culturally acquired knowledge (e.g., minimally counter-schematic concepts), see, e.g., Porubanova-Norquist, Shaw, and Xygalatas 2013.

35 Acts of John did not survive in its entirety, but several versions and fragments that allowed for its later reconstruction did, a possible testimony to the appeal of individual memorable narratives. See Lalleman 1998, 1–24; Pervo 2016, 1–16.

oretical framework with the notions of relevance and attraction, developed by Dan Sperber and Deirdre Wilson, which take into account varying social contexts.[36]

Sperber and Wilson study relevance from the perspective of human cognition.[37] According to them, the human mind is "geared to the maximization of relevance."[38] Some of the factors of relevance are distinct to a specific context and depend on the "cultural environment" and the "pool of cultural representations" in which an individual takes part. Others, on the other hand, are ingrained in human psychology and therefore essential regardless of the environment. The cultural environment thus causes humans to produce "mental representations,"[39] the density of which in a population is modified partly by the social situation, partly by human cognition.[40]

Cultural selection can also take place at the level of organisms. This means that cultural information can also spread because it benefits the individual organism. Content like this can, for example, be knowledge of how to make tools necessary for survival or symbolic material that benefits the individual in a less straightforward manner, such as information that offers the individual hope and comfort.[41] Czachesz takes up the Jewish Psalter prayers as an example of cultural content that offers the individual important cognitive coping mechanisms, thus enhancing the individual's wellbeing. According to Czachesz, the legal material of the Torah, on the other hand, enhances "the reproductive fitness of both individuals and society as a whole."[42]

The group level of selection was already taken up by Darwin and has since been hotly debated.[43] The idea may be defined as "the evolution of traits based on the differential survival and reproduction of groups."[44] Darwin noted that, while "a high standard of morality" is not beneficial to an individual within a group of people, a group that exhibits such behavior will be of great advantage to other groups.[45] Especially in the 1960s, it became a consensus view to deny that biological evolution took place at the level of groups. Instead, altruistic

36 Luomanen 2013, 51–52.

37 See Sperber and Wilson 1995, 118–171; Sperber 1996, 98–118.

38 Sperber and Wilson 1995, 260–266.

39 By mental representation, Sperber means a representation that exists "inside its users" and is "internal to the information-processing device." Sperber 1996, 32, 61.

40 Sperber 1996, 113–118.

41 See Czachesz 2017, 31.

42 Czachesz 2020.

43 For an overview of this debate, see Wilson and Wilson 2007.

44 Wilson and Wilson 2007, 329.

45 See Wilson and Wilson 2007, 328.

phenomena were explained as eventually effecting the individual either at the level of kin selection or as a consequence of reciprocity.[46] David Sloan Wilson and Edward O. Wilson, however, argued in 2007 that group selection can, after careful reconsideration, be adopted as a part of a sociobiological, multilevel model of evolution.[47]

The cultural sphere allows for easier detection of group level selection than biology.[48] Symbolic or behavioral identity markers, for instance, can contribute positively to the success of a group. The group level can also be approached through the theory of *costly signaling* as well as through social psychological theories such as the *social identity approach* (SIA). The former explains various time- or energy-consuming, or otherwise apparently noneconomical, behaviors as being signals of the individual's commitment to the group and, consequently, mechanisms that promote ingroup cohesiveness and cooperation.[49] The social identity approach, on the other hand, deals with various social and cognitive mechanisms that regulate group identity formation and maintenance as well as competition between groups.[50] It is especially noteworthy that figures like Paul the Apostle can play a crucial part in the process of identity construction of a social group, either as ideal prototypes or disreputable stereotypes. Cultural proto- and stereotypes may also be selected at the level of organisms, as they help individuals categorize themselves in relation to social groups and, consequently, offer them clarity and meaning.[51]

46 Wilson and Wilson 2007, 331.

47 Wilson and Wilson 2007 consider it particularly necessary to abandon ideas of "naïve group selection," which treats between-group selection as a stronger force than within-group selection.

48 Richerson and Boyd 2005, 197–211. Wilson and Wilson (2007, 343) note that cultural group selection is meaningful in that it enables faster phenotypic changes within and between groups than biological evolution.

49 On costly signalling, see Irons 2001. For further studies that examine costly behaviour in religion, see Czachesz 2017, 100–101.

50 For an introduction to the social identity approach (SIA), Esler 2014. For applications of SIA in the study of the New Testament, see Baker and Tucker 2014.

51 The self-categorization theory (SCT) is considered a part of the social identity approach (SIA). It explains how individuals become group members and experience themselves as such (see John Turner's foreword to Haslam 2004).

4 The Suffering and Dying Apostle as an Ingroup Prototype and a Memorable Idea

> Now you have observed my teaching, my conduct, my aim in life, my faith, my patience, my love, my steadfastness, my persecutions, and my suffering the things that happened to me in Antioch, Iconium, and Lystra. What persecutions I endured!
>
> 2 Tim 3:10–11

This quotation from The Second Epistle to Timothy is the work of a pseudonymous pro-Pauline author who ascribes many positive characteristics to Paul. While the author praises Paul's thinking, way of life, and love, one characteristic is particularly emphasized: Paul was persecuted and suffered for the Gospel. Even Paul's faith dims in comparison to his suffering. In the following, we offer examples of how Paul's role as a suffering and eventually dying Apostle was received in early Christian tradition. The later success of the theme has been noted by several scholars: Richard I. Pervo, for example, states that "later traditions glorify and magnify Paul's suffering, which becomes a leading means through which the gospel is spread."[52]

In his letters, Paul offers theological justifications for his suffering, emphasizing its role in his imitation of Christ.[53] He also ties it together with his main soteriological concept of "participation in Christ." In Philippians, for example, he portrays sharing in Christ's sufferings and "becoming like him in his death" as essential aspects of "knowing Christ" (3:10–11).[54] Early canonical Pauline pseudepigrapha frequently take up the topic of suffering and martyrdom. The author of Colossians not only stresses Paul's imprisonment ("Remember my chains!", 4:18),[55] but also gives Paul's afflictions atoning significance: "I am now rejoicing in my sufferings for your sake, and in my flesh I am completing what is lacking in Christ's afflictions for the sake of his body, that is, the church" (1:24). The author of 2 Timothy also remembers Paul's imprisonment (1:8), using sac-

52 Pervo 2010, 17. On Pervo, see note 3. For an extensive analysis of the formation of a culture of martyrdom in the early Christian collective memory, see Castelli 2004.

53 For early Christian martyr stories as re-enactments of Jesus's passion, see Moss 2010.

54 See Nikki 2018, 190–195. Paul's struggle with the Corinthian "Super Apostles" may have had a significant role for his theologizing on the meaning of suffering (Nikki 2018, 192).

55 Paul's imprisonment is strongly emphasized in later tradition. The image is evoked thrice in Ephesians (3:1, 4:1, 6:20). In 1 Clem 5, seven imprisonments of Paul are mentioned, while, in Acts of Paul, reports of imprisonments are given in Iconium, Ephesus, Philippi, and Rome. According to Pervo (2010, 16), for early Christian writers, "Paul's proper place was in jail."

rificial language to elevate the significance of Paul's death: "As for me, I am already being poured out as a libation, and the time of my departure has come" (4:6).

A prime example of an early Christian writer deeply invested in following Paul's example of suffering and martyrdom is Ignatius of Antioch.[56] His view of Paul as an imprisoned sufferer often repeats that of canonical pseudepigrapha, especially 2 Tim.[57] When addressing the Ephesians, Ignatius states: "You are a passageway for those slain for God; you are fellow initiates with Paul, the holy one who received a testimony and proved worthy of all fortune. When I attain to God, may I be found in his footsteps" (Ign. Eph. 12:2, transl. Ehrman). The author of 1 Clement also offers a powerful testimony to how Paul's afflictions soon came to define him:

> Because of jealousy and strife Paul showed the way to the prize for patient endurance. After he had been seven times in chains, had been driven into exile, had been stoned ... he thus departed from the world and went to the holy place, having become an outstanding example of patient endurance.
>
> 1 Clem 5, transl. HOLMES

Already in the fourth century, Eusebius writes about a full-blown martyr cult of Paul in Rome, where post-canonical tradition placed his death (*Theoph.* 4.7).[58] Eusebius also quotes the early third-century ecclesiastical writer Caius, who proclaims to know of Paul's tomb on the Ostian road.[59] The earliest Roman liturgical calendar *The Burying of the Martyrs* (written in 336 CE) places the remembrance of both Paul and Peter on June 29th.[60] According to David Eastman, "the Pauline cult was composed of a number of practices through which Christians created and re-created an image of Paul as a martyr worthy of vener-

56 According to Castelli (2004, 78), "Ignatius's letters are frequently used as one of the earliest sources for documenting both the historical experience of martyrdom and the emergent Christian theology of suffering and persecution."

57 See Smith 2011.

58 On the competing theories for the location of Paul's martyrdom, see Eastman 2011, 11: the site of the current Basilica of St. Paul Outside the Walls on the Ostian Road and the Catacombs of St. Sebastian on the Appian Road.

59 *Hist. eccl.* 2.25.7, transl. Cruse: "I can show ... the trophies of the apostles. For if you will go to the Vatican, or to the Ostian Road, you will find the trophies of those who have laid the foundation of this church."

60 Eastman 2011, 23.

ation." These practices included "places, stories, objects (relics, feast days) and rituals (pilgrimage), and patronage relationships."[61]

As a final, modern example, we can refer to the Jubilee of Paul in 2008–2009, mentioned at the beginning of this chapter. In his homily announcing the celebration, Pope Benedict XVI stated that "the extraordinary apostolic results that [Paul] was able to achieve cannot ... be attributed to brilliant rhetoric or refined apologetic and missionary strategies" but that they depended "above all on his personal involvement in proclaiming the Gospel with total dedication to Christ; a dedication that feared neither risk, difficulty nor persecution."[62] The comment relativizes Paul's intellectual efforts in the light of his personal willingness to suffer for the Gospel.

Why, then, has the idea of the suffering and dying apostle been so successful? If we look at cultural selection at the level of cultural bits and memes, the task is to look for features, such as minimal counterintuitiveness and emotionally provocative content that could have made the idea attention-grabbing and memorable. The mid-second-century Acts of Paul certainly fits these requirements in its depiction of the suffering and dying apostle: "turning toward the east, Paul lifted up his hands to heaven and prayed at length; and after having conversed in Hebrew with the fathers during prayer he bent his neck, without speaking any more. When the executioner cut off his head milk splashed on the tunic of the soldier" (Acts of Paul XI, 5, transl. Kennedy).[63] The story plays on the audience's emotions, offering fantastic elements such as the appearance of white, nurturing milk spilling from Paul's neck instead of blood.[64] Memorability can also be enhanced by plot twists that do not break ontological expectations. The *relevance* of the suffering Paul can be enhanced by the dissonance between the expectation of Paul as a great hero and the unexpected twist of his humiliating death.[65] In fact, at least one study has shown that vio-

61 Eastman 2011, 3. For an extensive introduction to early Christian and patristic references to Paul's (and Peter's) death, see Eastman 2015, 389–443.

62 For the full text, see http://www.vatican.va/content/benedict-xvi/en/homilies/2008/documents/hf_ben-xvi_hom_20080628_vespri.html.

63 On the magical enrichment of the character of Paul, especially in the Acts of Paul, see Nikki 2021.

64 On "disgust-based content bias," which may also be at play here, see Mesoudi 2011, 65.

65 Uchida (1998, 169) discusses relevance theory in connection to literary fiction, calling attention to instances where "the stories turn out to be quite the opposite to readers' anticipation, and as a result authors are able to achieve some kind of dramatic effect," referring to the phenomenon as a "twist." He distinguishes between local and global twists, the latter having to do with the general development of the story (Uchida 1998, 172–174).

lations in culturally acquired assumptions ("expectation-violating concepts") can be even more memorable than violations in ontological categories.[66]

Another factor proven to increase memorability has to do with the prominent role of agency detection and rationalizations concerning agency in human cognitive schemata. Humans have, through evolution, adapted to be able especially to understand, efficiently interpret, and purposefully track agency.[67] It has been suggested that there is a *hyperactive agency detection device* (HADD) in human cognition.[68] Thus, the presence of an agent in a story or a cultural representation elicits this basic human mode of thinking and increases its appeal and memorability.[69] That is, people are easier to remember than abstract ideas. This is perhaps why, surprisingly often, it is not ideas *by* Paul but the idea *of* Paul that crops up in later tradition.[70]

At the level of the organism, the idea of the suffering and martyred Apostle may have provided individuals with coping strategies in the face of various hardship. The idea of suffering for a greater cause and identification with a suffering role model can bring both consolation and a sense of meaning. A modern example is provided by Rachel Sing-Kiat Ting and Terri Watson, who studied the coping mechanisms of persecuted Chinese pastors.[71] Nearly half of the interviewees reported having been encouraged by identifying with the suffering Christ and his disciples. Another coping mechanism had to do with the belief that suffering was a normal part of life as a Christian—something to which the abundant representations of the afflicted Apostle have undoubtedly contributed. Paul himself also provides an example of meaning-making in Philippians 2, where the coincidental physical illness of the Philippians' envoy, Epaphroditus, is interpreted as undergoing Christ-like suffering.[72]

At a group level, the suffering Paul acts, first, as a prototype for the ingroup. According to the SIA, the significance of a prototype for a given group lies in the prototype's ability to (a) represent the group in the sense of being the same as the other members (as "one of us") and (b) in being optimally different

66 Porubanova-Norquist, Shaw, and Xygalatas 2013.

67 According to Alan Leslie (1993), children as young as six months show a good understanding of agents that move purposefully.

68 Leslie 1993.

69 See Czachesz 2017, 32–33. The study by Porubova-Norquist, Shaw, and Xygalatas 2013 also testified to the better memorability of the ontological category of human than categories of animals, plants, or objects (see esp. pp. 186, 189).

70 See also the role Pope Benedictus XVI gives to Paul as a person/agent in his speech.

71 Ting and Watson 2007.

72 Just as Christ (2:8) "became obedient to the point of death" (μέχρι θανάτου), Epaphroditus also "came close to death (μέχρι θανάτου) for the work of Christ" (2:30).

from relevant outgroups, creating a large *meta-contrast ratio*.[73] Prototypes thus serve to highlight the difference between the in- and outgroups and to promote ingroup cohesiveness. Depending on the outgroup, innocent suffering can form an extremely efficient contrast: Paul was killed by Romans (and, according to the sources, harassed by Jews), which makes him, and those who identify with him, their opposite. Another aspect of the appeal of the suffering Paul is that he is portrayed as following the prestigious Christ-type.[74] However, as a group prototype, Paul may even fare better than Jesus, who quickly became too counterintuitive and too otherworldly to optimally represent ingroup members in their daily lives.

Another way in which the image of the suffering Paul may have successfully spread through group-level selection is through the mechanism of costly signalling, an evolutionary biological theory that has been adapted to human group behaviour. The costly signal is understood as a time-, energy-, or health-consuming action that functions to deter free riders from a group.[75] Costly rituals and devotions have been linked in several studies to the better survival of religious groups, greater commitment by individual members, and more robust solidarity between members.[76] "The martyr Paul" may thus have been successful, since it offered a model for the manner and degree of expected costly signalling as proof of committed group membership. It is also possible that suffering and martyrdom (and eventually asceticism) became such strong signals in Paul-friendly tradition, because the lack of male circumcision and dietary regulations required that other signals be emphasized instead.[77]

---

73 Haslam, Platow, and Reicher 2011, 84–85.

74 On this typology in Philippians, see Bloomquist 1994.

75 An illustrative early discussion which can be interpreted in terms of costly signaling comes from Origen. In his *De Oratione* (29), Origen ponders why Jesus advises to pray for deliverance from temptations, if temptations are a natural part of Christian life. According to Origen, Paul and other apostles were tempted, because God *tested* them: "Even Paul, for all his riches, in all manner of discourse and in all manner of knowledge, is not released from the danger of sinning on their account through excessive exaltation, but needs a stake of Satan to buffet him in order that he may not be excessively exalted." In terms of costly signalling, temptations can be understood as tests of the individual's commitment to the group. Willingness to suffer plays a similar role as a token of group membership.

76 See, e.g. Iannaccone 1994; Sosis and Bressler 2003; Heimola 2013.

77 Nikki 2018, 194.

5 Anti-paulinism in Early Christianity

In explaining the success of the Gospel of Mark from an evolutionary perspective, Luomanen notes that the gospel includes many anecdotal accounts that are easy to remember and effective for oral transmission. These can be described as cognitively optimal.[78] Similarities appear when we compare the anecdotal stories in Mark to some anti-Pauline narratives. The claims about Paul attributed to the Ebionites, a "heretical" group mentioned in several patristic writings, are a good example: according to Irenaeus, the Ebionites call Paul "an apostate from the law."[79] In the *Panarion* ("Medicine Chest") by Epiphanius, they are said to claim that Paul was a proselyte who began to write against the law as a result of a failed romance with the high priest's daughter.[80] In addition to the Ebionites, other groups like Encratites,[81] Elcesaites,[82] and Severians[83] are accused of rejecting Paul and his writings. Cerinthus and his followers are also targeted in the work.[84] Epiphanius's account reports that Cerinthus lambasted Paul in Jerusalem (the two being contemporaries in the story) for having polluted the temple by bringing an uncircumcised person with him, a reference to Acts 21:28.[85] Not much can be said, however, for the historicity of said groups or persons.[86]

Even though the polemical texts mentioned above cannot be defined as *chreias* (miracle stories) in the Marcan style, they contain similar elements that increase their memorability: they are short, anecdotal references to Paul that include both counterintuitive (e.g., Paul as a gentile) and emotionally provocative (e.g., Paul as an apostate) elements. Other anti-Pauline narratives—for example, those in the Pseudo-Clementines—do not seem as cognitively optimal, however, as they are somewhat lengthy, such that the memorability of these narratives deserves more careful analysis.

Let us consider a passage in the Pseudo-Clementine Homilies as an example. In Homilies 17.19, we encounter a heated debate between Peter and Simon Magus. Even though the passage seemingly deals with Simon as the adversary,

78 Luomanen 2013, 56–59.
79 *Haer.* 1.26.2: "apostatam eum legis dicentes."
80 *Pan.* 30.16.9.
81 Origen, *Cels.* 5.65.
82 Eusebius, *Hist. eccl.* 6.38; Theodoret of Cyrus, *Haer. fab.* 2.7.
83 Eusebius, *Hist. eccl.* 4.29.
84 *Haer.* 1.26.1; Filaster, *Liber de haeresibus* 36.
85 Epiphanius, *Pan.* 28.4.1 For an extensive list of anti-Pauline narratives in patristic writings, see Klijn and Reinink 1973.
86 Epiphanius's report from Cyprus is a possible exception (see Luomanen 2012, 34–37).

Paul can easily be identified as the true target of criticism.[87] When discussing the value of visions and apparitions for receiving the true teaching, Peter's words are especially pointed:

> If, then, our Jesus appeared to you in a vision, made Himself known to you, and spoke to you, it was as one who is enraged with an adversary; and this is the reason why it was through visions and dreams, or through revelations that were from without, that He spoke to you. But can anyone be rendered fit for instruction through apparitions? … And how did He appear to you, when you entertain opinions contrary to His teaching? … If you were not opposed to me, you would not accuse me, and revile the truth proclaimed by me, in order that I may not be believed when I state what I myself have heard with my own ears from the Lord.[88]

This passage is usually considered the clearest case of anti-Paulinism in the Homilies, and the "you" of the text has been widely recognized as Paul. First, Paul's authority as an apostle is discounted by claiming that visions are not the right way to learn the true teachings of Jesus. Secondly, Paul is accused of maligning Peter by twisting his words. Gerd Lüdemann goes as far as claiming Paul is portrayed in the text as "an enemy of God."[89] The passage makes use of Paul's own accounts of Christ's appearance to him (Gal 1:11–12; 1 Cor 15:8), turning Paul's own cause against him. The logic of the attack can be understood using the notions of *relevance* and *attraction*. As stated above, Sperber and Wilson argue that so-called *cultural attractors* are important for making sense of the relevance of different representations. Alberto Acerbi and Alex Mesoudi give a helpful example:

> In an oral transmission of a story, say Cinderella, it is highly unlikely the story will be repeated verbatim at each passage. Still, some defining features, say the pumpkin coach or the wicked stepmother, perhaps because they are particularly memorable, will act as attractors, and will be repeated ("reconstructed") each time by different narrators.[90]

An attractor thus increases the density of mental representations around it, creating "buzz," which can either elevate or diminish its relevance. For example, an

87 Lüdemann 1996, 57–59; Stanton 2007, 315–316; Reed 2008, 196–198; Vähäkangas 2013, 223.
88 Hom. 19.17.1–5.
89 Lüdemann 1989, 188.
90 Acerbi and Mesoudi 2015, 483.

established practice is a strong *attractor* because of its familiarity. At the same time, its *relevance* might not be very high because of its high predictability. On the other hand, if a representation deviates from an established attractor, its relevance can increase significantly.[91] Accordingly, it can be observed that Paul, a well-known figure, is an established character and therefore a strong attractor in the early Christian context. Deviance from the established practice of writing about the apostle in positive terms, on the other hand, makes the polemical narrative highly relevant. In this case, Paul's established conversion story is turned on its head, increasing the relevance of the passage. Moreover, a personal attack on a popular figure would likely have provoked strong emotions for and against the claims being made.

A similar case is found in the *Book of the Rooster*, a fifth-century apocryphal Passion narrative that has survived in Geʿez.[92] The narrative contains all the familiar events prior to Jesus' crucifixion: the betrayal by Judas, Jesus's arrest and trials, and his journey to the place of execution. As such, the story might not be very relevant because of its familiarity, but the situation changes completely, when Paul (named in the text as Saul) appears. He is portrayed as a hostile figure who plots with Judas, leads the soldiers to arrest Jesus, takes Jesus from one court to another, and finally places the crown of thorns on his head.[93]

The masking of Paul as Simon Magus or an unnamed "enemy" (see Rec. 1.70–71 below) in the Pseudo-Clementine literature is also worth mentioning. The character of Simon Magus in the Pseudo-Clementine literature is built around earlier heresiographical traditions, such as Justin's *First Apology* (26) and Irenaeus's *Against Heresies* (1.23.2).[94] It is only later in the narrative that Paul's views are attributed to Simon, as seen from the example in the above passage. That is, the argumentation in the narrative relies first on a common and well-known "heretic" and only later reveals Paul to be that character.

A point of comparison can be found at the beginning of 2 Samuel 12, where the prophet Nathan describes of King David's misconduct, revealing his iden-

91 Sperber 1996, 114–115.

92 See Piovanelli 2003; Piovanelli 2006.

93 *Book of the Rooster* 4:15–8:34. See Piovanelli 2004, 429–431. Paul's appearance is only one of several inventive elements in the narrative. For instance, Jesus and his disciples are informed of the conspiracy against him by a cooked but ressurrected rooster, and Jesus takes vengeance for his failed escape attempt by turning the woman who betrayed him to stone.

94 See Rec. 2 (parallel in Hom. 2). Simon's character as an arch-heretic is already established in the Basic Writing, the common source text of Recognitions and Homilies/Klementia. This can be induced, for example, from the aforementioned parallels between Rec. and Hom.

tity only at the end. In the previous chapter, David had had Uriah the Hittite killed to make Uriah's wife, Bathsheba, his own. To show God's anger at David for his deed, Nathan tells him a parable of a rich and a poor man. The rich man owns an abundance of livestock but, when a guest arrives, slaughters the poor man's only lamb instead of one his own. David becomes enraged at the rich man and expresses a desire for his death, only to find out from Nathan that *he himself* is the villain of that parable. As a result, David understands his own crime and repents.[95]

It is also noteworthy that the character of Simon Magus seems to be developed from an amalgam of views considered heretical. F. Stanley Jones, for instance, notes Simon's similarity to Marcion and especially to his student Apelles.[96] The matter of who Simon Magus is or whom he represents therefore becomes unavoidably more complex. This kind of question, in which familiar elements are brought together but for which the identity of the individual is open to different interpretations, is a type of *relevant mystery*, a term coined by Sperber. Sperber, in fact, argues that relevant mysteries are the most successful type of cultural representations.[97] To Sperber's point, in the early Christian context, Luomanen has identified the original and sudden ending of Mark as a relevant mystery.[98]

Anti-Pauline narratives were especially relevant for those who disagreed with Paul's views about the Jewish law. The narratives demonstrate that a defamatory story about a person who represents a heretical order to the recipients can be cognitively very attractive. Such relevance would not, however, have been limited to the opponents of the apostle; polemical accounts about those who did not accept Paul's letters or insulted the apostle indicate that the anti-Pauline ideas attracted the attention of pro-Paulinists as well. The abundance of heresiological writings against those who rejected Paul illustrate this clearly.

At the group level of selection, the negative depictions of Paul served a significant role as a *negative group stereotype*. Both ingroup prototypes and out-

95 2 Sam 12:1–4. We thank Prof. Ismo Dunderberg for bringing this parallel to our attention.

96 In the context of the Pseudo-Clementines, the primary reason for attacking Paul might be the contemporary situation in Syria. In the Basic Writing, written at the beginning of third century CE, Marcionite concerns are at the forefront, even if the views of Marcion and his student Apelles are masked like those of Simon Magus (see above). Since Marcion held Paul in such high regard, the apostle could have been collateral damage in the Basic Writer's furious refutation of Marcionite views. The target of anti-Pauline polemic in the Pseudo-Clementines might then be the specifically Marcionite imagination of Paul. See Jones 2007.

97 Sperber 1996, 73.

98 Luomanen 2012, 57; Luomanen 2017, 131, 133.

group stereotypes[99] serve as repositories for relevant (and constantly changing) information about the groups.[100] As a stereotype, Paul embodies the negative characteristics of the outgroup and represents an antithesis to the ingroup. The antithetical character provides a tool for self-categorization at the individual level of selection as well and would thus have benefitted an individual's wellbeing and sense of meaning. In the Pseudo-Clementines, the figure of Paul is quite literally that of opponent and enemy. In the first book of Recognitions, Peter recounts the events that took place some years prior in Jerusalem.[101] There was a public debate over Jesus at the temple. James, the brother of Jesus and the leader of the congregation in Jerusalem, managed to convince the populace, as well as high priest Caiaphas, that Jesus is the Christ. Everyone in the city was to be baptized, but, before that could happen, "a certain hostile man" entered the temple and tried to invalidate the newfound agreement.[102]

When this man's arguments were refuted by James, the former began to raise disorder and even attempted to kill James by pushing him down the temple stairs. James survived, but chaos ensued. The congregation had to retreat from the temple and leave the city by night. In the subsequent chapter, the hostile man is revealed to be heading to Damascus, with authorization by Caiaphas to persecute the believers there, a clear allusion to Paul in Acts 9.[103] Paul's history as persecutor of the true faith, as described in Acts as well as in his own letters,[104] is not treated as an advantage or forgiven but used to attack him. Paul portrayal as a righteous sufferer in pro-Pauline material, which carries significance at the levels of both individuals and groups, is thus turned on its head, as Paul is denied this role and even depicted as the *cause* for righteous suffering.

A similar theme of Paul as opponent is seen in two other cases. In the first, Peter introduces a rule of good and evil counterparts. According to this rule, the evil one precedes its good equivalent and together form pairs that recur throughout history. Following the rule, Peter concludes that Simon, who started his mission to Gentiles before him, is his evil counterpart, but, because many are not familiar with the rule, "an enemy is received as a friend."[105] Secondly,

99 Although the term "stereotype" is sometimes viewed as a general category comprising both positive and negative generalizations (Bullock and Stallybrass 1977, 601), we use the term here exclusive to denote negative counterparts to prototypes.

100 Esler 2003, 175.

101 Recognitions 1.27–71 is part of an earlier source used originally by the Basic Writer but excluded from the Homilies as such.

102 Rec. 1.66–70.2.

103 Rec. 1.70.3–71.

104 Gal 1:13; Phil 3:6.

105 Hom. 2.18.2: "ὁ ἐχθρὸς ὡς φίλος ἀποδέδεκται."

in *The Letter of Peter to James*, one of the introductory letters to the Pseudo-Clementines, Peter laments that someone has already distorted his mission:

> Namely, some among the gentiles have rejected my lawful teaching and accepted the lawless and foolish teaching of my enemy.[106]

In the case of both counterparts and competing missions, therefore, a clear distinction is drawn between Paul and the righteous ones who oppose him and his later followers. These excerpts evidence a form of *social categorization*—that is, the construction of social identity by classifying people as ingroup and outgroup members and emphasizing the differences between the two. Such categories help to draw and strengthen the borders of the ingroup, thus making the group more unified.

Social identity can also be constructed by appealing to holy scriptures. In patristic sources, the Ebionites and other "heretical" groups are explicitly said to reject the letters of Paul, because the letters contain false teaching. In the Pseudo-Clementines, the true scriptures are correspondingly claimed to be in the possession of the ingroup as indicated in the accompanying letter texts. The aim of the author is to replace Paul and his writings and to legitimize his/her own view of the early Christian history, thus maintaining a distinct ingroup identity. Because of this tendency, parts of the Pseudo-Clementine writings have rightly been called "counter-history."[107]

As with scriptures, authoritative figures serve as a basis for identity construction. James, the brother of Jesus, and Peter are described in positive terms in the Pseudo-Clementines. Both are leading figures in the early Jerusalem community, and, notably, both strongly oppose Paul. James and Peter are exemplars, historical prototypes, whose anti-Paulinism justifies the hostility in the texts toward Paul, incorporating this animosity into the social identity of the group. While the Paul that is attacked in the Pseudo-Clementines is unambiguously opposed to the Jewish law, the historical Paul's relationship to Judaism is notoriously complicated. It is noteworthy that the anti-Pauline polemic does not challenge the image of "the apostle to the Gentiles" but instead uses this image to attack Paul and his legacy, depicting him similarly to how he is depicted in established tradition, with his supposed rejection of the Jewish law now considered a negative trait. The anti-Pauline rhetoric therefore indirectly recognizes the Gentile Christian view of Paul as normative.

---

106 *The Letter of Peter to James* 2.3.

107 Jones 1995b, 634–635; Reed 2008, 213–214.

To summarize, the rejection of Paul was a means for identity construction for some early Christians. At the group level of selection, Paul as a negative stereotype is a successful cultural representation, because it can unify the ingroup against a common enemy. The depiction of Paul as apostate and adversary is an overarching theme in the passages discussed, representing what his opponents do not want to be—followers of a false teacher who should have no place in early Christianity. Furthermore, a strong opposition is formed between Paul and alternative prototypical figures—e.g., Peter and James—by portraying them as enemies of Paul. As a result, the latter are seen as the true representatives of the Jerusalem church. We next compare these observations to some anti-Pauline views expressed in early Islamic writings and Toledot Yeshu.

6 Early Islamic Sources and the Jewish Toledot Yeshu

Perhaps the earliest case of hostility toward Paul in Islamic texts can be found in the writings of Sayf ibn ʿUmar al-Tamīmī.[108] *The Book of the Wars of Apostasy and Conquest*, dated to the late 2nd AH/8th CE century, contains a narrative where Paul of Tarsus, a Jewish king, corrupts Christianity by falsifying the teachings of Jesus and, afterwards, persecuting the few remaining true believers.[109] Sayf b. ʿUmar draws parallels from Paul to another figure, ʿAbd Allāh ibn Sabaʾ, whom he correspondingly alleges to have incited disputes among Muslims during the reign of Caliph ʿUthmān (reigned 24–36 AH/644–656 CE).

Sayf's narrative takes the form of a *khabar*, an independent account that is the usual genre of early Islamic historical writing. Despite dealing with Christian origins, it contains many elements of its author's Islamic context. It begins with a list of the transmitters of the story (*isnād*), increasing its authority by tracing its roots further back in history.[110] In the story, the rapid growth in the number of Christians after the ascension of Jesus is raising concerns among

108 Biographical details about Sayf ibn ʿUmar remain scarce. According to Donner (1997), even the traditional dating of his death to the reign of the Abbasid Caliph al-Rashīd (148–193/786–809), is only a guess. It is known with greater certainty that he was a member of the Usayyid clan, though there are here also contrasting accounts.

109 Qasim al-Samarrai discovered the manuscripts of *The Book of the Wars of Apostasy and Conquest* and *The Book of the Battle of the Camel and the Campaigns of ʿĀʾisha and ʿAlī* at a university library in Saudi Arabia and published critical editions of the texts in 1995 (Al-Samarrai 1995). Beforehand, Sayf b. ʿUmar's work was only indirectly available through citations by other early Islamic scholars, most notably al-Ṭabarī (d. 310/923). For a detailed analysis of the passage on Paul in *Book of the Wars*, see Anthony 2010; Barzegar 2011.

110 Anthony 2010, 173.

Jews, including for Paul, the king of Jews. He persecutes Christians, who survive by escaping to the mountains. Trying to put an end to his perceived threat, Paul goes to the Christians, feigning a conversion, and performing a sign showing God has sent him. The Christians, believing Paul's story, accept and welcome him among them. After joining them, Paul goes on to issue a series of new commands to distort their beliefs, and, over the course of the narrative, the Christians abandon the correct direction of prayer, dietary regulations, and warfare (*jihād*) because of him. Finally, the community is split into four factions, led by Ya'qub, Nestur, Malkun,[111] and the Believer (*al-Mu'min*), the last of whose following is the smallest. Each leader has different beliefs about the divinity of Jesus, but only the righteous Believer curses Paul and rejects his reforms. Paul provokes the others to attack the Believer and his followers, which forces them to leave for Syria. There, they live in peace in the mountains. The narrative ends with a Quranic quotation and a comparison between Ibn Sabaʾ and Paul's actions, which cause disarray among their communities. This is, according to the narrative, a warning for all the *umma* (Muslim community) to heed.[112]

According to Sean W. Anthony, in Sayf's account, Paul is not just plotting against a minor group of righteous believers but attempting to corrupt the universal message of Islam.[113] By including Quranic teaching into the narrative and drawing close parallels to a more contemporary "heretic," Ibn Sabaʾ, Paul is seen as a threat to the unity of *umma* and, similarly to many Christian writings mentioned above, a representative of later negative developments. Abbas Barzegar, too, argues that the text is part of "a grand historical narrative," which plays an important role in the formation of Sunni identity.[114] Contemporary concerns therefore have a strong influence on the story, but the effect is not unilateral; as Sayf is "an unlikely candidate for the invention of the tradition" on Paul,[115] the framework of the narrative also affects how Ibn Sabaʾ is understood and portrayed in the text. It is necessary, then, to look at the tradition history of Sayf's narrative.

There is a number of early Islamic sources mentioning the division of Christians into three sects.[116] It is, in fact, a common Muslim narrative on early

111 The first three factions are, from the point of view of the narrator, "heretical" and represent different eastern Christianities; Ya'qub is James, Nestur Nestorius, and Malkun presumably the leader of the Melkites. Barzegar 2011, 217.

112 Anthony 2010, 173–180; Barzegar 2011, 217–218.

113 Anthony 2010, 182–183.

114 Barzegar 2011, 209.

115 Anthony 2010, 194–195.

116 Among the historians writing about the event are al-Ṭabarī (d. 310/923), Ibn ʿAsākir (d. 571/

Christian history. As a rule, however, Paul is absent from the sources.[117] The cause for disagreements in some cases is a council that gathers to discuss Christological matters (e.g., Ibn al-Jawzī, d. 597/1201), elsewhere no reason for the disarray is given (e.g., al-Ṭabarī, d. 310/923). Some early references to Paul are more neutral in tone, where he does not play a role in the division of Christianity.[118] For instance, Ibn Isḥāq (d. 150/767), whose account is preserved through al-Ṭabarī, mentions Paul in close association with Peter in Rome.[119] The Islamic accounts where Paul *is* treated as a hostile figure, most notably ʿAbd al-Jabbār's (d. 415/1025) detailed writings, are mostly later and approach the matter from a more theological context compared to Sayf's historical account.[120]

There is, however, some comparable material: Ibn Ḥazm (d. 456/1064) presents Paul similarly to Sayf's account. In the text, Jewish rabbis bribe Paul to go to the Christians and convince them of Jesus's divinity.[121] Similarly, al-Damīrī, writing in the 15th century but claiming to cite a source from the 8th century (al-Kalbī), mentions a corresponding story of Paul leading the righteous Christians away from the truth.[122] Despite the agreements between the texts, Anthony argues that Sayf's narrative is independent from the others and posits a "pre-Islamic or non-Muslim" source for the story.[123] Since both Sayf and Ibn Ḥazm share parallels with Toledot Yeshu (see below) and both writers seem to be aware of non-Muslim sources, several scholars have identified the Jewish polemical life of Jesus as the source for the Islamic anti-Pauline tradition.

In some manuscripts of Toledot Yeshu, a Jewish polemical account of the life of Jesus, Paul (here named as Eliyahu) is indeed portrayed as a conspirator. He is a Jewish sage who is sent among followers of Yeshu, who are considered a threat, to lead them further away from true Judaism. Paul establishes new rules among Yeshu-believers, like changing the old holidays and abandoning circumcision and dietary regulations. It should be noted that Paul's actions are not described as negative in this case, as his mission to separate Christianity from Judaism leads to a positive outcome. The problem with Toledot Yeshu being the source for the Paul tradition is its timeline: the manuscripts that contain

1176), and Ibn al-Jawzī (d. 597/1201). For detailed references and discussions, see Rubin 1999, 117–167; Mourad 2002; Anthony 2010, 189–201.

117 Anthony 2010, 193.

118 Reynolds 2004, 170.

119 Whittingham 2015.

120 Anthony 2010, 196.

121 Anthony 2010, 193–194. Whittingham 2015.

122 Anthony 2010, 197–199. Whittingham 2015.

123 Anthony 2010, 194.

the Eliyahu story are from the medieval period.[124] Even if the narrative predates the extant texts containing it, however, literary dependence is difficult to prove.[125]

While there might not be enough direct evidence to draw a trajectory from Christian anti-Pauline texts to early Islamic or Jewish material (or from Jewish to Islamic polemics, for that matter), it is clear that the traditions influenced each other; Paul as a Jewish falsifier of true teachings (and a persecutor of the righteous in case of Christian and Islamic writings) is a recurring theme in all the above narratives. Even though the Christian groups hostile to Paul's letters and legacy eventually faded to obscurity, anti-Paulinism survived as a separate phenomenon, because it was memorable and useful for group identity construction.

This observation has a further, important consequence for the study Jewish Christianity, itself a difficult and criticized category, and its relationship to anti-Paulinism. Opposition to Paul has been associated with Jewish believers in Jesus throughout the history of research, though its importance to understanding the phenomenon as a whole has varied. Some scholars, initially John Toland and Ferdinand Christian Baur, and more recently Gerd Lüdemann, see the opposition to Paul as a defining feature of Jewish Christian groups.[126] This perspective is, in part, informed by heresiological patristic writings, where groups that adhere to Jewish dietary regulations and other customs are often accused of rejecting Paul. Recently, however, this traditional perspective on Jewish Christianity and anti-Paulinism has been challenged. Annette Reed and Pierluigi Piovanelli, for instance, have noted that, contra Baur, anti-Pauline traditions made their way into "mainstream" Christian literature, while Jewish Christian groups gradually faded away.[127]

124 Daniel Stökl ben Ezra (2009), however, gives a much earlier date, fourth or fifth century CE, to the narrative, based on a list of festivals included in the text. Another proponent of an early dating is Martin Whittingham (2020), who argues that the narrative of Toledot Yeshu influenced Sayf and other early Muslim authors. Anthony (2010, 201–202) suggests Sayf used an ancient version of the text. Scholars of the Princeton Toledot Yeshu project do not wholly agree with this line of thought (Schäfer et al 2011). Contra Stökl ben Ezra, they date the composition of the text to a late Medieval period. They, too, however admit that the narrative about Paul as a plotter could be much earlier.

125 Whittingham provides the best argument for it by noting verbal similarity in the changes Paul makes regarding food regulations. Both Sayf and Toledot state that according to Paul all animals from an insect to an elephant are lawful to eat. Whittingham 2020, 89.

126 See Lüdemann 1989; Carleton Paget 2012; Jones (ed.), 2012.

127 Piovanelli 2006; Reed 2008.

The observations made above support the interpretation of Reed and Piovanelli: some texts containing anti-Pauline ideas did indeed enjoy widespread circulation in the early centuries of Christianity. This shows that Jewish Christianity and anti-Paulinism have their own lives: anti-Pauline polemic in a text does not mean that the text is Jewish-Christian, nor can anti-Paulinism be seen purely as a feature of Jewish-Christianity. Hostility toward Paul has some cognitively attractive aspects that might explain its success, as demonstrated by its perseverance in narratives recorded in Jewish and Islamic sources. Other groups besides Jewish Christians could also have used the theme as a tool for group identification. The cultural evolutionary perspective is a useful research lens for this topic, since the notion of the meme-level selection allows us to understand the transmission of cultural variants beyond tradition within particular groups while still accounting for the importance of group-level selection.

7 Conclusion

This article applied a cultural evolutionary perspective to divergent traditions of Paul the Apostle—as either hero or villain. Cultural evolutionary theory treats the variation, selection, and transmission of cultural information as part of a wider process of human biocultural evolution, in which culture is understood as part of the human phenotype. Human cognition, in particular, is understood to mediate between biology and culture, which explains the close relationship between the cultural evolutionary approach and cognitive science—as well as, in the topic of religion, the cognitive science of religion (CSR).

The article has sought to showcase how the dissemination and perseverance of particular ideas of Paul can be explained through three levels of evolution: those of memes, individual organisms, and groups. The first level denotes the selection and transmission of ideas (or "memes") due to their conspicuous nature and memorability; the second level, their selection due to their capacity to enhance the wellbeing and survival of individuals; and the third level, their role in between-group competition. Both the pro- and the anti-Pauline traditions were shown to contain several types of elements that may have offered the themes a selective advantage. Both traditions contained counterintuitive and attention-grabbing features and both offered tools for individual self-categorization and meaning and provided groups with ways to distinguish themselves meaningfully from other groups by using Paul as a proto- or stereotype.

Evolutionary theory does not treat changes in biology or culture as improvement or development. Rather, evolution simply denotes any set of changes in a given population that emerges over a considerable period of time. While a species is understood to descend from common ancestors, change among the offspring is considered natural, not a deviation. For the variation, selection, and inheritance of the pro- and anti-Pauline traditions, this means that both represent equally valuable variations on a theme with a common origin. The heuristic categorization of pro- and the anti-Pauline themes eventually also blur together, revealing an overall tradition of Paul, which, in all its variety, is not "owned" by mainstream Christianity but rather shared between different forms of Christianity, Judaism, and Islam.

Bibliography

Acerbi, Alberto and Alex Mesoudi. "If We Are All Cultural Darwinians What's the Fuss about? Clarifying Recent Disagreements in the Field of Cultural Evolution." *Biology & Philosophy* 30 (2015), 481–503.

Anthony, Sean W. "The Composition of Sayf b. 'Umar's Account of King Paul and His Corruption of Ancient Christianity." *Der Islam* 85 (2010): 164–202.

al-'Aṭṭās, Sayyid Muḥammad Naqīb. *Islam and Secularism*. Kuala Lumpur: Muslim Youth Movement of Malaysia, 1978.

Baker, Coleman A. and J. Brian Tucker (eds.). *T&T Clark Handbook to Social Identity in the New Testament*. London: Bloomsbury T&T Clark, 2014.

Barrett, J.L. "Exploring the Natural Foundations of Religion." *Trends in Cognitive Sciences* 4 (2000): 29–34.

Barzegar, Abbas. "The Persistence of Heresy: Paul of Tarsus, Ibn Saba', and Historical Narrative in Sunni Identity Formation." *Numen* 58 (2011), 207–231.

Bloomquist, L. Gregory. *The Function of Suffering in Philippians*. Sheffield: JSOT Press, 1993.

Boyd, Robert and Peter J. Richerson. *Culture and the Evolutionary Process*. Chicago: The University of Chicago Press, 1985.

Boyer, Pascal. *The Naturalness of Religious Ideas: A Cognitive Theory of Religion*. Berkeley: University of California Press, 1994.

Boyer, Pascal. *Religion Explained: The Evolutionary Origins of Religious Thought*. New York: Basic Books, 2001.

Buckley, Christopher D. "Investigating Cultural Evolution Using Phylogenetic Analysis: The Origins and Descent of the Southeast Asian Tradition of Warp Ikat Weaving." *PLoS ONE* 7 (2012), available at https://journals.plos.org/plosone/article?id=10.1371/journal.pone.0052064.

Bullock, Alan and Oliver Stallybrass. *The Fontana Dictionary of Modern Thought.* London: Fontana/Collins, 1977.

Castelli, Elizabeth A. *Martyrdom and Memory: Early Christian Culture Making.* New York: Columbia University Press, 2004.

Czachesz, István. "Theologische Innovation und Sozialstruktur im Urchristentum: Eine Kognitive Analyse seiner Ausbreitungsdynamik." *Evangelische Theologie* 71 (2011): 259–272.

Czachesz, István. *Cognitive Science and the New Testament: A New Approach to Early Christian Research.* Oxford: Oxford University Press, 2017.

Czachesz, István. "The Bible as a Product of Cultural Evolution." In: U.E. Eisen and H. Mader (eds.), *Rede von Gott in Gesellschaft: Multidisziplinäres (Re)konstruieren antiker (Kon)texte/Talking God in Society: Multidisciplinary (Re)constructions of Ancient (Con)texts, FS Peter Lampe.* Vol. 1 Göttingen: Vandenhoeck & Ruprecht, 2020, 115–132.

Darwin, Charles. *The Origin of Species by Means of Natural Selection or Preservation of Favoured Races in the Struggle for Life.* London: John Murray, 1859.

Dawkins, Richard. *The Extended Phenotype.* Oxford University Press, 1982.

Donner, Fred M. "Sayf b. ʿUmar." In: C.E. Bosworth et al. (eds.) *Encyclopedia of Islam.* Leiden: Brill, 1997, volume IX, 102.

Drijvers, Han J.W. "Bardaisan's Doctrine of Free Will, the Pseudo-Clementines, and Marcionism in Syria." In: Guy Bedouelle and Olivier Fatio (eds), *Liberté chrétienne et libre arbitre.* Fribourg: Éditions Universitaires, 1994, 13–30.

Eastman, David L. *Paul the Martyr: The Cult of the Apostle in the Latin West.* Atlanta, GA: Society of Biblical Literature, 2011.

Esler, Philip Francis. *Conflict and Identity in Romans: The Social Setting of Paul's Letter.* Minneapolis, MN: Fortress Press, 2003.

Esler, Philip Francis. "An Outline of Social Identity Theory." In: Coleman A. Baker and J. Brian Tucker (eds.), *T&T Clark Handbook to Social Identity in the New Testament.* London: Bloomsbury T&T Clark, 2014, 13–40.

Geertz, Armin. "Brain, Body and Culture: A Biocultural Theory of Religion." *Method and Theory in the Study of Religion* 22 (2010): 304–321.

Gerstein, Mark B. et al. "What is a gene post-ENCODE? History and Updated Definition." *Genome Res.* 17 (2007): 669–681.

Guthrie, Stewart. *Faces in the Clouds: A New Theory of Religion.* Oxford: Oxford University Press, 1993.

Haslam, S. Alexander. *Psychology in Organizations. The Social Identity Approach.* London: SAGE Publications, 2004.

Haslam, S.A., Platow, M., and Reicher, S. *The New Psychology of Leadership: Identity, Influence, and Power.* Hove: Psychology Press, 2011.

Heimola, Mikko. *From Deprived to Revived: Religious Revivals as Adaptive Systems.* Boston: De Gruyter, 2013.

Heylighen, Francis and Klaas Chielens. "Cultural Evolution and Memetics." In: Robert A. Meyers (ed), *Encyclopedia of Complexity and System Science*. New York: Springer, 2009.

Iannaccone, Laurence. "Why Strict Churches are Strong." *American Journal of Sociology* 99 (1994), 1180–1211.

Irons, William. "Religion as a Hard-to-Fake Sign of Commitment." R.M. Nesse (ed.), *Evolution and the Capacity for Commitment*. New York: Russell Sage Foundation, 2001, 292–309.

Jablonka, Eva and Marion J. Lamb. *Evolution in Four Dimensions: Genetic, Epigenetic, Behavioral, and Symbolic Variation in the History of Life*. Cambridge, MA: MIT Press, 2005.

Jones, F. Stanley. *An Ancient Jewish Christian Source on the History of Christianity: Pseudo-Clementine "Recognitions" 1.27–71*. Atlanta, GA: Scholars Press, 1995a.

Jones, F. Stanley. "A Jewish Christian Reads Luke's Acts of the Apostles: The Use of the Canonical Acts in the Ancient Jewish Christian Source behind Pseudo-Clementine *Recognitions* 1.27–71." In: E.H. Lovering, Jr (ed), *Society of Biblical Literature 1995 Seminar Papers*. Atlanta, GA: Scholars Press, 1995b, 617–635.

Jones, F. Stanley. "Marcionism." In: Albert Frey and Rémi Gounelle (eds.), *Pseudo-Clementines. Poussières de christianisme et de judaïsme antiques: Études réunies en l'honneur de Jean-Daniel Kaestli et Éric Junod*. Publications de l'Institut romand des sciences bibliques 5. Lausanne: Éditions du Zèbre, 2007, 225–244.

Jones, F. Stanley (ed.). *The Rediscovery of Jewish Christianity: From Toland to Baur*. Atlanta: Society of Biblical Literature, 2012.

Klijn, A.F.J. and G.J. Reinink. *Patristic Evidence for Jewish-Christian Sects*. Leiden: Brill, 1973.

Leslie, A.M. "A Theory of Agency." *Technical Reports of the Rutgers University Centre for Cognitive Science* 12 (1993): 1–28.

Lüdemann, Gerd. *Opposition to Paul in Jewish Christianity*. Minneapolis: Fortress Press, 1989.

Lüdemann, Gerd. *Heretics: The Other Side of Early Christianity*. Louisville: Westminster John Knox Press, 1995.

Luomanen, Petri. *Recovering Jewish-Christian Sects and Gospels*. Leiden and Boston: Brill, 2012.

Luomanen, Petri. "From Mark and Q to Matthew. An Experiment in Evolutionary Analysis." In: Eve-Marie Becker and Anders Runesson (eds.), *Mark and Matthew II: Comparative Readings: Reception History, Cultural Hermeneutics and Theology*. Tübingen: Mohr Siebeck, 2013, 37–73.

Luomanen, Petri. "Morality and the Evolution of Christianity." In: Petri Luomanen, Anne Birgitta Pessi, and Ilkka Pyysiäinen (eds.), *Christianity and the Roots of Morality: Philosophical, Early Christian, and Empirical Perspectives*. Leiden and Boston: Brill, 2017, 113–139.

Porubanova-Norquist, Michaela, Daniel Joel Shaw, and Dimitris Xygalatas. "Minimal-Counterintuitiveness Revisited: Effects of Cultural and Ontological Violations on Concept Memorability." *Journal for the Cognitive Science of Religion* 1 (2013): 181–192.

Moran, Laurence A. "What Is Evolution?" 2007. Available at https://sandwalk.blogspot.com/2007/01/what-is-evolution.html. Accessed Jan 29, 2020.

Moss, Candida R. *The Other Christs: Imitating Jesus in Ancient Christian Ideologies of Martyrdom*. Oxford: Oxford University Press, 2010.

Nikki, Nina. *Opponents and Identity in Philippians*. NovTSup 173. Leiden: Brill, 2018.

Nikki, Nina. "Magic, Miracles, and the Cultural Evolution of Pauline Christianity." In: Kirsi Valkama and Nina Nikki (eds.), *Magic in the Ancient Eastern Mediterranean: Cognitive, Historical, and Material Perspectives on the Bible and Its Contexts*. Göttingen: Vandenhoeck & Ruprecht, 2021.

Origen, *De Oratione*. Transl. William A. Curtis. Available at https://www.ccel.org/ccel/origen/prayer.i.html.

Pervo, Richard I. *The Making of Paul: Constructions of the Apostle in Early Christianity*. Minneapolis, MN: Fortress Press, 2010.

Piovanelli, Pierluigi. "Exploring the Ethiopic *Book of the Cock*, An Apocryphal Passion Gospel from Late Antiquity." *The Harvard Theological Review* 96 (2003): 427–454.

Piovanelli, Pierluigi. "The *Book of the Cock* and the Rediscovery of Ancient Jewish-Christian Traditions in Fifth-Century Palestine." In: Ian H. Henderson and Gerbern S. Oegema (eds.), *The Changing Face of Judaism, Christianity, and Other Greco-Roman Religions in Antiquity*. Gütersloh: Gütersloher Verlagshaus, 2006, 308–322.

Reed, Annette Yoshiko. "Jewish-Christianity as Counter-History? The Apostolic Past in Eusebius' *Ecclesiastical History* and the Pseudo-Clementine *Homilies*." In: Gregg Gardner and Kevin L. Osterloh (eds.), *Antiquity in Antiquity: Jewish and Christian Pasts in the Greco-Roman World*. Tübingen: Mohr Siebeck, 2008, 174–216.

Richerson, Peter J. and Robert Boyd. *Not by Genes Alone: How Culture Transformed Human Evolution*. Chicago, IL: University of Chicago Press, 2005.

al-Sāmarrā'ī, Qāsim. *Kitāb al-Ridda wa'l-futūḥ and Kitāb al-Jamal wa masīr ʿĀ'isha wa-ʿAlī: A Facsimile Edition of the Fragments Preserved in the University Library of Imam Muhammad ibn Sa'ud Islamic University in Riyadh, Saudi Arabia*. Leiden: Smitzkamp Oriental Antiquarium, 1995.

Schäfer, Peter, Ya'aḳov Doiṭsch, David Grossberg, Avigail Manekin, Adina Yoffie, and Michael Meerson. *Toledot Yeshu: The Life Story of Jesus: Two Volumes and Database. Vol. 1, Introduction and Translation*. Tübingen: Mohr Siebeck, 2014.

Smith, Carl B. "Ministry, Martyrdom, and Other Mysteries: Pauline Influence on Ignatius of Antioch." In: Michael F. Bird, and Joseph R. Dodson (eds.), *Paul and the Second Century*. London and New York: T&T Clark, 2011, 37–56.

Sosis, Richard and E. Bressler. "Cooperation and Commune Longevity: A Test of the Costly Signaling Theory of Religion." *Cross-Cultural Research* 37 (2003): 211–239.

Sperber, Dan. Interview in Edge.org (2011). https://www.edge.org/3rd_culture/sperber05/sperber05_index.html. Accessed Feb 27, 2020.

Sperber, Dan. *Explaining Culture: A Naturalistic Approach*. Oxford: Blackwell, 1996.

Sperber, Dan and Deirdre Wilson. *Relevance: Communication & Cognition*. Oxford: Blackwell, 1995.

Stanton, Graham. "Jewish Christian Elements in the Pseudo-Clementine Writings." In: Oskar Skarsaune and Reidar Hvalvik (eds.), *Jewish Believers in Jesus: The Early Centuries*. Peabody, MA: Hendrickson, 2007, 305–324.

Stökl Ben Ezra, Daniel (2009). "An Ancient List of Christian Festivals in Toledot Yeshu: Polemics as Indication for Interaction." *The Harvard Theological Review* 102 (2009): 481–496.

Ting, Rachel Sing-Kiat and Terri Watson. "Is Suffering Good? An Explorative Study on the Religious Persecution among Chinese Pastors." *Journal of Psychology & Theology* 35 (2007): 202–210.

Turner, Jonathan H., Alexandra Maryanski, Anders Klostergaard Petersen, and Armin Geertz. *The Emergence and Evolution of Religion by Means of Natural Selection*. New York and London: Routledge, 2017.

Uchida, Seiji. "Relevance and Text." In: Robyn Carston, and Seiji Uchida (eds.), *Relevance Theory: Applications and Implications*. Amsterdam and Philadelphia, Pa.: J. Benjamins, 1998, 161–178.

Vähäkangas, Päivi. "Christian Identity and Intra-Christian Polemics in the Pseudo-Clementines." In: Raimo Hakola, Nina Nikki, and Päivi Vähäkangas (eds.), *Others and the Construction of Early Christian Identities*. Helsinki: The Finnish Exegetical Society, 2013, 217–235.

Whittingham, Martin. *Early Muslim Views of the Apostle Paul: Origins and Implications*. 24.2.2015. https://www.cmcsoxford.org.uk/resources/multimedia/early-muslim-views-of-the-apostle-paul-origins-and-implications. Accessed 27.2.2020. [Lecture recording].

Whittingham, Martin. *A History of Muslim Views of the Bible: The Bible and Muslim Identity Formation (7th to 11th century CE)*. Berlin: De Gruyter, 2020.

Wilson, D.S., and E.O. Wilson. "Rethinking the Theoretical Foundation of Sociobiology." *The Quarterly Review of Biology* 82 (2007): 327–348.

Ylikoski, Petri and Tomi Kokkonen. *Evoluutio ja ihmisluonto* ["Evolution and Human Nature"]. Helsinki: Gaudeamus, 2009.

CHAPTER 7

Death in the "Contact Zone": An Analysis of Ibn Ḥanbal's Hadith about a Hairdresser-Mother and Her Sons (*Ḥadīṯ al-Māšiṭa*)

Anna-Liisa Rafael and Joonas Maristo

The famous ninth-century hadith collector and jurist Ibn Ḥanbal (780–855 CE) relates a story about a woman, a hairdresser (*al-māšiṭa*) in the Pharaoh's court, who ended up being killed with her sons at the Pharaoh's command. We suggest that the story transmitted by Ibn Ḥanbal attests to the reception of the story of the mother and her seven sons in early Islamic tradition.* In other words, the hadith concerning the hairdresser and her sons—henceforth, *Ḥadīṯ al-Māšiṭa*—shares in the popular martyrological narrative tradition, well known in both late antique Christian and rabbinic literature.[1] By the time the story of the mother and her sons enters hadith literature, it has been connected with the Prophet Muhammad's nocturnal journey, as well as with a cluster of narratives relating stories of infants who spoke miraculously. These two narrative frames together with the story of the hairdresser and her sons itself are instructive of the ways in which the story of the mother and her seven sons was

* This article results from the cooperation between the authors and represents as a whole their shared views. As for the division of labour, Maristo has mostly worked on the hadith material discussed in this article, mapping out the references to the "beautiful fragrance" and the "infants who spoke" in hadith literature, and Rafael has brought to the analysis the comparative material from outside hadith literature, including biblical, early Jewish and Christian, rabbinic and early Islamic sources, as well as the theoretical background of the approach. While the reception history of the story of the mother and her seven sons in Islamic literature as a whole remains mostly an unexplored territory, we have not come across any attempts to trace it in hadith literature in particular. We wish to thank Dr. Ibrahim Bassal for bringing *Ḥadīṯ al-Māšiṭa* to our attention.

1 The earliest written versions of the story of the mother and her seven sons are preserved in the books of the Maccabees (2 Macc 7:1–41; 4 Macc 8 ff.). In Western scholarship, the mother and her seven sons are thus often called "Maccabean martyrs". Yet, both "Maccabean" and "martyrs" are notions that align with early Christian reception of this story, while the mother and her seven sons are not called Maccabean nor martyrs in the books of the Maccabees, rabbinic or Islamic literature. Our choice to speak generically about the story of the mother and her seven sons, not the Maccabean martyrs, in the context of the first millennium CE is an attempt to defy the boundaries of the early Christian tradition, Western versions of which often dominate in scholarly views of the period.

 | DOI:10.1163/9789004471160_008

integrated into the Islamic tradition and, perhaps, also of the ways in which it was transmitted to early Muslims.

Imagined boundaries and metaphors of exclusive identity construction are often dominant in the historical study of exchanges between adherents to different religions that are still often conceived of as separate. A study that seeks to understand the reception of a known Jewish-Christian story in Islamic literature would thus be expected to ask, how is the story "Islamicized", i.e., how it is made Islamic in a way that violates its previous Jewish and/or Christian character? We suggest, however, that the story of the mother and her sons not only has a life of its own in hadith literature, but that *Ḥadīṯ al-Māšiṭa* may also best be conceptualized as a product of a "contact zone" between and within religious traditions: in light of our analysis, *Ḥadīṯ al-Māšiṭa* becomes readable in conversation with other stories of the mother and her sons, the popular martyrological narrative tradition found within late antique Jewish and Christian literature, and frameworks attested within early Islamic hadith literature, namely the Prophet Muhammad's nocturnal journey and a narrative *topos* concerning "infants who spoke".[2]

1 The Story of the Mother and Her Sons as a Shared Narrative Tradition

The story of the mother and her seven sons is an established reference in both Jewish and Christian studies, though in the latter, it often goes by the name of "the Maccabean martyrs": the oldest known versions of this story are traced to Hellenistic Jewish literature, the books of the Maccabees,[3] which contain two different accounts of the execution of seven brothers by the order of

2 For the concept of "contact zone", see Pratt 2008, 7–8, and for its application to late antique encounters between Jews, Christians, and Muslims, see Hasan-Rokem 2016, 121–122.

3 Of the four books of the Maccabees found in the fifth-century Codex Alexandrinus, the second and the fourth relate the story of the mother and her seven sons. The books of the Maccabees are counted among the so-called Old Testament Apocrypha, or Pseudepigrapha, that is, Jewish Greek literature that was written during the late second temple period and was preserved by Christian communities. Most scholars hold that Hellenistic Jewish literature was received "again" in Jewish circles only towards the end of the first millennium, to a great extent due to a Hebrew paraphrase of "Josephus's history", *Sefer Yosippon*; see Stemberger 1992; Dönitz 2009. Viewed—anachronistically—from the perspective of Jewish and Christian canons, the books of the Maccabees are excluded from the Jewish canon of scriptures and partly included in Christian scriptures (sometimes distinguished there as the "Old Testament Apocrypha" or "deuterocanonical literature"). Yet, the canonicity/non-canonicity of scriptures does not indicate lack of renown or use of any scriptures; in contrast, many texts

the Seleucid ruler Antiochus IV Epiphanes and the subsequent death of their mother (2 Maccabees 7:1–41; 4 Maccabees 8:1 ff.).[4] 2 Maccabees tells the story of the mother and her seven sons as one incident among others that stem from the period that preceded the Maccabean Revolt and the rise of the semi-independent Hasmonean dynasty in Judea (ca. 140–116 BCE). The book's main focus is on Judas the Maccabee, the leader of the popular resistance movement against the Seleucids (see, e.g., 2 Macc 2:19–22); yet, the chapter concerning the mother and her seven sons becomes "the most famous chapter of our book, whether in the original, in translation, or in secondary versions, both Jewish and Christian, beginning with the Talmud and the midrash and through the Middle Ages" (Schwartz 2008, 298). 4 Maccabees places excessive emphasis on the mother and her sons, portraying this family as a representative of the whole Hebrew nation (Van Henten 1997, 212).

Regardless of various differences between the story of the mother and her seven sons in 2 Maccabees and 4 Maccabees, the basic story line is recognizably similar in both these books insofar as seven sons of a mother are taken captive by a "tyrant" who forces them to violate their ancestral commands by eating pork (2 Macc 7:1; 4 Macc 8:1–3). As they refuse the king's command, they are killed one by one. The mother stands at the scene, comforting and supporting her sons by her presence and words (2 Macc 7:5, 21–23; 4 Macc 8:4; 15:12, 14–15; 16:15–23). At the execution of her last, youngest son, the tyrant orders her to involve herself by persuading her son to save his life, but the mother only urges him on (2 Macc 7:25–28; 4 Macc 12:6–8). In the end, she too dies (2 Macc 7:41; 4 Macc 17:1).

From early on, Christians took this story "from the Maccabees" as a story of martyrdom that provided a useful example for Christians to admire and emulate.[5] Since the late fourth century, the mother and her sons have an annual feast in the Christian calendar of saints.[6] Their relics are discovered (or

---

dubbed "apocryphal" and "non-canonical" have been used more widely than "canonical" ones and, to state the obvious, rarely with these attributes.

4 Antiochus IV Epiphanes ruled the Seleucid Empire from 175 until 164 BCE. The uprising of the Jews in Judea during his reign and the establishment of the Hasmonean state that followed have a stronger historical basis than the persecution stories, some of which are most certainly legendary. On the growth of the persecution motif in the Maccabean historiography, see Honigman 2014, 229–258.

5 The earliest Christian writers, in whose works this idea emerges, are Hippolytus of Rome, Origen of Alexandria, and Cyprian of Carthage.

6 The earliest dated Syriac manuscript (British Library Add. 12150) contains a martyrology, which mentions the mother and her seven sons; see Witakowski 1994, 164. For the emergence of the cult of the Maccabees, see, e.g., Rouwhorst 2004.

invented) at Antioch during the same century and a commemorative shrine (or several) is established.[7] Christians regarded the Maccabees as martyrs of Christ: even though they had died for the Law of Moses, they had done so in a manner that was analogous with the manner in which Christians had died for Christ. The fact that Christians identified the Law of their Old Testament as the Christ further helped them to recognize the mother and her seven sons as martyrs. This story gained particular importance among Christians because its events had taken place before Christ: the mother and her seven sons could be taken as a prefiguration of the church and her martyrs, as protomartyrs who could miraculously bear witness to Christ before Christ, and as a bridge between "the old" and "the new" (from a Christian perspective).[8]

In rabbinic literature, the story of the mother and her seven sons is not explicitly associated with the Maccabees (books or people).[9] It is known in four versions, which are interrelated yet distinctive.[10] One version of the story is preserved in *Lamentations Rabbah* (1.16), a late antique rabbinic commentary on Lamentations, as a comment on the verse "For these things I weep" (Lam 1:16).[11]

---

7 Some scholars maintain that a Jewish cult of the Maccabees preceded the Christian cult at Antioch; see, e.g., Ziadé 2007, 55–65. Others find no evidence for a Jewish cult nor for the presence of any relics before Christians possessed them; yet, they argue for the significance of the memory of the mother and her seven sons for the Antiochene Jewish community; see, e.g., Rutgers 2009, 35–45; Joslyn-Siemiatkoski 2009, 42–50.

8 Such perceptions of these "Maccabees" and their martyrdom are reflected in late fourth- and early fifth-century Christian homilies that were delivered on the annual feast of the Maccabees. While many scholars have taken these homilies primarily as reflecting the difficulties Christians had to portray, or even recognize, the mother and her seven sons as martyrs, they rather convey a rich spectrum of theological meanings attested to the martyrdom of these celebrated pre-Christ individuals. For a detailed analysis of the late antique Christian homilies on the Maccabees and their theological reasoning, see Rafael 2021.

9 For an overview of the Maccabees' absence in rabbinic literature, see Stemberger 1992.

10 These versions are found in *Lamentations Rabbah* 1.16; *Pesiqta Rabbati* 43; the Babylonian Talmud, *Gittin* 57b; and *Seder Eliyahu Rabbah* 30; see Cohen 2007, 325; also 1991, 55–56 n. 3. They all locate the story under Roman rule, possibly Hadrianic persecution, and none report of any command to eat pork; instead, the protagonists are called to bow down to an idol. The mother is named Miriam in them, except for the Talmud where she remains anonymous. Only according to *Pesiqta Rabbati*, the mother is also slain like her sons. All, except for the one given in *Pesiqta Rabbati*, preserve the mother's rather remarkable greetings to Abraham, who had to build only one altar, while this mother did seven. All conclude with the Psalm verse, "a joyful mother of children" (Ps 113:9). These versions, just as the various versions of the story of the mother and her seven sons in Christian literature, are attended in our article only in so far as they help to explain certain aspects of *Ḥadīṯ al-Māšiṭa*.

11 As for the Hebrew text, we have been fortunate to consult the work of Paul Mandel, who is

Lamentations is traditionally understood as a work composed by the prophet Jeremiah at the sight of the destruction of the first temple; its rabbinic commentary works on the collective memories related to the destruction of the temple by the Romans in 70 CE. Accordingly, the seven sons of a mother—named here Miriam—are executed by the order of the Roman Caesar, not the Greek king, as in the books of the Maccabees. According to Daniel Joslyn-Siemiatkoski, the story of the mother and her seven sons was "orally transformed ... in the second-century framework of failed revolt," while in the context of the Maccabean history it preceded and celebrated a successful revolt. Its rabbinic versions "offered a critique of idolatry and the imperial cult, on the one hand, [and] contemporary Christian beliefs and practices, on the other hand" (2012, 130). Galit Hasan-Rokem reads this version of the story as both a lament of loss and a fierce critique of martyrdom that points to the brutality and futility of such an ideal (2000, 117–119). While the mother of 4 Maccabees and various Christian versions gladly and even enthusiastically escorts her sons to death, the mother of *Lamentations Rabbah* loses her mind at the sight of her sons' execution and death and commits suicide at the end of the story. The Holy Spirit adds to this tragic story a quote: "a joyful mother of children" (Ps 113:9). Hasan-Rokem reads this gesture as conveying irony: "As it were, the mourning of the human mother is now the fate of the Holy Spirit, whereas the mother is now joyful to play the heroine in a plot of martyrdom."[12]

Another rabbinic version of the story is preserved in *Pesiqta Rabbati* (43.4), a collection of homiletic Midrashim.[13] Again, the story of the mother of the seven children is told in the context of persecutions, but here Miriam, a mother of seven, is paralleled with other biblical women who had also been "made barren" for some period of time, among them Hannah the mother of Samuel and Sarah the mother of Isaac. In striking contrast to her ancestresses, whose barrenness God removed after a long time of waiting, Miriam was made barren from her already existing children, when they were slain. This version is less tragic, though, as the one told in *Lamentations Rabbah*: it suggests that the mother's task was to bear her barrenness and to deliver all her sons safely to

currently preparing a critical edition of *Lamentations Rabbah*. For an English translation, see Neusner 1989, 175–178, as well as Hasan-Rokem 2000, 115–117.

12 Hasan-Rokem 2000, 119.

13 The verse commented on is: "So the Lord remembered Hannah, and she conceived, and bore three sons and two daughters" (1 Sam 2:21) and it is joined to the Psalm verse "The Lord our God ... caused a woman to dwell barren in her house in order to make her the joyful mother of children" (Ps 113:9). The texts of all the extant Hebrew manuscripts are given in Ulmer 1999, 951–983; an English translation by Braude 1968, 745–768, is based on an eclectic text made up of the available manuscripts (see Braude 1968, 27–28).

"the bosom of Abraham," which functions here as a reference to the preferred place in the Hereafter.[14] Moreover, the mother's barrenness shall be removed eventually, though not in this life: she is slain after her sons and God promises to make her rejoice "in the time-to-come," to where she will follow her sons.

The rabbinic versions are mutually connected, for instance, by their application of the verse "a joyful mother of children" (Ps 113:9) to the mother.[15] But they also give indications of how the story could be viewed in many lights within the rabbinic tradition: *Lamentations Rabbah* utilizes the tragic dimension of the story, illuminating by the figure of the mother the gloomy fate of Jerusalem and her children, whereas *Pesiqta Rabbati* pays stronger attention to the possible brighter future to come. Moreover, as their analyses have shown,[16] both versions manifest partaking in conversations that go beyond the rabbinic tradition, suggesting that such popular narrative traditions could be shared and function as "significant sites for comparing [one's] cultural and literary corpus with others, whether contemporaneous and neighboring or more distant in time and space" and "emerge as possible constructions of narrative dialogue in which there is cultural borrowing" (Hasan-Rokem 2003, 31).

Jewish and Christian retellings of the story of the mother and her seven sons bear witness to the interpretative potential that allows a recognizably same story to sustain many meanings through its various versions. Such interpretative potential may occasionally point to shared conversations or subtler ways of coexistence. Although the story of the mother and her seven sons is hardly an established reference in Islamic studies, we suggest that *Ḥadīṯ al-Māšiṭa* transmitted to and by Ibn Ḥanbal's *Musnad* belongs to a Jewish-Christian-Muslim "'contact zone', … not always mark[ing] an interface between recognized groupings but possibly cut[ting] through some of the groups that are usually thought of as intact" (Hasan-Rokem 2016, 122).

---

14 Braude (1968, 761 n. 15) notes, a similar reference to "the bosom of Abraham," that is, the Hereafter, is also found in Luke 16:22. Cohen (1991, 49), following Saul Liebermann, notes this expression as "one of the stock martyrological phrases that were shared (with some slight variations) by both Jews and Christians" in late antique sources.

15 The reference to Ps 113:9 and their detachment from the Maccabean history may be noted as the central features that connect all known rabbinic versions of the story. See also note 11 above.

16 See especially Hasan-Rokem and Joslyn-Siemiatkoski on the story of the mother and her seven sons in *Lamentations Rabbah* quoted above.

2 Pharaoh's Daughter's Hairdresser and Her Children in Ibn Ḥanbal's *Musnad*

Aḥmad ibn Ḥanbal (780–855 CE) was a major collector of hadith, an advocate of Sunni theology and the founder of the Hanbali school of law. His *Musnad* is an extensive hadith collection: the modern printed edition contains about 27,600 hadiths (Melchert 2006, 43). The following Arabic text is taken from *Musnad* (1997 [vol. I], 309–310).[17] We have divided the text into six parts in order to clarify the structure of *Ḥadīṯ al-Māšiṭa*, as well as our references to the text in the analysis that follows.

حَدَّثَنَا عَبْدُ اللّٰه حَدثني أَبي ثنا أَبُو عُمَرَ الضَّرِيرُ أَنَا حَمَّادُ بْنُ سَلَمَةَ عَنْ عَطَاءِ بْنِ السَّائِبِ عَنْ سَعِيدِ بْنِ جُبَيْرٍ عَنِ ابْنِ عَبَّاسٍ قَالَ:

قَالَ رَسُولُ اللّٰهِ صَلَّى اللّٰهُ عَلَيْهِ وَسَلَّمَ: لَمَّا كَانَتِ اللَّيْلَةُ الَّتِي أُسْرِيَ بِي فِيهَا، أَتَتْ عَلَيَّ رَائِحَةٌ طَيِّبَةٌ، فَقُلْتُ: يَا جِبْرِيلُ، مَا هَذِهِ الرَّائِحَةُ الطَّيِّبَةُ؟ فَقَالَ: هَذِهِ رَائِحَةُ مَاشِطَةِ ابْنَةِ فِرْعَوْنَ وَأَوْلَادِهَا. قَالَ: قُلْتُ: وَمَا شَأْنُهَا؟

قَالَ: بَيْنَا هِيَ تُمَشِّطُ ابْنَةَ فِرْعَوْنَ ذَاتَ يَوْمٍ، إِذْ سَقَطَتِ الْمِدْرَى مِنْ يَدَيْهَا، فَقَالَتْ: بِسْمِ اللّٰهِ. فَقَالَتْ لَهَا ابْنَةُ فِرْعَوْنَ: أَبِي؟ قَالَتْ: لَا، وَلَكِنْ رَبِّي وَرَبُّ أَبِيكِ اللّٰهُ. قَالَتْ: أُخْبِرُهُ بِذَلِكَ قَالَتْ: نَعَمْ. فَأَخْبَرَتْهُ فَدَعَاهَا، فَقَالَ: يَا فُلَانَةُ، وَإِنَّ لَكِ رَبًّا غَيْرِي؟ قَالَتْ: نَعَمْ، رَبِّي وَرَبُّكَ اللّٰهُ. فَأَمَرَ بِبَقَرَةٍ مِنْ نُحَاسٍ فَأُحْمِيَتْ، ثُمَّ أَمَرَ بِهَا أَنْ تُلْقَى هِيَ وَأَوْلَادُهَا فِيهَا، قَالَتْ لَهُ: إِنَّ لِي إِلَيْكَ حَاجَةً. قَالَ: وَمَا حَاجَتُكِ؟ قَالَتْ: أُحِبُّ أَنْ تَجْمَعَ عِظَامِي وَعِظَامَ وَلَدِي فِي ثَوْبٍ وَاحِدٍ، وَتَدْفِنَنَا. قَالَ: ذَلِكَ لَكِ عَلَيْنَا مِنَ الْحَقِّ. قَالَ: فَأَمَرَ بِأَوْلَادِهَا فَأُلْقُوا بَيْنَ يَدَيْهَا، وَاحِدًا وَاحِدًا، إِلَى أَنِ انْتَهَى ذَلِكَ إِلَى صَبِيٍّ لَهَا مُرْضَعٍ، كَأَنَّهَا تَقَاعَسَتْ مِنْ أَجْلِهِ، قَالَ: يَا أُمَّهْ، اقْتَحِمِي، فَإِنَّ عَذَابَ الدُّنْيَا أَهْوَنُ مِنْ عَذَابِ الْآخِرَةِ، فَاقْتَحَمَتْ

قَالَ: قَالَ ابْنُ عَبَّاسٍ: تَكَلَّمَ أَرْبَعَةٌ صِغَارٌ: عِيسَى ابْنُ مَرْيَمَ عَلَيْهِ السَّلَامُ، وَصَاحِبُ جُرَيْجٍ، وَشَاهِدُ يُوسُفَ، وَابْنُ مَاشِطَةِ ابْنَةِ فِرْعَوْنَ.

---

17 The Arabic text, apart from the full *isnād*, is also printed in parallel with an English translation in Ibn Ḥanbal 2012 (vol. II: 615–616 / hadith no. 2821) and Ibn Ḥanbal 2001 (vol. V:30–31 / hadith no. 2821). These two editions are more readable. Other versions of *Hadith al-Māšiṭa*, which are later and shorter than Ibn Ḥanbal's version, are found in the collections of Ibn Ḥibbān (1988 VII, 163 / hadith no. 2903), al-Ṭabarānī (n.d. XIV, 450–451 / hadith no. 12279) and al-Ḥākim al-Naysābūrī (1997 II, 583–584 / hadith no. 3892).

(1) ʿAbdallāh narrated to us that my father narrated to me that Abū ʿUmar al-Ḍarīr narrated to us that Ḥammād b. Salama narrated from ʿAṭāʾ b. al-Sāʾib, who narrated from Saʿīd b. Jubayr, who narrated that Ibn ʿAbbās said:

(2) The Messenger of God, may peace be upon him, said: "In the night that I was taken into the nocturnal journey (*ʾusriya bī fī-hā*), a pleasant fragrance (*rāʾiḥa ṭayyiba*) came to me (*ʾatat ʿalayya*). I said: 'O Gabriel, what is this pleasant fragrance?' He responded: 'This is the fragrance of Pharaoh's daughter's hairdresser (*māšiṭa*) and her children.'
He [Ibn ʿAbbās] said: I [the Prophet] said: 'What is her story (*wa-mā šaʾnu-hā*)?'[18]
He [Gabriel] said:

(3) One day, when she was combing the hair of Pharaoh's daughter, the comb fell down from her hands.
Then she said: 'In the name of God (*bi-sm allāh*).'
The daughter of Pharaoh said: 'My father?'
She replied: 'No, rather my Lord and the Lord of your father, God (*allāh*).'
The daughter said: 'I will inform him about this.'
She said: 'Yes.'

(4) She informed her father and he summoned the hairdresser and said: 'O so and so (*yā fulāna*), do you have a Lord other than me (*wa-inna la-ki rabban ġayrī*)?'
She said: 'Yes, my Lord and your Lord is God (*allāh*).'
Then Pharaoh ordered a cow made of copper (*fa-ʾamara bi-baqarat min nuḥās*) to be heated (*fa-ʾuḥmiyat*). Then he ordered that the hairdresser and her children be thrown inside.
She said: 'I have one request for you (*inna lī ilayka ḥāja*).'
He said: 'What is your request.'
She said: 'I would like that you gather my and my children's bones in one cloth (*uḥibbu ʾan tajmaʿu ʿiẓāmī wa ʿiẓām waladī fī ṯawb wāḥid*) and that you bury us.'[19]

---

18 Interpreted in Ibn Ḥanbal 2012 (vol. 11), 615, as "their story".

19 Interpreted in Ibn Ḥanbal 2012 (vol. 11), 616, as a passive voice: "(…) to be gathered (…) and buried".

Pharaoh replied: 'You have a right to ask this from us (*ḏālika la-ki ʿalay-nā min al-ḥaqq*).'
He ordered her children to be thrown inside [the copper cow] one by one in front of her.

(5) This ended up to her young baby boy who was still being breastfed (*ṣabiyy la-hā murḍaʿ*). It was as if she hesitated because of him (*ka-ʾanna-hā taqāʿasat min ʾajli-hi*).
They boy said: 'O mother, go ahead, for the punishment of this world (*fa-inna ʿaḏāb al-dunyā*) is easier [to bear] than the punishment of the hereafter (*ʾahwan min ʿaḏāb al-ākhirat*).' Then she went ahead."

(6) He[20] said: Ibn ʿAbbās said: Four infants (*ṣiġār*) spoke: ʿĪsā ibn Maryam, may peace be upon him, companion of Jurayj (*ṣāḥib jurayj*), witness of Joseph (*šāhid yūsif*), and the son of the hairdresser of Pharaoh's daughter (*wa-bn māšiṭa ibnat firʿawn*).

3 The Structure of *Ḥadīṯ al-Māšiṭa*

A single hadith is made of two parts: *isnād*, the chain of transmitters, and *matn*, the actual text, which is allegedly said by the Prophet (Robson 1986, 24) or another important early Muslim. *Hadith al-Māšiṭa* is no exception. For analytical purposes, we have added more parts to this basic division, dividing the *matn* that follows the *isnād* into five distinctive parts. We thus conceive the structure and contents of *Hadīth al-Māšiṭa* as follows:

1) *Isnād*
2) The first narrative framework describes the situation in which the Prophet comes across the story including the dialogue with Gabriel.

The actual story, which begins by "He [Gabriel] said," divides further into three narrative scenes:

3) The first narrative scene introduces the hairdresser (*al-māšiṭa*) and the Pharaoh's daughter.
4) The second narrative scene focuses on the hairdresser in front of the Pharaoh.
5) The third narrative scene focuses on the hairdresser and her children, the youngest son, in particular.

---

20 The subject speaking here is ambiguous. However, looking at the *isnād*, Saʿīd b. Jubayr would be the most logical candidate since he precedes Ibn ʿAbbās.

Finally, after the story:

6) The second narrative framework related by Ibn ʿAbbās connects the hadith with a story cluster of infants who spoke.

In our analysis, we tackle the various aspects of *Ḥadīṯ al-Māšiṭa* reflected in these six parts. However, the order in which we proceed is not from the first to the sixth part. Instead, we shall first discuss the parts of the hadith that tell the story of the hairdresser and her sons (parts 3–5), paying particular attention to the benefit derived from reading this story in conversation with extant Jewish and Christian traditions of the story of the mother and her seven sons. The relative independence of *Ḥadīṯ al-Māšiṭa* from the known literary versions of the story of the mother and her seven sons suggests that it may have little if any bearing on them. Our analysis illuminates, however, ways in which the version of the story transmitted by Ibn Ḥanbal may be connected with the Jewish and Christian narrative traditions concerning the mother and her seven sons, by further discussing some prominent narrative emphases in them and, perhaps, by relating the story as embedded in the contemporaneous practices. Thereafter, we turn to analysing the remaining parts (1, 2, and 6), which not only make *Ḥadīṯ al-Māšiṭa* technically and characteristically a hadith but also suggest why and how the hairdresser's story had become worth relating within the context of early Islam. Our discussion scrutinizes the two distinctive ways in which the story is identified in hadith literature and thereby integrated into the Islamic tradition: by way of the "beautiful fragrance" that brings the story to Muhammad's awareness during his nocturnal journey accompanied by Gabriel (part 2) and by way of the story cluster that concerns "infants who spoke" (part 6).

4 The Story of the Pharaoh's Daughter's Hairdresser in Ibn Ḥanbal's *Musnad*

The story told in *Ḥadīṯ al-Māšiṭa* presents a hairdresser-mother of many children as a strong, public figure and, finally, eulogizes the courage and wisdom of her youngest son, who is intimately connected to and dependent on her. This overall narrative development is discernible in most versions of the story of the mother and her seven sons. Yet, *Ḥadīṯ al-Māšiṭa* transmitted by Ibn Ḥanbal, as well as the related versions preserved in hadith literature, is in many ways exceptional in comparison to Jewish and Christian versions of the story of the mother and her seven sons previous to or contemporaneous with it. To give an example, it is the only known version that provides the heroine of the story with a profession, other than being a single parent. The entire opening scene of the story that apparently takes place between women only (part 3) does not have any parallels in Jewish and Christian traditions, which begin directly from a public scene where a woman and her sons are taken to the king (cf. part 4). The mother figure is typically concerned with ensuring her offspring's eternal fate in the hereafter, rather than being worried about their more immediate needs; yet, her care-taking of her and her sons' remains *on earth* after their death takes her foresightedness to an unprecedented level.

Regardless of these and other various differences, we aim to demonstrate in what follows how *Ḥadīṯ al-Māšiṭa* shares in the popular narrative tradition concerning the mother and her seven sons known in the extant early and late antique Jewish and Christian literature and, in fact, converses with it in some quite remarkable ways. To grasp these narrative conversations, it is important to pay attention to both the similarities and the differences between the various versions of the story. We shall approach the story told in *Ḥadīṯ al-Māšiṭa* from three perspectives in order to show how it can be placed within the context of the popular narrative tradition concerning the mother and her seven sons shared by Jews and Christians. These perspectives are: (1) the testimonies of faith, which in the case of *Ḥadīṯ al-Māšiṭa* only the hairdresser-mother gives; (2) the mother's foresighted negotiations with Pharaoh concerning her and her sons' bones, which is a development that possibly reflects the interface with the cult of the saints; and, finally, (3) the mother's dialogue with her youngest son that contains both a surprising move from the subject of the mother to the subject of her last, infant son and the themes of final judgment and the earning of eternal life, which are typical of the popular narrative tradition concerning the mother and her seven sons.

4.1 *The Hairdresser's Testimonies of Faith* (*parts 3 and 4*)

In *Ḥadīṯ al-Māšiṭa*, the hairdresser gives a testimony of faith twice. First (in part 3), the setting seems rather private and harmless. Reportedly, only two women, the hairdresser and the Pharaoh's daughter, are present. The hairdresser is combing the Pharaoh's daughter's hair, when she accidentally drops the comb onto the floor. Spontaneously, she cries out: "In the name of God!" Somewhat unexpectedly, the event turns into a trial of faith by way of the Pharaoh's daughter's innocent response to her cry: "[Did you mean the Pharaoh,] My father?" The hairdresser answers: "No." Without further questions, she gives an account of her faith: "… rather my Lord and the Lord of your father, God." The Pharaoh's daughter responds, as if in a standard manner, that she shall have to inform her father about this incident. The hairdresser does not try to prevent her but consents. In the scene that follows (part 5), the Pharaoh's daughter informs her father about the incident. By this transition, she disappears and the attention shifts to the encounter between the hairdresser and the

Pharaoh; the setting of the events is no longer the private room of the Pharaoh's daughter but more public and thus more similar to persecution narratives in Jewish and Christian versions, which typically set their hero(ine)s in a public space.

The Pharaoh presents a straightforward question to the hairdresser, providing her with a new chance either to refute or to confirm her testimony: "Do you have another Lord than me?" She again answers more fully than necessary, now addressing the Pharaoh directly: "Yes, my Lord and your Lord is God." The resemblance between this brief dialogue and the one that takes place between the boys and Caesar in the version of the story told in *Lamentations Rabbah* (1.16) is worthy of attention. In it, the boys are told to "bow down before the idol". When they refuse, their persecutor asks: "Why not?" Each of the boys present as their grounds something that "is written in the Torah": the first, "I am the Lord, your God," and the second, "You shall have no other gods before me."[21] The boys' answers comprise the first of the commandments given to Moses at Sinai that forbids the worship of other gods than the one God: "I am the Lord your God, who brought you out of the land of Egypt, out of the house of slavery. You shall have no other gods before me" (Ex 20:2–3; Deut 5:6–7). Caesar does not further question their commitments but orders them to be slain.

The Pharaoh's question and the hairdresser's answer are reminiscent of the first commandment: the Pharaoh's question echoes God's command that the Israelites should have no other god than the one God, and the hairdresser's answer places God in the place which the Pharaoh wanted to reserve for himself.[22] The difference is that the boys in *Lamentations Rabbah* derive their principles from scriptures, identifying themselves with the Torah and as its careful students, whereas the confession of the hairdresser has no comparable point of reference. She shows no commitment to any scriptures but speaks, as it were, "from the tablet of her heart" (Prov 3:3; 2 Cor 3:3). The similarity of these confessions suggests, however, that the story told in *Ḥadīṯ al-Māšiṭa* also arises from the juxtaposition between monotheism and idolatry.

The hairdresser does not have a (particular) "religion" (*dīn*) or "law" (*šarīʿa*). The simple phrase "*bismillāh*"—"in the name of God"—counts as her initial

21 Trans. Neusner 1989, 175. These verses are also found in the version transmitted in the Babylonian Talmud (*Gittin* 57b), not however in *Pesiqta Rabbati* 43.4.

22 *Rabbuka*, according to Neuwirth (2016, 193), is the usual identification of God used throughout the Meccan *sūras*. It aligns, as she notes, with "the Lord" (*kyrios*), which is the standard translation of the *tetragrammaton* since the Septuagint. The phrasings in *Ḥadīṯ al-Māšiṭa* do not, however, resemble the Hebrew text of Exodus or Deuteronomy, nor its Greek, Aramaic or Syriac translations, nor the *šahāda* or the verse in *Sūra Ṭāhā* (20:14).

confession in front of the Pharaoh's daughter. Yet, it is enough to trigger the Pharaoh's daughter's question—"My father?"—and the further confession of the hairdresser, which leads her to a larger and more public arena. In the books of the Maccabees, as well as other accounts that put particular emphasis on the Jewishness of the protagonists, the trial has to do with eating pork, an act prohibited by the Mosaic Law. This theme often emphasizes the distinctiveness of Jews among all other nations, which they maintained by the observance of their own particular ancestral customs.[23] In various Christian versions of the story, the law (*nomos*) of the mother and her sons is taken as a direct reference to Christ, thus the pronounced Jewishness of the protagonists is converted into an as-pronounced Christian-ness.[24] In light of such readings, the cause of the mother and her seven sons introduces an identity-political dimension in the shared narrative tradition. In comparison to the above examples underlining the Jewishness or Christian-ness of the protagonists, the hairdresser's cause is "simply monotheistic" insofar as it claims that there is some higher being and authority than the Pharaoh. The confession serves to provoke the Pharaoh, but not to most Muslims, as well as Jews and Christians, who could have easily adhered to the mother's universal recognition of a higher God.

The story told in *Ḥadīṯ al-Māšiṭa* also utilizes the motif of an arrogant tyrant, also obvious in the books of the Maccabees and several other versions of the story: the hairdresser lowers the Pharaoh—who thinks of himself as a god—to the level of a human being. In the Qur'an, the Pharaoh is mentioned fifty times and seen negatively both as a tyrant and someone who denies the "signs of God" (3:11; 7:103; 8:52; 10:90; 14:6 etc.). According to the Qur'an, the Pharaoh and his people were a disobedient people who had rejected the divine signs and ridiculed them (e.g. 43:46–54). Situating the mother and her sons in this context, *Ḥadīṯ al-Māšiṭa* may suggest that their story had been another such sign, a message of the supremacy of the one God delivered to the Pharaoh and ignored by him. The hairdresser, then, would count as a kind of a prophetic figure, another chapter in the prophetic history. At the same time, however, the

23 This cause (*laḥm al-khinzīr*) is also found in a version preserved in al-Mālaṭī's *Kitāb al-tanbīh w'al-radd* (1936, 78), even though the mother of the seven sons is called Sāra in this story and the historical context is simply that of the "children of Israel".

24 In late antique Christian representations of this Maccabean story, the protagonists' extreme Jewishness is recreated in order that it may be "revealed" as their Christian-ness before Christ. Augustine even reports of Jewish claims of ownership of these martyrs in order that he may absolutely reject just claims. This should not be taken as adequate evidence in support of the proposition that actual Jews would have claimed or commemorated these figures as their martyrs but, rather, reflects the late antique Christian project of establishing a Christian identity vis-à-vis a Jewish one; see Rafael 2021.

story told in *Ḥadīṯ al-Māšiṭa* may seem to contradict *Sūra al-Baqara* (2:49): "the people of Pharaoh, who afflicted you with the worst torment, slaughtering your [newborn] sons and keeping your females alive"; according to *Ḥadīṯ al-Māšiṭa*, the Pharaoh shows no intention whatsoever to keep females alive.

In *Ḥadīṯ al-Māšiṭa*, the hairdresser's confession is presented as a rather accidental and spontaneous slip of the tongue in a markedly everyday situation; yet, its consequences show how the believers in one God could end up persecuted and might be slain at any given moment without any protection. It should be noted, however, that the Pharaoh's daughter appears as a friendly or, at least, neutral figure. In fact, as stories about her in the Hebrew Bible suggest that she converted to Judaism and took the name Bityah ("the daughter of the Lord"; cf. 1 Chron 4:18), one might speculate whether her encounter with her hairdresser's confession could have initiated her later conversion. The Pharaoh, instead, acts like any other tyrant: he gives an order that the means of torture are prepared—here, that a cow (*baqara*) made of copper be heated—so that the mother and her sons shall be punished.[25] This gesture suggests that such equipment was standardly on display at the Pharaoh's court. Thus, on the one hand, the narrative setting of *Ḥadīṯ al-Māšiṭa* with its strange place of events stands in stark contrast with other surviving versions of the story of the mother and her seven sons, each of which place the protagonists amidst famous persecutions of either Antiochus IV Epiphanes, the Roman Caesars, or kings in general.[26] On the other hand, however, the persecutions implied in *Ḥadīṯ al-Māšiṭa* may resemble the somewhat generic persecutions, characteristic of the time of ignorance (*jāhilīyya*). In Muslim memories, the pious people of the pre-Islamic past were constantly under the threat of persecution—a small group that survived in an ever-hostile environment—and thus the Pharaoh could be viewed as their persecutor as much as any other foreign power.[27] As

25 A "bronze bull", into which people were thrown to be roasted alive, is known from traditions concerning Phalaris, a sixth-century BCE ruler of Acragas. John S. Rundin (2004, 431) lists various ancient Greek authors who attest to this means of torture (see also Diehl & Donnelly 2011, 37). In other versions of the story of the mother and her seven sons, there are no mentions of a means of torture in the shape of any animal; the method of roasting or boiling is, however, common.

26 Notably, other versions of the story of the mother and her seven sons or references to it in Islamic literature attest to other historical contexts: al-Mālaṭī, for instance, simply situates the story in the time of *banū isrā'īl* (1936, 78); according to Vajda (1937, 96), this attribution originates within Islamic tradition. Regardless of the different possibilities regarding their historicity, the fame of the persecutions is quite legendary in both cases.

27 Michael Pregill discusses an interesting "Fāṭimid propaganda work", which could date to the ninth century CE (cf. Pregill 2014, 46). It contains a sympathetic interpretation of the situation of Moses and the Israelites in Egypt as that of persecutions by Pharaoh (see

we shall see, the theme of persecution is also prevalent in several Islamic narratives concerning the "infants who spoke".

Although the Pharaoh fits naturally into the role of the arrogant tyrant in the early Islamic context, the setting of the events would probably have struck fellow Christians and Jews as strange. Though familiar with Egypt at the time of the pharaohs as the "house of slavery", this historical context does not become persecutionized—to coin a verb—in the memories of Jews and Christians to an extent that popular persecution stories would be rooted into it. Instead, the Roman emperors are by far the most typical persecutors in late antique Jewish and Christian writings, in addition to the memories of the Seleucid ruler Antiochus IV Epiphanes; in the east, the kings of the Sasanian Empire and, later on, the Arab sultans would take on this role. Thus, both the Egypt of the pharaohs as the place of events and the Pharaoh's daughter's hairdresser as the profession of the mother are elements unattested in the narrative tradition concerning the mother and her sons, except for the versions preserved in hadith collections.

Yet, Egypt at the time of the pharaohs is not an insignificant place in the history of the "children of Israel". Biblical figures such as Joseph[28] and Moses,[29] as well as Jesus,[30] spent important periods of their life in Egypt. The Pharaoh's daughter features prominently in Moses's birth legend according to Exodus: Moses's mother put her baby in a plastered papyrus basket and placed the basket among the reeds on the bank of the river for the Pharaoh's daughter to

Pregill 2014, esp. 37–39). Pregill notes, however, that the Israelites were not persecuted "for their heroic principles or struggle for justice, as was the case with the *ahl al-bayt*; rather, they were passive victims of Pharaoh's tyranny, not being singled out for any particular beliefs or principled stance". Even so, and regardless of the overall critical stance adapted in the work towards the *sunna* of Israel, such a historical predecessor could be "a rather obvious and rhetorically useful one" from the *Šīʿite* perspective with respect to how they wanted to represent themselves and the Umayyads. In *Ḥadīṯ al-Māšiṭa*, the situation in Egypt is depicted as having to do not only with persecutions but also with "particular beliefs or principled stance", enabling an analogy between this historical context and later ones based on the similarity of the contents of the confession throughout times.

28 In the Hebrew Bible, the latter half of Genesis (Gen 37, 39–50) relates the stories concerning Joseph in Egypt; outside the surah dedicated to him (*Sūra Yūsuf*), his name is mentioned twice in the Qur'an (6:84; 40:34).

29 In the Hebrew Bible, the beginning of Exodus (Ex 2–13) relates stories about Moses in Egypt before he led the Israelites towards the "promised land"; Moses (*Mūsā*) is mentioned in the Qur'an 145 times by name.

30 The Gospel of Matthew (2:13–23) relates the story of baby Jesus and his parents' flight to Egypt after his birth in Bethlehem, and a wealth of traditions concerning this trip are preserved in Apocryphal Gospels later on. Rabbinic literature also suggest that Jesus spent a lengthy time in Egypt and that he "brought forth witchcraft from Egypt by means of scratches upon his flesh" (Schäfer 2007, 16).

find. Then Moses's mother sent Moses's sister Miriam to guide the Pharaoh's daughter, so that she might assign Moses's birth mother as his nurse before his adoption to the Pharaoh's daughter (Ex 2:1–10).[31] Coincidentally, some of the known rabbinic and Christian versions of the story of the mother and her seven sons call the mother by the name Miriam.[32] This name could have encouraged the location of the story of the mother and her seven sons in Egypt, Moses's sister being the most famous Miriam in Jewish tradition.

The profession of the heroine of *Ḥadīṯ al-Māšiṭa* as a hairdresser—unattested in no other surviving versions of the story of the mother and her seven sons—could also be intertwined with late antique traditions related to another Miriam. For some Talmudic passages present the mother of Jesus, definitely the most famous Miriam in the Christian tradition, as a women's hairdresser.[33] The rabbinic image of Miriam the hairdresser possibly confuses Mary the mother of Jesus with Mary of Magdala, the prostitute who became Jesus's close follower, whose name could have be transmitted into Aramaic as hairdresser (*megadla*). The result is an image of the mother of Jesus as a woman who had a son outside her marriage and who was a known harlot.[34] Thus, although the hairdresser-mother of the hadith and Miriam the hairdresser have a common profession, Miriam's profession serves in rabbinic literature together with references to her own long hair to connote her unchastity and even infidelity (Schäfer 2007, 17–18). Instead, the mother's profession in *Ḥadīṯ al-Māšiṭa* seems perfectly respectable: being the Pharaoh's daughter's hairdresser does not mean that her own hair would have been unfastened in public and it does not do away her implied exemplary morals and, consequently, her high status.[35]

---

31 Some of the versions of the story of the mother and her seven sons in rabbinic literature name the mother Miriam (*bat Naḥtum/Tanḥum*).

32 Indeed, the mother is known by this name it all the known rabbinic versions except for the Babylonian Talmud. Bensly and Barnes provide one Syriac version of the story in which the mother is called Miriam and which begins: "My beloved, there was in Antioch of Syria a certain woman of the children of Israel whose name was Mary and her seven sons in the days of the profane and wicked Antiochus" (1895, xxxv).

33 The Babylonian Talmud (*Shabbat* 104b) identifies Jesus's mother as "[Miriam], (the woman who) let (her) women's [hair] grow long (*megadla* [*seʿar*] *neshayya*)"; the text is reconstructed by Schäfer 2007, 16.

34 Schäfer (2007, 98–99) takes this image as "the Jewish answer to the Christian propaganda of the divine origin of Jesus." *Sūra Maryam* also reflects the accusations of unchastity that arouse when Mary gave birth to a fatherless son (19:27–28; the same section also calls Mary "sister of Aaron," possibly confusing her with Miriam, the sister of Moses and Aaron). Yet, as Jesus's miraculous birth is accounted and accepted in the Qur'an, its perspective on Mary is defensive.

35 In another Talmudic passage (*Hagigah* 4b), Miriam the women's hairdresser features

The story of the hairdresser and her sons fits well into the company of other so-called *isrāʾīliyyāt*, which often refer back to an unspecified past and the "pious [people] of the old".[36] The purpose of this past could be to provide not only edifying examples, but also the message revealed in the Qurʾan with a predecessor: to recount stories of "monotheists" who in their simple and straightforward faith were reminiscent of Muslims (though, as noted, not Muslims exclusively). The story of the hairdresser and her children highlights the timeless and universal character of the faith in one God, confirming that Muhammad did not invent something new but inherited and proclaimed something ancient and eternal. Thus, the hairdresser seems to function in *Ḥadīṯ al-Māšiṭa* in a way that is aligned to many other biblical characters (such as Abraham etc.): she roots the true faith in one God in a distant past and bears witness to it among the ignorant non-believers long before the Prophet proclaimed it.

This interpretation is in line with the elevated status of the mother in the narrative tradition shared by Christians and Jews alike and, perhaps, in particular in the Christian attempts to recast their story as foreshadowing faith in Christ. Yet, in *Ḥadīṯ al-Māšiṭa*, the mother is elevated in a distinct way: she is a woman with a profession who readily and cool-headedly presents her confession alone in front of the Pharaoh; her task is not to support silently the confessions of her sons. *Ḥadīṯ al-Māšiṭa* shows that the mother's popularity is greater than that of her sons. If, indeed, the hairdresser's confession was a sign of God (to the Pharaoh as well as later believers), she would in the hadith become a kind of prophetess.

4.2 *The Hairdresser's Foresighted Request (part 4)*

Having made her confession in front of the Pharaoh, the hairdresser-mother engages in a further conversation with the Pharaoh. A comparable dialogue is not attested in any of the extant Jewish and Christian versions of the story, in which the persecutor addresses the mother towards the end of the story, if

together with Miriam the raiser of babies without any connection to Jesus and also with no negative connotations.

36 *Isrāʾīliyyāt* is an Arabic term covering three types of narratives: complementary information of the often-summary accounts of the Qurʾan with respect to the personalities of the Bible; narratives of the ancient Israelites (*banū isrāʾīl*) and folklore fables sometimes borrowed from Jewish sources (Vajda 1997, 211–212). Albayrak (2001, 78–79) discusses the role of the *quṣṣāṣ* who would fashion "tales with a good moral around biblical and Qurʾanic stories and legends in which the stories of the prophets loom large, (…) supplemented by other legends from ancient stories and folklore." Characteristic of these tales was a focus on "the pious people of old" who would embody warnings and rebukes, as well as function as edifying examples. See also Abbot 1967, 14–15.

at all.[37] Thus, the short dialogue between her and the Pharaoh only strengthens the tendency already apparent in our story, namely, that the mother is in the centre of the narrative focus, a proactive character accompanied by her sons, not the other way around. Moreover, the hairdresser-mother's foresighted request may imply some points of convergence with other traditions concerning the mother and her sons.

After the woman learns from the Pharaoh's order that she and her sons are going to be thrown into the copper cow, she briefly interferes with the procedure, asking to make a request to the Pharaoh. Quite remarkably, the Pharaoh considers her wish appropriate and consents to hearing it. The woman asks the Pharaoh to gather her and her children's bones in one cloth and to bury them. Her request shows not only full acceptance of the Pharaoh's order and the forthcoming death of her and her children, but also her wise foresight. Unlike in several other extant versions of the story,[38] the mother's fear for her children's possible weakness in the face of death is not recorded in *Ḥadīṯ al-Māšiṭa* but, instead, her concern for the preservation of their remains on earth. The Pharaoh regards this request as reasonable, thus agreeing with her demand. He then orders her children to be thrown into the copper cow and the execution scene is resumed.

Ancient Egypt is known for its complex burial rituals, at least as far as the elite was concerned. According to Genesis, Joseph asks the children of Israel to carry his bones from Egypt, which is why he was embalmed and placed in a coffin in Egypt (Gen 50:25–26).[39] Yet, in late antique and early medieval contexts, bones wrapped in a cloth would most probably be associated with the relics of the saints. The cult of the saints seems to have been more or less a universal practice among Christians. The relics of saints were unearthed to be kept in churches or sanctuaries, and some of the churches or sanctuaries were built for

37 According to 2Macc 7:25–26, the tyrant urges the mother much but, according to 4Macc 12:6, there is hardly a verbal exchange between him and the mother. Gregory Nazianzen's homiletic retelling of the story in *Oration 15: In praise of the Maccabees* 9–10 makes a peculiar compromise: it does not mention any exchange between the tyrant and the mother, but presents the mother "like an Olympic champion" who "exclaimed in a loud and radiant voice" a speech of victory at the death of her sons (2003, 80–82). According to *Pesiqta Rabbati* 43.4, the last boy goes to his mother without any initiative of the persecutor. In *Lamentations Rabbah* 1.16, however, the mother addresses the Caesar without waiting to be addressed first.

38 See, e.g., Gregory Nazianzen's *Oration 15: In praise of the Maccabees* 4 & 8 (2003, 74, 79).

39 According to Exodus (Ex 13:19), moreover, "Moses took with him the bones of Joseph who had required a solemn oath of the Israelites, saying, 'God will surely take notice of you, and then you must carry my bones with you from here.'"

the purpose of their hosting. The process of making a cult of the saints was not dogmatic or abstract but involved practices concerned with the material reality and reshaping of the landscape. Tombs of the saints were mostly public places, accessible to all, and these shrines enabled forms of ritual which included the whole community.[40]

Based on late antique literary evidence, the best-known place of the relics of the mother and her seven sons was Antioch.[41] From the sixth century, there are sporadic references to the actual burial place of the mother and her seven sons at Antioch, and this city—founded by Antiochus IV Epiphanes—was sometimes even considered the place where they had been executed.[42] In addition to Antioch, the relics of the Maccabees—or, rather, parts of them—were also taken to Constantinople already in the fifth century and, later on, to Rome, as well as to the Rhineland; even today, these three sites recognize the traditions related to their possession of the so-called relics of the Maccabees.[43] Meanwhile in the east, the mother and her seven sons became very popular saints among Syriac-speaking Christians. The mother is usually called Šmūnī; this name appears already in Aphrahat's Demonstration 5 (*On Wars*, 20) and it continues to be used widely (Witakowski 1994, 153–164). Consequently, the mother often goes by the name Ašmūnī in Arabic (Abdalla, 2009). In *Murūj al-*

40 Peter Brown's classic study (1981) is focused on Western Christianity but gives a good idea about the culture that discovered relics and gave birth to saints. Fowden (1999) provides a much more detailed presentation of interactions at and around shrines, focused on St. Sergius's shrine at Rusafa. See also Fowden 2002 on sharing holy places.

41 John Chrysostom is the first known Christian orator who speaks, as it were, in the presence of the relics (probably in Antioch) in *Homily 1 on the Maccabees* 1 (Mayer 2006, 137). In a homily written in the beginning of the fifth century, Augustine declares that the church of the Maccabees is newly built and found in Antioch; *Sermon* 300: *On the Solemnity of the Maccabee Martyrs* 6 (Hill 2014, 279).

42 If the historicity of the persecutions told in the books of the Maccabees has been discussed, the two alternatives for locations have been Jerusalem, based on 4 Maccabees, and Antioch, based on the lack of geographic information in 2 Maccabees, as well as the later renown of these Maccabees at Antioch. John Malalas provides in his chronicle (the early sixth century) a historical narrative, explaining how the Maccabees were brought from Judea to Antioch and how Judas buried their relics; *Chronicle* 8 (1986, 108–109). There is, however, great complexity regarding the exact site of the Maccabean sanctuary and its possible ownership at Antioch and nothing, to be sure, has been found in excavations; cf. Mayer & Allen 2012, 90–94.

43 Patriarchal Church of St. George in Istanbul (https://www.patriarchate.org/saintgeorge); San Pietro in Vincoli in Rome (http://corvinus.nl/2017/04/04/rome-san-pietro-in-vincoli/); Church of St. Andreas in Cologne (https://gemeinden.erzbistum-koeln.de/st_andreas_koeln/kirche/kirchenfuehrer/english/). Interestingly, each website also expresses some doubts on those traditions.

dhahab wa maʿādin al-jawāhir, in an overview of Antiochene topography, the tenth-century historian and geographer al-Masʿūdi mentions a church highly esteemed among Christians, which is dedicated to *Ašmūnīt* (1864 [vol. III], 407). In addition, according to the tenth-century *Kitāb al-diyārāt* by al-Šābuštī (2008, 46 ff.), there was a monastery not far from Baghdad built in commemoration of a woman called Ašmūnī (*dayr Ašmūnī*). In Michael Abdalla's "incomplete list" of current sanctuaries devoted to (A)Šmūnī (and her sons), there are twenty-four items in the region of Northern Iraq alone, five in Turkey, and four in Syria (Abdalla 2009, 35–38). Though definitely an indicator of the popularity of the mother and her sons among Christians in the east, this list does not give us much help regarding the past.

Yet, it is well known that the saints had great appeal for people across religious traditions, and shrines, monasteries and other sites at which saints were feasted could be famous and popular regional attractions. In addition to festivities related to the annual feast of the saints, such as liturgy or outdoor processions, the site would flourish due to trade and various kinds of entertainment.[44] Josef W. Meri demonstrates the ambiguity of Muslim attitudes to relics of the saints. On the one hand, there are numerous instances where Muslims are explicitly forbidden to visit the shrines of Christian saints and warned not to be deceived by their appeal. On the other hand, the notion of a "blessing" (*baraka*) attained through a holy man/woman while visiting his/her tomb is not exclusive to any specific tradition, but the acknowledgment of positive powers connected to saintly figures or their remains—though diversely conceived—was part of the religious and cultural *koine* of the eastern Mediterranean (Meri 1999; 2002). Al-Šābuštī *Kitāb al-diyārāt* implies an interesting perspective onto the holiness of a saint's shrine. The book is organized into chapters named after monasteries and each chapter opens with a general description of the site, informing the reader about its attractions, including the time of its feast. These descriptions suggest that both Christians and Muslims would attend the monastery during its feast; yet, a Muslim visitor might enjoy from a distance the processions and other official festivities, smelling the incense, hearing the chanting and, perhaps, witnessing a local miracle, which would add to the natural attractions of the site.[45] As a *dayr* would stand not just for a church building

44 Hilary Kilpatrick (1999, 218) summarizes that the monastery was a pleasure garden which included all the dimensions of a paradise on earth, providing the visitor with an irresistible "combination of beautiful natural surroundings, freely available wine, and at least the prospect of amorous adventures." See also Fowden 2007, 12–13; Campbell 2009, 20.

45 *Kitāb al-diyārāt* is divided into three parts, two first of which seem to list monasteries geographically. The first of them has no title, or it has not been preserved, but the second one

but for cells for monks, for shops and taverns, and for fields and water supply (Sourdel 1965, 194), Muslims seemed, according to al-Šābuštī, be primarily encouraged to visit the site because the paradise-like atmosphere and the outdoor activities that provided such a contrast to the urban setting, as well as by the monastery's wine production;[46] as for the festivities, *Kitāb al-diyārāt* does not suggest that the Muslim visitors would have entered the sanctuaries or that they would have listened to any readings or homilies.[47]

The insertion of the hairdresser's request concerning their relics to Pharaoh could be observed against the backdrop of this religious and cultural *koine* of the eastern Mediterranean. Her plain but detailed instructions to the Pharaoh to wrap and bury the bodies could retrospectively explain why her and her children's bones would still be wrapped in a cloth and buried somewhere. At least, a reader or hearer of the hadith could imagine them still to exist and be kept somewhere. If he/she was familiar with a site that hosted their relics, the woman's instructions on their preservation could lend credibility to that site, while the site would reaffirm the historicity of the events described in the hadith. Existing relics would serve as the story's material documentation, while the story would narrate the significance of the site and authenticate the relics it hosted.[48] All in all, both the hadith and the relics would reinforce the hairdresser-mother's prophetic quality and authority: although the Pharaoh ordered her sons and herself to be killed, she had been foresighted enough to know that their relics need to be well taken care of and she, too, had made an order with lasting effects.

Now, if a site of the mother's and her sons' relics existed, could it have been not only known by but also accessible to Muslims? As we have no evidence for Muslim sites of veneration of the mother and her sons, apart from a few

is titled: "The monasteries of Egypt, which are intended for drinking and pleasure, including … [the description of the first monastery follows]" (2008, 284). The third part, then, is titled: "The monasteries famous for the miracles, according to what is remembered and characterized of them by their people. Among them are … [the description of the first monastery follows]" (2008, 300).

46 According to Sourdel (1965, 195), a Muslim visitor would be "free to drink as much wine as they wished" at the *dayr*.

47 Other Muslim accounts suggest a much closer contact and, at least, a more in-depth awareness of what was going on inside the churches (cf. Montgomery 1996).

48 John Malalas's (*Chron.* 8) retrospective description of the burial of the mother and her seven sons at Antioch, which contains a mention of some Judas who asked for their remains from their executors in order to bury them, probably reflects the authentication of their existing relics, providing them with a story of origins; the books of the Maccabees do not mention anything about their burial or relics.

contemporaneous examples,[49] it would seem appropriate to imagine a site maintained by Christians with the kind of the cultural and social atmosphere described by al-Šābuštī. Such a site could allow the possibility of maintaining two or more narrative backgrounds to the same site and its saints. The people who participated in the service, sang the songs and, perhaps, heard their story being told or saw their pictures on the walls of the sanctuary, might consider them to be saints who had died at the time of the Maccabees, whereas the people at a further distance could also take them as having once upon a time courageously confessed their faith in God at Pharaoh's court. Shared spaces could enable mutual contacts as well as relative distances.[50]

4.3 *The Hairdresser in Dialogue with Her Last Son (part 5)*

The third and the final scene of the story transmitted by Ibn Ḥanbal's *Musnad* focuses on the hairdresser and her children, the youngest son, in particular. The hairdresser's children are thrown into the copper cow, one by one (*wāḥidan wāḥidan*).[51] There is, however, so little interest in the individual children that by this time none of them has said a word nor been addressed and the story does not even mention their number. The situation takes a new turn when the last and the youngest one is about to be killed: the hairdresser suddenly hesitates. The plausible reason for this is that he is still being breastfed, lying in his mother's arms. The baby boy notices his mother's insecurity and gives her a persuasive piece of advice: "the punishment of this world (*fa-inna ʿaḏāb al-dunyā*) is easier [to bear] than the punishment of the hereafter (*ʾahwan min ʿaḏāb al-ākhira*)". After these words, the mother jumps into the fatal copper cow with her son.

The drama between the mother and the last son reminds one in many ways of the many other versions of the story of the mother and her sons. In most versions, something unexpected happens between the two and their private encounter is depicted as a particularly engaging moment. The young age of the boy is commented on—perhaps to stir the audience who by this point in

49 Abdalla (2009, 34–35) refers to a mosque in Mosul named "the mosque of the mother of nine", which had previously been a church commemorating Šmūnī and her sons, and there may be another, similar case in today's Iran; yet, both these cases are contemporary and, therefore, not decisive evidence for the medieval era.

50 See Fowden 2002 (esp. 125–129) on the example of Mamre and the Christians' multilayered experience of the site.

51 "One by one" is a common rhetorical expression in many versions of the story. Often it underlines the tortures of the brothers ("limb by limb", as in 2 Macc 7:7) or the difficult role of the mother in watching her children being tortured and killed one after the other (e.g. 4 Macc 14:15).

the story is quite accustomed to the thought of the boys being slain. According to 4 Maccabees (12:1), the seventh boy is "the youngest of [them] all".[52] The king employs the boy's mother to persuade him from choosing death, but the mother secretly only encourages him (4 Macc 12:7). According to *Lamentations Rabbah* (1.16), Caesar takes no special strategy with the youngest one but approaches him as severely as any of his brothers. When, however, he gives an order to put him to death, the mother interferes, as if reaching her limit: "By your life, Caesar, give me my son, so that I may hug him and kiss him." When she takes hold of her son and starts breastfeeding him, the shockingly young age of the boy is revealed. The mother then demands: "By your life, Caesar, kill me first, then him." But Caesar does not consent and the boy is killed first.

Although the drama of this scene is particularly flexible, the mother always assumes an active role, which is often shown by her being the focus of the story, as well as her role as her son's advisor. According to *Pesiqta Rabbati* (43.4), the boy even asks his persecutor: "May I go and take counsel of my mother?" In *Ḥadīṯ al-Māšiṭa*, however, the roles are reversed: the mother's courage seems to wither away and the boy takes on the active role, giving her a piece of advice that is effective, for the mother completes their trial. Needless to say, the speech of the boy who speaks in his mother's arms takes over the focus of the story and places the mother in a new light. Regardless of her courage so far, she, too, might hesitate. At the same time, this shift in the narrative stands in some contrast to the Jewish and Christian traditions that emphasize the high moral quality and steadfastness of the mother. 4 Maccabees assures us that "sympathy for her children did not sway the mother of the young men; she was of the same mind as Abraham" (4 Macc 14:20), praising her as "more noble than males in steadfastness, and manlier than men in endurance!" (4 Macc 15:30). This vein of thinking is also maintained in the much more emotional image of the mother in *Lamentations Rabbah*, in which the mother asks her dying son to tell Abraham not to take pride in his so-called sacrifice but look at her who "built seven altars and offered up seven sons in one day; yours was only a test, but I really had to do it".[53]

52 Of the sixth, it has already been said that he was a junior son; 4 Macc 11:13.

53 Moore & Anderson (1998, 266–267) interpret the relationship between the mother and Abraham in 4 Maccabees and *Lamentations Rabbah* in terms of gender, suggesting that the mother of 4 Maccabees albeit as courageous as the best of men still falls into the patriarchal challenge, whereas the mother of *Lamentations Rabbah* "dares" to take the comparison further. The verbal interference of the smallest boy could also be taken as a means by which the daring character of the mother is smoothened.

There may be various reasons why the boy speaks in the story of *Hadith al-Māšiṭa*. Yet, one of them could have to do with attempts to balance the overly promoted rank of the mother, for the mother's greater popularity is attested in various sources, often at the expense of her sons.[54] This, however, is not necessarily something that the hadith does, but it may be something that the hadith reflects. To say the least, the story transmitted in Ibn Ḥanbal's *Musnad* allows for a new dimension to develop within the relationship between the mother and her youngest son: the beginning of the story with the main emphasis on the hairdresser-mother indicates that she is a self-sufficient character and her children are her accessories; yet, the ending of the story suggests that she might not have been able to keep going without the sudden intervention of her son.

5 Reception of the Story of the Mother and Her Children in Hadith Literature

In addition to the actual story of the hairdresser-mother and her children, there are three parts in *Ḥadīṯ al-Māšiṭa* that we take as indicators of the story's reception in hadith literature. Of them, two set *Ḥadīṯ al-Māšiṭa* apart from the Jewish and Christian traditions and provide the story with an explicitly Islamic setting: the *isnād* (part 1) and the first narrative framework, that is, Muhammad's nocturnal journey (part 2).

To our knowledge, the second narrative framework, in which the hairdresser's youngest son is listed among the four infants who spoke (part 6), is not attested outside Islamic literature, although the notion of a miraculously speaking infant is found beyond Islamic literature. Moreover, the "infants who spoke" *topos* is not exclusive to Islamic narrative tradition but, rather, provides an interface for a wealth of narrative material shared by Jews, Christians and Muslims. In what follows, we shall scrutinize these various frames given to the story of the mother and her children in *Ḥadīṯ al-Māšiṭa* in order to understand what aspects of it they highlight and how they participate in telling the story.

54 Cf., e.g., 2 Macc 7:20. John Chrysostom's homily may be indicative of her irresistible popularity. He tries to shift the focus onto one of the mother's sons "[f]or yesterday we took the mother aside by herself and spent the entire sermon on her". To do so, he needs however to assure his congregation that "certainly the mother will come into [the sermon] for us today too, even if we don't touch her. For the progress of the sermon will attract her for sure and she won't be able to bear leaving her children." *Homily 2 on the Maccabees* 1 (2006, 148–149).

5.1 *The* isnād (*part 1*)

Isnād reports the chain of transmitters through which the hadith is transmitted. The transmitters mentioned in *Ḥadīṯ al-Māšiṭa* begin with the author himself, ʿAbdallāh Ibn Ḥanbal, who is the last one to have received the hadith and the one who wrote it down. According to the *isnād*, the hadith was transmitted to him through ʿAbdallāh, Ibn Ḥanbal's son,[55] who heard it from his father, who got the information from Abū ʿUmar al-Ḍarīr, who heard it from Ḥammād b. Salama (d. 783), who heard it from ʿAṭāʾ b. al-Sāʾib, Saʿīd b. Jubayr (665–714) and who heard it from Ibn ʿAbbās, who allegedly heard it personally from the Prophet Muhammad.

According to the Islamic tradition, Ibn ʿAbbās or Abū ʿAbdallāh b. ʿAbbās b. ʿAbd al-Muṭṭalib (d. ca. 687) was the Prophet Muhammad's cousin through his father, the Prophet's uncle, ʿAbbās. Ibn ʿAbbās is known to have been one of the greatest scholars of the first generation of Muslims, a renowned Qur'an scholar (Vaglieri 1960, 40) and to have transmitted a considerable amount of *Isrāʾiliyyāt* material (Colby 2008, 31). His name is also often linked to the traditions concerning Muhammad's nocturnal journey.

5.2 *Nocturnal Journey* (isrāʾ) *and the "Beautiful Fragrance"* (*part 2*)

According to the Islamic tradition, the Prophet Muhammad took the nocturnal journey from the mosque of Medina (*masjid al-ḥarām*) to the "further mosque" (*masjid al-aqṣā*). He was mounted on a winged animal called Barūq and led by the angel Gabriel. The story is briefly referred to in the *Sūra al-Isrāʾ* (17:1).[56] In the Islamic tradition, there are two main interpretations of the journey, which are often combined together. According to the first, the nocturnal journey is an allusion to Muhammad's ascension to heaven (*miʿraj*). According to the second, the "further mosque" is interpreted as Jerusalem (Horovitz & Schrieke 1993, 97–98). The core of the story remains the same regardless of the interpretation of the "further mosque". On the way, Muhammad encounters several good and wicked powers. At the further mosque, the Prophet meets Abraham, Moses, and Jesus and leads prayers before them, taking precedence over all the other prophets gathered there. He receives the duty of five daily prayers

---

55 According to the incipit of *Musnad*, Ibn Ḥanbal's son was called Abū ʿAbd al-Raḥmān ʿAbdallāh b. Aḥmad b. Muḥammad b. Ḥanbal and the name ʿAbdallāh without *kunya* or father's name probably refers to the son. As noted above, the two other printed editions without the full *isnad* are Ibn Ḥanbal 2012 (vol. II: 615–616/ hadith no. 2821) with an English translation and Ibn Ḥanbal 2001 (vol. V:30–31/ hadith no. 2821).

56 Other Qur'anic references which are often thought to describe *Isrāʾ* include 53:1–21 and 81:19–25.

during the nocturnal journey. However, it seems evident that there was a disagreement among the early scholars on the nature of the Prophet Muhammad's experience and many of the details in the journey. The *Isrā'* tradition within hadith and exegetic literature is extensive and includes many stories that provide details of the journey (Colby 2008, 23, 51–52, 80, 83). *Ḥadīṯ al-Māšiṭa* is one ramification of this large corpus.[57]

According to *Ḥadīṯ al-Māšiṭa*, Muhammad perceives a "beautiful fragrance" (*rā'iḥa ṭayyiba*) during the journey. Gabriel recognizes it immediately as the fragrance of the hairdresser and her children. In the Qur'an, there are no mention of Muhammad sensing a beautiful fragrance, but in the hadith and *tafsīr* literature a pleasant smell is sometimes associated with paradise during Muhammad's nocturnal journey (Furāt al-Kūfī 2011, 211; al-Suyūṭī 1996, 72). "The beautiful fragrance" of the hairdresser and her children could also be compared to another sensual attraction, namely "the sweet drop" described by Frederick S. Colby as follows: "As Muḥammad nears the divine throne in later versions of the Ibn ʿAbbās narrative, a drop of sweet liquid often falls from the throne onto his tongue. It either removes his fear or makes it easier for him to address the divinity, or else it conveys to him some type of secret knowledge" (Colby 2008, 238). Muhammad's dialogue with Gabriel also represents a "distinctive type of revelatory discourse" which "reflects the specific literary context of the otherworldly tour in which an *angelus interpres* serves as the visionary's heavenly guide" (Boustan 2005, 170).[58]

As the story tells us, the bodies of the hairdresser and her children were burned in the copper cow. This process could have resulted in the smell, imitated later on at martyr shrines with odours. According to Mary Thurlkill, both Christians and Muslims would recognize their high status as martyrs "after smelling glorious odours symbolic of their virtue and sanctity" (2016, 71–72). The "beautiful fragrance" of the hairdresser and her children should be interpreted as a positive token to convey the ideas of noble martyrdom, paradise, just sacrifice, and righteous action. In such a case, the first narrative framework of *Ḥadīṯ al-Māšiṭa* could, indeed, reflect the interface or contact zone between Muslims and the Christian cult of saints.

---

57 There is another hadith (no. 2819) reported in *Musnad* (Ibn Ḥanbal 2012 [vol. 11], 613–615), which also concerns the nocturnal journey or, rather, Muhammad's fears that the people would not find his report credible.

58 Boustan (2005, 170–171) names this type as "demonstrative explanations," following Martha Himmelfarb. The examples he gives from Jewish and Christian literatures are particularly intriguing, as they concern both visual and auditory sensations—"what is this?" or "what is this noise?"

5.3 *The "Infants Who Spoke"* topos (*part 6*)

The closing of the hadith attaches the hairdresser's son to a group of "four infants who spoke" (*takallama arbaʿa ṣiġār*): the hairdresser's son, Jesus, the witness of Yūsuf and the companion of Jurayj. In the Qurʾan, a child speaking "in the cradle" (*mahd*) appears three times (3:46; 5:110; 19:29), each time referring to Jesus. In the Islamic literature, however, the theme is elaborated and a *topos* of "infants who spoke" seems to emerge. The cluster of infants who spoke in *Ḥadīṯ al-Māšiṭa* is one among many similar clusters, in which the number of infants varies.[59] For instance, Muslim (d. 875) mentions four infants who spoke: Jesus, son of Maryam, the companion of Jurayj, and the companion of the tyrant (2000, 1118–1119 / 6509). Ibn al-Aṯīr (d. 1233) mentions four infants: the son of the Pharaoh's daughter's hairdresser (*wa-bn māšiṭat ibnat firʿawn*), the witness of Joseph, the companion of Jurayj and Jesus (1987, 108), just as Ibn Ḥanbal but in a different order. However, al-Suyūṭī (d. 1505) mentions three infants: the companion of Jurayj, Jesus, and the companion of al-Ḥabaša (2011 [vol. v], 508). Al-Qurṭubī (d. 1273) mentions six infants: the witness of Joseph (*šāhid yūsuf*), the son of the hairdresser of the Pharaoh's wife (*wa-ṣabī māšiṭa imraʾa firʿawn*), Jesus, John the Baptist (*yaḥyā*), the companion of Jurayj, as well as the companion of the tyrant (*ṣāḥib al-jabbār*) (2006 [vol. v], 140).

Joining the son of the Pharaoh's daughter's hairdresser to a group of infants who spoke introduces a completely new narrative framework. It also changes the focus from the hairdresser-mother to her son, suggesting that her infant son had a constitutive role in giving her the courage and wisdom to carry out her heroic task until the end. A closer familiarity with the other infants who spoke helps to understand this role. Who were ʿĪsā ibn Maryam, Joseph's witness and companion of Jurayj in Islamic context?

5.3.1 Jesus—*ʿĪsā ibn Maryam*

ʿĪsā ibn Maryam refers to Jesus. The Qurʾan mentions Jesus twenty-five times. He is regarded as a prophet among other prophets such as Moses (*mūsā*), Isaac (*isḥāq*), and John the Baptist (*yaḥyā*), and discussed widely in exegetic and hadith literature. In the Qurʾan, there are three references to Jesus speaking in the cradle (*mahd*). *Sūra al-ʾImrān* contains a promise, according to which Jesus "will speak to the people in the cradle and in maturity, and he will be of the righteous" (*wa-yukallimu al-nās fī al-mahd wa-kahlan wa-min al-ṣāliḥīn*) (3:46).

---

59 According to Parrinder (1965, 78), lists of up to eleven children who had spoken in their cradles are found in Islamic literature, and he also mentions a source according to which Jesus's mother Maryam also spoke in the cradle. The following examples are based on our tentative searches with this article in mind.

According to *Sūra Maryam*, Jesus first helps his mother survive the delivery (19:24–26) but a little later, when people accuse Mary of unchaste behaviour, she points at her new-born son, to which the people respond in a shocked fashion: "How can we speak to a child in the cradle (*kayfa nukallimu man kāna fī al-mahd ṣabiyyan*)?" (19:29). *Sūra al-Māʾida* refers to the miraculous act of Jesus:

> O Jesus, son of Mary, remember my favour upon you and upon your mother when I supported you with the pure spirit, and you spoke to the people in the cradle and in maturity (*iḏ ʾayyadtu-ka bi-rūḥ al-qudus tukallimu al-nās fī al-mahd wa-kahlan*); and remember when I taught you writing and wisdom and the Torah and the Gospel; and when you designed from clay what was like the form of a bird with my permission, then you breathed into it, and it became a bird with my permission; and you healed the blind and the leper with my permission; and when you brought forth the dead with my permission; and when I restrained the children of Israel from killing you when you came to them with clear proofs and those who disbelieved among them said, "This is nothing but mere magic."
>
> Qur'an 5:110

Jesus as a child is often depicted as a miracle maker in the Apocryphal Gospels. When he was five or seven years old, he made birds out of clay and breathed life into them (*The Infancy Gospel of Thomas* 1–2). This story is also referred to in the Qur'an (5:110 quoted above; 3:49). However, as Geoffrey Parrinder notes, the miracle of Jesus speaking *in the cradle* only seems to be attested in one of the Apocryphal Gospels, the *Arabic Infancy Gospel*, in a scribal note that precedes the actual narrative:

> He has said that Jesus spoke, and, indeed, when He was lying in His cradle said to Mary His mother: "I am Jesus, the Son of God, the Logos, whom thou hast brought forth, as the Angel Gabriel announced to thee; and my Father has sent me for the salvation of the world."[60]

60 For the *Arabic Infancy Gospel*, see Horn 2017, 61–64. Here we have used the translation by Alexander Walker (1886), which is available online: http://www.newadvent.org/fathers/0806.htm. Parrinder (1965, 78) remarks, in reference to the editor of the *Arabic Infancy Gospel*, that this anecdote must have been "current fairly early among Arab Christians". Yet, it could be that Jesus's fame according to the Qur'an had an impact on the Infancy Gospel; see Horn 2017, 68–69.

On this point, there are both similarities and differences between the *Arabic Infancy Gospel* and the Qur'an. In both texts Jesus, as an infant in the cradle, miraculously gives a theological testimony about himself. The main difference is that in the *Arabic Infancy Gospel*, he calls himself the son of God, whereas in the Qur'an he is a servant of God, a prophet, who receives heavenly revelation. These two attitudes go back to different theological principles, according to which the nature of Jesus and his relation to God were discussed in Late Antiquity. Interestingly, Ibn Ishāq mentions in the *Life of the Prophet* about the Christians of Najrān, who came to the Prophet Muhammad to debate about Jesus's miracle of speaking in the cradle, saying that it was "something that no child of Adam has ever done before" (Parrinder 1965, 78). Their point was to underline Jesus's unique nature: he had performed a miracle that no one else has ever done. Contrary to this, perhaps, we find in Islamic tradition numerous references to various children who speak in the cradle.

5.3.2 Joseph's Witness—*Šāhid Yūsuf*

Joseph (*Yūsuf*) is a figure known from the Qur'an, in which the *Sūra Yūsuf* (12) is dedicated to his story. The Qur'anic story shares much in content with the biblical story of Joseph and Potiphar's wife (Gen 39). In both stories, Potiphar's wife tries to seduce Joseph and, as he refuses her suggestions and tries to escape from her, she puts him in trouble. According to Genesis, Joseph forgets his clothes in a woman's room when he escapes (Gen 39:12) and the woman plots against him successfully, using Joseph's clothes as evidence of him having tried to rape her, leading to Joseph's imprisonment (Gen 39:13–20). While the Genesis story allows for such damage to Joseph's reputation, later Jewish literature abounds with attempts to vindicate Joseph: the Qur'anic story of Joseph attests to one common attempt, namely, the introduction of witnesses into the narrative who testify to Joseph's innocence (Goldman 1995, 110). Such a witness also makes an appearance in *Ḥadīṯ al-Māšiṭa*.

According to *Sūra Yūsuf* (12:25–26), the woman only succeeds in tearing the back of his shirt and when she reports her version of events to her husband, Joseph defends himself by saying that it was the woman who tried to seduce him, not the other way around. To this "a witness from her family testified" (*šahada šāhid min ʾahl-i-hā*): "If his shirt is torn from the front, then she has told the truth, and he is a liar. But if his shirt is torn from the back, then she has lied, and he is being truthful" (12:26–27). Due to this witness, the man believes Joseph and the woman is publicly disgraced (12:28–30). The Qur'an contains no further details on the witness apart from his descent in the wife's family. He is simply an anonymous person who saves Joseph's honour. However, exegetical literature on the Qur'an specifies that the witness was a child in the cradle: al-

Ṭabarī gives various accounts according to which the child was an infant in the cradle (*ṣabiyy fī al-mahd*) (2011 [vol. XIII], 105–111) and al-Qurṭubī also affirms that the witness was a child in the cradle (*ṭifl fī al-mahd*) (2006 [vol. XI], 321–323).[61]

Unlike Jesus and the hairdresser's son who speak as infants to protect or encourage their mothers, the infant witness of Joseph is not, at least explicitly, related to him. Nonetheless, each of the speaking infants assure the moral success of an important past figure at a critical moment in their lives.

5.3.3 Companion of Jurayj the Ascetic—*Ṣāḥib Jurayj*

The fourth infant who spoke in the *Ḥadīṯ al-Māšiṭa* is the companion of Jurayj (*ṣāḥib jurayj*). Neither Jurayj nor his companion are known from the Qur'an or the Bible. Yet, famous hadith collectors such as Muslim (2000, 1118 / 6508, 6509), al-Bukhārī (2002, 852 / 3436) and Ibn Ḥibbān (1991 [vol. XIV], 411–412 / 6489), as well as the historian al-Maqdīsī ([vol. III], 135 / 139), tell a story of an ascetic man called Jurayj.[62] According to Muslim, the story of Jurayj goes as follows:

> Jurayj was a pious monk who spent his days praying. Her mother came to him twice but Jurayj turned her away and continued praying. On the third time when Jurayj turned his mother away, she stated: "O God, please do not kill him before he has seen the faces of the prostitutes." Then, one day a prostitute came to him and offered her services. Jurayj declined her, but she insisted. Then she went to a shepherd who was pasturing around Jurayj's hermitage. The shepherd made her pregnant, and she gave birth to a baby boy. Later, the woman claimed that the father of the boy was Jurayj. Consequently, the people in the village accused him of fornication and beat him. Jurayj asked to bring out the baby boy in question. The baby was brought and Jurayj addressed a question to him even though he was still in his mother's womb: "Who is your father?" The boy answered that his father is a shepherd called so-and-so. After the testimony, people believed Jurayj and in order to recompense his pains they promised to rebuild his hermitage in gold.

Josef Horovitz recognizes a comparable narrative in Syriac Christian hagiography. He suggests, moreover, that the character of Jurayj that circulates in

---

61 Alternatively, both Jewish and Muslim sources also suggest that the witness was a female cousin of Potiphar's wife; see Goldman 1995, 110.

62 For a discussion on the various versions of the legend of Jurayj in Muslim literature, see Horovitz 1905, 78–81.

Muslim literature could be too derived from the figure known in eastern Christianity as Gregorios Thaumaturgos, in whose life a dramatic false accusation also plays an important role. In Gregorios's case, however, there is no infant speaking from the cradle or womb, but a figure of prostitute who attempts to disgrace Gregorios. Thus, according to Horovitz, the details concerning the infant are added to the legend of Jurayj later on, due to the influence of other speaking infants, such as Jesus and Joseph's witness (1905, 82–83).

The situations of Joseph and Jurayj are, indeed, comparable insofar as both are being accused of crossing moral boundaries related to sexual affairs and saved by the witness of an infant or, in Jurayj's case, a foetus who spoke. Moreover, the growth of the hairdresser's son's role into a decisive player in *Ḥadīṯ al-Māšiṭa* could have been inspired by already existing legendary infants who spoke in a way similar to that which Horovitz suggests for the growth of the Gregorios/Jurayj narrative.

5.3.4 Companion of the Pit (*ṣāḥib al-ʾukhdūd*) and Companion of the Tyrant (*ṣāḥib al-jabbār*)

As it was mentioned above, in addition to the four infants of *Ḥadīṯ al-Māšiṭa*, there are other infants who appear in the clusters of infants who spoke in Islamic tradition. Also it is worth of mentioning that the hairdresser's son, Jesus, the witness of Yūsuf and the companion of Jurayj appear together or separately in various clusters of infants who spoke. While it is unclear if any motif other than the miracle of an infant speaking holds these clusters together, it is useful to briefly investigate two more stories. Companion of the pit is one of those stories. Like the son of the hairdresser, the companion of the pit is persecuted and may thus shed some light on the interface between the story of *Ḥadīṯ al-Māšiṭa* and the cluster of infants who spoke.

The companion of the pit (*ṣāḥib al-ʾukhdūd*) refers to the *Sūra Al-Burūj* (85:4), in which the companions of the pit (*aṣḥāb al-ʾukhdūd*) are mentioned. Through an exegesis of the Qur'anic verse, al-Ṭabarī gives multiple explanations of the companions (al-Ṭabarī, 2011 [XIV], 270–277). Al-Ṭabarī provides nine different explanations of which some are shorter and some more detailed. In four of them the companions of the pit are identified as victims of religious persecution (al-Ṭabarī, 2011 [XIV], 271, 272, 273–275, 276) and in two of them they are referred to as Israelites (*banī isrāʾīl*) (al-Ṭabarī, 2011 [XIV], 272, 273). On two occasions, al-Ṭabarī provides information that links the persons to themes that are prevalent in *Ḥadīṯ al-Māšita*.

On one of the two occasions, al-Ṭabarī refers to a hadith of Muslim (2000, 1297 / hadith 7511). The hadith is too long to be quoted here entirely but the contents may be summarized as follows: the story includes the figures of a boy, a sorcerer, a monk, and a king. The boy is a believer, and the king questions him. The king asks: "Do you have another Lord besides me (*ʾa-wa la-ka rabban ġayrī*)?" The boy answers: "Yes, your Lord and my Lord is God (*rabbī wa-rabbi-ka allāh*)." The king then sets up a series of trials for the boy to make him renounce his faith. The boy insists, and other people join his faith. Finally, the king kindles a fire and says: "Whoever abandons his religion, let him go, and whoever does not, throw him into the fire." The hadith closes with the following scene:

> They were struggling and scuffling in the fire until a woman, and her baby whom she was breastfeeding came, and it was as if she was somewhat hesitant (*fa-taqāʿsat*) to be cast into the fire, so her baby said to her: "Be patient mother! For verily, you are following the truth (*fa-inna-ki ʿalā al-ḥaqq*)!"

Al-Ṭabarī also relates the following story (2011 [XIV], 272):

> It has been told to us (*ḥuddiṯa-nā*) that ʿAlī b. Abī Ṭālib, may God be pleased with him, has said: There were people in the semi-cultured lands (*bi-miḏāriʿ*) of Yemen. Believers of the land fought with unbelievers. The believers overcame the unbelievers, then they fought back, and the believers overcame the unbelievers [again]. Then they made agreements and treaties with one another so that they would not act treacherously with one another. Then the unbelievers betrayed [the believers] and took them as prisoners (*fa-ʾakhaḏū-hum ʾakhaḏan*). A man among the believers said to them: "Do you have any good intentions (*hal la-kum ʾilā khayr*)? You should light a fire and expose us to the fire. Some will follow you in your religion, and that is what you desire and some will not, and they will jump into the fire, and you will be saved from it." They set a fire alight, and the [believers] were exposed to it. Their leaders started to jump into the fire until only an old woman remained of them and it was as if she hesitated (*ka-ʾanna-hā talakkaʾat*). An infant in her lap said to her: "O mother, go forward and shun hypocrisy."

While the plot is different, there are some significant similarities in the underlying motives between the two hadiths transmitted by al-Ṭabarī and *Ḥadīṯ al-Māšiṭa*. For one, each story is dated back to pre-Islamic times, which can be deduced from the fact that the context is devoid of distinctively Islamic characteristics: the king, his kingdom and the protagonists are not named. Secondly, in all cases there is a tyrant who oppresses his subjects including the pious people. Thirdly, the oppression is so intense that people are publicly executed for their faith. Fourthly and, indeed, quite strikingly, each hadith features a mother and her infant son. Even though in the hadiths mentioned by al-Ṭabarī the mother and her son are not properly introduced, their resemblance with the hairdresser-mother and her youngest son is obvious.

In addition to these thematic similarities, the two hadiths transmitted by al-Ṭabarī share with *Ḥadīṯ al-Māšiṭa* some verbatim passages. For one, the boy and the hairdresser-mother are asked exactly the same question (*ʾa-wa la-ka rabban ġayrī*) and they respond identically (*rabbī wa rabbi-ka allāh*). Such a dialogue may well suggest a common, standardized context of persecutions, perhaps especially in the Muslim memories of pre-Islamic times. In addition, the mother figure seems to hesitate (*taqāʿasat* and *talakkaʾat*) in both Muslim's hadiths and *Ḥadīṯ al-Māšiṭa*, as well as in the other hadith transmitted by al-Ṭabarī. This gesture strengthens the literary connection between these mother figures and, consequently, their infants who encouraged them. This suggests that such a pair, if not any specific version of their story, was widely spread in the hadith literature.

In addition to the companion of the pit (*ṣāḥib al-ʾukhdūd*), the companion of the tyrant (*ṣāḥib al-jabbār*) also often appears in the list of "infants who spoke". According to both Muslim and al-Bukharī, this figure was a baby boy (*ṣabiyy*) breastfed by his mother. This following hadith appears in connection to the story of Jurayj (al-Bukharī 2002, 852 / hadith 3436; Muslim 2000, 1119 / hadith 6509):

> [...] A lady from the children of Israel was nursing her child at her breast when a handsome rider passed by her. She said: "O God! Make my child like him." On that, the child left her breast, and facing the rider said: "O God! Do not make me like him." The child then started to suck her breast again. Abu Hurayra [the transmitter of the hadith] further said: "As if I were now looking at the Prophet sucking his finger by way of demonstration." After a while, the people passed by with a lady slave and she [the child's mother] said: "O God! Do not make my child like this [slave girl]!" On that, the child left her breast and said: "O God! Make me like her." When the mother asked why, the child replied: "The rider is one of the tyrants while this slave girl is falsely accused of theft and illegal sexual intercourse."

An obvious parallelism with *Ḥadīṯ al-Māšiṭa* is the child speaking as well as the connection to pre-Islamic times. Instead of a context of persecutions, this story seems to resemble the prominent themes of Jurayj's story, namely false accusations and sexual intercourse. The role of the mother figure here is to be ignorant and, perhaps, superficial, in contrast to her child's wisdom, which clearly surpasses her own. In any case, this hadith is yet another example of an infant who speaks. These examples of the "children who spoke" motif attest to a widespread use of this theme in Islamic literature: they show us glimpses of how this motif has evolved, changed and been employed in different contexts.

6 Conclusions and Reflections

The story of the mother and her sons has a life of its own in hadith literature. By analysing one example of it, *Ḥadīṯ al-Māšiṭa* transmitted in Ibn Ḥanbal's *Musnad*, we have sought to understand the ways in which the story was integrated into the Islamic tradition and transmitted to early Muslims. In this aim, we have provided a division of *Ḥadīṯ al-Māšiṭa* into six parts, three of which (3–5) comprise the story as it is told in hadith literature. In comparison to the versions of the story of the mother and her seven sons known from Jewish and Christian literature, the story of the hairdresser-mother and her children is exceptional in many ways. It contains, for example, an opening narrative scene in which the mother is alone with the Pharaoh's daughter, practising her profession and fulfilling her daily routines. The opening scene confirms the centrality of the mother to the story, which is manifested in various late antique versions of the story of the mother and her seven sons. Yet, as we have observed, the contextualization of the story in the Egypt of the pharaohs, as well as the manifestation of the mother's profession, are features that are unique to the story in hadith literature. These may be explained by the need to weave the story into a past that is known and recognized in the Bible as well as the Qur'an.

Ḥadīṯ al-Māšiṭa is an independent story that cannot and should not be reduced to any Jewish or Christian source. Yet, it becomes readable in conversation with other stories of the mother and her sons, the popular martyrological narrative tradition found within late antique Jewish and Christian literature. We maintain that *Ḥadīṯ al-Māšiṭa* does not "Islamicize" the story of the mother and her sons in any way that would attest an exclusively Islamic identity to the figures. Rather, the story underlines generic pious features that may be considered shared among Jews, Christians, and Muslims, such as the recognition of one God and the refusal of idolatry or the expectation of afterlife judgment. Although the hairdresser-mother and her children are not explicitly Muslims, they provide the faith revealed in the Qur'an with a predecessor, adding to the wealth of ancient and eternal documentation supports Muhammad's proclamation. Their function in the hadith is comparable in some ways to the function early Christians attested to their "Old Testament" when they took it as prophesies of Christ. As some Christians took the mother and her seven sons as a prefiguration of the church and her martyrs, in the Islamic tradition the mother and her sons are conceived retroactively as proto-Muslims who died for the sake of the religion. This is the case with *Ḥadīṯ al-Māšiṭa*, our main reference, as well as the hadith of the monk and the apprentice of the king's magician transmitted by Muslim (7148 /3005).

The story of the hairdresser-mother and her children can also be read in conversation with the narrative frameworks attested to it in *Ḥadīṯ al-Māšiṭa*, which are specific to the Islamic context, namely the Prophet Muhammad's nocturnal journey and the "infants who spoke" *topos*. The reference in the hadith to the nocturnal journey and, in particular, the motif of the "beautiful fragrance" in it connects the story to paradise, putting the figures in high esteem. It may also support our suggestion to contextualize the reception of the story in an environment in which the mother and her children were venerated as martyr-saints and worshipped with scents.

As for linking the hairdresser's son to other "infants who spoke", it may further emphasize the identification of the story of the mother and her seven sons as *isrāʾīliyyāt*. Jesus the son of Maryam, the witness of Joseph, the companion of Jurayj, and the son of the Pharaoh's daughter's hairdresser belong to the time before the life of the Prophet Muhammad, and so do the companions of the pit (*ṣāḥib al-ukhdūd*) and of the tyrant (*ṣāḥib al-jabbār*). While Jews, Christians, and Muslims alike may have connected the theme of infants who spoke with the pious ones, the idea of clustering such infants seems to be an Islamic innovation, possibly both a continuation and relativization of the Qur'anic miracle of Jesus. We should also note that there are remarkable similarities between Ibn Ḥanbal's *Ḥadīṯ al-Māšiṭa* and the hadith of the boy, the sorcerer, the monk, and the king transmitted by Muslim. Although the stories are entirely different, they share some short phrases, as well as a common narrative element, namely the gripping final scene between an infant and his hesitant mother. The spread of the *topos* of infants who spoke in general and these literary features in particular suggest that the story of the mother and her children formed an identifiable entity within early Islamic literature.

Within the Islamic tradition, *Ḥadīṯ al-Māšiṭa* could be classified as *isrāʾīliyyāt*, referring back to an unspecified past and the pious people of former times (Albayrak 2001, 78–79). As for the transmission of the story, we have not even attempted to identify a written original text behind Ibn Ḥanbal's version. Instead, relying on the known fact of a shared narrative tradition concerning the mother and her seven sons among Jews and Christians, we have conceptualized this story as a product of a "contact zone" that attests to various and multidirectional influences, borrowings and sharing among Jews, Christians, and Muslims (cf. Hasan-Rokem 2016). By this theoretical tool, our analysis of *Ḥadīṯ al-Māšiṭa* hopefully adds to the understanding of the interfaces of the Jewish-Christian-Muslim contact zone, that is, the interfaces of shared traditions and common conversations.

We may, moreover, have identified a potential subtle hint in *Ḥadīṯ al-Māšiṭa* at one means of transmission of the story to Muslims, for we take the mother's request to the Pharaoh that she and her children be wrapped in a cloth and buried and the Pharaoh's consent to this request as indicative of the ongoing veneration of the mother and her seven sons as martyr-saints and the presence of their relics in the environment in which the story was transmitted. Considering all the various differences between the story told in *Ḥadīṯ al-Māšiṭa* and those connected to their cult, one cannot speak of textual and perhaps not even of oral transmission without taking into account other auditory as well as visual means of transmission. We suggest that the story transmitted to hadith literature may result from relative familiarity with the highly-esteemed figures of the mother and her children who once upon a time had been martyred; that is, it may have been shaped in relative proximity to one of their local cults, yet at a relative distance from it that would have enabled the development of the story.

Bibliography

Abbot, Nabia. *Studies in Arabic Literary Papyri: Qur'anic Commentary and Tradition.* Chicago: University of Chicago Press, 1967.

Abdalla, Michael. "The Cult of Mart Shmunie: A Maccabean Martyr in the Tradition of the Assyrian Churches of Mesopotamia." *Journal of Assyrian Academic Studies* 23 (2009): 22–39.

Albayrak, Ismail. "Re-Evaluating the Notion of Isra'iliyyat." *D. E. U. Ilahiyyat Fakiltesi Dergisi* 14 (2001): 69–88.

Augustine of Hippo. "Sermon 300: On the Solemnity of the Maccabee Martyrs." Translated (from *Patrologia Latina* 38, 1376–1380) by Edmund Hill in *The Works of Saint Augustine (4th Release): Electronic edition: Sermons (273–305A) on the Saints*. Charlottesville, Va.: InteLex Corporation, 2014, vol. III/8, 277–281.

Bensly, R.L. and W.E. Barnes. *The Fourth Book of Maccabees and kindred documents in Syriac: First edited on manuscript authority by the late R.L. Bensly, with an introduction and translations by W. E. Barnes*. Cambridge: Cambridge University Press, 1895.

Brown, Peter. *The Cult of the Saints: Its Rise and Function in Latin Christianity*. London: SCM Press Ltd, 1981.

Boustan, Ra'anan S. *From Martyr to Mystic: Rabbinic Martyrology and the Making of*

Merkavah Mysticism. Text and Studies in Ancient Judaism 112. Tübingen: Mohr Siebeck, 2005.

Al-Bukharī, Muḥammad b. Ismāʿīl. *Ṣaḥīḥ al-Bukhārī*. Beirut: Dār Ibn Kaṯīr, 2000.

Campbell, Elizabeth. "A Heaven of Wine: Muslim-Christian Encounters at Monasteries in the Early Islamic Middle East." Dissertation at the University of Washington, 2009.

Cohen, Gerson D. "Hannah and Her Seven Sons." In: M. Berenbaum and F. Skolnik (eds.), *Encyclopaedia Judaica*. 2nd ed. Detroit: Macmillan Reference USA, 2007, vol. VIII, 325.

Cohen, Gerson D. *Studies in the Variety of Rabbinic Cultures*. New York: The Jewish Publication Society, 1991.

Colby, Frederick S. *Narrating Muhammad's Night Journey: Tracing the Development of the Ibn Abbas Ascension Discourse*. Albany: State University of New York Press, 2008.

Diehl, Daniel and Mark P. Donnelly. *The Big Book of Pain: Punishment and Torture through History*. Stroud: History Press, 2011.

Dönitz, Saskia. "Sefer Yosippon and the Greek Bible." In: N. de Lange, J. Krivoruchko, and C. Boyd-Taylor (eds.), *Jewish Reception of Greek Bible Versions: Studies in Their Use in Late Antiquity and the Middle Ages*. Tübingen: Mohr Siebeck, 2009, 223–234.

Fierro, Maribel. "Al-Ṭabarānī." In: P.J. Bearman et al. (eds.), *The Encyclopaedia of Islam*. Leiden: Brill, 2010, vol. X, 10–11.

Fowden, Elizabeth Key. *The Barbarian Plain: Saint Sergius between Rome and Iran*. Berkeley: University of California Press, 1999.

Fowden, Elizabeth Key. "Sharing Holy Places." *Common Knowledge* 8 (2002): 124–146.

Fowden, Elizabeth Key. "The Lamp and the Wine Flask: Early Muslim Interest in Christian Monasticism." In: A. Akasoy, J.E. Mongomery, and P.E. Pormann (eds.), *Islamic Crosspollinations: Interactions in the Medieval Middle East*. Cambridge: Gibb Memorial Trust, 2007, 1–28.

Fück, J.W. "Ibn Ḥibbān." In Bernard Lewis et al. (eds.), *The Encyclopaedia of Islam*. Leiden: Brill, 1986, vol. III, 799.

Furāt al-Kūfī, Abū al-Qāsim Furāt b. Ibrāhīm. *Tafsīr Furāt al-Kūfī* I–II. Edited by Muḥammad al-Kāẓim. Beirut: Mu'assasat al-Ta'rīkh al-ʿArabī, 2011.

Goldman, Shalom. *The Wiles of Women/The Wiles of Men: Joseph and Potiphar's Wife in Ancient Near Eastern, Jewish, and Islamic Folklore*. Albany: State University of New York Press, 1995.

Gregory Nazianzen. "Oration 15: In praise of the Maccabees." Translated (from *Patrologia Graeca* 35, 912–933) by Martha Vinson in *St. Nazianzen of Nazianzus: Selected Orations*, Fathers of the Church 107. Washington: The Catholic University of America Press, 2003, 72–84.

Hasan-Rokem, Galit. *Web of Life: Folklore and Midrash in Rabbinic Literature*. Translated by B. Stein. Stanford: Stanford University Press, 2000.

Hasan-Rokem, Galit. *Tales of the Neighborhood: Jewish Narrative Dialogues in Late Antiquity*. Berkeley: University of California Press, 2003.

Hasan-Rokem, Galit. "Ecotypes: Theory of the Lived and Narrated Experience." *Narrative Culture* 3 (2016): 100–137.

Henten, Jan Willem van. *The Maccabean Martyrs as Saviours of the Jewish People: A Study of 2 and 4 Maccabees*. Leiden: Brill, 1997.

Honigman, Sylvie. *Tales of High Priests and Taxes: The Books of the Maccabees and the Judean Rebellion against Antiochos IV*. Oakland: University of California Press, 2014.

Horn, Cornelia B. 2017. "Apocrypha on Jesus' Life in the Early Islamic Milieu: From Syriac into Arabic." In: Miriam L. Hjälm (ed.), *Senses of Scripture, Treasures of Tradition: The Bible in Arabic among Jews, Christians and Muslims*. Leiden: Brill, 58–78.

Horovitz, Josef. *Spuren griechischer Mimen im Orient*. Berlin: Mayer & Müller, 1905.

Horovitz, Josef and Bertram Schrieke. "Miʿrādj." In: C.E. Bosworth et al. (eds.), *The Encyclopaedia of Islam*.

Leiden: Brill, 1993, vol. VII, 97–99.

Al-Ḥākim al-Naysābūrī, Muḥammad b. ʿAbdallāh. *Al-Mustadrak ʿalā al-Ṣaḥīḥīn*. Edited by Abū ʿAbd.

al-Raḥmān Muqbil al-Wādi ʿī. Al-Qāhira: Dār al-ḥaramayn, 1997, vol. II.

Ibn al-ʾAṯīr. *Kāmil fī al-Taʾrīkh*. Edited by Abū al-Fidāʾ ʿAbdallāh al-Qāḍī. Beirut: Dār al-Kutub al-ʿIlmiyya, 1987, vol. I.

Ibn Ḥanbal, Aḥmad. *Musnad Imām Aḥmad Ibn Ḥanbal—wa bi-hāmišihi muntaḫab kanz al-ʿammāl fī sunan al-aqwāl wal-afʿāl*. Beirut: Dār Ṣādir, 1997, vol. I.

Ibn Ḥanbal, Aḥmad. *Musnad Imām Aḥmad Ibn Ḥanbal* I–L. Šuʿayb al-Arnaʾūṭ & ʿĀdil Muršid (toim). Beirut: Muʾassasa al-risāla li-l-ṭibāʿa wa-l-našr wa-l-tawzīʿ, 2001.

Ibn Ḥanbal, Aḥmad. *English Translation of Musnad Imam Ahmad Bin Hanbal*. Vols. I–III. Edited by Huda al-Khattab and translated by Nasiruddin al-Khattab. Riadh: Darussalam, 2012.

Ibn Ḥibbān. *Al-Iḥsān fī Taqrīb Ṣaḥīḥ Ibn Ḥibbān*. Vols. I–XVIII. Edited by Šuʿayb al-ʾArnaʾūṭ. Beirut: Muʾassasat al-Risāla, 1988–1991.

Ibn Khallikān, Abū al-ʿAbbās Šams al-Dīn.*Wafayāt al-Aʿyān wa-Abnāʾ Abnāʾ al-Zamān*. Vols. I–VII. Edited by Iḥsān ʿAbbās. Beirut: Dār al-Ṯaqāfa, 1972.

John Chrysostom. "Homily 1 on the Maccabees 1." Translated (from *Patrologia Graeca* 50, 617–624) by Wendy Mayer in *The Cult of the Saints: Selected Homilies and Letters*. New York: St Vladimir's Seminary Press, 2006, 137–145.

John Chrysostom. "Homily 2 on the Maccabees 1." Translated (from *Patrologia Graeca* 50, 623–626) by Wendy Mayer in *The Cult of the Saints: Selected Homilies and Letters*. New York: St Vladimir's Seminary Press, 2006, 148–153.

John Malalas. *The Chronicle of John Malalas*. Translated (from *Patrologia Graeca* 97, 88–717) by E. Jeffreys, M. Jeffreys, and R. Scott in *The Chronicle of John Malalas: A Translation*. Melbourne: Australian Association for Byzantine Studies, 1986.

Joslyn-Siemiatkoski, Daniel. *Christian Memories of the Maccabean Martyrs*. New York: Palgrave Macmillan, 2009.

Joslyn-Siemiatkoski, Daniel. "The Mother and Her Seven Sons in Late Antique and Medieval Ashkenazi Judaism: Narrative Transformation and Communal Identity." In: G. Signori (ed.), *Dying for the Faith, Killing for the Faith: Old-Testament Faith-Warriors (1 and 2 Maccabees) in Historical Perspective*. Leiden: Brill, 2012, 127–146.

Kilpatrick, Hilary. "Representations of Social Intercourse between Muslims and Non-Muslims in Some Medieval Adab Works." In: J. Waardenburg (ed.), *Muslim Perceptions of Other Religions: A Historical Survey*. Oxford: University Press, 1999, 213–224.

Laoust, H. "Aḥmad b. Ḥanbal." In: H.A.R. Gibb et al. (eds.), *The Encyclopaedia of Islam*. Leiden: Brill, 1986, I, 272–277.

Lamentations Rabbah. Editied by Paul Mandel, forthcoming. Translated by Jacob Neusner, *Lamentations Rabbah: An Analytical Translation*. Atlanta: Scholars Press, 1989.

Al-Mālaṭī, Abū al-Ḥusayn. *Kitāb al-Tanbīh wa-l-Radd ʿala ahl al-aḥwāʾ wa-l-bidʿa*. Ed. S. Dedering. Istanbul: Staatsdruckerei, 1936.

Al-Maqdisī, al-Muṭahhar b. Ṭāhir. *Kitāb al-Badʾ wa-l-Taʾrīkh*. Edited and translated by Clément Huart. Paris: Éditions Ernest Laroux, vol. III, 1903.

Al-Masʿūdi, Abū al-Ḥasan ʿAlī ibn al-Ḥusayn. *Murūj al-dhahab wa maʿādin al-jawāhir*. Edited and translated by Barbier de Meynard and Pavet de Courteille. Paris: Société asiatique de Paris, 1861–1877.

Mayer, Wendy. *The Cult of the Saints: Selected Homilies and Letters: St John Chrysostom*. New York: St Vladimir's Seminary Press, 2006.

Mayer, Wendy and Pauline Allen. *The Churches of Syrian Antioch (300–638 CE)*. Leuven: Peeters, 2012.

Melchert, Christopher. *Ahmad ibn Hanbal*. Oxford: Oneworld Publications, 2006.

Meri, Josef W. "Aspects of Baraka (Blessings) and Ritual Devotion among Medieval Muslims and Jews." *Medieval Encounters* 5 (1999): 46–69.

Meri, Josef W. *The Cult of Saints among Muslims and Jews in Medieval Syria*. Oxford: Oxford University Press, 2002.

Montgomery, James E. "For the Love of a Christian Boy: A Song by Abū Nuwās." *Journal of Arabic Literature* 27 (1996): 113–124.

Musa, Aisha Y. *Ḥadīth as Scripture: Discussions on the Authority of Prophetic Traditions in Islam*. New York: Palgrave Macmillan, 2008.

Muslim, al-Ḥajjāj b. Muslim. *Ṣaḥīḥ Muslim*. Riyadh: Dār al-Salām, 2000.

Neuwirth, Angelika. "Qurʾanic Studies and Philology: Qurʾanic Textual Politics of Staging, Penetrating, and Finally Eclipsing Biblical Tradition." In: A. Neuwirth & M.A. Sells (eds.), *Qurʾanic Studies Today*. New York: Routledge, 2016, 178–206.

Parrinder, Geoffrey. *Jesus in the Qurʾan*. Oxford: Oneworld Publications, 1965.

Pesiqta Rabbati: A Synoptic Edition of Pesiqta Rabbati Based upon All Extant Manuscripts and the Editio Princeps. Vols. I–III. Edited by Rivka Ulmer. Atlanta: Scholars Press, 1997–2002. Translated by William G. Braude, *Pesikta Rabbati: Discourses for Feasts, Fasts, and Special Sabbaths*. Vols. I–II. New Haven: Yale University Press, 1968.

Pratt, Mary Louise. *Imperial Eyes: Travel Writing and Transculturation*. Second edition. London: Routledge, 2008.

Pregill, Michael. "Measure for Measure: Prophetic History, Qur'anic Exegesis, and Anti-Sunnī Polemic in a Fāṭimid Propaganda Work (BL Or. 8419)." *Journal of Qur'anic Studies* 16 (2014): 20–57.

Al-Qurṭubī, Muḥammad b. Aḥmad al-Anṣarī. *Al-Jāmiʿ al-Aḥkām al-Qurān*. Vols. I–XXIV, Beirut: Al-Resalah Publishers, 2006.

Al-Qurṭubī, Muḥammad b. Aḥmad al-Anṣarī. *Al-Mufhim li-mā ʾAškala min Talkhīṣ Kitāb Muslim*. Vols. I–VII. Damascus: Dār Ibn Kaṯīr, 1996.

Rafael, Anna-Liisa. "Since When Were Martyrs Jewish? Apologies for the Maccabees' Martyrdom and Making of Religious Difference" In: Outi Lehtipuu and Michael Labahn, *Models of (In-)Tolerance in the Early Christian Age: Encountering Others in Early Judaism and Christianity*. Amsterdam: Amsterdam University Press, 2021, 139–168.

Robson, J. "Ḥadīth." In: Bernard Lewis et al. (eds.), *The Encyclopaedia of Islam*. Leiden: Brill, 1986, III, 23–28.

Rouwhorst, Gerhard. "The Cult of the Seven Maccabean Brothers and their Mother in Christian Tradition." In: M. Poorthuis & J. Schwartz (eds.), *Saints and Role Models in Judaism and Christianity*. Leiden: Brill, 2004, 183–204.

Rundin, John S. "Pozo Moro, Child Sacrifice, and the Greek Legendary Tradition." *Journal of Biblical Literature* 123 (2004): 425–447.

Rutgers, Leonard V. *Making Myths: Jews in Early Christian Identity Formation*. Leuven: Peeters, 2009.

Al-Šābuštī, Abu al-Hasan Ali. *The Shabushti's Book of Monasteries: Al-Diyarat*. Edited by George Awwad. Piscataway: Gorgias Press, 2008.

Schäfer, Peter. *Jesus in the Talmud*. Princeton: Princeton University Press, 2007.

Schwartz, Daniel R. *2 Maccabees*. Berlin: De Gruyter, 2008.

Siddiqi, Muhammad Zubayr. *Ḥadīth Literature: Origin, Development and Special Features*. Cambridge: Islamic Texts Society, 1993.

Stemberger, Günter. "The Maccabees in Rabbinic Tradition." In: F.G. Martínez, A. Hilhorst, and C.J. Labuschange (eds.), *The Scriptures and the Scrolls: Studies in Honour of A. S. van der Woude on the Occasion of his 65th Birthday*. Leiden: Brill, 1992, 193–203.

Al-Suyūṭī, ʿAbd al-Raḥmān Kāmil al-Dīn. *Al-Durr al-Manšūr fī al-Tafsīr al-Maʾṯūr*. Vols. I–VIII. Beirut: Dār al-Fikr, 2011.

Al-Suyūṭī, ʿAbd al-Raḥmān Kāmil al-Dīn. *Laʾālīʾ al-Maṣnūʿa fī al-Aḥādīṯ al-Mawḍūʿa*. Edited by ʿAbd al-Raḥmān Ṣalāḥ b. Muḥammad b. ʿUwayḍa. Beirut: Dār al-Kutub al-ʿIlmiyya, 1996.

Al-Ṭabarānī, Abū al-Qāsim. *Al-Muʿjam al-Kabīr*. Vol. XIV. Edited by Ḥamdī ʿAbd al-Majīd al-Salafī. Al-Qāhira: Maktaba Ibn Taymiyya, n.d.

Al-Ṭabarī, Abū Jaʿfar Muḥammad b. Jarīr. *Tafsīr al-Ṭabarī: Jāmiʿ al-Bayān ʿan Taʾwīl Āy al-Qurʾān*. Vols. I–XXVI. Ed. ʿAbdallāh b. ʿAbdalmuḥsin al-Turkī. Cairo: Dār al-Hijr, 2011.

Thurlkill, Mary. *Sacred Scents in Early Christianity and Islam*. London: Lexington Books, 2016.

Vaglieri, Veccia L. "ʿAbd Allāh b. al-ʿAbbās" In: Bernard Lewis et al. (eds.) *The Encyclopaedia of Islam*. Leiden: Brill, 1986, I, 40–41.

Vajda, G. "Une versio arabe du martyre des fréres 'Macchabées'." *Revue des Études Juives* 101 (1937): 95–96.

Vajda, G. "Isrāʾīliyyāt." In: Bernard Lewis et al. (eds.), *The Encyclopaedia of Islam*. Leiden: Brill, 1997, IV, 211–212.

Witakowski, Witold. "Mart(y) Shmuni, the Mother of the Maccabean Martyrs, in Syriac Tradition." In: R. Lavenant (ed.), *VI Symposium Syriacum 1992. University of Cambridge, Faculty of Divinity 30 August–2 September 1992*. Rome: Pontificio Istituto Orientale, 1994, 153–168.

Ziadé, Raphaëlle. *Les Martyrs Maccabées: de l'histoire juive au culte chrétien: Les homélies de Grégoire de Nazianze et de Jean Chrysostome*. Leiden: Brill, 2007.

CHAPTER 8

Little Big Gods: Morality of the Supernatural in Lydian and Phrygian Confession Inscriptions

Jarkko Vikman

In the Abrahamic traditions, their ideas of the supernatural and human identities related to them often entwine with morality.* Abrahamic gods are omnipotent supernatural agents who are primarily interested in human prosocial behaviour. These kinds of gods are sometimes described as "big gods." However, they are not the only kind of supernatural agents found in our cultures. Evolutionary studies of religion emphasize that we have long done well without these watchers of morality. Recently, the discussion about the rise of big gods has been related to the birth of complex societies: Did the notion of big gods advance the birth of large-scale societies? Or did the large-scale societies come first, with big gods being born to keep these societies together?

In this article, I will first read Anatolian confession inscriptions (written in Greek, dated 120–250 CE) in the light of evolutionary studies on religion and then present some comments on the recent discussion. Confession inscriptions come from non-Abrahamic traditions often labelled traditional cults of Asia Minor. They describe how a transgressor has received a punishment from god, and now asks for forgiveness by erecting a stele. I argue that big gods not only evolve in the growth of well-being in new larger societies, but also in the crises of rural contexts. Furthermore, the morality of a big god may be surprisingly closely entwined with domains of etiquette and good manners—areas that are often neglected in studies of religion and morality.

1 Big Gods

In their *Oxford Handbook of Evolutionary Psychology and Religion* article from 2016, Pascal Boyer and Nicolas Baumard state that the birth of morally inter-

* The article is based on a paper given in the session *Do the Gods Make us Moral? Psychological, Ecological and Cognitive Exploration* at the conference of the European Association for the Study of Religions (Tartu, Estonia, June 2019). I would especially like to thank Roosa Haimila and Nina Nikki for their comments on an earlier version of the article.

DOI:10.1163/9789004471160_009

ested gods occurred simultaneously in various parts of the world due to common changes in economic contexts. A life with more available resources was also a longer and healthier life. In the era known as the Axial Age, approximately from 600 BCE to 100 CE, upper social classes in complex societies had the need for religiously based ethics due to their globally enhanced well-being and its future-oriented way of life. According to Boyer and Baumard, the social elite of the large-scale Axial Age societies was keen to conserve the benefits offered by the new situation. This created a need for morally interested gods who had their word on sharing (or not sharing) the new resources. Similarly, the longer life expectancy increased the orientation towards the future, thus creating thoughts on an afterlife ruled by the same resource-sharing gods.[1] However, the great masses of this Axial Age continued to believe in powerful yet amoral supernatural agents.[2] Yet, other explanations for the interdependence of big gods and big societies have recently been given as well.

Partly, this recent interest in big gods is due to new possibilities gained with the use of big data from historical databases. Partly, the new interest has arisen from Ara Norenzayan's influential studies on big gods.[3] Norenzayan states that big gods were not just a result of growing societies but helped build these societies. Therefore, they may even have preceded the large-scale societies. In the spring of 2019, analyses conducted on *Seshat*, a global history databank, gained larger publicity as an article by Whitehouse et al. concluded that complex societies preceded the birth of moral gods.[4] Since the article was published, discussions on its methodological and statistical preferences have remained active.[5]

While I do not endeavour to offer an answer to this chicken-or-egg question, I do argue that a closer look at confession inscriptions and their birth context can sharpen the discussion on morally interested gods. I will next contrast my examples with the views of Boyer and Baumard. Confession inscriptions share the moral concern of the gods, but their social setting differs from the description of Boyer and Baumard. I argue that population decrease, economic stress, and common problems with health may have created a need for morally interested gods in the confession inscriptions.

1 Boyer and Baumard 2016, sec. "The Axial Age Movements."

2 Boyer and Baumard 2016, sec. "Kingdoms and City States."

3 Norenzayan 2013; Norenzayan 2015; Norenzayan et al. 2016. Norenzayan's theory has aroused wider interest, as Yuval Noah Harari has presented similar thoughts in his popular non-fiction work (Harari 2015, 77–98).

4 Whitehouse et al. 2019.

5 See the critique in Beheim et al. 2019. The discussion has since stayed active on social media and in preprint versions of various articles. However, most of the arguments had not yet appeared in research journals at the time this article was written.

2 The Confession Inscriptions of Rural Anatolia

Approximately 130 inscriptions from rural regions of Lydia and Phrygia, modern central Turkey, have been catalogued as confession inscriptions.[6] The majority of them indicate a date for their erection, in modern terms equivalent to 120–250 CE.[7] These inscriptions share the same structure as the pig theft confession below: a transgression by a person has led to punishment from a god.

> Hermogenes and Apollonius ... from Syros Mandrou, when three pigs belonging to Demaneitus and Papias from Azita wandered off and got mixed up with the sheep belonging to Hermogenes and Apollonius, while a 5-year-old boy was pasturing them, and they were herded back inside, and therefore Demaneitus and Papias were looking for them, they did not confess through some ingratitude. The staff of the goddess (Anaitis) and the lord of Tiamou (Mēn) was therefore set up, and when they did not confess the goddess duly showed her powers, and when Hermogenes died, his wife and child and Apollonius brother of Hermogenes implored her mercy and now bear witness to her and with the children sing her praises. In the year 199 (AD 114/15).[8]

The punishment—or in some inscriptions, a vision about it—created a need for the transgressor to confess his or her wrongdoing in a temple and to erect an inscription praising the god.[9] The religious expert responsible for the confession ritual is often depicted in the inscriptions with a sceptre held high, which is a common ritual element in traditional Greek religion. Eckhard Schnabel has catalogued the transgressions described in the inscriptions:

> Theft of clothes from a bath house, theft of weapons, theft of money, in one case from a granary, theft of pigs and sheep, theft of nets for fishing or hunting, theft of animal hides from a temple, infuriating one's mother, cheating orphans out of their inheritance, cheating a temple out of an inheritance where a deceased person had promised part of the family vineyards to the god, driving a stepson mad by poisoning him,

---

6 There are 124 inscriptions in the collection of Petzl 1994 and 135 inscriptions in Ricl 1995.
7 Gordon 2004, 179.
8 Siglum TAM V 1:317, translation: Mitchell 1993, 192.
9 Belayche 2006, 67.

> evicting one's sister from the household, bringing false charges against foster-children, violating foster-children, swearing of oaths and perjury, lying, defamation, failure to keep a vow, making an imprudent vow, idle talk and perjury (of a woman), refusal to acknowledge a debt involving perjury, non-payment of debts, sexual misconduct, sexual intercourse during a forbidden time, masturbation (perhaps in the temple), neglecting religious duties by absenteeism, being late for an appointment in the sanctuary, cutting down and selling wood from sacred groves, stoning sacred pigeons, stealing sacred pigeons, illegally pasturing flocks in a sacred grove, failure to appear before a god, visiting a temple without fulfilling the necessary preconditions, i.e. in a state of defilement, failure of a female temple official to obey purity laws after intercourse, engaging in cultic ablutions outside the appointed dates, breaking into a sanctuary, visiting the temple of a god in rags, carousing in a temple, removal of a holy slave from the temple (of Meter Hipta and Sabazios), bringing soldiers into a temple, eating the meat of a goat that had not been properly sacrificed, adultery with women attached to a temple, failure to transfer ownership of a slave who had been promised to the god, failure to provide labor to the god for a certain amount of days, mocking the god, unwillingness to take part in the mysteries of the god, refusal to obey a divine command to assume a priesthood, attempting to make a god assert something that is knowingly false, failure to erect a stele after being healed as a result of prayer to the god, refusal to believe in the power of the god.[10]

The ritual of confession is rather unusual in traditional Greco-Roman religious life. Usually the gods of Greeks and Romans are comprehended as morally disinterested. This is especially how the matter is understood in the cognitive science of religion. Jennifer Larson states that the role of Greek gods was not to define personal conduct.[11] According to Joseph Watts and colleagues, "The ancient Greeks and Romans did not have M[oralizing] H[igh] G[od]s."[12] Boyer and Baumard link the moral teaching to Greek philosophers, but do not consider it as part of the average religious life in Greco-Roman antiquity.[13] While the confession rituals cast a shadow of doubt on the pervasiveness of

10 Schnabel 2003, 169–171.
11 Larson 2016, 5.
12 Watts et al. 2015, 6.
13 Boyer and Baumard 2016, sec. "The Axial Age Movements."

this amoral gods argument,[14] it is worth noting that evidence about the ritual has not been found in any larger cities outside Lydia or Phrygia. Therefore, one should not overestimate the historical significance of this phenomenon. In addition, several confessions deal with transgressions that the modern reader would label ritual failures rather than moral flaws. However, I will later question how fruitful this common separation of ritual rules and moral laws is in the case of ancient religions.

The inscription MAMA IV 285 not only gives an example of these ritual failures, but Mitchell's translation also conveniently reveals the literary plainness of these rural monuments:

> I went up to the place and I went through the village twice unpurified. I forgot. I went back into the village. I announce that no one else will despise the god since he will have the stele as an example. The aforementioned Eutycheis did this of his own accord and confessed and has supplicated.[15]

The rural nature of this ritual innovation of confession and stele erection becomes most visible on a map of northwest Asia Minor. Confession inscriptions centre on settlements near the towns of Saittai, Silandus, Kollyda, and Motella. Only one confession inscription is found near Sardis and none from Ephesus or Smyrna. Some perspective on the population differences of these sites can be gained from *The Barrington Atlas of the Greek and Roman World*. The Atlas divides sites into five different categories according to their size, physical remains, literary references and civic status. None of the largest metropolises from the first category are located in western Asia Minor—the area relevant for this study. Whereas Sardis, Smyrna and Ephesus belong to the second category of a city, Saittai and Silandus represent the third category (a town), Motella the fourth category (a village), and finally Kollyda the fifth category (isolated villa, farm, bath, or hamlet). The rest of the smaller locations near Saittai and Silynda belong to category five.[16] J.W. Hanson's analysis of the urban demographics of Asia Minor does not mention these sites. However, it estimates the population of other settlements, which are ranked in the third category of the *Barrington Atlas*. Based on Hanson's statistics, the average population of a third category town could have ranged between a thousand and

14 Belayche (2003, 241; 2006, 72–73) parallelizes morally interested gods of the confession inscriptions with the ones in Homer, *Od.* 13.214.

15 Translation: Mitchell 1993, 193.

16 Talbert 2000, maps 56, 61; Hanson 2011, 236.

ten thousand inhabitants.[17] Most of the confession inscriptions were erected outside these towns.

Scholars have interpreted the significance of this rural context in various ways. According to Richard Gordon, tenants who worked on estates of the city elites erected the steles.[18] Amongst several others, Angelos Chaniotis sees the confession inscriptions as the continuation of a millennium-old tradition that had originated amongst the Hittites and continued in the periphery.[19] Eckhard Schnabel criticizes this view, as it has not been able to explain the thousand-year gap between the Hittite tradition and the Anatolian inscriptions. He sees the rise of a new epigraphic habit as a response to early Christian and Judean influences on the region. Schnabel considers the praising songs of the ritual (also described in our first example) as an example of this influence.[20] A scholarly consensus seems to rest on the importance of a priestly class for the erection of the inscriptions: the effort was encouraged by the temple officials and they dictated (at least partly) the wording of the steles.[21]

Schnabel's critique of the Hittite background deserves to be taken seriously, as the confession inscriptions do seem to appear from nowhere during the second century CE. Yet, I would be more cautious about drawing straight lines between early Christian influences and these steles. First, the early Christian material culture does not seem to pay attention to questions of guilt and confession in the first centuries of the Common Era. According to the pre-Constantine sources catalogued and interpreted by Graydon Snyder, the emphasis of early Christian art and inscriptions lay stronger on questions of health, wealth and security.[22] Second, even if we suppose the steles were a reaction to Christianity, Schnabel's thesis fails to explain the rural context of the confession inscriptions. Religious innovations are usually more rapidly adopted in urban contexts.[23] If one considers the urban settlements of Eph-

17 Hanson 2011, 254–257; compared to all 3rd category settlements in 269–271.

18 Gordon 2004, 180–181.

19 Chaniotis 2009, 146. The Hittite origin was first suggested by Raffaele Pettazzoni (see, e.g., Pettazzoni 1967). Nicola Belayche (2006, 70) joins to this view. Yet, she also emphasizes Greco-Roman influences: many of the names mentioned in the inscriptions are Greek and Roman.

20 Schnabel 2003, 178–188. For the links between Judeo-Christian praising and the εὐλογία of the confession inscriptions, Schnabel refers (i.a.) to Mitchell 1999, 112.

21 Schnabel 2003, 176, 178; Gordon 2004, 183, 190. However, Mitchell (1993, 194–195) emphasizes the direct relationship between the confessor and the god in the act.

22 Snyder 2003, 298: "From 180 to 400 [CE] artistic analogies of self-giving, suffering, sacrifice or incarnation are totally missing."

23 Rogers 1983, 294–300: Inhabitants of larger living units are enmeshed in more complex social networks in which innovations "diffuse" faster.

esus and Smyrna as key areas for the spread of early Christianity—as scholarly opinion usually does—then one would also expect to find confession steles from these cities.[24]

My contribution to the discussion on the question of "religion and evolution of morality" links to the enigmatic socio-historical context of these inscriptions. Inspired by Boyer and Baumard, I endeavour to understand what kind of socioeconomic and health-related factors could explain the novel need for the confession of personal guilt. One of the most common answers is written in the inscriptions: fear of punishment. The historical reasons related to this fear remain more tentative by nature—yet still worth pursuing.

3 In Sickness, Not in Wealth: Birth of the Anatolian Moral Gods

One potential reason behind the rise of the new inscriptional habit is the fear of death and disease. Angelos Chaniotis has linked confession inscriptions to ancient medicinal habits. Chaniotis has listed 30 confession inscriptions which explicitly mention a mental or physical illness. Some features are described in the texts, others in pictures on steles. For example, TAM V.1 322 has breasts, a leg (probably the right one), and eyes pictured in it. One could enlarge Chaniotis's list by adding inscriptions describing the death of a relative. According to Chaniotis, ocular problems are the most common issue in these descriptions (14 inscriptions), but ailments concerning other body parts, such as breasts, buttocks, legs and arms, are also depicted. Furthermore, mental illnesses, and even one loss of virginity are interpreted as divine punishments in the inscriptions.[25] Chaniotis explains the popularity of confession behaviour by the costliness, painfulness, and uncertainty linked to the methods of proper physicians. In a rural context, the help of the temple might have been an easier option for uneducated people.[26]

Chaniotis's argument of health-promoting inscriptions can be supported with psychological studies that have shown a connection between ritualistic

24 For the research history on the significance of Ephesus to early Christianity, see Trebilco 2004, 1–4; for Smyrna, Neufeld 2005, 33–37. In addition, Stephen Mitchell's map illustrates the unlikelihood of early Christian or Jewish influences for confession inscriptions (Mitchell 1993, 190): Evidence of Jewish communities and Montanist Christians is concentrated in the larger cities of Lydia and Western Phrygia. Apollo Lairbenos's temple site near Motella marks the only exception, as both confession inscriptions and remnants of Montanist influences have been discovered near the site.

25 Chaniotis 1995, 338–339.

26 Chaniotis 1995, 332–333.

behaviour and coping with anxiety. Richard Sosis and W. Penn Handwerker have investigated the ritualized behaviour of modern Israelis who had experienced the horrors of rocket attacks. According to the study, those who sang psalms during the attack feared less than those who did not sing.[27] Sosis and Handwerker interpret the phenomenon through Malinowski's theory of magic as an individual's means of controlling unpredictable situations. They also list 14 other psychological studies linking magical rituals and uncontrollable conditions.[28] Sosis and Handwerker complement these studies by emphasizing that in these situations the stressors need to be both uncontrollable and unpredictable. "Reciting psalms (it is believed) can protect your house from destruction by a Katyusha [rocket], but psalms cannot make the floor space your family is sleeping on grow larger, keep your children busy, or make your belongings suddenly appear in your new residence."[29] Before modern medicine, matters of health were out of the control of and not predictable by an individual, and therefore prone to ritualized behaviour.

Carol Nemeroff and Paul Rozin have defined magical thinking as "Cognitive intuition or belief in the existence of imperceptible forces or essences that transcend the usual boundary between mental/symbolic and physical/material realities."[30] Israeli psalm singing and Anatolian stele erecting fit this description: through symbolic action and invisible powers one wishes to effect concrete physical states or prevent further health-related problems. In our first example above, the family of the deceased thief may hope to avoid the fate of Hermogenes.[31] This intuitive process not only describes the protective powers of magico-religious rituals, but also human strategies to explain life experiences as a series of causes and effects—even non-visible ones. This phenomenon has been labelled as "superstitional conditioning" in behavioural studies.[32] It was originally discovered in test conditions with pigeons. Even though the birds were fed regularly every five minutes, they rapidly developed a ritual-like habit of repeating the gesture which they happened to be making

27 Sosis and Handwerker 2011. The birth of the cognitive theory relating ritualization and anxiety is often linked to the articles of Pascal Boyer and Pierre Liénard (Boyer and Liénard 2006; Liénard and Boyer 2006).

28 Sosis and Handwerker 2011, 41.

29 Sosis and Handwerker 2011, 48.

30 Nemeroff and Rozin 2000, 5.

31 Belayche (2006, 79–80) observes how the steles may have functioned as guarantees for memory: the monument helped to memorize god's powers. God who was remembered and praised was a satisfied god. He or she did not need to cause further misfortunes.

32 The following summary of "superstitional conditioning" is based on the definition in Czachesz 2013, 166–167.

when the first food dose was given.[33] Likewise, pre-school children started to act ritually in front of a mechanical clown that gave them marbles at fixed intervals.[34] It has been suggested that this phenomenon arises from hypersensitivity to causality, which might have been an evolutionary benefit to several organisms (such as the pigeons and human children in the examples above). Besides this adaptive function, some "superstitious" actions may also arise from "ecological traps": a predator might have gone extinct, but its prey still hides from it after several generations.[35]

In the case of confession inscriptions, Chaniotis's thoughts on their medicinal nature concentrate on the relevance of the confession to the confessors. I continue the thought by stating that this could also help us understand the birth of this ritual. Hypersensitivity to causality bends individuals to seek the cause and effect behind uncertain and unpredictable situations. Some studies have shown that this can benefit an individual's coping during misfortunes. For example, Chris Sibley and Joseph Bulbulia discovered this among earthquake survivors: those who sought guidance from religious explanations for the disaster experienced their subjective health as better than other participants of the test did.[36]

What kind of misfortunes could have caused the common demand for ritual confession in rural Anatolia? In the footsteps of Boyer and Baumard, I approach this question through information from population dynamics. Two possible explanations arose from this view: first, Peter Turchin and Sergey Nefedov's view on the carrying capacity of the Roman Empire, and second, possible effects related to the Antonine plague.

In their research, Turchin and Nefedov have compiled statistical data from various sources,[37] and through the data they aim to describe the populational and governmental life cycles of different empires. They designate the years 96–165 CE as "stagflation" of the Roman population cycle. The high political stability lead to a "golden age" of the empire but also created overpopulation and high inflation, as can be witnessed from official censuses and Egyptian wheat pricelists: The Roman population had grown in about seventy years (28 BCE–48 CE) from 4.063 million to 5.894 million, the implied growth rate at year

33 Skinner 1948; Morse and Skinner 1957.

34 Wagner and Morris 1987.

35 Foster and Kokko 2009, 36.

36 Sibley and Bulbulia 2012.

37 To mention some of the most often quoted (in the chapter considering the Roman principate): Duncan-Jones 1994; Frier 2000; McEvedy and Jones 1978; Scheidel 2001; Ward et al. 2003.

48 CE being 0.5% per year. The average price of wheat in private transactions was increased from 7.2 drachmas per *artaba* (18 BCE–47 CE) to 15.6 d/a (150–200 CE).[38] In official transactions the rise was from 3.3 d/a (13 BCE–65 CE) to 9.0 d/a (99–162 CE).[39]

According to Turchin and Nefedov, in times of overpopulation and high inflation inhabitants tend to cluster in metropolitan areas. These kinds of situations make individuals interested in possibilities for social mobility: they have witnessed the lives of the elite in the age of new well-being. Many want to have their own share of the lifestyle of the rich and famous. Likewise, stagflation resulted in "elite overproduction" in the Roman empire: even though the number of high-ranking offices in the empire seems to have as much as tripled during the first and second centuries CE, still more senatorial descendants were rivalling for open offices than ever before. The agricultural situation mirrors this competition: in the Latin west, the number of inhabited rural sites decreased by 32 percent from the second century to the late third century CE.[40]

The stagflation lead to a phase Turchin and Nefedov call "crisis" in 165–197 CE when the Antonine plague carried by Parthian War veterans struck from the east. Even without the plague, the social system had been at the limits of its carrying capacity with a highly competitive and insecure elite and an inflation-struck non-elite. The plague likely hit the latter harder. Turchin and Nefedov state that this socio-political instability probably caused further population decline even after the Antonine plague. They label the resulting phase as "depression" (197–285 CE), a phase that was ravished by the plague of Cyprian (named after the church father whose written record of the epidemic has survived to us).[41]

This dark era led to the gradual recovery of rural areas, as the number of mouths to be fed decreased. Egyptian documents from Theadelphia witness that the size of farmed land areas grew. This may also signal a higher standard of living in the agricultural context of the third century, especially as the areas for orchards and vineyards grew significantly ("from 140 ha in 158 to 415 ha in 216"). Egyptian price data imply that the amount of cereals decreased in the commoners' diet, which points to diversified nutrition. Steep inflation of course alters the picture, but the trend can be perceived when the prices are announced in silver: in private transactions, the average price was 124 grams

38 *Artaba* is an Egyptian unit of dry capacity. During the Roman era it would have equalled approximately 25 litres: Smith et al. 1890, *ad locum*.

39 Turchin and Nefedov 2009, 183–184, 199–200.

40 Turchin and Nefedov 2009, 196–198; on elite overproduction: 201–202.

41 Turchin and Nefedov 2009, 203–205.

per quintal between 150 and 200 CE, but only 44 g/q between 250 and 300 CE. In official prices, the average prices are 94 g/q (99–162 CE) and 73 g/q (246–294 CE). Similar diversification of nutrification has also been perceived in studies concerning European diets after the Black Death.[42]

The description above generalizes the situation of an enormous empire rather roughly. Situations must have varied in different areal contexts. Still, even as a wide generalization, it can illuminate the context of confession inscriptions more sharply than other rough generalizations of Christian or Hittite influences. In the light of theories on rituals as relievers of uncontrollable and unpredictable situations, the innovation of a ritual (or recovery of an ancient one) becomes understandable.

Following Turchin and Nefedov, one can situate the confession inscriptions within a rural context that has begun to lose wealth-seeking inhabitants to larger cities. Inflation is pushing prices up, which creates an interest in coveting one's neighbour's possessions. Most of the property transgression described in inscriptions are dated between 164 and 222 CE: during the time of the Roman crisis and the early phases of the depression. The high price of nutrition leads to monotonous diets, and consequently, to health issues. At the turn of the third century, the Antonine plague strikes. It might not be as severe in loosely populated areas as in cities, but it still leaves its mark.

Uncontrollable and unpredictable events lead to rituals. Magical thinking, moreover, creates causality where none can empirically be perceived. According to the prior literature on magical thinking, it may alleviate anxiety by increasing a sense of control over seemingly random events. The other side of magical thinking is that the same person is also responsible for the worrisome situation. The ritual patient becomes an agent as he or she evaluates former actions again and pursues altering them in the future. The ritual itself is a part of this process by enacting this agency in a visible mode. The concrete inscriptions are a manifestation of this enactment. Singing the praise hymns also belongs to this process—the singing may have worked in a similar vein as psalms in the modern Israeli context.

As the socioeconomic factors alter through the impacts of the plague and economic depression, the rural sites begin to recover. Nutrition diversifies, farmed areas grow, and life becomes more controllable. The erecting of confession steles seems to stop as quickly as it began. The last dated confession inscription available to us was erected in 263 CE—at the advent of Cyprian's plague.[43]

42 Turchin and Nefedov 2009, 200–204.
43 Petzl 1994, no. 11 = Robert 1983, 516–520. Concordance of the dates: Petzl 1994, 145.

4 Confession Inscriptions and the Discussion on Big Gods

If the view of confession inscriptions as a magico-religious response to Roman resources is accepted, it raises interesting (yet anecdotal) perspectives on the recent discussion on the birth of moralizing gods. I categorize these perspectives in three concluding remarks:

First, the situation of confession inscriptions differed from the context Boyer and Baumard give for the rise of moral gods. They see their birth being related to new wealth, bigger populations and securing the resources. I consider the moralistic gods of my source inscriptions as being summoned out of fear, death and sickness. This may merely specify Boyer and Baumard's theory, as even in the Anatolian context the surrounding cities experienced a season of rapid population growth and inflation caused by it.[44] Still it is worth noting that the birth of morally interested gods is plausible in contexts other than large-scale societies. In fact, the interpersonal (and thus small-scale) relations of temple personnel and confessors may have played a significant role in the act of the ritual: the priest may have known of the wrong deeds already through rumours. The social pressure to compensate for them was more strongly experienced if the religious expert had to be encountered in daily interactions.

Second, my analysis seems to deurbanize the birth of at least the Anatolian moral gods. This calls us to remember other potential explanations for the birth of gods of justice. They are not born only from theologians' writing skills or extended memory—even though both of these surely play their part in the case of confession inscriptions. The unadorned causal logic of these inscriptions reminds me of a rivalling narrative behind big gods offered by Harvey Whitehouse fifteen years ago. Whitehouse suggested that the repetitive, technical and causal nature of agriculture may have created logical and "doctrinal" gods even before literacy.[45]

Third, and in my opinion most importantly, my view applies magical thinking and the ritualistic control of the uncontrollable as paths to moral actions. By this, I question the strong differentiation between moral and amoral traditions. In confession inscriptions, morality does not merely relate to the abstract theology of religious experts, but also to the survival techniques of the human mind. For example, the theory of charismatic signalling has emphasized this

44 Belayche (2003, 239; 2006, 80) insightfully notes that the epigraphic habit was mostly an urban phenomenon. The gods of the confession inscriptions were portrayed in a vein which the illiterate majority could have interpreted as symbols of the urban elite.

45 Whitehouse 2004, 77–82.

relation. According to its formulators, etiquette secures trustworthiness in cooperation. Therefore, supernatural sanctioning is needed to enable the etiquette:

> The majority of evolutionary theories of religion focus on how supernatural concerns of morality, and punishments to breaches of morality, enable cooperation. However, these theories ignore the fact that the concerns of supernatural entities often extend far beyond obvious issues of morality. Indeed, supernatural entities are often very concerned that group members adhere to very specific sets of behavioral etiquette. The charismatic signaling model explains why etiquette is perceived as a moral breach: Breaches to etiquette pose a threat to coordination. Adherence to a broad set of norms—across various types of social interaction—helps resolve risks to cooperation ... By providing information to anonymous individuals who engage in various forms of interaction, etiquette reinforced by supernatural sanctioning enables cooperation across large groups.[46]

Likewise, Natalie and Joseph Henrich's work on cultural evolution of human prosociality has seen a close link between seemingly irrelevant (or even dangerous) ancestral customs and our capability to act together. They see the connection in reputation management: deficiencies in etiquette effect the way others value us as members of society. This reputation then defines which kind of prosocial networks we are able to join.[47]

Etiquette and morality are also combined in confession inscriptions. The wrong clothes in the temple bring about similar reactions as pig theft, gossiping, and even disbelief in the god's power. Whether interested in the magical rituals or adaptive cooperation, one operates wisely in keeping the etiquette

---

46 Shaver et al. 2017, sec. "The Puzzle of Why the Gods Punish Etiquette Violations Explained."

47 Henrich and Henrich 2007, 71: "[T]his effect can stabilize lots of noncooperative (even maladaptive) behaviors by linking them to reputation in the indirect-reciprocity game. For example, the practice of giving daughters clitoridectomies could be linked to a family's reputation such that families who fail to perform the ritual circumcision would get a bad reputation in their communities, and would thereby not receive aid if disaster were to strike them. This potentially answers the question of how noncooperative and sometimes maladaptive behaviors are maintained in a population by reputation. ... If different (via the randomness in cultural evolution) groups have linked reputation to a mutual aid game (for example) and to other behaviors ... then groups that happened to link reputation to cooperative behavior, especially those related to the *n*-person situations that are otherwise difficult to solve (e.g., cooperation in warfare, defense, and large-scale economic endeavors), will spread relative to other groups via the cultural group selection processes discussed above."

and ethics together. We should at least define sharply what we mean by the word moral, and how it differs or tangles with our own definitions of morality. For example, when Boyer and Baumard state that gods of archaic societies were only interested in stabilizing the political and societal norms, how does this differ from morality?[48] Reasons may exist for cropping this function outside the definition of moral gods, but they need to be explicated. Philosophical discussions on the theme of moral agency seem to continue (possibly more than ever before) because of the need to define the ethics of artificial intelligence. We will do wisely to consult these discussions in the case of historical nonhuman agency too.

5 Conclusion

Finally, it needs to be asked: Should we count the Anatolian supervisors of pig thieves and temple desecraters among the elite league of big gods? Do they fit into the group of guarantors of long-time investments in prosocial behaviour? Certainly, they do. However, they do not act as we would wish moral gods to function. They are interested in issues that seem marginal to us. They do not try to universalize their opinions or find common rules for their actions. Nor did they become great ones in urban settlements.

Walter Burkert was one of the first to apply evolutionary approaches to the field of Greco-Roman religions. His perspective is easy to dismiss as one grand theory of religion among the others. Yet, in the case of confession inscriptions, my analysis seems rather close to Burkert's, as he is writing on evolutionary perspectives of guilt and causality. "People are quite inclined to accept their own guilt, a readiness which makes the course of events understandable and offers a way to handle or refashion one's own fate."[49] According to him, this readiness exists still today in matters of health and disease, bringing "the surplus of causality and sense" as mediators of the phenomenon.[50] Burkert states that

48 Boyer and Baumard 2016, sec. "Kingdoms and City States": "People in archaic societies imagined gods with extensive powers over them but little moral concern. These gods were said to monitor what people do, but mostly to check that they provided the prescribed ceremonies or sacrifices, and conformed to established political and social norms. Also, in many cases the gods themselves were described as unencumbered with moral conscience and uninterested in human morality." In my opinion, statements like these would function more efficiently if the differences between monitoring, norm-checking and morality were explicitly stated.

49 Burkert 1996, 128.

50 Burkert 1996, 128.

science is in conflict with these cause-and-effect charlatans, as science tends to offer complicated and chaotic responses and therefore "will not easily prevail."[51] The case of Lydian and Phrygian confession inscriptions might remind us that big gods do not have to be popular gods. For some, they may even look like local charlatans.

Bibliography

Beheim, Bret et al. "Corrected Analyses show that Moralizing Gods Precede Complex Societies but Serious Data Concerns Remain." *PsyArXiv Preprints* (2019). DOI: 10.31234/osf.io/jwa2n.

Belayche, Nicole. "Résumé des conférences et travaux." *Annuaire de l'EPHE, Section des sciences religieuses* 111 (2003), 238–242.

Belayche, Nicole. "Les steles dites de confession: Une religiosité originale dans l'Anatolie impériale?" In: Lukas de Blois, Peter Funke, and Johannes Hahn (eds.), *The Impact of Imperial Rome on Religions, Ritual and Religious Life in the Roman Empire: Fifth Workshop of the International Network Impact of Empire, June 30–July 4, 2004, at Westfälische Wilhelms-Universität Münster, Germany*. Leiden: Brill, 2006, 66–81.

Boyer, Pascal and Nicolas Baumard. "The Diversity of Religious Systems Across History: An Evolutionary Cognitive Approach." In: James R. Liddle and Todd K. Shackelford (eds.), *The Oxford Handbook of Evolutionary Psychology and Religion*. New York: Oxford University Press, 2016. DOI: 10.1093/oxfordhb/9780199397747.013.5.

Boyer, Pascal and Pierre Liénard. "Why Ritualized Behavior? Precaution Systems and Action Parsing in Developmental, Pathological and Cultural Rituals." *Behavioral and Brain Sciences* 29 (2006): 595–613.

Burkert, Walter. *Creation of the Sacred: Tracks of Biology in Early Religions*. Cambridge: Harvard University Press, 1996.

Chaniotis, Angelos. "Illness and Cures in the Greek Propitiatory Inscriptions and Dedications of Lydia and Phrygia." In: Philip J. van der Eijk, H.F.J. Horstmanshoff, and P.H. Schrijvers (eds.), *Ancient Medicine in its Socio-Cultural Context: Papers Read at the Congress Held at Leiden University 13–15 April 1992*. Amsterdam: Rodopi, 1995, II, 323–344.

51 Burkert 1996, 128. In a similar vein, Legare et al. 2012 describe "multiple epistemologies" as a common tool to interpret singular events. In their study, natural and supernatural explanations affect in us side by side when explaining the origin of species, causes of illnesses, and the event of death.

Chaniotis, Angelos. "Ritual Performances of Divine Justice: The Epigraphy of Confession, Atonement, and Exaltation in Roman Asia Minor." In: Hannah M. Cotton, Robert G. Hoyland, Jonathan J. Price, and David J. Wasserstein (eds.), *From Hellenism to Islam: Cultural and Linguistic Change in the Roman Near East*. Cambridge: Cambridge University Press, 2009, 115–153.

Czachesz, István. "A Cognitive Perspective on Magic in the New Testament." In: István Czachesz and Risto Uro (eds.), *Mind, Morality and Magic: Cognitive Science Approaches in Biblical Studies*. Durham: Acumen, 2013, 164–179.

Duncan-Jones, Richard. *Money and Government in the Roman Empire*. Cambridge: Cambridge University Press, 1994.

Foster, Kevin R. and Hanna Kokko. "The Evolution of Superstitious and Superstition-like Behaviour." *Proceedings of the Royal Society B* 276 (2009), 31–37.

Frier, Bruce W. "Demography." In: Alan K. Bowman, Peter Garnsey and Dominic Rathbone (eds.), *The Cambridge Ancient History: The High Empire, AD 70–192*. Second edition. Cambridge: Cambridge University Press, 2000, 787–816.

Gordon, Richard. "Raising a Sceptre: Confession-Narratives from Lydia and Phrygia." *Journal of Roman Archaeology* 17 (2004), 177–196.

Hanson, J.W. "The Urban System of Roman Asia Minor and Wider Urban Connectivity." In: Alan Bowman and Andrew Wilson (eds.), *Settlement, Urbanization, and Population*. Oxford: Oxford University Press, 2011, 229–275.

Harari, Yuval Noah. *Sapiens: A Brief History of Humankind*. Translated by the author with the help of John Purcell and Haim Watzman. London: Vintage Books, 2015.

Henrich, Natalie and Joseph Henrich. *Why Humans Cooperate: A Cultural and Evolutionary Explanation*. Oxford: Oxford University Press, 2007.

Larson, Jennifer. *Understanding Greek Religion: A Cognitive Approach*. London: Routledge, 2016.

Legare, Cristine H. "The Coexistence of Natural and Supernatural Explanations Across Cultures and Development." *Child Development* 83 (2012): 779–793.

Liénard, Pierre and Pascal Boyer. "Whence Collective Rituals? A Cultural Selection Model of Ritualized Behavior." *American Anthropologist* 108 (2006), 814–827.

McEvedy, Colin and Richard Jones. *Atlas of World Population History*. London: Allen Lane, 1978.

Mitchell, Stephen. *Anatolia: Land, Men, and Gods in Asia Minor: Vol. 1, the Celts in Anatolia and the Impact of Roman Rule*. Oxford: Clarendon Press, 1993.

Mitchell, Stephen. "The Cult of Theos Hypsistos between Pagans, Jews, and Christians." In: Polymnia Athanassiadi and Michael Frede (eds.), *Pagan Monotheism in Late Antiquity*. Oxford: Oxford University Press, 1999, 81–148.

Morse, W.H. and B.F. Skinner. "A Second Type of Superstition in the Pigeon." *American Journal of Psychology* 70 (1957), 308–311.

Nemeroff, Carol and Paul Rozin. "The Makings of the Magical Mind: The Nature and

Function of Sympathetic Magical Thinking." In: Karl S. Rosengren, Carl N. Johnson and Paul L. Harris (eds.), *Imagining the Impossible: Magical, Scientific, and Religious Thinking in Children*. Cambridge: Cambridge University Press, 2000, 1–34.

Neufeld, Dietmar. "Christian Communities in Sardis and Smyrna." In: Richard S. Ascough (ed.), *Religious Rivalries and the Struggle for Success in Sardis and Smyrna*. Waterloo: Wilfried Laurier University Press, 2005, 25–39.

Norenzayan, Ara. *Big Gods: How Religion Transformed Cooperation and Conflict*. Princeton: Princeton University Press, 2013.

Norenzayan, Ara. "Big Questions about Big Gods: Response and Discussion." *Religion, Brain and Behavior* 5 (2015): 327–342.

Norenzayan, Ara et al. "The Cultural Evolution of Prosocial Religions." *The Behavioral and Brain Sciences* 39 (2016), 1–65.

Pettazzoni, Raffaele. "Confession of Sins and the Classics." In: Raffaele Pettazzoni, *Essays on the History of Religions*. Translated by H.J. Rose. Leiden: Brill, 1967, 55–67.

Petzl, Georg. *Die Beichtinschriften Westkleinasiens*. Bonn: Habelt, 1994.

Ricl, Marijana. *La conscience du péché dans les cultes anatoliens à l'époque romaine* [in Serbian, with a French Summary]. Belgrade: University of Belgrade, 1995.

Robert, Louis. "Documents d'Asie Mineure." *Bulletin de correspondance hellénique* 107 (1983): 497–599.

Rogers, Everett M. *Diffusion of Innovations*. Third edition. New York: Free Press, 1983.

Scheidel, Walter. "Progress and Problems in Roman Demography." In: Walter Scheidel (ed.), *Debating Roman Demography*. Leiden: Brill, 2001, 1–81.

Schnabel, Eckhard J. "Divine Tyranny and Public Humiliation: A Suggestion for the Interpretation of the Lydian and Phrygian Confession Inscriptions." *Novum Testamentum* 45 (2003): 160–188.

Shaver, John H., Gloria Fraser, and Joseph A. Bulbulia. "Charismatic Signaling." In: James R. Liddle and Todd K. Shackelford (eds.), *The Oxford Handbook of Evolutionary Psychology and Religion*. New York: Oxford University Press, 2017. DOI: 10.1093/oxfordhb/9780199397747.013.17.

Sibley, Chris G. and Joseph Bulbulia. "Faith After an Earthquake: A Longitudinal Study of Religion and Perceived Health before and After the 2011 Christchurch New Zealand Earthquake." *PLoS ONE* 7:12 (2012): 1–10.

Skinner, B.F. "'Superstition' in the Pigeon." *Journal of Experimental Psychology* 38 (1948): 168–172.

Smith, William, William Wayte, and G.E. Marindin (eds.). *A Dictionary of Greek and Roman Antiquities*. London: John Murray, 1890.

Snyder, Graydon F. *Ante Pacem: Archaeological Evidence of Church Life before Constantine*. Second edition. Macon: Mercer University Press, 2003.

Sosis, Richard and W. Penn Handwerker. "Psalms and Coping with Uncertainty: Religious Israeli Women's Responses to the 2006 Lebanon War." *American Anthropologist* 113 (2011): 40–55.

Talbert, Richard J.A. *Barrington Atlas of the Greek and Roman World*. Princeton: Princeton University Press, 2000.

Trebilco, Paul. *The Early Christians in Ephesus from Paul to Ignatius*. Tübingen: Mohr Siebeck, 2004.

Turchin, Peter and Sergey A. Nefedov. *Secular Cycles*. Princeton: Princeton University Press, 2009.

Wagner, Gregory A. and Edward K. Morris. "'Superstitious' Behavior in Children." *Psychological Record* 37 (1987): 471–488.

Ward, Allen Mason, Fritz M. Heichelheim, and Cedric A. Yeo. *A History of the Roman People*. Fourth edition. Upper Saddle River: Prentice Hall, 2003.

Watts, Joseph et al. "Broad Supernatural Punishment but Not Moralizing High Gods Precede the Evolution of Political Complexity in Austronesia." *Proceedings of the Royal Society B* 282 (2015). DOI: 10.1098/rspb.2014.2556.

Whitehouse, Harvey. *Modes of Religiosity: A Cognitive Theory of Religious Transmission*. Walnut Creek: AltaMira, 2004.

Whitehouse, Harvey et al. "Complex Societies Precede Moralizing Gods Throughout World History." *Nature* 568 (2019): 226–243.

CHAPTER 9

"One Letter *yud* Shall not Pass Away from the Law": Matthew 5:17 to Bavli *Shabbat* 116a–b

Holger Zellentin

This article first briefly summarizes previous arguments that Matthew, especially in the famous passage Matt 5:17, urged Jewish followers of Jesus to keep the commandments of "the Law," i.e. the entirety of Biblical law as applicable to them, and that he modifies the Law only by placing it within a moral framework he considered to be stricter than the one he associates with his Pharisaic opponents.* The study will then focus on how the passage was received, on the one hand, in Greek and Latin and, on the other hand, in Syriac and Aramaic communities, and how it shaped Late Antique Christian legal thought. It will argue that the Matthean passage was understood as affirming the Law throughout late antiquity, as evidenced by the vehement attempts by many church fathers to deny just such a reading. The chapter will place special emphasis on those works—such as Faustus's *Disputationes* in Latin (as transmitted by Augustine), the *Clementine Homilies* in Greek, and the *Didascalia Apostolorum* in Syriac—that understood Matthew as confirming legal observance as necessary for salvation, and it will trace the relationship of Matt 5:17 to the development of the notion of satanic falsification of Scripture. The study will conclude by arguing that the Babylonian Talmud, in *Shabbat* 116a–b, restates and transforms aspects of both Eastern (i.e., Syriac) and Western (i.e. Latin and Greek) Christian traditions based on Matt 5:17.

* This chapter is part of a project that has received funding from the European Research Council (ERC) under the European Union's Horizon 2020 research and innovation programme (Grant agreement Grant agreement ID: 866043). Many translations in this chapter have been slightly modified to give a more literal sense of the text; unattributed translations are my own. I transliterate Syriac as well as rabbinic Aramaic and Hebrew in accordance with the early defective (i.e. non-vocalized) tradition, as follows: *ʾ b g d h w z ḥ ṭ y k l m n s ʿ p ṣ q r sh t*; Biblical texts follow the SBL transliterations; Arabic follows IJMES. I am grateful for the perceptive and encouraging comments and corrections offered by the anonymous reviewer of this volume and by Volker Drecoll to an earlier draft of this article; as well as to Sergey Minov and Alison Salvesen for their helpful guidance. I am moreover indebted to the resources offered by the Digital Syriac Corpus (⟨syriaccorpus.org⟩) and of the Friedberg Project for Talmud Bavli Variants (⟨bavli.genizah.org⟩).

 | DOI:10.1163/9789004471160_010

1 Matthew 5:17–18 in the Greek, Latin and Syriac Gospels

Numerous scholars, myself included, have suggested that Matthew's gospel was originally written from within an ethnically Jewish framework, which includes gentiles, if at all, only as a secondary audience—with some exceptions such as the gospel's plausibly secondary ending.[1] Matthew, in this view, presupposes that Jews must remain obedient to "the Law," i.e., to the entirety of the legal obligations which the Hebrew Bible imposes upon the Israelites—even if Jesus is portrayed as questioning Pharisaic additions to this law, especially when it comes to Kashrut and Shabbat observance.[2] While the consensus on the matter seems to be moving towards the view that Matthew wrote within a Jewish law-affirming context, Matthew's Christian readers, by contrast, long understood his polemics against Pharisaic law as directed against all of Jewish law, and some continue to do so.[3] We will see that most hermeneutical positions occupied by contemporary academics have at least a close parallel already among Matthew's late antique readers.

In the Sermon on the Mount, Matthew presents Jesus as summing up his legal philosophy. The passage Matt 5:17–20 is densely structured through a series of repetitions, here rendered in italics:

17	Think not that *I have come to abolish the Law* and the prophets,	mē nomisēte *oti ēlthon katalusai ton nomon* ē tous prophētas,
	I have come not *to abolish* but to fulfil.	*ouk ēlthon katalusai* alla plērōsai.

1 Central studies that have contributed to a better understanding of the clear distinction between Jewish and gentile ethnicity in the early church include John R. Van Maaren (2019); Suzanne Watts Henderson (2018, 145–168); Todd Berzon (2018, 191–227); Todd S. Berzon (2016); Anders Runesson (2016); and Isaac Oliver (2013). I have sought to trace the implications of their insights for Jewish and Christian ritual observance in a number of studies, e.g. Holger Zellentin (2013c; 2018, 117–159; 2019, 115–215). On the gentiles in Matthew, and on the gospel's ending, see note 7 below.

2 On this extensive debate, which involves the respective views of the historical Jesus on the one hand and that of his evangelists on the other, see esp. John VanMaaren (2017, 21–41); see also the useful summaries by Lutz Doering (2008, 213–241) and by Yair Furstenberg (2008, 176–200). For my own assessment of Matthew's views, perhaps most closely aligned with Runesson's recent study, see Holger Zellentin (2013b, 379–403). The reading here of Matthew as considering Biblical—though not necessarily "Jewish"—law to be applicable for Jews—though not necessarily for gentiles—is at least compatible with important strands in other areas of New Testament scholarship as presented, for example, in Mark D. Nanos and Magnus Zetterholm (2015).

3 The literature on the topic is vast, a good overview can be gleaned from Ulrich Luz (2007, 210); Hans Dieter Betz (1995, 166–197); see also Roland Deines (2008, 53–84) and the two in-depth studies by Roland Deines (2004) and Robert Banks (1975).

18	*For* truly, *I tell you*, *until heaven* and earth *pass away*, not an iota or *a* dot will *pass* from *the Law* *until* all is accomplished.	amēn *gar legō umin*, *eōs an parelthē o ouranos* kai ē gē, iōta en ē *mia* keraia ou mē *parelthē* apo *tou nomou* *eōs an* panta genētai.
19	Whoever then *dissolves* one of *the least* of these commandments and *teaches* men so, *shall be called least in the kingdom of heaven*, but he who does them and *teaches* them *shall be called great in the kingdom of heaven*.	*os ean* oun *lusē* mian tōn entolōn toutōn *tōn elachistōn* kai *didaxē* outōs tous anthrōpous, *elachistos klēthēsetai en tē basileia tōn ouranōn*, *os d'an* poiēsē kai *didaxē* outos megas *klēthēsetai en tē basileia tōn ouranōn*.
20	*For I tell you*, unless your righteousness exceeds that of the scribes and Pharisees, you will never *enter the kingdom of heaven*	*legō gar umin oti ean* mē perisseusē umōn ē dikaiosunē pleion tōn grammateōn kai pharisaiōn, ou *mē eiselthēte eis tēn basileian tōn ouranōn*.[4]

A literary as well as a literal reading of Matthew's message, if understood within a Jewish context, suggests that Matthew meant what he wrote: Jesus teaches that Jews must uphold what the Law and the prophets command.[5] Matthew seems to be aware that Jesus's criticism of Pharisaic law could be misunderstood as implying the dissolution of Biblical law.[6] He therefore repeats emphatically: Jesus has not come to abolish to the Law, but to fulfil the Law of the

4 The citation follows Eberhard Nestle, Erwin Nestle, Barbara Aland and Kurt Aland (2004, 10). The variants of the Greek text are few and hardly significant, with the exception of the omission of the second part of verse 19 (from *os d'an poiēsē* ...) in the *Codex Sinaiticus* and a few minor witnesses as noted in NA[27].

5 Matthew Thiessen explains the passage as a reaction to the charge that Jesus's alleged abrogation of the Law led to the destruction of the Temple; see Thiessen (2012, 543–556); for a brief history of scholarship see Betz (1995, 166–197) and Zellentin (2013b, 379–403); cf. Luz (2007, 210–225) and Deines (2008, 80–82).

6 Luz argues that Matthew's statement "do not think" does not constitute "evidence of a direct polemic, for example, against antinomians" (see Luz 2007, 213), yet this statement strikes me as at odds with both Matthew's literary structure and the parallel polemics against neo-Pauline antinomianism, for example, in the *Book of Revelation*, see David Frankfurter (2001, 403–425). Betz therefor correctly emphasises that the verses Matt 5:17–20 "respond to specific accusations with regard to Jesus's interpretation of the Torah," see Betz (1995, 173). Von Harnack (1912, 185) has also drawn attention to the respective parallel between Matt 5:17 and the palpable reaction to a different charge in Luke 23:2, "we found this man (i.e., Jesus) perverting

Bible in all its minute commandments, none of which Matthew presents Jesus as breaking, and none of which he demands of gentiles to keep.[7] "Until all is accomplished," in this reading, means that the Torah will last as long as heaven and earth will last (see also Luke 16:17). As some ancient commenters (on which more below) already noted, heaven and earth have not yet passed away: therefore, since "all" has not yet been accomplished, one must not relax any of the Torah's commandments, not even a minor one, as long as the earth persists.

Matthew's message is reinforced by a series of parallelisms indicated by italics in the rendering above, which are woven around the five-fold repetition of the verb *erchomai*, "to come," thereby linking the transformation of the Law to Jesus's "coming." These repetitions culminate and, by repetition and alliteration, point to the dramatic denial of entry to the kingdom of heaven to those who think otherwise: do not think I have *come* (*ēlthon*) to abolish; I have *come* (*ēlthon*) to fulfil; until heaven and earth *have passed* (*an parelthē*); not one iota *will pass* (*mē parelthē*); you will not *enter* (*mē eiselthēte*). All occurrences of the verb *erchomai* are based on its *e-l-th* root, making the alliteration readily audible to the audience. The "coming" of Jesus is thereby connected to the "passing" of the earth and of the Torah at the end of times, highlighting both Jesus's cosmic significance and the endurance of both cosmos and Law. The repetition of the central verb *erchomai*, moreover, is embedded in a complex web of further parallelisms that highlight Jesus's tight connection to the impending kingdom of heaven.[8]

---

our nation (*diastrefonta to ethnos ēmōn*), forbidding us to pay taxes to the emperor (*koluonta forous kaisari didonai*)"; see also Warren Carter (1998, 44–62).

7 Luz (2007, 211) downplays the role of Matt 5:17 by focusing on the historical Jesus rather than on Matthew, stating that "it is risky to attribute this saying to Jesus and to make it the central point for interpreting Jesus' understanding of the Law". Betz (1995, 167), by contrast, holds that Matt 5:17–20 "state the hermeneutical principles underlying [the Sermon on the Mount's] interpretation [of the Torah],". A crucial point for the discussion is obviously Matthew's attitude towards the inclusion of gentiles in the realm of God, beyond the more specific issue of their potential conversion. While the present context does not allow for a full elaboration of the issue, it should be noted that Matthew's ethnically charged depiction of gentiles as dogs (see Matt 15:21–28 and 5:47), as well as his general openness towards them (see e.g. Matt 8:5–13), points to a development in the gospel towards greater openness, as is also evident in the tension prevalent between the exhortation to focus only on the house of Israel (Matt 10:5–6) and the gospel's (perhaps secondary) ending, telling its audience to "make disciples of all gentiles" (Matt 28:18–20). Runesson (2016, 343–428), by contrast, finds important arguments that the ending marks an integral denouement of the gospel. Suffice it to say that this tension between Israelite particularism and universalism marked much of Hellenistic Judaism, and that openness towards the salvation of gentiles *qua gentiles* does by no means imply the abolishment of the Torah.

8 In detail, the following repetitions structure the passage Matt 5:17–20: *kataluō*, twice in

While the term *kataluō* clearly indicates that the abrogation of the Torah is denied, the term *plēroō* has a wide range of meaning. It may well co-note the beginning of a new era in the Pauline sense of the word, yet more centrally to its meaning it clearly denotes legal fulfilment and a specific type of augmentation of law, as the passage's immediate context indicates.[9] Matthew has Jesus insists that the "righteousness" of his disciples exceeds that of the Pharisees, which is achieved by simultaneously reducing Pharisaic additions to the Law and by placing it within a stricter moral framework. Jesus's disciples, not distracted by misleading additions, can fulfil the letter of the Law with greater exactness than the Pharisees. Throughout the Septuagint and Hellenistic Jewish literature, and also in Matthew, the Greek term he uses to describe "righteousness," *dikaiosyne*, signifies the keeping of the commandments; it denotes legal observance and connotes moral integrity.[10] Matthew hence insists that his disciples keep the biblical laws with greater stringency, and with greater moral integrity, than the Pharisees.

Matt 5:17–20, to summarize, presents a key element in Matthew's view that the Law must be kept strictly, and with moral integrity. Jesus adds to the Law and reduces it at the same time as prohibiting to add to or to reduce the Law. What has perplexed readers for millennia is relatively simple if one distinguishes between God's Law and the added "traditions of the elders." Jesus adds to God's Law by emphasizing moral integrity, but he does not add any new laws. He reduces previous human additions to the legal corpus, but he does not reduce God's Law. The remainder of the gospel, or at least its manifold discussions of Biblical and Pharisaic law, can be understood as a putting Matthew's respective teaching into legal practice.[11]

---

verse 17, anticipating the use of the verb *luō* in verse 19; *nomos*, twice in verse 17; *gar legō umin* in verse 17 and, with slightly inverted word order in verse 20; *eōs an*, twice in verse 18, *ouranos* in verse 18, preparing the repetition of *en tē basileia tōn ouranōn* in verses 19 and 20; *os ean*, twice in verse 19, *elachistos*, twice in verse 19; *didaskō*; twice in verse 19 (same form); and *kaleō*, twice in verse 19 (same form). The ensuing literary structure warrants an analysis beyond the confines of this contribution; it is enough here to state that we are dealing with a carefully composed unit. For a useful guide to Matthew's literary qualities see Wilhelmus Johanis Cornelius Weren (2014, 13–90).

9 Discussion of the terms *kataluō* and *plēroō*, with different emphases, can be found in Luz (2007, 217–219) and Betz (1995, 173–179).

10 See e.g. the Septuagint on Genesis 15:6. Paul's innovative reading of the Genesis passage in Romans 4 attests to the regular meaning of *dikaiosunē* as pious observance; it is used in this way by Paul himself in Philippians 3:5–6. For a discussion of the term in the context of Matthew see, e.g., Betz (1995, 190–193); for starkly different reading cf. Deines (2008, 73–84).

11 See Runesson (2016) and Zellentin (2013b, 379–403) both of which offer several case studies on the issues of Shabbat, divorce and dietary law.

Most later renderings of the Gospel, unfamiliar with the first- and second century CE discourse on Jewish law, tended to miss, or at least to modify, Matthew's distinction between Biblical and Pharisaic law and between law as applicable to Jews and to gentiles, and instead read Matt 5:17–20 either as endorsing or abrogating the Law in broader terms.[12] Likewise, the later renderings of the Matthean passage in other languages have no means to maintain the full literary complexity of Matthew's Greek text. The passage's rudimentary literary form, however, proved central to its reception history, as it can be reconstructed by its translations, its paraphrases, as well as by the many commentaries on it.

Regarding the passages' translations, it suffices to note that the key translations of Matthew into Latin and Syriac rendered the text in a way that allowed for a law-affirming reading of it, and that they maintained only some the repetitions we find in the Greek. Jerome's revision of the Old Latin gospels, for example, renders Matthew 5:17–18 as follows:

17	Do not think that I am come to dissolve the Law or the prophets.	*nolite putare quoniam veni solvere legem aut prophetas*
	I have note come to dissolve but to fulfil.	*non veni solvere sed adimplere*
18	For amen I say unto you,	*amen quippe dico vobis*
	until heaven and earth pass away	*donec transeat caelum et terra*

12 The gospels' statements about Pharisaic law did of course note escape their late antique audience entirely. While this issue is too complex to be treated here, we can find a good, if idiosyncratic, example in the views of Ptolemy, recorded in Epiphanius's citation of the *Letter to Flora*, which, with some historical justification, uses Matt 5:17 in order to distinguish between divine law and human additions. After quoting Matt 15:4–9 and Isaiah 29:13, Ptolemy argues that "from these passages, then, it is plainly shown that that Law as a whole is divided into three. For in it we have found Moses's own legislation, *the legislation of the elders*, and the legislation of God himself (*Mōseōs te gar autou* kai tōn presbuterōn *kai autou tou theou euromen nomosthesian en autō*, my emphasis). And this division (*ē diairesis*) of that Law as a whole which I have made here has made clear what in it is true. But the one portion, the Law of God himself, is again divided into some three parts. It is divided into the pure legislation with no admixture of evil, which is properly termed the "law," which the saviour came not to destroy but to fulfil (*on ouk ēlthe katalusai o sōtēr alla plērōsai*, Matt 5:17)," see Epiphanius, *Panarion* 33.3.14–5.1, translation according to Williams (1994, 218), Greek text according to Holl (1915, 453). Ptolemy associates the Decalogue alone with "God's law," a common theme that we will find in the Syriac tradition as well, see note 88 below as well as Salvesen (2012). The two further parts of the divine law are one part that is good but mixed up with evil (such as the talion) and a third, ritual part which is to be spiritualized; for a discussion on the identity of God as a law-giver in Ptolemy's letter see e.g. Herbert Schmid (2011, 249–271) and Markschies' rebuttal (2011, 411–430); see also von Harnack (1912, 193–194).

One *iota* or one tittle shall pass from the Law	*iota unum aut unus apex non praeteribit a lege*
until all will be done.	*donec omnia fiant.*[13]

Jerome's Latin rendering does not obviate the potential to understand Jesus as affirming the Law seen in the Greek original. The verb *solvere*, designating the "dissolution" of the Law, follows the Greek *kataluō* quite closely; the rendering of *plēroō* as *adimplere*, likewise, allows for a reading in terms of the legal fulfilment of any individual obligation, or of the Law as a whole.[14] When it comes to the parallelisms, however, the Latin text is much impoverished: Jerome's repetition of *veni* and *non veni*, for example, captures only one of the first repetitions of the Greek verb *erchomai*, "to come." Jerome does not connect this "coming" with the "passing," or "transition" of the heaven and the earth and of the Law, which the Greek text does by repeating the term *parerchomai*, for which Jerome, in turn, uses two different other verbs—*transeo* and *praetereo*.[15]

Around the fifth-century, the *Peshitta* became the accepted Gospel in the West Syrian tradition. Like Jerome's Vulgate, the New Testament Peshitta was a careful revision of a number of earlier Syriac translations.[16] The Peshitta equally renders the passage Matthew 5:17 in a way that allows for its understanding as endorsing the fulfillment of the Law, paying slightly more attention to the Greek's original repetitions than Jerome:

13 Cited according to Robert Weber and Roger Gryson (2007, 1531). While this is not the place to discuss the complex Old Latin Biblical tradition which Jerome was asked to replace, the witness of *Codex Bezae Cantabrigensis* is a good representative for its distinctness, see notes 14 and 15 below. Matt 5:17–18 can be found on folio 25 and 27 of Codex Bezae, published here: https://cudl.lib.cam.ac.uk/view/MS-NN-00002-00041/26.

14 Note that the Old Latin of *Codex Bezae* uses the verb *dissolvere* instead of Jerome's *solvere* and *inplere* instead of Jerome's *adimplere*, which both times is very close in meaning, see *Codex Bezae*, folio 25 and 27, https://cudl.lib.cam.ac.uk/view/MS-NN-00002-00041/26.

15 Jerome's use of different verbs for *parerchomai* is especially noteworthy since the Old Latin version of *Codex Bezae* renders the verb twice as *transeo*, maintaining some of the parallelism that structures the Greek original, see *Codex Bezae*, folio 25 and 27, https://cudl.lib.cam.ac.uk/view/MS-NN-00002-00041/26.

16 Among the ancient Syriac witnesses of the four Gospels, the Sinaiticus and Curetonianus predate the Peshitta, while the Harklean version post-dates it. On the importance of the Peshitta's witness see Piet B. Dirksen, and Arie van der Kooij (1995); all four Gospels have been edited in George Anton Kiraz (2004); the all citations in this paper are given according to ibid., vol. 1, 53–55.

17	Do not think that I have come to loosen the Law or the prophets	*lʾ tsbrwn dʾtyt dʾshrʾ*[17] *nmwsʾ ʾw nbyʾ*.[18]
	I have not come to loosen but to fulfil.	*lʾ ʾtyt dʾshrʾ*[19] *ʾlʾ dʾmlʾ*.[20]
18	For truly I tell you,	*ʾmyn gyr ʾmr ʾnʾ*[21] *lkwn*
	Until heaven and earth pass away,	*dʿdmʾ dnʿbrwn*[22] *shmyʾ wʾrʿʾ*
	not even one *yud* or a dash shall pass away from the Law	*ywd ḥdʾ ʾw ḥd srṭʾ*[23] *lʾ nʿbr*[24] *mn nmwsʾ*
	until all of it is fulfilled.	*ʿdmʾ dkl nhwʾ*.[25]

The distinct character of the Peshitta's translation is best understood by comparing it to earlier Syriac translations, and especially to the second-century Diatessaron, which proved far more central to the Syriac understanding of Matt 5:17, and especially for the Syriac emphasis on the enduring value of the Law. While we do not have the original version of the Diatessaron, a few citations in the works of Aphrahat give us a rough sense of the ancient Syriac reading of the Matthean passage.[26] The Peshitta's version of both Matt 5:17 and 18 is different from the Diatessaron's likely rendering in few but important ways. Aphrahat renders "I have not come to loosen the Torah or the prophets but to fulfil them" as *dlʾ ʾtyt lmshrʾ ʾwrytʾ wnbyʾ ʾlʾ lmmlyw ʾnyn*, using infinitive rather than imperfect forms of the same verbs we see in the Peshitta and, importantly, using the term *ʾwrytʾ*, Torah, rather than the more common term *nmwsʾ*, "law" we see in the Peshitta.[27] Likewise, a citation of the Diatessaron's rendering of Matt 5:18

---

17 Attested also in Curetonianus; Sinaiticus and the Harklean version read *lmshrʾ*.

18 Attested also in the Harklean version, Sinaiticus and Curetonianus read *wnbyʾ*.

19 Attested also in Curetonianus. Sinaiticus reads *dʾshrʾ ʾnwn*; the Harklean version reads *lmshrʾ*.

20 Sinaiticus and Curetonianus read *lmmlyh ʾnwn*; the Harklean version reads *lmshmlyh*.

21 Attested also in the Harklean version. Sinaiticus and Curetonianus read *ʾmrnʾ*.

22 Attested also in Curetonianus. Sinaiticus reads *ʿdmʾ dnʿbrwn*; the Harklean version reads *dʿdmʾ dtʿbr*.

23 Attested also in the Harklean version. Sinaiticus reads *ywd ʾtwtʾ ḥdʾ*, "one letter *yud*;" Curetonianus reads *ywd ʾtwtʾ ḥdʾ ʾw qrnʾ*, "one letter yud or one tittle," see also notes 28 and 33 below.

24 Attested also in the Harklean version. Sinaiticus an Curetonianus read *tʿbr*.

25 Sinaiticus reads *dkwl nhwʾ*, Curetonianus reads *dkl mdm nhwʾ*, and the Harklean version reads *dklhyn nhwyn*.

26 On the importance of the Diatessaron see William L. Petersen (1994), see also note 27 below.

27 Aphraat, *Demonstration 2* (*On Charity*) 5, see Jean Parisot (1894, 56–57). Aphrahat's reading is confirmed by Ephrem's truncated rendering of the same verse as "I have come to fulfil them" (*ʾtyt lmmlyh ʾtnwn*), see Ephraem, *Commentary on the Diatessaron* 15:4, Leloir (1963, 142). Elsewhere, however, Ephrem renders the passage as first briefly as *lʾ gyr ʾtyt dʾshrʾ ʾlʾ*

can be found in the same passage from Aphrahat: "Not one letter *yud* will pass away from the Torah and the prophets until all is fulfilled" (*dywd ʾtwtʾ ḥdʾ mn ʾwrytʾ wnbyʾ lʾ tʿbr ʿdmʾ dkl nhwʾ*), crucially translating as "one letter *yud*" what the Peshitta had translated as "one *yod* or dash."[28] Four elements of the Syriac translations of Matt 5:17 found in the Diatessaron, in the Peshitta and in previous translations proved consequential for its history of interpretation.

- First, the verb *sh-r-y*, used both by the Diatessaron and the Peshitta (in the *paʿel* and *peʿal* form, respectively), does not quite correspond to the Law's "dissolution" in the Greek text, in as far as it can be understood more easily in terms of gradual "loosening" the Law, as well as in shared sense of "breaking," or "destroying" the Law—an important difference in light of the respective Syriac interpretation of Matt 5:17 that reads Jesus as effectively "diminishing" the Law, which we will discuss below.[29]
- At the same time, the verb *m-l-ʾ*, used for the Law's "fulfilment," both in the Diatessaron and in the Peshitta (in the infinitive and imperfect *paʿel* form, respectively) renders the Greek very well, in as far as it allows for understanding Jesus both as fulfilling the Law as a whole and for the fulfilment of individual commandments, thereby offering a firm basis for the Syriac interpretations that saw the "fulfilment" of God's Law as prerequisite of gaining eternal life.[30]

---

dʾmlʾ, and then again slightly longer as *dlʾ ʾtyt dʾshrʾ ʾwrytʾ wnbyʾ ʾlʾ dʾmlʾ*, using the same imperfect verb form we see in the Peshitta in a possible later emendation, see Ephrem, *Commentary on the Diatessaron* 6.3a, see Louis Leloir (1990, 60), and see note 81 below.

28 *Aphrahat Demonstrations* 2 (*On Charity*) 7, see Parisot (1894, 61); the phrase is paraphrased again towards the end of the passage as *dlʾ tʿbr ywd ʾtwtʾ mn nmwsʾ wmn nbyʾ*, here using the more common term *nmwsʾ* rather than the Diatessaron's *ʾwrytʾ*. Ephrem discusses Matthew 5:18 also in one of his genuine *memre* (1.3.238, see Edmund Beck, 1969) vol. 1 and 2, ad loc.; see also note 33 below.

29 See Michael Sokoloff (2009, 1608–1609). The Arabic Diatessaron 8:46 renders the verb in Matt 5:17 with *naqaḍa*, "to break," which is used in the sense of breaking God's covenant in the Qur'an (e.g. in Q2:27, Q4:155, and Q5:13); see P. Augustinus Ciasca (1888, 32) and A.-S. Marmadji (1935, 76). On the relevance of the Arabic Diatessaron see also Georg Graf (1944, 150–155); and more recently John Granger Cook (2006, 462–471). Petersen points out the enduring importance of the Arabic translations as the only complete Eastern witness of the Diatessaron. While the language of many of the Arabic readings seems to have been influenced by the Peshitta and the Qur'an, the Arabic seems to preserve the original sequence of Tatian's work, which is of value to my considerations below; see Petersen (1994, 133–138).

30 Sokoloff (2009, 768–769), note that the Harklean version uses the verb *sh-m-l-y*, which has a similar meaning, see ibid, 1573. The Arabic Diatessaron 8:46 renders the verb in Matt 5:17 with *kamala* in the fourth form, "to complete," which is used in the same form and the sense of fulfilling God's law in the Qur'an (Q 5:3), see Ciasca (1888, 33) and Marmardji (1935, 76).

- Moreover, just like Jerome, the Peshitta repeats the verb "coming" (*ʾ-t-y*), pointing out its importance—without, however, structurally connecting Jesus's coming to the passing of the heaven and earth by the use of repetitions of the same root, as we saw in the Greek text.[31] We cannot be sure whether or not the Diatessaron repeats the verb *ʾ-t-y*; the extant citations do not suggest that it would.[32]
- A final important detail is the Syriac rendering of the Greek "not an *iota or* a dot," which the Peshitta translates, precisely, as constituting two elements: "one *yud or* one dash" (*ywd ḥdʾ ʾw ḥd srṭʾ*). The Diatessaron, however, along with two other older Syriac versions, understands the latter part of the phrase as describing the former one, and the two elements together become *ywd ʾtwtʾ ḥdʾ* "one letter *yud*," thereby laying the ground for the central Syriac interpretation of the *yud* in Matt 5:17 as designating the supreme commandment, the ten commandments along with certain additions, and, ultimately, Jesus himself.[33]

We will see that, overall, the translation of the Diatessaron proved far more important for the development of the Syriac thought on law than the Peshitta. At the same time, it has become evident that there are three elements in the

31 The Peshitta, however, does use the repetition of the root *ʿ-b-r* to connect the earth's "passing" with the "passing" of "one *yud or* dash," which is in turn reinforced by the repetition of the conjunction "until" (*ʿdmʾ*). The text thereby captures one further aspect achieved in the Greek by the repetition of the Greek verb *erchomai*, "to come," a feature we have equally seen in the Old Latin of *Codex Bezae*, see above, note 15.

32 The Arabic Diatessaron 8:46 renders the verbs in Matt 5:17 with two different verbs, first with *jāʾa* and then with *atā*, both of which simply mean "to come," see Ciasca (1888, 32), Marmardji (1935, 76).

33 Among the Syriac versions, the Curetonianus, usually seen as the oldest of the Syriac renderings, reads *ywd ʾtwtʾ ḥdʾ ʾw qrnʾ*, "one letter *yud* or one tittle," maintaining the two-partite version of the Greek, yet adding another element specifying that the *yud* is a "letter," *ʾtwtʾ*. The Diatessaron as attested by Aphrahat and Ephrem, along with the Sinaiticus, modifies this fuller rendering by truncating the second part entirely, reading *ywd ʾtwtʾ ḥdʾ*, "one letter *yud*." The Peshitta and the Harclean version then attempt to return closer to the Greek original, reading "one *yud* or one dash" (*ywd ḥdʾ ʾw ḥd srṭʾ*, see notes 23 and 28 above). It is noteworthy that the Arabic translation of the Diatessaron, idiosyncratic and possibly corrupted as it may be, renders the verse by specifying "one (letter?) *sīn* (*sīnah wāḥidah*, sic!) or one sign (*ḥarf wāḥid*) of the Law" that will not pass away (see Ciasca 1888, 33; the female ending of *sīnah* may indicate a *nomen unitatis*, this could well be a *hapax legomenon* unless it is a corruption), see Ciasca (1888, 32), Marmardji (1935, 76). The Arabic Diatessaron, by retaining two elements, one a named letter and one a generic description of a sign, thus stands close to the Greek original and its precise rendering in the Peshitta and Harkelan version, making it likely that the Arabic text was updated in light of the later Syriac translations.

dominant Greek, Latin and Syriac renderings of Matt 5:17 that remained stable across linguistic and cultural boundaries:
- Jesus is portrayed as orally presenting his role in legal salvation history, by relating his "coming" to the Law, in the first person.
- This role is then specified by the repetition of the verb "to come."
- The statement concludes with a bi-partite statement, first endorsing the Law's general validity and secondly describing Jesus's role in qualifying the validity and scope of the Law.

The Greek, Latin and Syriac text of Matt 5:17 thus all allow for a law-affirming reading of the passage, which proved to be troubling for many of its Christian readers. We will explore first the Greek and Latin and then the Syriac range of late antique responses to Matt 5:17 which, in turn, prepared the Talmud's own renderings of this tradition. We will see that the Jewish version of Jesus' Matthean saying echoes many aspects of its Christian history of interpretation, yet clearly stand apart from them both as located more firmly in an oral context and as representing unique and unprecedented perspectives on Jesus's relationship to the Law.

2 Fulfilment or Falsification? Matthew 5:17–18 in the Greek and Latin Tradition

The reading of Matthew as a fully law-abiding Jewish text, needless to say, was not an option usually entertained by his gentile Christian audience.[34] We can locate three reactions to Matthew 5:17 in the Greek and Latin Christian tradition.
- First, most church fathers tended to read Matthew's term "to fulfil" not in terms of fulfilling legal observances by enacting them, but rather as having "fulfilled" the purpose of the Hebrew Bible as a whole, leading to the abrogation of its commandments by Jesus coming itself. This majority reading should best be understood in reaction to a second option.

34 This article revisits and broadens the foundational study by Adolf von Harnack on what he calls "The history of a programmatic word," namely Matt 5:17, see von Harnack (1912, 184–207). Harnack (1912, 203) summarizes the Christian attitude towards the passage by stating that "den ursprünglichen, einfachen Sinn von Matth. 5,17 hat kein Kirchenvater mehr zu konstatieren gewagt, weil die Entwicklung der Kirche über diesen Sinn hinweggeschritten war". This is false in as far as many church fathers did state what Matthew meant, even if they attributed this viewpoint to their "heretical" opponents. A related useful broad overview which, unlike von Harnack, pays close attention to the Syriac tradition is Alison G. Salvesen (2012, 47–66).

- A minority of Christians throughout late antiquity, such as Marcion and the followers of Mani, as well as the Emperor Julian, understood Matt 5:17 as affirming the Law.[35] These readers, at the same time, questioned the passage's authenticity, and the Christians among them excised it from their Gospel, designating it as a satanic falsification of Scripture.
- Finally, a minority tendency in the Greek tradition combined the two aforementioned options by reading Matthew 5:17–18 both as a genuine passage and in a law-affirming way—at the same time as using it in order to argue that *other* Biblical passages are falsifications of, i.e. human or satanic additions to the Hebrew Bible.

Many Christians, moreover, put Matthew 5:17–18 to polemical and heresiological use, often testifying to its meaning as abrogating the Law, the reading which they endorsed, and as affirming the Law, namely by quoting, paraphrasing or referring to the reading which they rejected.

Most church fathers, to reiterate, understood Matt 5:17 in neo-Pauline terms. Already Irenaeus, writing in Greek, in the south of France, in the second half of the second century, seeks to combine his understanding of Matthew's message with that of his understanding of Paul, thereby establishing the mainstream Greek and Latin Christian understanding of the passage. In his refutation of Marcion (to whom we will return presently), Irenaeus connects the "fulfilment" of the Law not with the keeping of its precepts, but with Jesus's coming itself. The early Latin translation of the lost original offers the following:

> But the servants would have turned out to be false, and not sent by the Lord, if Christ in his advent (*adveniens*) had not fulfilled (*adimplesset*)

---

35 An early Greek patristic reading Matt 5:17 with a positive attitude towards the Law is Hippolytus of Rome, who wrote at the turn of the third century C.E. A relevant note in his commentary on Gen 49:14 states: "For they who keep the commandments (*oi tas entolas fulassontes*), and do not disclaim the ordinances of the Law (*ouk apotaxamenoi tois nomikois diatagmasin*), enjoy rest both in them and in the doctrine (*didaskalia*) of our Lord … As the Lord says, I am not come to destroy the Law and the prophets, but to fulfil them (*ouk ēlthon katalusai ton nomon ē tous prophētas alla plērōsai*, Mt. 5:17). For even our Lord, in the fact that He keeps the commandments, does not destroy the Law and the prophets, but fulfils them (*en tō tas entolas fulassein ou kataluei ton nomon kai tous prophētas alla plēroi*), as He says in the Gospels," see Hippolytus of Rome, Fragment 29 line 5, translation according to S.D.F. Salmond (1868, 413); Greek text according to H. Achelis (1897), ad loc., see also von Harnack (1912, 203). While the fragmentary nature of Hippolytus' statements makes it difficult to assess his broader views, his attitude clearly contrasts with that of later "Western" fathers and more closely corresponds to the Syriac Christian readings of Mt. 5:17 we will discuss below.

> their words and been exactly what had been promised. That is why he said, "Do not think that I have come to abolish the Law or the prophets (*ne putetis quoniam veni dissolvere legem aut prophetas*); I have come not to abolish but to fulfil (*non veni dissolvere sed adimplere*). For truly I tell you, until heaven and earth pass away, not one letter, not one stroke of a letter, will pass from the Law until all is accomplished" (Matt 5:17–18). By his advent he fulfilled all things (*omnia enim ipse adimplevit veniens*), and in the Church he still fulfils (*et adhuc implet in ecclesia*) the new covenant foretold by the Law and will do so until the consummation. To this effect also Paul, his apostle, says in the *Letter to the Romans*, "But now, apart from law, the righteousness of God has been disclosed, and is attested by the Law and the prophets," for "the one who is righteous will live by faith" (Rom 3:21; 1:17, cf. Habakkuk 2:4). This fact, that the righteous shall live by faith, had been previously announced by the prophets.[36]

Irenaeus's reading of the passage shows how dramatically the content of Matthew changes if one reads the Gospel without its original ethnic Jewish context. Paul's letter was originally addressed to the gentile Romans, whom he sought to dissuade from following the Jewish law in its entirety—which, of course conforms to the legal position found in the Hebrew Bible as well as that of some texts in the New Testament (such as Acts) and the later rabbis.[37] Matthew, by contrast, addressed at least a predominantly Jewish audience as he tried to disassociate Jesus from a tradition that portrayed the Messiah as dissuading *Jews* to follow the Law. Matthew's focus is not necessarily incompatible with that of Paul, as long as one distinguishes between Jews and gentiles. Irenaeus, however, conflates Paul's address to gentiles with that of Matthew to his Jewish audience, as if both made universal, ethnically homogenizing statements.[38] In the ensuing legal tension, it is the Matthean side that gives. The only "fulfilment" that seems reasonable from Irenaeus's perspective, if fulfilling the

36 Irenaeus, *Against Heresies* 4.34.2, translation according to James R. Payton (2012, 139–140), Latin text according to Adelin Rousseau and Louis Doutreleau (1965, 848–850). On Irenaeus, Matt 5:17 and the Law see also von Harnack, (1912, 199–203) and Salvesen, (2012, 51–52).

37 See e.g. Stanley Stowers (1994); see also Zellentin, (2018, 117–132; 2019, 115–133).

38 Von Harnack surmises that Paul's teaching on the Law responds to Matt 5:17 in some way, yet it seems very likely that the Gospel post-dates the Apostle by several decades if not longer, and that the Matthean passage should at least partially be understood in response to Neo-Pauline anti-nomian tendencies as suggested in note 6 above, cf. von Harnack (1912, 187–188).

Torah's commandments is not an option, may well be that one must consider the Torah as already "fulfilled" by the coming of Christ.

Irenaeus inaugurated the reading of Matt 5:17 that remained dominant in the Greek and Latin Christian tradition: Jesus's coming itself is the fulfilment of the Torah, or, as Irenaeus's Latinate contemporary Tertullian puts it elegantly, "if the gospel has not fulfilled the Law, even so the Law has fulfilled the gospel (*si evangelium legem non adimplevit, ecce lex evangelium adimplevit*)."[39] Clement of Alexandria, slightly younger than Irenaeus and Tertullian, likewise states that "to fulfil (*plērōsai*)," i.e. the Laws, in Matt 5:17 "does not mean that it was defective (*ouch ōs endeē*)," rather, "the prophecies which followed the Law were accomplished through (Christ's) presence, since the qualities of an upright way of life were announced to people of righteous behaviour—before the Law, by the Word (*pro tou nomou dia tou logou*)."[40] We find a similar reading in Origen in the third century, who sees the Law as "completed in the Gospels and, through the apostles, in the words of Christ" (*peplērōtai ... en tois euaggeliois kai tois christou dia tōn apostolōn logois*).[41] Other Greek and Latin church fathers could be marshalled to support this reading. John Chrysostom, for example, writing in Eastern Rome in the fourth century, unsurprisingly evoked the passage in his anti-Jewish polemics, and we find similar uses in Eusebius of Caesarea, Gregory of Nyssa, Basil of Caesarea and others.[42]

The most exemplary of the "Western" understanding of Matthew, however, may be the one church father who seemed to have returned to Matt 5:17 the most often: Augustine, the late fourth and early fifth-century father writing, in Latin, in North Africa, repeatedly invoked the passage throughout his life.

39 Tertullian, *Against Marcion* 5.14.14; translation and Latin text according to Ernest Evans (1972, 602–603); on Tertullian and the Law see also Salvesen (2012, 53–54).

40 Clement of Alexandria, *Stromata* 3.6.46.2 (see also 3.9.63), translation according to John Ferguson (2010, 284), Greek according to L. Früchtel, O. Stählin, and U. Treu (1970), ad loc; see also idem, *Stromata* 3.9.63; on Clement of Alexandria, Matt 5:17 and the Law see von Harnack (1912, 193) and Salvesen (2012, 54–56).

41 Origen, *Commentary on the Gospel of Matthew*, 10.12; Greek text according to Robert Girod (1970, 140–386); see also Origen, *De pascha* 92.11; on Origen and the Law see also Salvesen (2012, 56–57).

42 For John Chrysostom, see *In Matthaeum* (homiliae 1–90) 57.237.62 and 241.54; *In Joannem* (homiliae 1–88) 59.276.18; *De Christi precibus* (= *Contra Anomoeos*, homilia 10) 48.788.52 and 789.17 and *Expositiones in Psalmos* 55.288.14. For Gregroy of Nyssa see *In Canticum canticorum* (homiliae 15) 6.371.14, *Theol. Encomium in sanctum Stephanum protomartyrem* 1.20.6 and 2.46.728.34. For Basil of Caesarea, see *Regulae morales* 31.761.31. For Eusebius see *Demonstratio evangelica* 1.7.1.10 and 8.2.33.1 and *Commentaria in Psalmos* 23.81.17. Von Harnack (1912, 197) observes, importantly, that Justin Martyr by and large ignores Matt 5:17; see also Salvesen (2012, 51).

As importantly, Augustine preserved the arguments of a Manichean opponent who read Matt 5:17 plainly as confirming the Law—and as a Satanic falsification of Scripture.[43]

Augustine pushed the earlier readings of his Christian predecessors further and declared, inspired by Paul, that "the Law of the Lord is none but Himself (*Lex ergo Domini ipse est*), who came to fulfil the Law, not to destroy it (*qui venit legem implere, non solvere*)."[44] Augustine sees Christ *as* the Law.[45] Notably, Augustine also incorporated the view of Christ's fulfilment of the Law in his understanding of original sin:

> Hence it is [not!] gratuitous (*non gratis*) that Christ died, so that the Law be fulfilled (*impleretur*) through Him who declared, "I am not come to destroy the Law but to fulfil it" (*non veni legem solvere, sed implere* Matt 5:17) and the nature that was lost through Adam would be recovered through Him, Who said that He came "to seek and to save what had been lost" (Matt 18:11, Luke 19:10). Even the fathers of old, who loved God, believed in Him who was to come (*in quem venturum*).[46]

Augustine thus sees Christ as the Law, and the Law's fulfilment in turn becomes the redemption from original sin. Augustine can therefore be said to epitomize the dominant reading of Matt 5:17 in the Greek and Latin tradition.

For Augustine, Matt 5:17 remained a statement that related Jesus to God's law, yet if Jesus *became* God's law, then the latter is thereby relegated to a mere type and relieved of any positive soteriological value it may have retained for previous fathers. At the same time, Augustine participated in the broad tendency to put Matthew 5:17 to polemical and heresiological use, as we have already seen in Irenaeus. Both church fathers, namely, polemicize against those Christians

43 See for example Augustine, *c. Faust.* 17, 5; *en. Ps.* 68, 10; *spir. et litt*; 7, 10; and *util. cred.* 3.

44 Augustine, *First Exposition on Psalm 18*, 8, translation according to Dame Scholastica Hebgin and Dame Felicitas Corrigan (1960, 178), Latin text according to Jacques-Paul Migne (1861, 155, vol. 4a).

45 Augustine, like Irenaeus, read Matt 5:17 in light of Paul, see, e.g., *On Baptism, Against the Donatists* 3.26 (using Romans 13:10, see also ibid, verse 8 and Gal 5:14). Von Harnack has already drawn attention to the Pauline phrase of the "law of Christ" (*ton nomon tou christou*, Gal 6:2) in this respect (see von Harnack 1912, 187); he also points to the respective tradition in the *Shepherd of Hermas* 3[69]:2 and in the *Preaching of Peter* (cited by Clement of Alexandria, *Stomata* 1.29.182 and 2.15.68), see von Harnack (1912, 197).

46 Augustine, *On Grace and Free Choice*, 13.25, translation according to Peter King (2010, 162), Latin according to Volker Henning Drecoll and Christoph Scheerer (2019, 148, 16–25). Augustine, of course, seeks to liberate Christians not only from the divine laws but also from the moral guidance inherent in human law, see e.g., Daniel Burns (2015, 273–298).

who view the verse both as affirming the Law and as spurious—i.e. against the view constituting the second of the three tendencies to read Matthew 5:17 in the Greek and Latin tradition, and the one more important for its Talmudic rendering.

The tendency to use Matt 5:17 for heresiological purposes is already evident in the passage by Irenaeus quoted above, which he formulated "to address all the heretics, and chiefly the followers of Marcion and their likes."[47] Irenaeus's use of Matt 5:17 against "the Marcionites" is noteworthy since also Tertullian, Irenaeus's contemporary, claimed that Marcion had indeed "blotted this (i.e., Matt 5:17) out as an interpolation (*hoc enim … ut additum erasit*)."[48] Likewise, Cyril of Jerusalem, in the fourth century, enjoined his audience to use Matt 5:17 against those who sought to excise the Hebrew Bible from the canon, which is the central position the fathers connected with Marcion: "And so, if ever thou hear any heretic blaspheming the Law or the Prophets (*blasfēmountos nomon ē profētas*), quote that saving word against him: Jesus came not to destroy the Law, but to fulfil it (*ouk ēlthen iēsous katalusai ton nomon alla plērōsai*)."[49] We should note that if Irenaeus already reacts to Marcion, then the latter's erasure of Matt 5:17 may well constitute one of the earliest Greek Christian reaction to Matthew. Regardless of the difficult chronology, it seems that a substantial part of the Greek and Latin reading of Matt 5:17 seems to respond to arguments for the rejection of the passage.

There is no clear record of how Marcion understood Matt 5:17, yet he was not the only reader of Matthew to doubt the veracity of the passage, as becomes clear when turning, again, to Augustine.[50] Augustine quotes a text composed

---

47 Irenaeus, *Against Heresies* 4.34.1; translation according to Payton (2012, 139).

48 Tertullian, *Against Marcion* 4.7.4, translation and Latin text according to Evans (1972, 278–279). Note that Matt 4:17 is central for Tertullian's argument throughout the chapter, see also 4.2 (ibid, 262–263), 4.8 (ibid, 292–293), 4.9 (ibid, 294–295), 4.12 (ibid, 316–317), 4.22 (382–383), 4.34 (448–449), 4.36 (4.68–69), and 4.40 (ibid., 490–491). Marcion, of course, eliminated the entire Gospel of Matthew, but apparently saw it as necessary to negate Matt 5:17 independently. On Tertullian's record on the passage see already von Harnack (1912, 191), on Marcion's views of the Gospel see Judith M. Lieu (2015, 367–386).

49 Cyril of Jerusalem, *Catechetical Lecture 4* (*On the Ten Points of Doctrine*) 33, translation according to Leo P. McCauley and Anthony A. Stephenson (1969–1970, 135), Greek according to W.C. Reischl and J. Rupp (1848), ad loc.; see also Cyril of Jerusalem, *Catechetical Lecture 10*, 18.

50 Note also that the otherwise anonymous Adamantius, writing at the beginning of the fourth century, changed rather than disputed Matt 5:17, citing the verse "I have not come to fufill the Law but to abolish (*ouk ēlthon plērōsai ton nomon alla katalusai*)," see Willem van de Sande Bakhuyzen (1901, 88, 31–33). On comparable attitudes testified to in the *Acta Archelai* (XLIV) and by Isidore of Pelusium (Epp. 1, 371) see von Harnack (1912, 191–192); see

by his interlocutor Faustus of Mileve, with whom he met around 383 CE. In an arresting passage, Faustus points to the hermeneutical tension inherent in Augustine's position simultaneously to defend the text of Matt 5:17 and to refute its law-affirming meaning:

> 1. Faustus said: "'I have come not to destroy the Law, but to fulfil it (*non veni solver legem et prophetas, sed adinplere* Matt 5:17).' But unless this perhaps means something else, you should know that to believe Christ said this contradicts you as much as it contradicts me. For each of us is a Christian under this assumption: we have taken it for granted that Christ came to destroy the Law and the prophets (*in destructionem legis ac prophetarum venisse*). This is the reason that you yourself also hold the commandments of the Law and the prophets in contempt (*quod legis ac prophetarum praecepta et ipse contemnis*); this is the reason that both of us say that Jesus established the New Testament (*novum testamentum condidisse*). And what else do we imply by that but the destruction of the Old Testament (*destructionem ... veteris testamenti*)? Since this is so, how shall we believe that Christ said these words unless we first .... observe the Law in its entirety along with the prophets (*obsequamurque legi de integro ac prophetis*), and are careful to observe (*curemus*, i.e. the commandments) ...? When we have done that, then it will at last be true that we believe that Jesus said that he came not to destroy but to fulfil the Law (*quia non venerit legem solver, sed adinplere*). But now it is not true, because not even you believe what you accuse me alone of.
>
> 2. ... Do you want to be subject to the Law (*sub legem*) if Christ did not destroy it but fulfilled it (*non tam solvit sed adinplevit*)? Do you want to be circumcised .... Do you want to observe the Shabbat rest ...? In order to feed the demon of the Jews (*Iudaeorum daemonis*)—for he is not God—do you want to slay with knives now bulls, now rams, now even goats ...? Do you want to regard certain foods from animals as clean (*munda*) and regard others as unclean and defiled (*inmundis et contaminatis*), among which the Law and the prophets claim that pork is the more polluted? ... But notice that Christ did not himself observe (*nec ipsum servasse*) the Sabbath and never commanded that it be observed (*nec usquam mandasse servandum*). Likewise, listen to him saying, with regard to foods, that a person is not defiled by any of the things that enter his mouth

---

also Moiseeva (2018), and Lieu (2015, 398–432). For further examples of rewritings of Matt 5:17 see also note 68 below.

> … (Matt 15:11). Likewise, regarding sacrifices (*de sacrificiis*), listen to his frequent statements that God wants mercy, not sacrifice (*misericordium velle, non sacrificium*, Matt 9:13, 12:7). If these statements are true, where will that saying be that he came not to destroy but to fulfil the Law and the prophets (*non eum venisse solvere legem et pophetas, sed adinplere*)."[51]

Faustus's testimony on his reading of Matt 5:17, is extensive and coherent, and it seems to me that it is most likely representative of his actual *Disputationes*.[52] It may constitute the most fully argued case for the implications of a law-affirming reading of Matt 5:17 preserved from antiquity. Faustus, unaware of Matthew's distinctions between biblical and Pharisaic law and between Jews and gentiles, reads Matthew like most of his Christian interpreters did after him: he understands Matthew's criticism of Pharisaic Shabbat rules as the dissolution of the Shabbat, he sees Matthew's criticism of Pharisaic purity requirements as the abolition of food laws, and so on. Since Faustus, consequentially, can understand Matt 5:17 only as demanding the observances of the Law, including the usual triad of circumcision, Shabbat and Sacrifice, he concludes that the passage must be spurious.[53] The response Augustine eventually gives is comparatively tame, and focuses on typology: "Christians do not do the things from the Law and the prophets," he argues at some length, "that were signs of the things (*quibus significate sunt*) that they now do."[54]

Faustus suggests a different solution to the conundrum Matt 5:17 poses to him: Matthew's endorsement of the Law lead him to the conclusion that the text must have been corrupted by the forces of evil, according to the Manichean theory of Satanic interpolations of Scripture, as he sets out in the sequel to the passage cited:

51 Augustine, *Contra Faustum* 18.1–2, translation according to Roland J. Teske (2007, 232–233), Latin text according to Iosephus Zycha (1891, 490–491). On Faustus's own initial attraction to Judaism see e.g., Jacob Albert van den Berg (2010, 197–200); on Faustus' rare use of the title "Manichaen" in this passage see Nils Arne Pedersen (2013, 183).

52 Augustine's rendering of Faustus's citation of Matt 5:17 does not fully correspond to either the Old Latin version of Codex Bezae nor to Jerome's translation which was produced later; see note 13 above. On the title of Faustus's work see Gregor Wurst (2001, 307–324).

53 On the pivotal shifts in late antique attitudes towards sacrifice see Guy G. Stroumsa (2009; 2016, 23–42). See now also Mira Balberg (2017, 223–250); David L. Weddle (2017, 100–154) and Daniel C. Ullucci (2017, 95–136).

54 Augustine, *Contra Faustum* 18.4, translation according Teske (2007, 233), Latin text according to Iosephus Zycha, *Sancti Aurli Augustini*, 492; see also Volker Drecoll and Mirjam Kudella, *Augustin und der Manichäismus* (Tübingen: Mohr Siebeck, 2011), 49–51.

> 3. “And yet Manichean faith (*Manichaea fides*) has made me safe in face of the difficulty of this passage. For, to begin with, it has convinced me not to believe indiscriminately all the things that we read were written under the name of the saviour but to test whether they are true, sound and incorrupt (*si sint … vera, si sana, si incorrupta*). For there are many weeds that the sower of the night has scattered in almost all the scriptures in order to spoil the good seed …. I am still permitted explicitly to test whether this comes from the good sower of the day (*interdiani satoris et boni*) or from that most evil one of the night (*an noturni illius et pessimi*). But you who rashly believe everything (*qui temere omnia credis*), who denounce human reason (*rationem ex homnibus damnas*), which is nature’s gift to us, who are afraid to judge what is true and what is false …. what are you going to do when logic forces you into difficulties over this statement (i.e. Matt 5:17)? I mean when a Jew (*Iudaeus*) or anyone else aware of this statement asks you why you do not observe the commandments of the Law and the prophets (*quid ita legis et prophetarum praecepta non serves*), since Christ says that he came not to destroy but to fulfil these same commandments (*non se venisse solvere dicat sed adinplere*), you are of course forced either to yield to a silly superstition, or to admit that this passage is spurious (*aut capitulum profiteri falsum*), or to deny that you are a disciple of Christ (*aut te Christi negare discipulum*).”[55]

Faustus, like Marcion before him, discounts Matt 5:17 as spurious, yet he emphasizes the more sinister side of the falsification of Scripture: according to Mani’s teaching, even the true Scriptures are interspersed with falsehoods, a teaching that was widespread among Marcionites and Manicheans alike, and will find another iteration in the so-called Clementine Homilies.[56] Faustus’s testimony proves crucial for the present inquiry in one further way, namely when highlighting the danger residing in Matt 5:17 in terms of its usefulness for anti-Christian polemics. He asks Augustine how he would answer if “a Jew or anyone else aware of this statement asks you why you do not observe the commandments of the Law and the prophets.” This scenario of “Jews and oth-

55 Augustine, *Contra Faustum* 18.3, translation according to Teske, *The Works of Saint Augustine*, 233, Latin text according to Zycha (1891, 492).

56 On this doctrine in Manichaeism see esp. Andreas Hoffman (1997, 149–182), for broader discussions see also Shuve (2018, 171–206), Evgenïa Moiseeva (2018, 274–297); Gabriel Said Reynolds (2010, 189–202); Angela Standhartinger (2013, 122–149); Christian Hofreiter (2013, 44–55); Donald Henry Carlson (2013); Giovanni Battista Bazzana (2012, 11–32); F. Stanley Jones (2012, 152–171); and Kevin M. Vacarella (2007).

ers" making use of Matt 5:17 was not far-fetched, and indeed remains a central issue for the remainder of our survey of Greek and Latin readings of Matt 5:17. We will turn to Jewish uses of the passage presently; much closer to Faustus in time and place, the neo-pagan emperor Julian had already argued along the very same lines, paraphrasing Matt 5:17 and 19 as follows:

> Therefore when He (i.e. Christ) has undoubtedly commanded that it is proper to observe the Law (*tērein ton nomon*), and threatened with punishment those who transgress one commandment, what manner of defending yourselves will you devise, you who have transgressed them all (*oi sullēbdēn apasas*) without exception? For either Jesus will be found to speak falsely (*pseudoepēsei*), or rather you will be found in all respects and in every way not to preserve the Law (*ou nomofulakes*).[57]

Julian and Faustus, and before them likely Marcion and Mani, thus agree on the reading of the passage in principle, with one important difference: they all hold the text to demand legal observance, they all hold that this teaching is incompatible with Christian practice, and they all suggest that the passage may well be spurious. The one difference is that while Faustus, along with Marcion and Mani's likely reading, are certain of the passage's falsified character, Julian merely evokes the possibility that Jesus may have been speaking falsely.[58]

Faustus's question to Augustine, how he would react if "anyone ... aware of this statement asks you why you do not observe the commandments of the Law and the prophet," was thus based on precedent. This also proves true regarding the more concrete possibility that "a Jew" would ask the same question. Before turning to the Syriac and eventually the Talmud's view on the matter (which

57 Julian, *Against the Galileans* 351 C, translation and Greek text according to Wilmer Cave Wright (1923, 420–423); see also John Granger Cook (2000, 292–293) and von Harnack (1912, 203).

58 In Cyril of Alexandria's quotation of Julian's *Against the Galileans*, the same passage is preceded by a quote of Matt 5:17, which, however, is not attributed to Julian, see Cyril of Alexandria, *Against Julian* 10.31.17–22, in Th. Brüggemann, W. Kinzig, and C. Riedweg (2017), ad loc. John Granger Cook notes that in one Syriac fragment of Cyril of Alexandria, Julian pointed to the discrepancy between Christ's saying that he "came to fulfil the Law (*dnshml' nmws' 't'*) and that whoever loosed one of the least of the commandments (*wkl dpwqdn' z'wr' nshr'*) and so taught people would be called least" on the one hand and, on the other, the fact that Christ allegedly loosed (*shr'*) the Sabbath in Matt 12:8 and the food-laws in Matt 15:11 (translations according to Granger Cook 2000, 293, Syriac text according to Karl Johannes Neumann 1880, 56). This translation stands much closer to the Greek text of Matt 5:17 yet there is no way of corroborating whether the Syriac tradition is based on any passage in Julian's Greek original, which does not transmit this passage.

again comes close to this very scenario evoked by Faustus), we should consider the testimony provided by Faustus himself and others regarding "Jewish" readings from within the Jesus-movement. Faustus, namely, goes on to relate that "the Nazoreans" (*Nazoraeorum*) also insist that Jesus "said that he had not come to destroy the Law" (*non se venisse solvere legem*), since they, too were "also deceived by this same passage (i.e. Matt 5:17), that is, because Christ said that he had come not to destroy but to fulfil the Law" (*decepti etiam ipsi … hoc ipso capitulo … quia Christus non ad solvendam legem se venisse dixerit, sed ad inplendam*).[59] Faustus emphasizes that he had not actually met any Nazoreans, and his respective testimony cannot be verified. We should note, however, that Epiphanius of Salamis, in his portrayal of this same alleged group he calls Nazareans, made use precisely of Matt 5:17 in order to *refute* what he considers to be their misguided observance of the Law.[60] Epiphanius, moreover, contextualizes his reading of Matt 5:17 in a historical way that proves important also for the way in which his actual (rather than perceived) opponents read the passage:

> But they too are wrong to boast of circumcision, and persons like themselves are still "under a curse" (Gal 3:10) since they cannot fulfil the Law (*mē dunamenoi ton nomon plērōsai*). For how can they fulfil the Law's provision (*plēroun ta en tō vomō eirēmena*), "Thrice a year thou shalt appear before the Lord thy God, at the feasts of Unleavened Bread, Tabernacles and Pentecost," on the site of Jerusalem? (see Exod 34:32 and Deut 16:16). As the site is closed off, and the Law's provisions cannot be fulfilled (*kai tōn en tō nomō mē dunamenōn plērousthai*), anyone with sense can see that Christ came to be the Law's fulfiller (*oti christos ēlthen plērōtēs tou*

59 Augustine, *Contra Faustum* 19.4, translation according to Teske (2007, 239), Latin text according to Zycha (1891, 500).

60 According to Epiphanius, to Nazoreans were a group of followers of Jesus whom he claims followed the Law and were circumcised. There is no direct evidence for either Nazoreans or Ebionites, another alleged group constituting a favourite topic of the heresiologists. For an affirmative view on the existence of the former group, see Wolfram Kinzig (2007, 463–487), for the latter see Oskar Skarsaune (2007, 419–462). A more cautious note is struck e.g., in Petri Luomanen (2007, 81–118); on the Ebionite's alleged rendering of Matt 5:17 see below. Some of the patristic evidence likely resembles actual Christian thought in late antiquity. However, those followers of Jesus who did not conceive of Jesus in terms of the abrogation of Jewish law *for Jews* would have maintained the traditional distinction between Jews and gentiles embodied in this very law. This important distinction is never reported by the church fathers, their testimony thus likely mischaracterizes a traditional strand within mainstream Christian thought at the same time as projecting it on an imagined group outside the fold, see e.g., Zellentin (2013c, 1–54; 2018, 117–121; 2019, 115–117).

> *nomou*)—not to destroy the Law, but to fulfil the Law (*ou ton nomon katalusōn alla ton nomon plērōsōn*, cf. Matt 5:17)—and to lift the curse that had been put on transgression of the Law (cf. Gal 3:22). For after Moses had given every commandment he (i.e. Moses) came to the end of the book (*ēlthen epi to terma tēs biblou*) and "included the whole in a curse" with the (Pauline!) words "cursed is he that continues not in all the words that are written in this book to do them" (Gal 3:10, see Deut 27:26). Hence, he (i.e., Christ) came to free (*ēlthen oun luōn*) what had been fettered with the bonds of the curse. In place of the lesser commandments which cannot be fulfilled (*tōn mē dunamenōn plērousthai*), he granted us the greater, which are not inconsistent with the completion of the task (*ou machomena thateron thaterō pros tēn tou ergou plērōsin*) as the earlier ones were. For I have discussed this many times before, in every sect, in connection with the Sabbath, circumcision and the rest—how the Lord has granted something more perfect to us.[61]

Epiphanius's argument against the Nazaranes follows that of Faustus quite closely, in as far as he marshals circumcision, Sabbath and sacrifice against those who seek to fulfil the Law. Like his predecessors, Epiphanius combines Matt 5:17 with the letters of Paul, yet Epiphanius adds an important historical perspective: if it is impossible to fulfil the Law because the Temple is destroyed, he argues, it must follow that Christ already had fulfilled it, since one otherwise would unavoidably fall short of the Law's commandments, incurring the Deuteronomistic curse used so effectively in Paul's *Letter to the Galatians*.

Epiphanius's historic contextualization of Matt 5:17 thus falls broadly within the parameters set out by his predecessors, yet it stands out in as far as it is closely related to a third instance in which a law-affirming reading of the passage has been recorded in the Western tradition. The reading of the Matthean passage we find in the Clementine Homilies, namely, combines the view of the passage as affirming the keeping of the commandments in principle with the Manichean view of Satanic interpolations—and with Epiphanius's argument that the destruction of the Temple proves the temporal nature of Sacrifice.

The Clementine Homilies are a fourth or fifth century novel which, unlike any other rendering of Matt 5:17 from within the Jesus-movement, continue to distinguish between Jews and gentiles in a way of requiring diverging law-codes to be followed by each group, in a way comparable to the one we find in

61 Epiphanius, *Panarion* 29.8.1 translation according to Frank Williams (1994, 142), Greek text according to Holl (1915) vol. 1, 330.13–331.16; for Epiphanius further uses of Matt 5:17 see also *Panarion* 1.244.13; 2.125.8; 2.151.25; and 3.94.3.

the Hebrew Bible, in Acts, and likely in the Gospel of Matthew.[62] The Clementine Homilies, like so many of their predecessors paying close attention to that gospel's repetition of the verb *erchomai* in 5:17, read the passage in a way that is only partially anticipated by Faustus:

> And also that (Jesus) said, "I am have not come to abrogate the Law" (*ouk ēlthon katalusai ton nomon*, Matt 5:17) and appeared to be abrogate it (*fainesthai auton kataluonta*), indicates that what he abrogated were not from the Law (*oti a kateluen ouk ēn tou nomou*). And (Jesus's) saying, "The heaven and the earth shall pass away, but one jot or one tittle shall not pass from the Law (*o ouranos kai ē gē pareleusontai iota en ē mia keraia ou mē parelthē apo tou nomou*)," indicates that what passes away before the heaven and the earth (*ta pro ouranou kai gēs parerchomena*) is not from the Law (*mē onta tou ontōs nomou*, see Matt 5:17).[63]
>
> Since, then, while the heaven and the earth still stand (*ouranou kai gēs eti sunestōtōn*), sacrifices have passed away (*parēlthan thusiai*), and kingdoms, and prophecies among those who are born of woman, and such like, as not being ordinances of God; hence therefore He says, "Every plant which the heavenly Father has not planted shall be rooted up" (Matt 15:13) … and to those who supposed that God is pleased with sacrifices, He said, "God wishes mercy, and not sacrifices" (Matt 9:13)—the knowledge of Himself, and not holocausts.[64]

The Clementine Homilies, like Faustus, Epiphanius, and so many others unaware of (or uninterested in) the distinction between biblical and Pharisaic law, hold that Jesus, despite Matthew's wording, at first sight may well appear to be abolishing the Law in its entirety.[65] Like Faustus, the Homilies cite Matt 9:13 against sacrifices, and like Epiphanius, the Homilies argue against them from a historical perspective: sacrifices have passed before heaven and earth have done so, and must accordingly have fallen into Jesus's purview of abroga-

62 See Clementine Homilies VIII:5–7 and Karin Zetterholm (2019, 68–87), and see Zellentin (2013c, 1–54; 2018, 142–148; and 2019, 146–152).

63 Note that the Clementine Homilies, as well as the *Letter of Peter to James* (see note 66 below), slightly modify the Greek text of Matt 5:18, using a future form of *parerchomai*, plausibly in line with the usage of the same word in Mark 13:31 and Luke 21:33.

64 Clementine Homilies 3:51–56, translation according to Thomas Smith (1870, 79–81), Greek text according to Bernhard Rehm (1969, 75–77).

65 On the distinction between Biblical and Pharisaic law in Matthew see note 12 above.

tion.[66] For the Homilies, however, Jesus's abrogation of the Law largely pertains to sacrifice alone. The simple argument, here as well as in Epiphanius, is that since sacrifice was factually abrogated by the destruction of the Temple, it cannot have been part of God's enduring law—the similarity of the arguments, indeed, makes one wonder if Epiphanius may have read the Homilies, to which he may make explicit reference, or if the author of the homilies was familiar with Epiphanius's heresiological exploits, to which the Homilies show intriguing parallels.[67]

According to Epiphanius, for example, the Ebionites read the Gospel of Matthew as a law-abiding "Jewish" text, yet with noteworthy changes which Epiphanius designates to be "guileful inventions" (*ta par autois dolia epinoēmata*). Matt 5:17 in the alleged Ebionite version reads "I came to abolish the sacrifices (*ēlthon katalusai tas thusias*) and if you cease not from sacrifices, wrath will not cease from you."[68] To a degree, this corresponds to the teachings

66 Note that the Clementine *Letter of Peter to James* 2:3–5 have Peter declare that "some from among the Gentiles (*tines gar tōn apo ethnōn*) have rejected my legal preaching (*to di'emou nominon apedokimasan kērugma*), attaching themselves to certain lawless and foolish (*anomon tina kai fluarōdē*) teaching of the man who is my enemy ... to transform my words by certain various interpretations, for the dissolution of the Law (*tines poikilais tisin ermēneiais tous emous logous metaschēmatizein eis tēn tou nomou katalusin*), as though I myself were of such a mind .... For such a thing were to act in opposition to the Law of God which was spoken by Moses, and was borne witness to by our Lord in respect to its eternal continuance; for thus he spoke: "The heavens and the earth shall pass away, but one jot or one tittle shall will not pass from the Law" (*o ouranos kai ē gē pareleusontai iōta en ē mia keraia ou mē parelthē apo tou nomou*)," translation according to Smith (1870, 2), Greek text according to Rehm (1969, 2). This statement, as idiosyncratic as it may be from a historical point of view, may well capture some important aspects of Matthew's original message. Note that the *Clementine Recognitions*, a text slightly more in line with dominant patristic discourse than the Homilies, describes God as temporarily having had sanctioned the Temple in the past, with its eventual end in mind (1.37), which is then brought by Christ's abolition of sacrifice (1:54)—an attitude also shared by the Didascalia Apostolorum and the Apostolic Constitutions, as we will see below.

67 Many of these parallels between Epiphanius and the Clementine Homilies are already noted in Holl (1915, 28, 205, 214, 296, 321–382). The close affinity of the respective heresiology presented by both has been noted in Annette Yoshiko Reed (2008, 273–298).

68 Epiphanius, Panarion 30.16.5 translation according to Williams (1994, 144), Greek text according to Holl (1915, 354.3–9), see also Simon J. Joseph (2017, 92–110) and von Harnack (1912, 192). Another text modifying Matt 5:17 in such a way (already noted by von Harnack 1912, 193) is the purported *Gospel of the Egyptians*, which, according to Clement, rephrases the passage as "I have come to dissolve the works of the female (*ēlthon katalusai ta erga tēs thēleias*)," see Clement of Alexandria, *Stromata* 3.9.63, translation according to John Ferguson (2010, 284), Greek according to L. Früchtel, O. Stählin, and U. Treu (1970, 225). For further examples of similar Gospel rewritings see also note 50 above.

of the Homilies on sacrifice—yet the Homilies, we have seen, do teach that the "standard" Matthean passage is the genuine one, making a direct exchange between this text and Epiphanius less likely.

Other than when it comes to sacrifice, the Homilies are a unique text in as far as they continue to hold the view shared with earlier Christian texts, such as the Gospel of Matthew, that Moses's Law is still incumbent upon Jews. The Homilies also hold that only a concise part of the Law—following an "expansive" reading of the so-called *Decree of the Apostles*—has always been incumbent upon gentiles, and remains so regardless of the coming of Jesus.[69] In this distinction between Jews and gentiles, the Homilies come very close indeed to Matthew's original view as portrayed above, of which they prove to be a more attentive recipient in both literary and legal terms than many of their predecessors.

The Clementine Homilies' distinction between Jewish and gentile ethnicity make a mockery of Faustus's and Epiphanius's testimony about "Jewish-Christian" Nazoreans or Ebionites, and vice versa. It is the emphatically "gentile" self-identity so dominant in the Western tradition that had made Matthew's original thinking very difficult to access already since the time of Marcion and Irenaeus. Epiphanius seems to grasp that some of his contemporaries within the Jesus movement do not see themselves as gentiles, and notes the tension between this group and "the Jews" at large, which seems an astute observation in as far as it goes. However, instead of recognizing the clear ethnic distinction between Jewish and non-Jewish believers in Christ one can observe within the Clementine Homilies, Epiphanius then projects an ethnic amalgamation onto his Nazoreans, thereby making it nearly impossible to understand, on their own terms, those believers that he successfully recasts as what later scholars would call "Jewish-Christian". The heresiologists' arguable invention of Jewish Christianity, namely, proved as consequential as that of the invention of Gnosticism, the internal cohesion of which became understandable only after the finding of the Nag Hammadi texts.[70] Epiphanius portrays groups that do not fit his definition of Jewish or Christian orthodoxy as hopelessly embroiled in an

69 Irrespective of the abrogation of the "Jewish" law and the ensuing rhetoric, most Christians in Late Antiquity endorsed a broad reading of the purity laws which Leviticus 17–18 and the Acts of the Apostles impose upon gentiles. While most Christians appreciated these laws and only few dismissed them, the Clementine Homilies endorsed an "expansive" understanding of these laws; see notes 1 above and 95 below.

70 For a perceptive view of the "gnostic" tradition see Karen King (2005, 5–19). The comparison between the heresiological constructs has been made by several scholars in the past; for a lucid yet slightly different presentation of the usefulness of the category "Jewish-Christian" see esp. Annette Yoshiko Reed (2018).

unclear grasp of the Law, as standing "in all evil, in the midst of the church and the synagogue (*meson ekklēsias kai sunagōgēs*)"—a view not so dissimilar from the one we will find in the Talmud.[71] The only primary source in Epiphanius's time that remotely resembles this description to a degree are the Clementine Homilies, which, in partial contrast, argue precisely for a *distinction* between Jewish and gentile ethnicity and between their respective legal requirements and even faith commitments.[72] Intriguingly, just as Epiphanius, the Homilies turn to Matt 5:17, which they consider as genuine, in order to refute their opponent, and just like him, they invoke the evidence of history itself.

At the same time, the Homilies take up the Marcionite and more specifically the Manichean argument that parts of Scripture are indeed the result of their satanic falsification we have already seen in Faustus. They explain satanic falsification of Scripture as fully compatible with God's omnipotence, holding that "the falsehoods of the Scriptures have been permitted to be written for a certain righteous reason, at the demand of evil" (*aitēmati kakias*).[73] While humans may be the agents of these falsification, they all are initiated by the devil.[74] The reason the Clementine Homilies' indicate is that the "mystery of the books which are able to deceive" (*tōn apatan dunamenōn biblōn to mustērion*) have been allowed by God in order to test the believers: "nothing happens unjustly, since even the falsehoods of Scripture are with good reason presented for a trial" (*pros dokimēn*).[75] This "test" is constituted by the believers' misplaced trust on a literal reading of the Bible (quite in line with Faustus's respective views):

> Worthy, therefore, of rejection is everyone who is willing so much as to hear anything against the monarchy of God (*tēs theou monarchias*). If any one dares to hear anything against God, as trusting in the Scriptures (*ei d'ōs grafais tetharrēkōs*), let him first of all consider with me that if any one, as he pleases, form a dogma agreeable to himself (*oti an tis eulogon*

71 Epiphanius, *Panarion* 11.30.1.4; Williams (1994, 131), Greek text according to Holl (1915, 334). Epiphanius uses the Septuagint rendition of Proverbs 5:14 to describe Ebion's double commitment to Jesus and purity, to the Christian church and the Jewish synagogue, which are presented as mutually exclusive.

72 See note 60 above.

73 Clementine Homilies 3:5, Smith (1870, 58), Greek text according to Rehm (1969, 58).

74 The "proclaimers of error," according to the Homilies, have one chief, "the chief of wickedness" (*ton tēs kakias ēgemona*), namely the devil, ibid. 3:16, Smith (1870, 63), Greek text according to Rehm (1969, 62).

75 Clementine Homilies 3:4, Smith (1870, 58), Greek text according to Rehm (1969, 58).

> *eautō dogma ōs bouletai anaplasē*), and then carefully search (the Scriptures), he will be able to produce many testimonies from them in favour of the dogma that he has formed (*pollas uper ou eplasato dogmatos ap'autōn marturias ferein*). How, then, can confidence be placed in them against God, when what everyone wishes is found in them (*en ais ē pantōn boulē eiseurisketai*)?[76]

It is within this context that the Clementine Homilies' reading of Matthew 5:17 can be seen as constituting the third way of reading the passage in the Greek and Latin tradition: the Clementine Homilies, just like Marcion, Faustus and Julian, read the passage as affirming the Law. Yet the Homilies place the passage in three contexts that dramatically changes their understanding of Matthew.

- First, they maintain Matthew's original distinction between Jews and gentiles, thereby making the demands for gentile law observance much softer than those for Jews—in line with the Christian tradition of gentile purity law they do not include circumcision or Shabbat.
- Secondly, the Homilies read the passage within the historical framework shared with Epiphanius, agreeing that Jesus cannot have endorsed sacrifice and must therefore have intended it as the subject of his abolishment of the Torah.
- Thirdly, the Homilies place their reading within the Manichean-Marcionite framework of satanic falsification of Scripture, which relegates the respective scriptural passages on sacrifice to be of demonic origin. The Homilies, moreover, point out that human readers will find confirmation for erroneous doctrines in these false Scriptures—echoing Faustus rather precisely.

The Homilies thus refute Epiphanius's argument that the end of sacrifice implies the end of the Law. They equally adopt the teaching of the satanic falsification of Scripture, yet rather than applying it to Matt 5:17, as Marcion and Faustus did, the Homilies apply it to the Torah's laws on sacrifice and other statements that may question God's absolute unity or His omniscience or omnipotence.[77]

---

76 *Clementine Homilies* 3:9, Smith (1870, 60–61), Greek text according to Rehm (1969, 60); the wording may intentionally mimic the rabbinic tradition attributed to Ben Bag Bag, who *invites*, in relationship to the Torah, to "turn it, turn it, for everything is in it," see Mishna *Avot* 5:24.

77 Philip Schaff (1914, 439) already summarized the viewpoint of the Clementine Homilies quite accurately: "[Pseudo-Clement] sees in Christianity only the restoration of the pure primordial religion, which God revealed in the creation, but which, on account of the obscuring power of sin and the seductive influence of demons, must be from time to time renewed. The representatives of this religion are the pillars of the world: Adam, Enoch, Noah, Abraham, Isaac, Jacob, Moses, and Christ. These are in reality only seven different

The Homilies thereby solve the historical challenge to the observance of the Law after the Temple's destruction that Epiphanius had levelled against his imaginary—or at least grossly distorted—interlocutors, whom he recast as tantamount to what modern scholars perceive as "Jewish-Christian." The Homilies, in short, may constitute a minority tradition in the Christian reception history of Matt 5:17, yet they should not be seen as marginal in as far as they combine aspects of the Western majority tradition with that of their Marcionite and Manichean opponents.[78] The Homilies thus constitute the one instance in the Western tradition that most fully corresponds to the case evoked by Faustus, namely that of a Jewish reading of Matt 5:17. The Homilies, along with the testimony of Faustus himself and that of Julian, will help us contextualize the ways in which the Talmud will employ the passage. Yet in order to understand their respective readings most fully, we first need to turn to the Syriac Christian tradition of understanding the Matthean passage.

3 Matthew 5:17 in the Syriac Tradition

It is noteworthy how little attention Matt 5:17 has received in the Syriac tradition when compared to the Greco-Latinate record. Still, there is ample evidence to reconstruct a distinct Syriac reading, which since, Ephrem and Aphrahat, placed a somewhat different emphasis on the passage's legal implications than the Western one, especially when it comes to the enduring value of the Law. At the same time, the mainstream Christian Syriac reading of Matt 5:17, like the Greek and Latin one, took the passage to be genuine, and largely connected Jesus's coming to the "fulfilment" of the Law, which left it transformed. Moreover, the Syriac fathers, like their Greek and Latinate contemporaries, tended to respond to Marcionism and Manichaeism, along with a refutation of the teachings of Bardaisan, yet they spent far less time quoting and refuting their opponents than the Western traditions.[79]

incarnations of the same Adam or primal man, the true prophet of God, who was omniscient and infallible. What is recorded unfavourable to these holy men, the drunkenness of Noah, the polygamy of the patriarchs, the homicide of Moses, and especially the blasphemous history of the fall of Adam, as well as all unworthy anthropopathic passages concerning God, were foisted into the Old Testament by the devil and his demon".

78 The Clementine Homilies likewise integrate a broad range of Christian legal thought, see Zellentin (2018, 143–144; 2019, 148–149).

79 See, e.g., Moiseeva (2018); Alberto Camplani (2016, 9–66); Lieu (2015, 143–180); Lucas van Rompay (2007, 77–90); and Sidney Griffith (2002, 5–20).

In order to comprehend the Syriac attitudes towards Matt 5:17, one needs to understand its views of Israelite ethnicity. Ephrem and the majority of Syriac writers, it is true, consider "the peoples" to have replaced "the People," just as the Western church understood itself has having superseded Israel. In partial contradistinction to the Western Christian tradition, however, the Syriac tradition retained a view that saw the church as the result of an ethnic amalgamation: after Jesus's coming, "the nations" have *joined* rather than *replaced* "the nation," a vision close to the Pauline image of the olive tree which has wild branches grafted onto it. This is the view put forward by Aphrahat, which, in the words of Sebastian Brock, "held that that the Church derived from both the People and the Peoples, and constituted a 'new People.'"[80] Aphrahat's model was explicitly retained by the Didascalia Apostolorum (on whose later dating see below), the Syriac tradition that will prove most important for the present inquiry. Moreover, we will see that the Syriac tradition seems to endorse the enduring value of the Law, which it defines in its own way. Most importantly for the present purpose, this tradition uses Matt 5:17 in increasing clarity as a passage to express precisely how much of the Law remained after Jesus's coming, and how, precisely, Jesus reduced the divine law by partially abrogating some of its punitive aspects. We will briefly consider Ephrem's views of the Law, which come closest to the Western tradition, and then trace the more conservative approach favoured by Aphrahat, the Book of Steps, and the Didascalia Apostolorum.

Ephrem, writing in the Eastern Roman Empire in the fourth century, stands closest to the Western tradition both when it comes to his views of ethnicity and when it comes to his reading of Matt 5:17. Yet even he points out that Jesus's "fulfilment" should not be understood as abrogation:

> So that the disciples should not think that the perfect commands, which our Lord was introducing, were to dispense from the Law, he first said to them, "If you hear that I am setting forth perfection, do not imagine that I am abolishing the Law. Indeed I am fulfilling it. For I have not come to abolish, but to fulfil" (*lʾ gyr ʾtyt dʾshrʾ ʾlʾ dʾmlʾ*). For the scribe who completes a child's education does not engage in contention [that a child should remain with] an instructor, nor does a father wish that his son should always be a child. Or a nurse, that her infant should always ask for milk. Milk is appropriate in its time. But when a child has grown strong, he no longer needs milk.

80 See Sebastian Brock (2019, 9), and see note 90 below.

> He said to the scribes and Pharisees who were rising up and seeking a pretext, "I have not come to abolish the Torah and the Prophets, but to fulfil them" (*dlʾ ʾtyt dʾshrʾ ʾwrytʾ wnbyʾ ʾlʾ dʾmlʾ*, Matt 5:17). This was fulfilment with regard to what was lacking (*wmwlyʾ lḥsrywtʾ hw hwʾ*). He made it known what kind of fulfilment (*mwlyʾ*) this was: "Behold we are going up to Jerusalem (*lʾwrshlm*) so that everything written concerning me may be fulfilled (*lshlm*)" (Luke 18:31). With regard to those things that were lacking (*ḥsyrtʾ*), he said "The former things have passed away (*dqdmytʾ ʿbr lhwn*," 2 Cor 5:17). Concerning those things which have entered into fullness (*dʿl bmlywtʾ*), and are absorbed into growth (*wʾtblʿ btwsptʾ*), and renewed in abundance (*wʾtḥdtʾ bytyrwtʾ*), he said, "it is easier for heaven and earth to pass away (*tʿbr*) than that one of the letters of the Torah (*ḥdʾ mn ʾtwtʾ dʾwrytʾ*) be dropped" (Luke 16:17) and "whoever relaxes one of the commandments" (*dnshrʾ lm ḥd mn pwqdnʾ*, Matt 5:19)—of the New Testament (*ddytqʾ ḥdtʾ*).[81]

Ephrem here dismisses the sense that Jesus would abolish the Law in its entirety. Instead, he indicates that the Law serves a specific purpose as preparatory nourishment, evoking Paul's language of the schoolmaster (see e.g., Gal 3:24) and quoting 2 Cor 5:17 as Jesus's own words. Ephrem also speaks about the "fulfilment" and the passing away of the Law as a whole through the crucifixion, staying very close to the Pauline interpretation of the term. There is, however, one central difference in emphasis between Ephrem's interpretation and that of the "Western" tradition: for him, some part of the Torah has remained in what he, uniquely, calls the "commandments of the New Testament," which must not be relaxed. While he does not specify what these commandments are, his interpretation nevertheless upholds the value of law, and even speaks of the Law's "growth" and "abundance." Ephrem thereby opened the door to a distinct Syriac legal tradition that eventually stood apart from the Western one. It is this Syriac tradition which is primarily reflected in the Talmud. The exegetical pathway of this interpretation, however, began not only with Ephrem, but also with Aphrahat.

---

81 Ephrem, *Commentary on the Diatessaron* 6.3a–b, English translation according to Carmel McCarthy (1993, 111), Syriac text according to Leloir (1990, 60), see also note 27 above. Ephrem also emphasizes that "[w]hat was lacking therefore in the old [law] has been fulfilled in the new (*ḥsyrwth hkyl dʿtyqtʾ mlyt ḥdtʾ*). This is why [he said], "I have come to fulfil these" (*ʾtyt lmmlyh ʾtnwn*, Matt 5:17), Ephrem, *Commentary on the Diatessaron* 15.4, translation according to McCarthy (1993, 231), Syriac according to Leloir (1990, 142). See also Salvesen (2012, 61–64).

The early fourth century church father Aphrahat, who wrote in Adiabne, in the north of the Sasanian Empire, slightly predates Ephrem. Like the latter and like so many Greek and Latin fathers, Aphrahat read Matt 5:17 in conjunction with the letters of Paul. Yet Aphrahat's perceptive and independent reading, even more so than Ephrem's, is remarkably different from the Western fathers in his emphasis on the *keeping* of parts of the Law, as he explains in detail in his *Demonstration on Charity*:

> 5. And 430 years before the Law (*qdmy ... mn nmwsʾ*), the promise existed that in the seed of Abraham all the peoples will be blessed (Gal 3:17). The Law could not cancel (*dnbṭl*) the promise, hence the Law was an addition (*twsptʾ*) to this word of promise until its time (*ʿdmʾ dʾtʾ zbnh*) should come. And this word was kept for 1794 years from the time that it was promised to Abraham and until it came (*wʿdmʾ dʾtʾ*). And this word was kept in reserve for 1304 years after the giving of the Law (*mn btr sym nmwsʾ*). And the word preceded (*wqdmyʾ*) 430 years before the Law and when it came it cancelled the observances of the Law (*wbd ʾtt bṭlt ʾnyn lnṭwrtʾ dnmwsʾ*). The Law and the prophets were contained in these two commandments (*tryn pwqdnyn*) about which our Lord said, "All the Law and the prophets (*dklh nmwsʾ wnbyʾ*) until John the Baptist prophesied" (Matt 11:13). And our Lord said, "I have not come to dismiss the Torah and the prophets but to fulfil them (*dlʾ ʾtyt lmshrʾ ʾwrytʾ wnbyʾ ʾlʾ lmmlyw ʾnyn*," Matt 5:17). It is also written that the truth of the Law was through Jesus (John 1:17).
>
> 6. How indeed was the Law and the prophets lacking (*ḥsyr*), and in need to be fulfilled (*dntmlwn*)? If not, on account of the testament which was hidden in them, which itself is the word of promise. For, that testament was not sealed which was given to Moses till this latter testament came, which is the first, which was promised from above and was sealed down below. ... The first testament was fulfilled in the last (*wʾtmlyt lh dytqʾ qdmytʾ bʾḥrytʾ*). Aged and antiquated are the works which are in the Law and they are for destruction (*lḥblʾ*, cf. Heb 8:13). For, from the time the new (*ḥdtʾ*) was given, the old was made obsolete (*bṭlt lh ʿtyqtʾ*). It was not only from the time of the arrival of our Saviour, that the sacrifices were rejected (*ʾstlyw dbḥʾ*), but also from before that time their sacrifices were not pleasing him as it is written, ... "I have not delighted in sacrifices and also I am not pleased with whole burnt offerings" (Jer 6:20; Ps 51:16). ... The prophet Isaiah also said, ... "I hate and reject your feasts and I will not perceive the odour of your religious assembly" (Amos 5:21; Isa 1:14).
>
> 7. And also this word which our Saviour said, on which the Law and the prophets hang (*dbh tlyn ʾwrytʾ wnbyʾ*, cf. Matt 22:40), is beautiful, good

> and fair, because our Lord said as follows, "Not one letter *yud*, will pass away from the Torah and the prophets until all is fulfilled" (*dywd ʾtwtʾ hdʾ mn ʾwrytʾ wnbyʾ lʾ tʿbr ʿdmʾ dkl nhwʾ*, Matt 5:18). For, he took the Law and the prophets and hung them on the two commandments (*wtlʾ ʾnwn btryn pwqdnyn*, cf. Matt 22:40), and cancelled nothing from them (*wmdm lʾ bṭl mnhwn*). But when you look well at this word, it is so in truth. The observance which is in the Law and everything which is written in it is under this word, "You shall love the Lord your God with all your soul, with all your strength and with all your heart" (Deut 6:5; Matt 22:37). Everything which was done in the Law was in order that they should be brought to love the Lord their God and that a person should love his neighbour in the flesh as himself. And these two commandments are above all the Law .... For, whoever keeps righteousness is above the commandment and the Law and the prophets (*dmn dnṭr bzyqtʾ lʿl mn pwqdnʾ hw wnmwsʾ wnbyʾ*). And the word which our Lord said is true, "That no letter *yud* will pass away from the Law and from the prophets" (*dlʾ tʿbr ywd ʾtwtʾ mn nmwsʾ wmn nbyʾ* see Matt 5:18), because he set a seal and hung them on the two commandments (*wtlʾ ʾnwn btryn pwqdnyn*, cf. Matt 22:40).[82]

Aphrahat reads Matthew 5:17 in the light of Paul's view of the extension of God's blessing through Abraham's seed. For Aphrahat, the Law is thus secondary to the "promise," in a precise chronological way—reading we will find spelled out in more detail later in the Syriac tradition. Aphrahat, on the one hand, reads the "fulfilment" of the Law very much like the Greek and Latin fathers as a final fulfilment pertaining to its entirety, rather than as the ongoing partial fulfilment of any particular legal obligations. Along with the Clementine Homilies and other Western texts, Aphrahat holds that sacrifices were not a good idea to begin with, going very far in his rejection of the Torah.[83] Like Clement of Alexandria, he emphasizes that the Law was not defective; rather, it needed to be transformed in order to release the promise that had been contained in it all along.

At the same time, however, we have seen that "the Church," for Aphrahat, "derived from both the People and the Peoples, and constituted a 'new People'," as Brock puts it. Aphrahat describes Jesus as married to "the community

82 Translation according to Kuriakose Valavanolickal (2005, 43–46), Syriac according to Parisot (1894, 55–64), on Aphrahat's view of law see also Salvesen (2012, 59–61).

83 See note 53 above.

of the People (*knwsht ʿmʾ*) and the community of the Peoples (*knwsht ʿmmʾ*)."[84] Aphrahat's ethnic self-identification with Israel, to the best of my knowledge, is not yet fully appreciated in scholarship, as is another aspect in his thought, namely his endorsement of a redefined Law. Aphrahat maintains a cognizance that even Christ's "fulfilment" of the Law in its entirety does not necessarily cancel Matthew's emphasis on the "fulfilment" of its individual commandments. Aphrahat therefore takes up another stream of the Christian tradition spelled out in Matt 22:36–40 (see also John 13:34–35 and James 2:8), which holds that Christ combined the entire law in two commandments—the love of God along with the love of one's neighbour. Aphrahat, following the Diatessaron translation in this regard, emphasizes that "not one letter *yud* (*dywd ʾtwtʾ hdʾ*), will pass away from the Torah and the prophets until all is fulfilled." Aphrahat thereby reads the *yud* of Matt 5:18 as designating the endurance of law itself. He recasts the abrogation of the Law as keeping it by the different means of two specific commandments which include all the others, the love of God and the love of one's neighbour—a view famously shared, *mutatis mutandis*, by the rabbis.[85] Aphrahat's law-affirming language, along with that of Ephrem, thereby prepared a central element of the affirmative Syriac attitude towards law and towards Matt 5:17 in particular—and this attitude became more explicit in the later tradition.

Unlike many Greek and Latin Christian commentators, who tended to see any symbolic endorsement of the Law as diminishing the status of Christ, Aphrahat thus endorsed the idea of the enduring validity of a divine law at least in principle. The difference, of course, could be said to be one of emphasis rather than of content, since the Syriac tradition saw much of the Jewish law just as much as abrogated as the majority of the Latin and Greek tradition.[86] Yet the difference in emphasis proved consequential in the long run. While Aphra-

84 Aphrahat, *Demonstration* 21 (On Persecution) 13; Syriac text according to Parisot (1894, 965), English translation according to Brock (2019, 13).

85 See e.g. Sifra *Qodashim* 4:12, *Bereshit Rabbah* 24:7 and Bavli *Shabbat* 31a, see also Serge Ruzer (2002, 371–389).

86 A good example of this is the summary offered by Ishoʿdad of Merv in his Commentary on Matthew 5:17 "He promises two things in this; one, that all the previous voices of the Law (*mqdmtʾ dnmwsʾ*), those that were spoken about Me have been fulfilled (*dʾtmr ʿly mtgmrn*), in that the Law has taught about My coming (*mʾtyt*); second, that until, I say, these things happen, the Law remaineth Mine, and from now henceforth all things are made new (*mtḥdt klmdm*), and with them also the Heavens and the Earth in a type and a mystery (*bṭwpsʾ wbʾrzʾ*);" translation and Syriac text according to Margaret Dunlop Gibson (1911), vol. 1, 35 (English), vol. 3, 59 (Syriac). Further discussions of law can be found, for example, in Philoxenus of Mabbug's *Letter to Patricius*, in Cyrus of Edessa, *Explanation of the Passion* 7.5–9 and in his *Explanation of Pentecost Sunday* 3:10; and in many works of

hat, in his views on law as well as in his reading of Matt 5:17, remains largely in line with the Western Christian tradition, we find a very different point of view in the *Book of Steps*, a central Syriac text composed in the fourth or fifth century. The *Book of Steps* follows the language of Aphrahat very closely, but uses Matt 5:18 in order to emphasize the endurance of law through which one "lives"—the Syriac term of eternal salvation. Again, the *yud* of Matt 5:18 is central for the issue:

> 21. When he said, "He made both of them one" Testament (*dʿbd trtyhwn ḥdʾ dytyqy*, see Eph 2:14), and he annulled the Law of the commandments by his commandments (*wnmwsʾ dpwqdnʾ bpwqdnwhy bṭl*, Eph 2:14), so that he might make everything new with one testament. From then on, namely (*mkyll lm*) "not a single letter *yud* will pass away from the Law and the prophets" (*ywd ʾtwtʾ ḥdʾ lʾ tʿbr mn nmwsʾ wmn nbyʾ*, Matt 5:18). As for the rest, "The whole Law and Prophets up to John were established in order to serve and then pass away" (Matt 11:13). "For the thing that has become old is worn out and close to destruction" (*lḥblʾ*, Heb 8:13) and from then on we ought not to speak about these (Heb 9:5). From then on, namely (*mkyll lm*), one letter *yud* (*ywd ʾtwtʾ ḥdʾ*, Matt 5:18) will remain—which is the ten commandments (*ʿsrʾ ptgmyn*), which are called *yud*, for there are Ten Commandments in the number of the signs. These ten commandments, which I will enumerate here, are the *yud* that do not pass away from the Torah or from the prophets (*dlʾ ʿbrʾ mn ʾwrytʾ wmn nbyʾ*) ... This is the letter *yud*, and look, it is recorded in the Gospel (*bʾwnglywn*). So from then on let no one serve these other commandments that have been abolished (*pwqdnʾ ʾḥrnʾ dʾtbṭlw*), or these by which a person does not live (*dlʾ ʾysh ḥyʾ bhwn*), because they were given on account of the stubbornness of the people (*dmṭl qrḥwthwn dʿmʾ*) and their contentiousness (*wmṭl mmrmrnwthwn*).
>
> 22. In summary, these ten commandments are sufficient for the (eternal) life of humans (*hlyn ʿsrʾ ptgmyn spqyn lḥyyhwn dbnynshʾ*), so that whoever does them will live by them (*dmn dʿbd lhwn ḥyʾ bhwn*, cf. Lev 18:5, Gal 3:12, Rom 10:5). For all the wearisomeness of the Law and the prophets (was intended) so that people might come to these commandments of this *yud* (*pwqdnʾ dhdʾ ywd*). As our Lord said, "All the power of the Law and the prophets hang upon these two commandments (*dklh ḥylh dnmwsʾ*

Severus of Antioch, e.g., in his *Letter to John of Bostra*. My gratitude to Sergey Minov for pointing me to these sources.

> *wnby' bhlyn tryn pwqdnyn tl'*, Matt 22:40), and whoever does these two commandments fulfills the whole law" (*wmn dʿbd hlyn tryn pwqdnyn klh nmws' mml'*). As Paul said, "The whole (Law) is spoken with a few (words), "you shall love your neighbor as yourself" (Gal 3:19)."
>
> 23 … Therefore, let us fulfill the Gospel and the *yud* (*nshlm … l'wnglywn wlywd*), which are one testament by which people conduct themselves in a new way. But whatever is outside (*dlbr*) of this *yud* is in the Law and in the prophets, being called the testament of debts (*dytyqy dḥwb'*), for on account of the debts of the people (*ḥwbwhy dʿm'*) it is designated the testament of debts.[87]

We can see a clear development in the Syriac legal thought, from Aphrahat to the *Book of Steps*. The former one, entrenched as he was in anti-Jewish polemics, understood the *yud* of the Law that remains, according to the Diatessaron's rendering of Matt 5:18, solely in terms of the dual commandment of love of God and love of one's neighbor. The *Book of Steps* follows this interpretation, but takes it one step further: here, the "one letter *yud*" (*ywd 'twt' ḥd'*), according to its numerical value of ten, designates the Decalogue.[88] While endorsing the Decalogue's validity as such is unsurprising, the language used by the *Book of Steps* is unique: it promises eternal life, i.e., salvation of the soul, through the observation of law. At the same time, the *Book of Step* mitigates the radical endorsement of the Law we have seen in Matt 5:17: by adding "from then on (*mkyll lm*)," the text endorses the permanence of the Law—yet only after Jesus's coming. The Book of steps thus endorses "the Law" by expanding what Aphrahat already saw the Law's enduring value. The enduring law now includes the "two commandments," the love of God and one's neighbor according to Matt 22:40, as well as the Ten Commandments.

One further step in the development of a positive Syriac Christian attitude towards law, and yet another use of Matt 5:17, can be found in the *Didascalia apostolorum*, a text of central significance in the West Syrian tradition whose development can be traced from third-century Greek fragments to a fifth-century Latin palimpsest and a broadened Syriac version that predates

87 *Book of Steps* 22, 21, translation according to Robert Kitchen (2004, 269–271), Syriac text according to Michael Kmosko (1926, 682–686); citations from the letters of Paul largely follow the Peshitta, on the attitude towards law in the *Book of Steps* see also Salvesen (2012, 64–66).

88 Associating the Decalogue alone with the enduring part of the Law, of course, has precedence in the Greek tradition, see note 12 above as well as Salvesen (2012).

the eighth century CE.[89] The Didascalia, like Aphrahat, sees the church as composed of both "the people (*ʿmʾ*) and of the peoples" (*ʿmmʾ*), the church, therefore, must follow the Law:

> Indeed, the Law (*nmwsʾ*) is a yoke, because like a plow-yoke of oxen it is laid upon the former people (*sym ʿl ʿmʾ qdmyʾ*, i.e., of Israel) and upon the present church of God (*ʿl ʿdtʾ dʾlhʾ dhshʾ*), even as now also in the church it is upon us, upon those who are called from the people (*mn ʿmʾ*) and upon you and upon those who from among the peoples (*dmn byt ʿmmʾ*) who have (obtained) mercy for them; it has gathered and held us both, together in one accord.[90]

Just as for Aphrahat, the Didascalia sees the church as mixture of Israel and of the nations, upon which it is to keep the Law. Elsewhere, it presents the necessity of keeping the Law for salvation along with Jesus's role in the history of law by using Matt 5:17 as a prooftext. Importantly, it juxtaposes "the Law" and the "Second Legislation," which Jesus came to abrogate:

> Indeed, you know that He gave a simple and pure and holy law of life (*nmwsʾ pshyṭʾ wdkyʾ wqdyshʾ dḥyʾ*), wherein our Savior set his name. He spoke the ten utterings (*ʿsrʾ … ptgmyn*) to point out Jesus (*lyshwʿ*)—for ten represents *yud*, but *yud* is the beginning of the name of Jesus (*dyshwʿ*) … And again our Saviour, when he cleansed the leper, sent him to the Law (*lwt nmwsʾ shdrh*) and said to him: "Go, show yourself to the high priest, and offer the offerings (*wqrb qwrbnʾ*) of your cleansing, as Moses commanded, for a testimony unto them (Mark 1:44 and parallels)" that he might show that He does not abrogate the Law (*dlʾ shrʾ nmwsʾ*), but

89 On the use of Matt 5:17 in the Didascalia see already von Harnack (1912, 202–203). Salvesen's (2012, 57–59) helpful comments on law in the Didascalia differ from my understanding since, based on the early fragments, she dates the entirety of the text earlier than Aphrahat and Ephrem, a defensible yet ultimately speculative presupposition still common in the scholarship; for my own views on the Didascalia see Zellentin (2013c, 77–154).

90 *Didascalia Apostolorum* XXVI 249.11–15; translation and Syriac text according to Arthur Vööbus (1979), vol. I–IV, henceforth "DA." Note that the entirety of chapter XXVI is (at least formally) addressed to those "who have been turned from the (Israelite) people to believe in God our Saviour Jesus Christ" (*ʾylyn dʾtpnyw mn ʿmʾ lmhymnh bʾlhʾ prwqn ʾshwʿ mshyḥʾ*, DA XXVI 241.9–10). For the fusion of "people" and "peoples" see also, e.g. DA XV, 159.14 and DA XXV 239.11–12; see also Zellentin (2013c, 164). The Didascalia also voices the contrasting idea, that God abandoned "the people of the Jews (*lʿmʾ dywdyʾ*) and the Temple and has come to the church of the gentiles" (*lʿdtʾ dʿmmʾ*, DA XXII 226 19–20), which stands closer to Ephrem and the Western tradition of replacement; see also note 80 above.

teaches what is … the Law[91] and what the second legislation (*tnyn nmys'*). Indeed, he (Jesus) said thus: "I am not come to abrogate the Law nor the prophets, but to fulfill them" (*dl' 'tyt d'shr' nmws' wl' nby' 'l' d'ml' 'nwn*, Matt 5:17). The Law therefore is not abrogated (*nmws' hkyl l' mshtr'*), but the second legislation is temporary, and is abrogated (*tnyn nmws' dyn dzbn' hw wmshtr'*).[92] Now the Law is the ten utterings and the judgments (*'sr' ptgmyn wdyn'*), to which Jesus bore witness (*d'shd*) and said thus: "One letter *yud* shall not pass away from the Law (*dywd 'twt' ḥd' l' t'br mn nmws'*, Matt 5:18)." It is the *yud*, however, which passes not away from the Law (*dl' 'br' mn nmws'*), even that which may be known from the Law itself through the ten sayings (*'sr' ptgmyn*), which is the name of Jesus (*dyshw'*). The letter (*'tyt'*), however, is the extension of the wood of the cross (*mtḥh hy dqys' dṣlyb'*). And again on the mount also Moses and Elijah appeared with our Lord—that is, the Law and the prophets (*nmws' wnby'*).

The Law thus consists of the ten words and the judgments (*'sr' ptgmyn wdyn'*), these which God spoke before that the people made the calf (*'gl'*) and worshipped idols. Indeed, also that it is called the Law (*nmws'*), truly on account of the judgements (*dyn'*). This is the simple and light law (*nmws' pshyṭ' wqlyl'*). In it there is no burden, no distinction of meats, no incenses, no offerings of sacrifices and burnt offerings (*wl' qwrbn' ddbḥ' wdyqd'*) …. Indeed, he said about sacrifices (*'l dbḥ'*) thus: "If you shall make me an altar" (*'n t'bd ly mdbḥ'*) … Then he does not say "make for me," but "if you shall make an altar" (*'l' 'nhw t'bd mdbḥ'*). He did not set up this as a necessity (*l' hd' 'nnq' sm*), but showed what was about to be … On this account He signified here: "If you desire to sacrifice, whereas I need it not (that) you sacrifice to Me" (*d'n r'g 'nt lmdbḥ kd l' snyq 'n' dbḥ 'nt ly*).[93]

Again, in contrast to the Western Christian tradition, and in line with the *Book of Steps*, the Didascalia speaks of a "law of life" (*nmws' … dḥy'*). The Didascalia again cites the Diatessaron's version of Matt 5:17, with one small but telling modification that shows the influence of the Peshitta: the "one letter *yud*" that "shall not pass away" does not do so from the "Torah" (*'wryt'*), as in the Diatessaron, but from "the Law" (*nmws'*), which is the term the Peshitta here uses, and which the Didascalia endorses not once.[94] Its reading of the passage, moreover,

91 Following Vööbus's emendation, based on the Latin texts and the majority of manuscripts.
92 The phrase, "and abrogated," is missing in the Latin, which simply states: "lex ergo indestructibilis, secundatio autem legis temporalis," see R.H. Connolly (1929, 219).
93 *Didascalia Apostolorum*, XXVI 242.5–244.9.
94 The Didascalia unfailingly uses the term *nmws'* to designate "the Law," with only one

develops that found in Aphrahat and the *Book of Steps*. The "one letter *yud*" (*dywd ʾtwtʾ ḥdʾ*) remains to include "the ten sayings" yet to this, "the judgments" (*dynʾ*), are added, namely those parts of the Law that remain legally binding. The Didascalia here expands the teaching of the *Book of Steps* on the Law that is not abrogated in a significant way, just as the *Book of Steps* had expanded Aphrahat's teaching. At the same time, the Didascalia develops the meaning of the *yud*, which now corresponds to Jesus himself, whose letter begins with a *yud*; the Didascalia here echoes Augustine's identification of Jesus and the Law. It also adds a typological meaning to the *yud*: since the term *ʾtytʾ* in Matt 5:18 can denote both "letter" and "sign," the Didascalia holds that the *yud* constitutes the "extension" or "reach" (*mtḥʾ*) of the cross (see Mishna *Sanhedrin* 6:4).

According to the Didascalia, then, the enduringly valid "primary" law corresponds to the Ten Commandments and a number of ritual and social laws based on a variety of Biblical passages, including Ezekiel 18 and the Decree of the Apostles.[95] The "secondary," temporal law, by contrast, is the ritual part of the Law that the Didascalia portrays as abrogated, including sacrifice, washing after intercourse, and "distinction of meats" beyond the strict avoidance of blood.[96]

The Didascalia's idea of an eternal and a temporal law is thus essential in order to understand how it understands Jesus's partial confirmation and partial abrogation of the Law. By and large, the Didascalia presents Jesus as "confirming" the Law. It states that:

> indeed, in the Gospel (*bʾwnglywn*) (Jesus) renewed and fulfilled and confirmed the Law (*lnmwsʾ hw ḥdt wmly wwshrr*), but the second legislation he abrogated and abolished (*wltnyn nmwsʾ shrʾ wbṭl*). Truly it was to this end, indeed, that (Jesus) came (*ʾtʾ*), that the Law be confirmed (*dnshrr nmwsʾ*), and that the second legislation be abrogated (*wtnyn nmwsʾ nbṭl*) …[97]

exception: the passage just cited, which places the wilful disregard of "Torah and the Prophets" in the mouth of antinomian ascetic "heretics," see DA XXIII, 230.9.

95 See Zellentin (2013c, 1–54; 2018, 133–134, 147–148; 2019, 135–143).

96 In its temporal distinction of a primary and eternal law from a secondary and temporal one, the Didascalia could be understood as constituting a later parallel to Matthew's distinction between the original Biblical law and the later Pharisaic additions, which Jesus came to scale back—yet its implementation of this temporal understanding of law proves starkly different from Matthew. Note that we find a similar teaching about a "primary" law—consisting of the Decalogue—given before and a "secondary" law after the Golden Calf—abrogated by Jesus—in the Apostolic Constitutions 1.6 (citing Matt 5:17), a church order incorporating parts of the Didascalia Apostolorum; on the relationship between the two texts see Zellentin (2013c, 46–69).

97 DA XXVI, 246.21–24. The Syriac verb for "confirmation," *sh-r-r*, ranges in its meaning from

The notion of "confirmation" of the Law, and continuity of legal thought, is thus central to the Didascalia. Presenting its own writing as a confirmation of previous teachings, the Didascalia states that "those things which were said before (*mnqdym*), hear also now."[98] Affirmation here occurs amidst alteration of current practice; its implied apostolic authors portray the correction of heretical teachings by stating that "we had established and confirmed and set down" (*'tqnn wshrrnn wsmnn*)—namely the words of the Didascalia.[99] The Didascalia sees Jesus's "coming" as inherently tied to the Law's "confirmation", both when citing and when alluding to Matt 5:17.

The Didascalia thus affirms the Law even more fully than the *Book of Steps*, in further development of the thought we have seen in Aphrahat, yet differently from both. Intriguingly, the Didascalia's conception comes closest to that of the Clementine Homilies, with whose teaching it may or may not have had contact.[100] Unlike the Homilies, the Didascalia does not differentiate between Jewish and gentile law, or between Jews and gentiles. It does not, however, see its own congregation as "gentile" either, as most Western fathers did. Rather, the Didascalia takes another unique position on the relationship between Jews and gentiles: for this text, "the nation," a common Syriac term used for Israel, has been split. A part of Israel has believed Jesus and was joined by "the nations," forming the new community. Another part, "the Jews", rejected Jesus. In line with this ethno-religious concept (which stands in far closer continuity with Israel than the merely "spiritual" Israel of the gentile Western Christian traditions), the Didascalia distinguishes between two types of law, which it relates temporally. On the one hand, there is the eternal primary Law, which it unreservedly affirms, and which it sees as untouched by Jesus's coming, and which all humans now must keep. On the other hand, there is the "second legislation," which was a punitive law given to the Jews after the Golden Calf and other sins, which the Israelites were supposed to keep until Jesus's coming, and which the

"establishing," to "fulfilling," "guarding," and "strengthening;" see Sokoloff (2009, 1612); on the "confirmation" of law in the Didascalia see also Zellentin (2013c, 127–174).

98 DA IX, 103.3–4.

99 DA XXV 240.6. The object of the sentence is missing; the Latin Didascalia explicates what is obvious in the Syriac: the apostles confirmed *haec statuentes*; see Connolly (1929, 215). The *af'el* form of the verb *t-q-n*, used by the Didascalia here to denote the "establishing" of tradition, can also denote "fixing" or "repairing;" see Sokoloff (2009, 1662).

100 The Didascalia and the Clementine Homilies share a broad range of purity laws based on the tradition of Leviticus 17–18 and Acts of the Apostles. The Homilies, however, endorse an "expansive" understanding of these laws which the Didascalia *specifically* reject. This is most likely the result of both texts' participation—with different emphases—in a shared oral tradition and practice; see note 1 and 69.

Jews erroneously continue to keep to this day.[101] This, of course, does not happen at the expense of Jesus's importance for salvation: rather, the Law itself contains the reference to both the enduring part of the Law and to the cross.

4 Matthew 5:17 in the Aramaic Tradition

We can now turn to the rabbis of the Babylonian Talmud and their sense of Jesus's saying on the law and its abrogation. Just like the Western tradition of reading Matt 5:17, the Talmud put the passage to heresiological use, yet its very formulation corresponds more closely to its Eastern, Syriac Christian understanding.[102] The famous passage Bavli *Shabbat* 116a–b occurs in the midst of a satirical story about a corrupt judge, which itself is a narrative illumination of the meaning of the Syriac term *ʾwnglywn*, "Gospel," which the Talmud, playfully, renders as *ʾwn glywn*, designating a "margin of error."[103] The Talmudic story explicates that the Gospel is a heretical book; it opens with a parodic enactment of Luke 12:13–14—Jesus refusal to judge an inheritance case—and ends with satirical use of Matt 5:15–16—"let your light shine." These two gospel references work as bookends for the Talmud's parody of Matt 5:17.[104] In the Talmudic

101 See Zellentin (2013c, 127–154); similar ideas about the Golden Calf and punitive laws can be found in the Western tradition, see e.g., Irenaeus, *Against Heresies* IV.15–16 and Justin Martyr, *Dialogue with Trypho*, 19.

102 On this passage see most recently Yakir Paz (2019, 517–540); Zellentin (2011, 137–166; 2008, 339–363) and the previous literature cited there; von Harnack (1912, 203–204) is missing here. Paz, in turn, makes valuable additions to my previous study and rightly expands my respective suggestion for the relevance of the *Syro-Roman Law Book*—a collection of Eastern Roman law composed in Greek after 474 CE that is only preserved in Syriac translation—for reconstructing the context of the Bavli. His conclusion, however, that the Talmud would polemicize against any Christian work of law, leave alone a specific one, presupposes a greater interest in Christian literature on the part of the rabbis than even I would be willing to countenance. In my view, Christian inheritance law functions as pars pro toto for the rabbis' view of Christian law and its relationship to the Torah. On the dating of the Syro-Roman Lawbook see Walter Selb and Hubert Kaufhold (2002, 43–46).

103 The Talmud explores the various unseemly meanings of the Syriac term "Gospel" *ʾwnglywn*, a Greek loan word, if understood as Hebrew *ʾwn glywn*, "margin" or "message of oppression," or as Aramaic *ʿwn glywn*, "margin of perversion," "wrong," or "penalty;" see Zellentin (2011, 145–146); the Babylonian pronunciation does not distinguish between *ʿayin* and *aleph*.

104 The Talmudic story retells a Palestinian rabbinic story from the Pesiqta deRav Kahana in light of the Lukan tradition that sees Jesus as *refusing* to act as a judge in an inheritance case, and ends with an invocation of the "light" one should let "shine forth," from the Sermon on the Mount, see Zellentin (2011, 153–159, 163–165).

story, a rabbinic Jewish woman named Imma Shalom seeks to ridicule (*lʾḥwky*) a judge who styles himself as "a philosopher" (*pylwspʾ*) in order secure a favorable ruling regarding her inheritance.[105] While she is eligible for inheritance according to Christian law, Jewish law denies her this inheritance in favor of her brother, Rabban Gamliel.[106] The woman bribes the judge with a silver lamp, and the judge therefore initially leans towards favoring her case. He states the following (in the version of manuscript Munich, with important variants noted in the footnotes):

"From the day that you (m. pl.) were exiled from your land	*mywmʾ dglytwn mʿl ʾrʿkwn*[107]
the Torah of Moses was taken away,	*ʾynṭylt*[108] *ʾwryytʾ dmshh*[109]
and the Gospel was given,	*wʾtyhyb(t) byh*[110] *ʿwn glywn*[111]
and it is written in it: 'Daughter and son inherit equally.'"	*wkty(b) byh brtʾ wbrʾ ʾrtwn kḥdʾ*

105 The term "philosopher" is broadly attested across rabbinic and Syriac Christian literature in a variety of spellings. Importantly, the term tends to describe outsiders in rabbinic literature (see e.g. *Mekhilta deRabbi Ishmael* 20:5, *Genesis Rabbah* 1:9 and 11:76; Yerushalmi *Shabbat* 3,4 (6a) and *Betsa* 2,5 (61c); Bavli *Avodah Zarah* 44b and 54b). In Syriac literature, however, the term "philosopher" (*pylwspʾ*) is an inside one, as perhaps best evidenced by the ways in which the Syriac tradition deals with several notables bearing it as a title; cases include Secundus the Silent Philosopher, see Sebastian Brock (1978, 94–100); Pantænus the Philosopher, see Eusebius, *Ecclesiastical History* Book 5.10, Syriac, in William Wright and Norman McLean (1898, 246); or even Bardaisan, the "Aramaic philosopher," see Han J.W. Drijvers (1970, 190–210). Note that Ephraim alleges that when his ignorant nemesis, i.e. Bardaisan, proclaimed himself "philosopher," he made himself "the laughingstock" (*gwḥkʾ*) of Syriacs and Greeks, using the same verb as we find in the Talmud's ridicule of the corrupt philosopher, see Ephrem, *Prose Refutations of Mani, Marcion and Bardaisan* (in C.W. Mitchell, 1921, vol. II, 7, line 45); see also note 120 below.

106 See the lucid treatment of Christian inheritance law in Paz (2019, 522–527) and my previous observations in Zellentin (2011, 143–159).

107 Following Ms. Munich, Ms. Oxford, Bodleian Opp. Add. fol. 23 (366), Ms. Vatican ebr. 487/82–85 and JTS fragment ENA 2069/5–6; Ms. Vatican 108 is slightly corrupted; on the quality of the manuscripts see Zellentin (2011) 149.

108 Following Ms. Munich and Vatican ebr. 487/82–85; Ms. Oxford, Bodleian Opp. Add. fol. 23 (366), Ms. Vatican 108 and JTS fragment ENA 2069/5–6 read *ʾytntylt*.

109 Ms. Oxford, Bodleian Opp. Add. fol. 23 (366) adds "from you" (*mnkwn*).

110 Following the slightly abbreviated Ms. Munich and Ms. Vatican 108. Ms. Oxford, Bodleian Opp. Add. fol. 23 (366) reads "to you" (*lkwn*); Ms. Vatican ebr. 487/82–85 reads *wʾtyhyb lhn* ("was given to them"), JTS fragment ENA 2069/5–6 reads *wʾtyhyb lnʾ*.

111 Ms. Oxford, Bodleian Opp. Add. fol. 23 (366) reads *ʾwrytʾ dʿwn gylywn*, "the Torah of the Gospel".

The judge here summarizes a particular take on the abrogation of the Law, connecting it not with the coming of Jesus but rather with the exile of the Jews, which the rabbis as well as Christian writers connected with the destruction of the Temple.[112] The Bavli specifies that in this view, which corresponds largely to Ephrem and to the dominant strand of the Western Christian tradition, the Torah has been completely replaced by the Gospel, or, as one manuscript has it, "the Torah of the Gospel" (*ʾwrytʾ dʿwn gylywn*)—a formulation with a deep pedigree especially in Syriac Christian thought. The notion of "the Torah of the Gospel" clearly evokes Ephrem's view of the "commandments of the New Testament" (*pwqdnʾ ddytqʾ ḥdtʾ*) and the "commandments of this *yud*" (*pwqdnʾ dhdʾ ywd*), i.e. of Jesus, which take the place of the Law that we saw in the Book of Steps and especially in the Didascalia. To these sources, we may add the notion of the "Law of the Messiah" (*nmwsʾ dmshyḥʾ*) which abrogates "the Law of Moses" (*nmwsʾ dmwshʾ*) along with all other forms of Mosaic inheritance law as detailed in the Syro-Roman Lawbook's introduction (which of course does not cite Matt 5:17 or any other Biblical source).[113] The conflation of the Gospel and Jesus becomes complete in the sequel of the Bavli's story.

Here, Rabban Gamliel, Imma Shalom's brother, resorts to offering a Libyan donkey, an even more valuable bribe, to the judge, in order to expose the latter's corruption.[114] In response to this second bribe, the judge then favors the "orthodox" Jewish side of Jesus and promptly changes his ruling—by evoking Matt 5:17. Again following manuscript Munich, he states:

"I went down to the end of the Gospel,	*shpyly lyh lsypyh*[115] *dʿwn gylywn*
and it is written in it: 'I am the Gospel;	*wktyb by ʾnʾ ʿwn glywn*
Not to reduce the Torah of Moses did I come	*lʾ lmypḥt mʾwryytʾ dmshh ʾtyty*

112 See e.g. Naftali Cohn (2012) and Holger Zellentin (2013a, 319–367).

113 The formulation "Torah of the Gospel" in the Bavli follows Ms. Oxford, Bodleian Opp. Add. fol. 23 (366), see note 109 above. In the introduction to the Syro-Roman Lawbook, "the law of the Messiah" as instituted by Constantine, functions as the replacement not only of the "law of Moses" but also of all the diverging types of Greek, Roman and Egyptian law that had in turn been based on Mosaic law (sic!). This is especially interesting for the current considerations since the juxtaposition of law introduces the volume's focus on inheritance law as, as noted by Paz (2019, 532–536); for the text and a German translation see Selb and Kaufhold (2002, 20), vol. II.

114 Whether Imma Shalom is part of this sting operation, or herself exposed, depends on the Bavli's manuscript tradition; see Zellentin (2011, 148–149).

115 Following Ms. Munich. Ms. Vatican 108 has *shplyt lsyp(h)*, Ms. Oxford, Bodleian Opp. Add. fol. 23 (366) and JTS fragment ENA 2069/5–6 has *shpylyt lswpyh*, Ms. Vatican ebr. 487/82–85 is corrupted.

but to add [or: and not to add] did I come,'	*ʾlʾ lwswpy*[116] *ʾtyty*
and it is written in it: 'If there is a son, the daughter does not inherit.'"	*wktyb byh bmqwm brʾ brtʾ lʾ tyrwt*[117]

The corrupt judge now revises his ruling, since he "went to the end of the gospel." We should not understand this as reference to a putative version of the Gospel that places Mt 5:17 at its end. Rather, the judge here is portrayed as employing a technical rabbinical phrase. Elsewhere in the Bavli, we find the order "go to the end of the verse," *shpyl lsypyh dqrʾ*, hurled at interlocutors, including heretics, in order to point them to the perceived tension between their interpretation of one part of a *biblical* verse and another one they overlooked (see e.g. Bavli *Berakhot* 10a, *Sukkah* 52b, and Eruvin 101a). In the present case, the judge, himself a heretic, applies the phrase to himself, substituting the gospel for the Bible yet eagerly employing the hermeneutical tool where it suits his fancy. When he came "to the end of the Gospel," he realized that the meaning of Jesus' words about the importance of his "coming" must be that the Torah of Moses is still valid, and that the sister therefore inherits nothing.[118]

The Bavli here does not quite cite the Matthean passage, yet repeats all its key stylistic elements that we have seen throughout its Christian, and especially its Syriac reception history:

- Jesus is portrayed as presenting his role in legal salvation history by relating himself to the Law, in the first person, fusing the person of Jesus with the Gospel in a way that goes beyond even the formulation of Augustine, Aphrahat and the Didascalia, echoing the notion of the "Law of the Messiah" in the Syro-Roman Lawbook.
- This role is then specified by the repetition of the verb "to come," unsurprisingly using the shared Aramaic root *ʾtʾ*, just as in the Peshitta's rendering.
- The statement concludes with a bi-partite statement endorsing the Law's general validity and describing Jesus's role in qualifying the validity of the Law, in this case without any restriction.

---

116 Following Ms. Munich; the version in parenthesis is that of Ms. Oxford, Bodleian Opp. Add. fol. 23 (366), which has *wlʾ lʾwspy ʿl ʾwrytʾ dmshh*; Ms. Vat ebr. 487/82–85 and JTS fragment ENA 2069/5–6 have *wlʾ* "and not to;" the entire phrase is missing in Ms. Vatican 108.

117 Ms. Vatican ebr. 487/82–85 is slightly corrupted.

118 We should also note the inicidental parallelism between the way in which the judge "went down to the end of the Gospel" in the Bavli and the phrase of Epiphanius who, when discussing the impossibility of law observance according to Matt 5:17, narrated that Moses "came to the end of the book" (*ēlthen epi to terma tēs biblou*) in order to add the curse. While the parallel is intriguing, only a small part of the Panarion was translated into Syriac, see Luise Abramowski (1983).

The Bavli's version of Matt 5:17 echoes the Christian tradition in more than one way. Like Epiphanius and the Clementine Homilies, the Bavli also places Matt 5:17 in a historical context by relating the passage to the Temple's destruction, yet only indirectly so—and only in order to point out the original meaning of Matthew which, in the eyes of the Bavli, clearly contrasts with any sense that Jesus would have abrogated the Law.

There are, at the same time, two remarkable differences between the Bavli and Matthew. First, the Bavli speaks of the "the Torah of Moses" (*ʾwryytʾ dmshh*) which is slightly different from Matt 5:17, yet closer to the Diatessaron's "the Torah and the Prophets" (*ʾwrytʾ wnbyʾ*) than to the Peshitta's "the Law and the Prophets" (*nmwsʾ ʾw nbyʾ*); it matches nicely, in turn, with the Syro-Roman Lawbook's abrogated "Law of Moses" (*nmwsʾ dmwshʾ*). Second, the Bavli's quotation of the Gospel, when qualifying Jesus's relationship to the Law, does not repeat the traditional juxtaposition of "destroying" and "fulfilling" the Law. Instead the Bavli portrays Jesus, in the quoted version from manuscript Munich, as having come "not to reduce … *but* to add" (*lʾ lmypḥt … ʾlʾ lwswpy*, my emphasis) which, in other manuscripts, is rendered as "not to reduce … *and not* to add" (*lʾ lmypḥt … wlʾ lwswpy*, my emphasis). Both the reading of manuscript Munich and the alternative reading evoke aspects of the Christian tradition on Matt 5:17.

The majority reading, to begin with, sees Jesus as "neither adding nor reducing" the Torah, departs far from Matthew's idea of "not abrogating but fulfilling." Yet, the reading stands very close to Matthew's original intent as discussed above: here, Jesus does not reduce any aspects of God's law, and he does not allow for any of its additions, such as the traditions of the Pharisees, either. Yet we should hardly assume the Bavli to be interested in Matthew's original message as presented above. A different way of explaining this discrepancy between Matt 5:17 and the Bavli in terms of the latter's quite precise reference to Deuteronomy 4 (partially mirrored in Deuteronomy 13:1):

> 1 So now, Israel, give heed to the statues and ordinances that I am teaching you to observe so that you may live to enter and inherit the land that G-d, the God of your ancestors, is giving you.
>
> 2 You must neither add anything to it (*lw tspw*), nor take away anything from it (*wlʾ tgrʿw*) but keep the commandments of the Lord your God with which I am charging you.

The Bavli, indeed, reverses the order of the sentence from Deuteronomy and replaces Matthew's "to abolish" with "to cut away" and "to fulfill" with "to add." The passage Deut 4:1–2, moreover, is often cited in Christian sources; yet given the Talmud's brevity, it is difficult to know whether it alludes to other Jesus traditions in this context.[119]

In the context of Deuteronomy 4:1, however, the author of the Imma Shalom story would have an excellent reason to amend its rendition of the Gospel with a Deuteronomic quotation. Namely, in Deuteronomy, the inheritance the Holy Land is clearly tied to the very issue under discussion, the observance of the commandments. The Talmudic story thereby associates the siblings' inheritance with the inheritance of the Land of Israel, which was at the time ruled by Christians who did not observe the Israelite law—but perhaps should have according to the Bavli's reading of Matthew, which parallels that of several Western sources we have seen above. In this sense, the citation itself satirizes Christian supersessionism, as becomes evident to any reader familiar with its basic tenets and with the Book of Deuteronomy.

Most importantly, the Bavli's majority reading, understanding Jesus as "not coming to add and not coming to reduce," regards the philosopher's revised ruling as equivalent to Matthew's view that the emergence of Jesus did not abrogate the validity of the Torah—just as the Marcion, Faustus, Julian and the Clementine Homilies did in another strand of the Western reading of Matt 5:17. Hence, sons still take precedence over daughters in matters of inheritance (which they did not do in Syriac Christian law). In other words, the philosopher argues at first that the Law had been abrogated, although his own tradition can easily be understood as saying that this was not the case.[120] Then he returns to

119 It should be noted that some "Christian" texts, such as the "Two Ways" tractate in the *Didache* (4.13) and Revelation 22.18, explicitly refer to Deuteronomy 4:1; the tradition itself is broadly attested in early Judaism and Christianity, see Betz (1995, 183), note 112.

120 The anonymous peer reviewer of this volume has kindly pointed out to me that one relevant Talmudic manuscript I had consulted, Vat. ebr. 487/82–85, calls the Christian judge not "philosopher" (*plsp'*, see note 105 above) but *pwl' sb'*, which they suggest translating as "Paul the Elder." While the term *sb'* is broadly attested as designating either a father or a grandfather across the rabbinic and Syriac corpora, the name Paul does not appear in rabbinic literature. Given the context of our story, the suggestion that at least one Talmudic copyist here entered a reference to the Apostle Paul, often credited with the Torah's abrogation, is indeed intriguing. One could object that the name of Paul is usually rendered as *pwlws* rather than *pwl'* in Syriac sources, yet the latter form occurs as an appellative for the apostle in the Peshitta of Acts at 26:24 and 27:24. Moreover, later Christian figures, such as Paul of Samosata and Paul of Constantinople, are at times spelled as *pwl'*, as is "Paul the Jew" (*pwl' yhwdy'*), the controversial sixth-century patriarch of Antioch; see e.g. Wright and McLean (1898, 311) and the respective passages in the post-Talmudic *Chronicle of Zouqnin*, see Jean Baptiste Chabot (1927, 146, 170, 174, and 176 and 1952, 19–24). The apostle, moreover, is portrayed as referring to himself as "I, Paul, being an old man (*'n' pwlws d'yty sb'*) .... and now also a prisoner (*dyn ap 'syr'*) of Christ" in the letter to Philemon, 1:9, here cited according to the Peshitta rendering. Narsai, in his *Homily on Peter and Paul*,

the "plain" meaning of Matthew, according to which the Torah had not been abrogated. Being able to choose among the two interpretive alternatives that are both part of the Christian tradition, the judge accepts the highest bid and adjusts his ruling accordingly. The Bavli's majority reading, hence, can be said to reflect the Western minority reading of Matt 5:17, which understands the passage as affirming the Law.

The version of manuscript Munich, by contrast to the Bavli's majority reading, states that Jesus does not come to reduce *but to add* to the Torah, and thereby stands closer to the mainstream of the Eastern tradition. To begin with, this version follows the juxtaposition in the Syriac versions of Matthew, which is equally indicated with the particle *ʾlʾ*, "but" (both in the Diatessaron and in the Peshitta). Moreover, we have seen the inverse image of Jesus "adding" to the Law in Ephrem, who, like the Bavli, uses the root *y-s-p* in order to explain Matt 5:17–18, when speaking about the elements of the Law "which have entered into fullness (*dʿl bmlywtʾ*), and are absorbed into growth (*wʾtblʿ btwsptʾ*), and renewed in abundance (*wʾtḥdtʾ bytyrwtʾ*)."[121]

The two Talmudic variants of Jesus' words thus shine a very different light on the Bavli's take on Matt 5:17. What both readings share, however, may be the most important aspect: they portray Jesus not as denying to *abrogate* the law in its entirety, but as denying to *reduce* it. The denial of precisely this reading in a parodic context—out of the mouth of a corrupt judge—in turn evokes the Bavli's awareness of the saying's usage in specific strands of the Christian tradition. The image of Jesus as "reducing" the Law, namely, corresponds rather precisely to the understanding of his role, as expressed in the Syriac tradition most concretely by the Didascalia's understanding of Matt 5:17, which in turn echoes aspects of Greek tradition as expressed in the Clementine Homilies' partial reduction of the Torah.[122] This fact places the Bavli's rendering firmly within the mainstream of the Syriac Christian tradition of reading the Matthean passage, and plausibly also in dialogue with some strands of Greco-Latinate Christian thought.[123] We can thus take the Talmudic story as witness

---

makes reference to this passage when referring to "Paul, in his old age, a prisoner on behalf of faith" (*pwlws sbʾ ʾp ʾsyrʾ dḥlp qwshtʾ*, see Mingana 1905, 83). We cannot therefore dismiss the possibility that Paul, after all, appears in the Talmud, yet neither can we exclude the possibility that the phrase merely constitutes a scribal error.

121 Ephrem, *Commentary on the Diatessaron* 6.3a–b, English translation according to McCarthy (1993, 111), Syriac text according to Leloir (1990, 60).

122 The teaching that Jesus both upholds and reduces the Torah also echoes the Clementine Homilies' idea of destroying sacrifice at the same time as following the commandments as laid out above, see above.

123 Note that the medieval Jewish tradition continued to employ the witness of Matthew

to how central the passage remained in Syriac Christian discourse, and how it was perceived in a cultural context outside Christianity:

- The Bavli shows a clear echo of Matt 5:17, yet not of 5:18, and understands the passage as affirming Biblical law and perhaps also of its partial abrogation (at least in Ms. Munich),
- It shows an accurate sense of Christian law in inheritance and a good sense of varying Christian attitudes towards law, and
- it rephrases Matt 5:17 in a way that makes sense within its own literary, linguistic and cultural paradigms.

It may thus not be an overstatement to assert that the many ways in which Jews, Christians and pagans understood Jesus' saying according to Matt 5:17 offers a unique mirror of some of the most polarized strands of late antique thought. Ancient authorities struggled with the saying every bit as much as contemporary scholars still do. The passage, moreover, puts into sharp relief how divergent late antique notions were not only regarding Jesus and his role in "fulfilling," "abrogating," "curtailing" or even "expanding" "the Law," but also regarding the content and applicability of "the Law" itself.

Bibliography

Abramowski, Luise. "Die Anakephalaiosis zum Panarion des Epiphanius in der Hs. Brit. Mus. Add. 12156." *Le Muséon* 96 (1983): 217–230.

Achelis, H. *Hippolyt's kleinere exegetische und homiletische Schriften. Die griechischen christlichen Schriftsteller* 1.2. Leipzig: Hinrichs, 1897.

Balberg, Mira. *Blood for Thought: The Reinvention of Sacrifice in Early Rabbinic Literature.* Oakland, CA: University of California Press, 2017.

Banks, Robert. *Jesus and the Law in the Synoptic Tradition.* Cambridge: Cambridge University Press, 1975.

Bazzana, Giovanni Battista. "Apelles and the Pseudo-Clementine Doctrine of the False Pericopes." In: Gabriella Aragione and Rémi Gounelle (eds.), *"Soyez des changeurs avisés": controverses exégétiques dans la littérature apocryphe chrétienne.* Cahiers de Biblia Patristica 12. Strasbourg: Université de Strasbourg, 2012, 11–32.

Beck, Edmund. *Des heiligen Ephraem des Syrers, Sermones*, vol. 1, 2. Louvain: Secretariat du Corpus Scriptorum Christianorum Orientalium, 1969.

against Christianity, the witness of works such as *Qissat Mujādalat al-Usquf*, *Sefer Nestor ha-Komer*, *Sefer Milhamot ha-Shem*, *Sefer Yosef ha-Meqanne*, *Nizzahon Vetus*, *Even Bohan*, *Kelimmat ha-Goyim*, and *Hizzuq Emunah* has been treated by Christoph Ochs (2013).

Berzon, Todd S. *Classifying Christians: Ethnography, Heresiology, and the Limits of Knowledge in Late Antiquity*. Berkeley: University of California Press, 2016.

Berzon, Todd S. "Ethnicity and Early Christianity: New Approaches to Religious Kinship and Community." *Currents in Biblical Research* 16 (2018): 191–227.

Betz, Hans Dieter. *A Commentary on the Sermon on the Mount, including the Sermon on the Plain (Matthew 5:3–7:27 and Luke 6:20–49). Hermeneia: A Critical and Historical Commentary on the Bible*. Minneapolis: Fortress Press, 1995, 166–197.

Brock, Sebastian. Synagogue and Church in Dialogue: Four Syriac Poems from Late Antiquity. *Journal of Jewish Studies Supplement Series* 3. Oxford: Journal of Jewish Studies, 2019.

Brock, Sebastian. "Secundus the Silent Philosopher: some notes on the Syriac Tradition." *Rheinisches Museum für Philologie* (Neue Folge) 121 (1978): 94–100.

Brüggemann, Th., W. Kinzig, and C. Riedweg. Kyrill von Alexandrien: Gegen Julian, Buch 1–10 und Fragmente. *Die Griechischen Christlichen Schriftsteller der ersten Jahrhunderte Neue Folge 21*, vol. 2. Berlin: De Gruyter, 2017.

Burns, Daniel. "Augustine on the Moral Significance of Human Law." *Revue d'Études Augustiniennes et Patristiques* 61 (2015): 273–298.

Camplani, Alberto. "Traces de controverse religieuse dans la littérature syriaque des origines: peut-on parler d'une hérésiologie des "hérétiques"?" In: Flavia Ruani (ed.), *Les controverses religieuses en syriaque*. Études syriaques 13. Paris: Paul Geuthner, 2016, 9–66.

Carlson, Donald Henry. *Jewish-Christian Interpretation of the Pentateuch in the Pseudo-Clementine Homilies*. Minneapolis: Augsburg Fortress, 2013.

Carter, Warren. "Jesus' 'I have come' Statements in Matthew's Gospel." *The Catholic Biblical Quarterly* 60 (1998): 44–62.

Cave Wright, Wilmer. *The Works of the Emperor Julian*, vol. 3. London: G.P. Putnam's Sons, 1923.

Chabot, Jean Baptiste. *Chronicon Anonymon. Pseudo-Dionysianum vulgo dictum* (I). CSCO 91; Scriptores Syri 43; Louvain: Durbecq, 1953.

Chabot, Jean Baptiste. *Incerti Auctoris Chronicon. Pseudo-Dionysianum vulgo dictum* (II). CSCO 104; Scriptores Syri 53; Louvain: Durbecq, 1952.

Ciasca, P. Augustinus. *Tatiani Evangeliorum Harmoniae Arabica nunc primum ex duplici codice edidit et translatione Latina*. Rome: S. C. De Propaganda Fide, 1888.

Cohn, Naftali. *The Memory of the Temple and the Making of the Rabbis*. Philadelphia: University of Pennsylvania Press, 2012.

Connolly, R.H. *Didascalia Apostolorum: The Syriac Version Translated and Accompanied by the Verona Latin Fragments*. Oxford: Clarendon Press, 1929.

Deines, Roland. *Die Gerechtigkeit der Tora im Reich des Messias*. Tübingen: Mohr Siebeck, 2004.

Deines, Roland. "Not the Law but the Messiah: Law and Righteousness in the Gospel of Matthew—An Ongoing Debate." In: Daniel M. Gurtner and John Nolland (eds.), *Built Upon the Rock: Studies in the Gospel of Matthew*. Grand Rapids: Eerdman, 2008, 53–84.

Dirksen, Piet B., and Arie van der Kooij, eds. *The Peshitta as a Translation: Papers Read at the 2. Peshitta Symposium held at Leiden 19–21 August 1993*. Leiden: Brill, 1995.

Doering, Lutz. "Much Ado About Nothing? Jesus's Sabbath Healings and their Halakhic Implications Revisited". In: Lutz Doering, H.-G. Waubke and F. Wilk (eds.), *Judaistik und Neutestamentliche Wissenschaft: Standorte, Grenzen, Beziehungen*. Göttingen: Vandenhoeck Ruprecht, 2008, 213–241.

Drecoll, Volker and Christoph Scheerer, *Augustinus: Späte Schriften zur Gnadenlehre. De Gratia et Libero Arbitrio, De Praedestinatione Sanctorum Libri Duo (Olim: De Praedestinatione Sanctorum, De Dono Perseverantiae). Corpus Scriptorum Eclclesiasticorum Latinorum* 105; Berlin: De Gruyter, 2019.

Drecoll, Volker and Mirjam Kudella. *Augustin und der Manichäismus*. Tübingen: Mohr Siebeck, 2011.

Drijvers, Han J.W. "Bardaisan of Edessa and the Hermetica: The Aramaic Philosopher and the Philosophy of his Time." *Jaarbericht Ex Oriente Lux* 21 (1970): 190–210.

Dunlop Gibson, Margaret. *The Commentaries of Isho'dad of Merv, Bishop of Ḥadatha (c. 850 A.D.) in Syriac and English*, vol. 1, 3. Cambridge: Cambridge University Press, 1911.

Evans, Ernest. *Tertullian: Adversus Marcionem*. Oxford: Clarendon Press, 1972.

Ferguson, John. *Stromateis. The Fathers of the Church: a New Translation Series 85*. Washington: Catholic University Press, 2010.

Frankfurter, David. "Jews or Not? Reconstructing the "Other" in Rev 2:9 and 3:9." *The Harvard Theological Review* 94 (2001): 403–425.

Früchtel, L., O. Stählin and U. Treu. Clemens Alexandrinus. *Die griechischen christlichen Schriftsteller* 52. Berlin: Akademie Verlag, 1970.

Furstenberg, Yair. "Defilement Penetrating the Body: A New Understanding of Contamination in Mark 7:15." *New Testament Studies* 54 (2008): 176–200.

Girod, Robert. *Origène: Commentaire sur l'évangile selon Matthieu*, vol. 1. *Sources chrétiennes* 162. Paris: Éditions du Cerf, 1970.

Graf, Georg. *Geschichte der christlichen arabischen Literatur*, vol. 1. Vatican City: Biblioteca Apostolica Vaticana, 1944.

Granger Cook, John. *The Interpretation of the New Testament in Greco-Roman Paganism*. Tübingen: Mohr Siebeck, 2000.

Granger Cook, John. "A note on Tatian's Diatessaron, Luke, and the Arabic Harmony." *Zeitschrift für antikes Christentum* 10 (2006): 462–471.

Griffith, Sidney. "Christianity in Edessa and the Syriac-Speaking World: Mani, Bar Daysan, and Ephrem; the Struggle for Allegiance on the Aramean Frontier." *Journal of the Canadian Society for Syriac Studies* 2 (2002): 5–20.

Hebgin, Dame Scholastica and Dame Felicitas Corrigan. *St. Augustine on the Psalms. Ancient Christian Writers* 29. London: Longman's Green, and Co., 1960.

Hoffman, Andreas. "Verfälschung der Jesus-Tradition. Neutestamentliche Texte in der manichäisch-augustinischen Kontroverse." In: L. Cirillo and A. Van Tongerloo (eds.), *Manichaeism and Early Christianity*. Turnhout: Brepols, 1997, 149–182.

Hofreiter, Christian. *Reading Herem Texts as Scripture*. PhD diss., University of Oxford, 2013.

Holl, Karl, ed. *Epiphanius (Ancoratus und Panarion)*, vol. 1. *Die griechischen christlichen Schriftsteller* 25. Leipzig: Hinrichs, 1915.

Jones, F. Stanley. *Pseudoclementina Elchasaiticaque inter judaeochristiana: Collected Studies*. Leeuven: Peeters, 2012.

Joseph, Simon J. "'I Have Come to Abolish Sacrifices' (Epiphanius, Pan. 30.16.5): Re-examining a Jewish Christian Text and Tradition." *New Testament Studies* 63 (2017): 92–110.

King, Karen. *What is Gnosticism*. Cambridge, MA: Harvard University Press, 2005.

King, Peter. *Augustine: On the Free Choice of the Will, On Grace and Free Choice, and Other Writings*. Cambridge: Cambridge University Press, 2010.

Kinzig, Wolfram. "The Nazoreans." In: Oskar Skarsaune and Reidar Hvalvik (eds.), *Jewish Believers in Jesus: The Early Centuries*. Peabody, MA: Hendrickson Publishers, 2007, 463–487.

Kiraz, George Anton. *Comparative Edition of the Syriac Gospels Aligning the Sinaiticus, Curetonianus, Peshitta and Harklean Versions*, vol. 1. Piscataway, NJ: Gorgias, 2004.

Kitchen, Robert. *The Book of Steps: The Syriac Liber Graduum*. Collegeville, MN: Cistercian Studies, 2004.

Kmosko, Michael. *Liber Graduum. Patrologia Syriaca*. Paris: Firmin-Dido et Socii, 1926.

Leloir, Louis. *Conmentaire de l'Evangile Concordant: Texte syriaque. Chester Beatty Monographs* 8. Dublin: Hodges Figgis, 1963.

Leloir, Louis. *Saint Éphrem: Conmentaire de l'Evangile Concordant: Texte syriaque: Folios Additionnels. Chester Beatty Monographs 8*. Leuven: Paris, 1990.

Lieu, Judith M. *Marcion and the Making of a Heretic: God and Scripture in the Second Century*. Cambridge: Cambridge University Press, 2015.

Luomanen, Petri. "Ebionites and Nazarenes." In: Matt Jackson-McCabe (ed.), *Jewish Christianity Reconsidered*. Minneapolis: Fortress Press, 2007, 81–118.

Luz, Ulrich. *Hermeneia: A Critical and Historical Commentary on the Bible. Matthew 1–7: A Commentary*. Minneapolis: Fortress Press, 2007.

Markschies, Christoph. "Individuality in Some Gnostic Authors: With a Few Remarks on the Interpretation of Ptolemaeus, Epistula ad Floram." *Zeitschrift für Antikes Christentum* 15 (2011): 411–430.

Marmadji, A.-S. *Diatessaron de Tatien*. Beyrouth: Imprimerie Catholique, 1935.

McCarthy, Carmel. *Saint Ephrem's Commentary on Tatian's Diatessaron: An English Translation of Chester Beatty Syriac MS 709*. Oxford: Oxford University Press, 1993.

McCauley, Leo P. and Anthony A. Stephenson. *The Works of Saint Cyril of Jerusalem. The Fathers of the Church: A New Translation*, vol. 1. Washington: Catholic University of America Press, 1969–1970.

Migne, Jacques-Paul. *Sanctie Aurelii Augustini, Hipponensis Epicsopi, Opera Omnia*, vol. 4a. Paris: Migne, 1861.

Mingana, Alphonse. *Narsai doctoris syri homiliae et carmina*, vol. 2. Mosul: Fratrum Prædicatorum, 1905.

Mitchell, C.W. *S. Ephraim's Prose Refutations of Mani, Marcion and Bardaisan: Transcribed from the Palimpsest B.M. Add. 14623*. London: Williams and Norgate, 1921, vol. II.

Moiseeva, Evgenïa. "The Old Testament in Fourth-Century Christian-Manichaean Polemic." *Journal of Late Antiquity* 11 (2018): 274–297.

Nanos, Mark D. and Magnus Zetterholm. *Paul within Judaism: Restoring the First-Century Context to the Apostle*. Minneapolis: Fortress Press, 2015.

Neumann, Karl Johannes. *Iuliani Imperatoris: Liborum Contra Christianius que supersunt*. Leipzig: Teubner, 1880.

Nestle, Eberhard, Erwin Nestle, Barbara Aland and Kurt Aland. *Novum Testamentum Graece post Eberhard et Erwin Nestle: Editione Vicesima Septima Revisa*. Stuttgart: Deutsche Bibelgesellschaft, 2004.

Ochs, Christoph. *Matthaeus Adversus Christianos: The Use of the Gospel of Matthew in Jewish Polemics Against the Divinity of Jesus*. Tübingen: Mohr Siebeck, 2013.

Oliver, Isaac. *Torah Praxis after 70 CE: Reading Matthew and Luke-Acts as Jewish Texts*. Tübingen: Mohr Siebeck, 2013.

Parisot, Jean. *Aphraatis sapientis demonstrations. Patrologica Syriaca*. Paris: Firmin-Didot et socii, 1894.

Payton, James R. *Irenaeus on the Christian Faith: A Condensation of Against Heresies*. Cambridge, UK: James Clarke Company, 2012.

Paz, Yakir. "The Torah of the Gospel: A Rabbinic Polemic against The Syro-Roman Lawbook." *Harvard Theological Review* 112 (2019): 517–540.

Pedersen, Nils Arne. "Manichaen Self-Designations in the Western Tradition." In: Johannes van Oort, ed. *Augustine and Manichean Christianity: Selected Papers from the First South African Conference on Augustine of Hippo*. University of Pretoria, 24–26 April 2012. Leiden: Brill, 2013, 183.

Petersen, William L. *Tatian's Diatessaron: Its Creation, Dissemination, Significance, and History in Scholarship*. Leiden: Brill, 1994.

Rehm, Bernhard. *Die Pseudoklementinen I: Homilien*. Berlin: Akademie Verlag, 1969.

Reischl, W.C. and J. Rupp. *Cyrilli Hierosolymorum archiepiscopi opera quae supersunt omnia*, vol. 1. Munich: Lentner, 1848.

Reynolds, Gabriel Said. "On the Qurʾānic Accusation of Scriptural Falsification (taḥrīf) and Christian anti-Jewish Polemic." *Journal of the American Oriental Society* 130 (2010): 189–202.

Rousseau, Adelin and Louis Doutreleau. Irénée de Lyon, Contre les Hérésies. *Sources chrétiennes* 100, vol. 4. Paris: Cerf, 1965.

Runesson, Anders. *Divine Wrath and Salvation in Matthew: The Narrative World of the First Gospel.* Minneapolis: Fortress, 2016.

Ruzer, Serge. "From "Love Your Neighbour" to "Love Your Enemy": Trajectories in Early Jewish Exegesis." *Revue Biblique* 109 (2002): 371–389.

Salmond, S.D.F. *The Refutation of all Heresies by Hippolytus ... with Fragments from His Commentaries on Various Books of Scripture. Ante-Nicene Christian Library*, vol. 6.1. Edinburgh: T & T Clark, 1868.

Salvesen, Alison G. "Early Syriac, Greek and Latin Views of the Decalogue." In: Jeffrey P. Greenman and Timothy Larson (eds.), *The Decalogue Through the Centuries: From the Hebrew Scriptures to Benedict XVI*. Louisville, KY: Westminster John Knox Press, 2012, 47–66.

Schaff, Philip. *History of the Christian Church, vol. II. Ante-Nicene Christianity*. New York: Charles Scribner's Sons, 1914.

Schmid, Herbert. "Ist der Soter in Ptolemäus' Epistula ad Floram der Demiurg? Zu einer These von Christoph Markschies." *Zeitschrift für Antikes Christentum* 15 (2011): 249–271.

Selb, Walter and Hubert Kaufhold. *Das Syrisch-Römische Rechtsbuch*, vol. I, II. Vienna: Verlag der Österreichischen Akademie der Wissenschaften, 2002.

Skarsaune, Oskar. "The Ebionites." In: Oskar Skarsaune and Reidar Hvalvik (eds.), *Jewish Believers in Jesus: The Early Centuries*. Peabody, MA: Hendrickson Publishers, 2007, 463–487.

Smith, Thomas. *The Clementine Homilies. The Apostolic Constitutions, Ante-Nicene Christian Library, The Clementine Homilies* (Volume XVII). Edinburgh, T & T Clark, 1870.

Sokoloff, Michael. *A Syriac Dictionary: A Translation from the Latin, Correction, Expansion, and Update of C. Brockelmann's Lexicon Syriacum.* Winona Lake, IN: Eisenbrauns, 2009.

Standhartinger, Angela. "Ptolemaeus und Justin zur Autorität der Schrift." In: Markus Lang (ed.), *Ein neues Geschlecht? Entwicklung des frühchristlichen Selbstbewusstseins*. Göttingen: Vandenhoeck & Ruprecht, 2013, 122–149.

Stowers, Stanley. *A Rereading of Romans: Justice, Jews, and Gentiles.* New Haven: Yale University Press, 1994.

Stroumsa, Guy G. *The End of Sacrifice: Religious Transformations in Late Antiquity.* Chicago: Chicago University Press, 2009.

Stroumsa, Guy G. *The Making of the Abrahamic Religions in Late Antiquity.* Oxford: Oxford University Press, 2016.

Teske, Roland J. *The Works of Saint Augustine. A Translation for the 21st Century. I/20: Answer to Faustus, a Manichean.* New York: New City Press, 2007.

Thiessen, Matthew. "Abolishers of the Law in early Judaism and Matthew 5:17–20." *Biblica* 93 (2012): 543–556.

Ullucci, Daniel C. *The Christian Rejection of Animal Sacrifice*. Oxford: Oxford University Press, 2017.

Vacarella, Kevin M. *Shaping Christian Identity: The False Scripture Argument in Early Christian Literature*. PhD diss. Tallahassee, FL: Florida State University, 2007.

Valavanolickal, Kuriakose. *Aphrahat Demonstrations 1*. Baker Hill, Kottayam: St. Ephrem Ecumenical Research Institute (SEERI), 2005.

Van den Berg, Jacob Albert. *Biblical Argument in Manichaean Missionary Practice: The Case of Adimantus and Augustine*. Leiden: Brill, 2010.

Van de Sande Bakhuyzen, Willem. Der Dialog des Adamantius "De recta in Deum fide". *GCS 4*. Leipzig: Hinrichs, 1901.

Von Harnack, Adolf. "Geschichte eines programmatischen Worts Jesu (Matth 5,17) in der ältesten Kirche." *Sitzungsberichte der Königlichen Preussischen Akademie der Wissenschaften*. Berlin: De Gryuter, 1912.

Van Maaren, John R. "Does Mark's Jesus Abrogate Torah? Jesus' Purity Logion and its Illustration in Mark 7:15–23." *Journal for the Jesus Movement in Its Jewish Setting* 4 (2017): 21–41.

Van Maaren, John R. *The Gospel of Mark within Judaism: Reading the Second Gospel in its Ethnic Landscape*. PhD diss. MacMaster University, 2019.

Van Rompay, Lucas. "'Bardaisan and Mani in Philoxenus of Mabbog's Mēmrē against Habbib." In: Wout van Bekkum (ed.), *Syriac Polemics: Studies in Honour of Gerrit Jan Reinink*. Orientalia Lovaniensia Analecta 170. Leuven: Peeters, 2007, 77–90.

Vööbus, Arthur. *The Didascalia Apostolorum in Syriac*. Corpus Scriptorum Christianorum Orientalium 401–402 and 407–408, vol. I–IV. Louvain: Secrétariat du Corpus Scriptorum Christianorum Orientalium, 1979.

Watts Henderson, Suzanne. "Was Mark a Supersessionist? Two Test Cases from the Earliest Gospel." In: Lori Baron, Jill Hicks-Keeton, and Matthew Thiessen (eds.), *The Ways That Often Parted: Essays in Honor of Joel Marcus*. Atlanta: Society of Biblical Literature, 2018, 145–168.

Weber, Robert and Roger Gryson. *Biblia Sacra iuxta vulgatam versionem*. Stuttgart: Deutsche Bibelgesellschaft, 2007.

Weddle, David L. *Sacrifice in Judaism, Christianity, and Islam*. New York: New York University Press, 2017.

Weren, Wilhelmus Johanis Cornelius. *Studies in Matthew's Gospel: Literary Design, Intertextuality, and Social Setting*. Leiden: Brill, 2014.

Williams, Frank. *The Panarion of Epiphanius of Salamis*, vol. 1. Leiden: Brill, 1994.

Wright, William and McLean, Norman. *The Ecclesiastical History of Eusebius in Syriac*. Cambridge: Cambridge University Press, 1898.

Wurst, Gregor. "Bemerkungen zu Struktur und *genus litterarium* der *Capitula* des Faustus von Mileve." In: Johannes van Oort, Otto Wermelinger and Gregor Wurst, *Augustine and Manichaeism in the Latin West: Proceedings of the Fribourg-Utrecht Symposium of the International Symposium Association of Manichaean Studies* (IAMS). Leiden: Brill, 2001, 307–324.

Yoshiko Reed, Annette. "Heresiology and the (Jewish-)Christian Novel: Narrativized Polemics in the Pseudo-Clementine Homilies." In: Eduard Iricinschi and Holger Zellentin (eds.), *Heresy and Identity in Late Antiquity*. Tübingen: Mohr Siebeck, 2008, 273–298.

Yoshiko Reed, Annette. *Jewish-Christianity and the History of Judaism*. Tübingen: Mohr Siebeck, 2018.

Zellentin, Holger. "Margin of Error: Women, Law, and Christianity in Bavli Shabbat 116a–b." In: Eduard Iricinschi and Holger Zellentin (eds.), *Heresy and Identity in Late Antiquity*. Tübingen: Mohr Siebeck, 2008, 339–363.

Zellentin, Holger. Rabbinic Parodies of Jewish and Christian Literature. *Texts and Studies in Ancient Judaism* 139. Tübingen: Mohr Siebeck, 2011.

Zellentin, Holger. "Jerusalem Fell After Betar: The Christian Josephus and Rabbinic Memory." In: Ra'anan Boustan, Klaus Herrman, Reimund Leicht, Giuseppe Veltri, and Annette Yoshiko Reed (eds.), *Envisioning Judaism: Studies in Honor of Peter Schäfer on the Occasion of his Seventieth Birthday*, vol. 1. Mohr Siebeck, Tübingen, 2013a, 319–367.

Zellentin, Holger. "Jesus and the Tradition of the Elders: Originalism and Traditionalism in Early Judean Legal Theory." In: Eduard Iricinschi, Lance Jenott, Nicola Denzey Lewis, and Philippa Townsend (eds.), *Beyond the Gnostic Gospels: Studies Building on the Work of Elaine H. Pagels*. Studies and Texts in Antiquity and Christianity. Tübingen: Mohr Siebeck, 2013b, 379–403.

Zellentin, Holger. *The Qur'ān's Legal Culture: The Didascalia Apostolorum as a Point of Departure*. Tübingen: Mohr Siebeck, 2013c.

Zellentin, Holger. "Judaeo-Christian Legal Culture and the Qur'ān: The Case of Ritual Slaughter and the Consumption of Animal Blood." In: Francisco del Río Sánchez (ed.), *Jewish Christianity and the Origins of Islam*. Turnout: Brepols, 2018, 117–159.

Zellentin, Holger. "Gentile Purity Law from the Bible to the Qur'an: The Case of Sexual Purity and Illicit Intercourse." In: Holger Zellentin (ed.), *The Qur'ān's Reformation of Judaism and Christianity: Return to the Origins*. Routledge Studies in the Quran. New York: Routledge, 2019, 115–215.

Zetterholm, Karin. "Jewish Teachings for Gentiles in the Pseudo-Clementine Homilies: A Reception of Ideas in Paul and Acts Shaped by a Jewish Milieu." *Journal for the Jesus Movement in Its Jewish Setting* 6 (2019): 68–87.

Zycha, Iosephus. *Sancti Aureli Augustini De utilitate credendi, De duabus animabus, Contra Fortunatum, Contra Adimantum, Contra Epistulam Fundamenti, Contra Faustum, De natura boni, Epistula Secundini, Contra Secundinum, accedunt Evodii De fide con-*

tra Manichaeos, et Commonitorium Augustini quod fertur praefatione utriusque partis praemissa. Corpus Scriptorum Ecclesiasticorum Latinorum XXV.V.I. Vienna: F. Tempsky, 1891.

General Index

1 Clement 125
2 Maccabees 147
2 Samuel 131
4 Maccabees 147, 149, 167
ʿAbbāsids 102
ʿAbdallāh 152, 169
ʿAbd al-Jabbār 137
ʿAbd Allāh ibn Sabaʾ 135–136
Abraham 6–7, 12, 82, 95, 150, 161, 167, 169, 234–235
Abrahamic 3, 6, 10–11, 100, 108, 186
Abu Hurayra 177
Abū ʿUmar al-Ḍarīr 152, 169
Acropolis 9, 45
Acts of John 121
Acts of Paul 126
Acts of the Apostles 85
Adam 173, 218
Adiabne 234
ʿAdī ibn Zayd 82
Against Heresies 131
Agathodaimon 99, 102, 105
Alexander the Great 25, 43
Alexandria 21, 23, 25–27, 34, 36
Al-Andalus 95
Al-Damīrī 137
Al-Fārābī 93
Al-Ḥabaša 171
Alī b. Abī Ṭālib 176
Al-Kalbī 137
Al-Kindī 92–95, 98–101, 105–109
Al-Marwa 81
Al-Masʿūdī 96
Al-Muʾmin (The Believer) 136
Al-Šābuštī 164–166
Al-Ṣafā 81
Al-Sarakhsī 9, 92, 95, 98–101, 105, 107, 109
Al-Suyūṭī 171
Al-Ṭabarī 137, 173–177
Al-Tawḥīdī 108
Al-Qurṭubī 171, 174
Ammianus Marcellinus 21, 25–27, 32
Anatolia 188, 194
Anatolian 186, 191–193, 197, 199
Antioch 17, 124–125, 148, 163
Antiochus IV Epiphanes 147, 158, 163
Anti-Pauline 5, 10, 116, 129, 132, 134–135, 137–140
Anti-Paulinism 116, 129–130, 134, 138–139
Apelles 132
Aphrahat 211–212, 231–239, 241–242
Aphrahat's Demonstration 163
Aphrodite 58–59
Apocryphal Gospels 172
Apodeictic 101
Apollonius 22–23, 32, 188
Arabian 3–4, 68, 81–82, 92, 95, 97–99, 101, 105, 109, 159
Arabic Infancy Gospel 172–173
Arānī 99
Aratus 102
Aristotelian 93, 96, 99, 101–103, 107
Aristotelianism 94
Asclepius 21, 34, 104
Asia Minor 11, 186, 190
Ašmūni 163–164
ʿAṭāʾ b. al-Sāʾib 152, 169
Atheist 71
Athenian 48
Athens 41, 48, 96
Augustine 204, 217–223, 241, 246
Avicenna 93

Babylonian 102
Babylonian Talmud 2, 204, 243
Bacchic devotees 51
Bacchus 45, 55
Baghdad 92, 94, 98, 164
Bahá'í 6
Bakcheion 45, 55–57
Bardaisan 231
Barūq 169
Basil of Caesarea 217
Bathsheba 132
Bavli 3, 11, 204, 243, 245–250
Benedict XVI, the Pope 115, 126
Berossus 22–23, 30–32
Berytus 19
Bileam 121
Bityah 158
Book of the Rooster 131
Books of the Maccabees 146, 149, 157

Brethren of Purity 9, 92–95, 98, 102, 104–109
Buddhism 95

Caesarea 19
Caiaphas 133
Caius 125
Camarini 24–25, 30, 33
Catalogue of Ibn al-Nadīm 98
Cerinthus 129
Chaldaeans 22–23, 26–27, 31–32
Children of Israel 78, 162, 177
Clementine Homilies 204, 222, 225–226, 228–230, 235, 242, 247–249
Clement of Alexandria 217, 235
Colossians 124
Constantinople 163
Constantius 22
Constantius II 18, 34
Cyril of Jerusalem 219

Damascius 96
Damascus 133
Darwin, Charles 117–118, 120, 122
Darwinian 116–117
David 131–132
Decalogue 34, 238
Decree of the Apostles 241
Demaneitus 188
Demonstration on Charity 234
Description of the Doctrines of the Sabians 98
Determining the Appropriate Time in which the Prayer is Answered from the View Point of Astrology 105
Deuteronomy 247–248
Diatessaron 211–213, 236, 240, 247, 249
Didascalia Apostolorum 204, 232, 239–242, 245–246, 249
Dionysiac-identity 52
Dionysian association 44, 47, 55–57
Dionysian ritual 57
Dionysos 5, 9, 41, 43–45, 48, 58–59
Discourse on the Macarini 25
Disputationes 204

Eastern Mediterranean 8, 16, 26, 33, 36, 164–165
Ebionites 129, 134, 227–228
Egypt 21, 25–29, 33, 156, 159–160, 162, 178
Egyptian 22–23, 26–27, 32, 34, 102, 194–195
Elcesaites 129
Elijah 240
Eliyahu 137–138
Encratites 129
Epaphroditus 127
Ephesians 125
Ephesus 190
Ephrem 231–234, 236, 245, 249
Epicureans 102
Epiphanius 129, 224–231, 247
Epistles of the Brethren of Purity 94–95, 102, 105, 108
Europe 1, 72
European 196
Eusebius of Caesarea 125, 217
Eutycheis 190
Expositio and Descriptio totius mundi et gentium (E/DTMG) 8, 16–25, 29–36
Ezekiel 241

Faustus 204, 220–226, 228–231, 248
First Apology 131
France 215

Gabriel 152–154, 169–170, 172
Gaul 17–18
Geʿez 131
Genesis 162, 173
Gentiles 4, 67, 69, 74, 129, 133–134, 205, 207, 209, 214, 216, 221, 225, 228–230, 242
Gnosticism 228
Gospel of Luke 207, 218, 233, 243
Gospel of Mark 121, 129, 132, 239
Gospel of Matthew 11, 121, 204–210, 214–219, 221, 226–228, 230–231, 235–236, 243, 247–249
Greco-Roman association 4, 9, 41–43
Greco-Roman religion 189, 199
Greeks 24, 34, 95–96, 102, 189
Gregorios Thaumaturgos 175
Gregory of Nyssa 217
Gyges 102

Hades 44
Ḥadīṯ al-Māšiṭa 145, 160, 178–179
Ḥammād b. Salama 152, 169
Ḥanīf 9, 95–96, 100, 102, 105

Hannah, the mother of Samuel 149
Ḥarrān 92, 94–98, 101–102, 105–107, 109
Ḥarrānians 9, 92–98, 100–102, 109
Hasmonean 147
Hebrew Bible 85, 158, 205, 214–216, 219, 226
Heliopolis 19
Hellenistic 96–97, 101, 146, 208
Hermes 99, 101–102, 105
Hermetic 96, 101, 105
Hermogenes 188, 193
Herodes Atticus II 48–49, 54
Herodotus 22–23
Historia Augusta 18
Hittite 191, 196
Homer 102

Ibn ʿAbbās 152–154, 169–170
Ibn al-Aṯīr 171
Ibn Ḥazm 137
Ibn Isḥāq 137
Ibn al-Jawzī 137
Ibn al-Nadīm 98–99
Ibn Ḥanbal 10, 145, 150–151, 154, 166, 168–169, 171, 178–179
Iconium 124
Ignatius of Antioch 125
Imma Shalom 244–245, 248
India 25, 27, 30, 33
Indian 24, 28, 33
Iobakchoi 42, 47, 50–51, 53–55, 61
Iran 2
Iraq 92, 95, 164
Iraqian 95
Irenaeus 129, 215–219, 228
Isaiah, the prophet 235
ʿĪsā ibn Maryam (Jesus) 153, 171
Israel 159, 172, 247
Israelite 3, 78–79, 156, 175, 205, 242
Itineraries from the Paradise of Eden to the Land of the Romans 25, 30

James, the brother of Jesus 133–135
Jeremiah, the prophet 149
Jerome 209–210, 213
Jerusalem 80–81, 129, 133–135, 150, 169, 224, 233
Jesus Christ 3, 11, 69, 84, 115–116, 121, 128, 130–131, 133–138, 159–160, 169, 171–175, 179, 204–208, 210, 212–220, 223–228, 230–235, 238–243, 245–250
John Chrysostom 217
John the Baptist 171, 234
Joseph 153, 159, 162, 171, 173–175, 179
Josephus 20, 22, 23, 24, 31, 32
Jovian 34
Judas Iskariot 131
Judas the Maccabee 147
Judea 147
Judean 191
Julian 18, 26, 34, 215, 223, 230–231, 248
Jupiter 21
Jurayj 153, 171, 174–175, 177, 179
Justin 131
Justinian 96

Kaʿba 68, 80–83
Karaite Jews 6
Khosrow Anūshirwān 96
Kindian 95
Kitāb al-diyārāt 164–165
Kollyda 190
Kore 58, 59

Lamarckian 119
Lamentations 148–149
Lamentations Rabbah 148–150, 156
Letter to the Galatians 225
Levantine 19
Libyan 245
Life of the Prophet 173
Lydia 188, 190
Lydian 186, 200
Lystra 124

Maccabean 146–147, 149
Magianism 66
Magians 86
Mālik b. ʿUqbūn 97
Malkun 136
Mandeans 95
Manetho 22–23, 32
Manichean 218, 221–222, 225, 229–231
Manichaeism 231
Marcion 132, 215, 219, 222–223, 228, 230, 248
Marcionism 231
Marcionites 219, 222, 229–231
Mary of Magdala 160

Mary, the mother of Jesus (Maryam) 84, 153, 160, 172, 179
Mecca 67–68, 80–82
Medina 67–69, 74, 81, 169
Mediterranean 1, 5, 7, 43
Menander 22–23
Mesopotamia 92
Mesopotamian 96
Metaphysics 101
Meteorology 100
Meter Hipta 189
Midrash 147
Midrashim 149
Miriam 149, 160
Mormon 6
Moses 22, 24, 31, 148, 156, 159–160, 169, 171, 225, 228, 234, 239–240, 244–247
Motella 190
Mount Lebanon 19
Muhammad, the Prophet 2, 4, 10, 68–69, 71, 73, 75, 77, 79–80, 82, 84–86, 145–146, 168–170, 173, 179
Mu'minūn (Believers) 67, 73, 74
Munich 244–245, 247, 249–250
Murūj al-dhahab wa maʿādin al-jawāhir 163–164
Musnad 150–151, 154, 166, 168
Muʿtazilite 99

Nag Hammadi 228
Najrān 173
Nathan, the prophet 131–132
Nazoreans 224, 228
Near East 5
Neo-Darwinian 119
Neo-pagan 223
Neo-Pauline 215
Neoplatonic 94
Neo-Pythagorean 94, 96
Nestur 146
New Testament 85, 210, 216, 220, 233
Nikomachos 49, 58

Old Testament 148, 179, 220
Olympus 44
On First Philosophy 108
On Generation and Corruption 100
On Senses and the Sensibles 101
On the Heavens 100
On the Soul 101
On the Quantity of Aristotle's Works 107
Origen 217
Oxford Handbook of Evolutionary Psychology and Religion 186

Pagan 3–4, 9–10, 17, 20, 22, 25, 29, 34–36, 82, 92, 95, 108–109
Palaimon 58–59
Panarion 129
Pannonia 17
Papias from Azita 188
Paradise 24, 70, 77–78, 170, 179
Pauline 115–116, 124–125, 133, 208, 225, 232–233
Paulinism 116
Paul, the apostle 3, 10, 115–117, 123–140, 215–216, 218, 225, 233–235, 238
People of the Book 9, 68, 74–77, 79–80, 84, 86–88
Persia 32, 96
Persians 31, 96
Pesiqta Rabbati 149–150, 167
Peshitta 210–213, 240, 246–247, 249
Peter, the apostle 125, 129, 130, 133–135, 137
Peutinger Table 30
Phaedo 104, 106
Pharisaic 204–206, 208–209, 221, 226
Philippians 124, 127
Phrygia 188, 190
Phrygian 186, 200
Physics 100
Plato 97, 99, 102
Platonic 3, 94, 96–97, 99, 101, 103
Platonists 102
Potiphar 173
Proteurythmos 58–59
Pseudo-Clementine 10, 129, 131, 133–134
Ptolemaic-Aristotelian 103
Pythagoras 102, 105, 107
Pythagoreans 102

Rabban Gamliel 244–245
Recognitions 133
Republic 102
Rhineland 163
Roman 3, 6, 8–9, 19–20, 27, 29–33, 36, 48, 96, 125, 128, 149, 158–159, 189, 194–197, 216, 232

Rome 8, 21–22, 36, 125, 137, 163
Rule of the Iobakchoi 9, 41, 46

Sabazios 189
Sabian 9–10, 78, 86, 92–109
Saʿīd b. Jubayr 152, 169
Saittai 190
Samaritans 6
Sarah, the mother of Isaac 149
Sardis 190
Sasanian Empire 2, 159, 234
Sāsānid 96
Sayf ibn ʿUmar al-Tamīmī 135
Sea of Ṭāwus 103
Seleucid 147, 159
Serapeum of Alexandria 25–26
Serapis 21, 26, 28
Severians 129
Silandus 190
Simplicius 97
Simon Magus 129, 131–133
Smyrna 190, 192
Socrates 104, 106
Solon 99
Spain 33
Sūra al-Baqara 158
Sūra Al-Burūj 175
Sūra al-ʾImrān 171
Sūra al-Isrāʾ 169
Sūra al-Māʾida 172
Sūra Maryam 172
Sūra Yāsuf 173
Syria 20, 136, 164, 210
Syriac 2, 11, 97, 163, 174, 204, 209–214, 223, 231–233, 235–238, 242–243, 245–246, 248–250
Syriac Gospels 205
Syrian 27, 37, 210, 238
Syrian coast 19
Syro-Palestinian area 19
Syros Mandrou 188

Talmud 6, 11, 147, 160, 214, 219, 223, 229, 231, 233, 243, 248–249
see also "Babylonian Talmud"
Tertullian 217, 219
Thābit Ibn Qurra 92, 98, 101, 107
Theadelphia 195
Thebais 28
The Barrington Atlas of the Greek and Roman World 190
The Book of Steps 232, 237–238, 240–242, 245
The Book of the Wars of Apostasy and Conquest 135
The Burying of the Martyrs 125
The followers of Mani 215
The Infancy Gospel of Thomas 172
The inscription IG $II^2$1368 9, 41, 45, 52, 61
The inscription MAMA IV 285 190
The Letter of Peter to James 134
The Scribes and Pharisees 206, 233
The Second Epistle to Timothy (2 Tim.) 124–125
The Septuagint 208
Thucydides 22–23
Tiamou 188
Toledot Yeshu 135, 137
Torah 6, 11, 83–84, 122, 156, 172, 207–208, 211–212, 217, 230, 233–237, 240, 244–249
Trier 17
Turkey 164, 188
Tyre 19

Umar II, the Caliph 70
Uriah the Hittite 132
ʿUthmān, the Caliph 135

Venus 106
Vestal virgins 21
Vulgate 210

Western Arabia 9, 81–82

Yemen 176
Yūsuf 171, 173, 175

Yaʿqub 136
Zoroaster 32
Zoroastrianism 66
Zoroastrians 2, 70

Printed in the United States
by Baker & Taylor Publisher Services